Jean-Luc Godard,
Cinema Historian

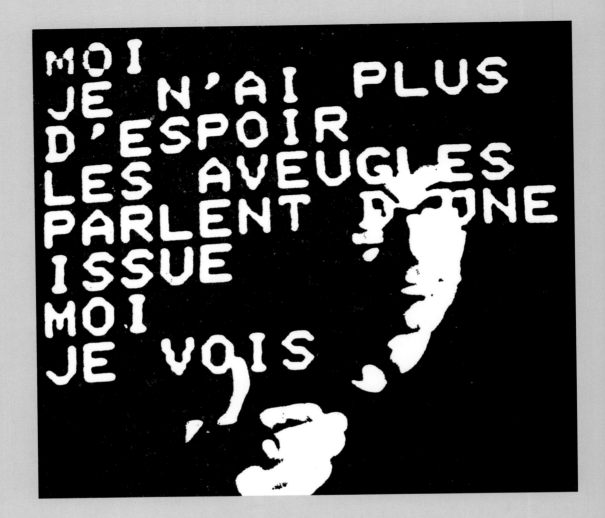

"Me / I no longer have any / hope / the blind / speak of a / way out / me / I see." From *Jean-Luc,* episode 2b of *Six fois deux (Sur et sous la communication)* (Anne-Marie Miéville and Jean-Luc Godard, 1976). Reproduced in Godard, *Introduction à une véritable histoire du cinéma* (Éditions Albatros, 1980).

Jean-Luc Godard, Cinema Historian

MICHAEL WITT

INDIANA UNIVERSITY PRESS

Bloomington & Indianapolis

This book is a publication of

Indiana University Press
Office of Scholarly Publishing
Herman B Wells Library 350
1320 East 10th Street
Bloomington, Indiana 47405 USA

iupress.indiana.edu

Telephone orders   800-842-6796
Fax orders   812-855-7931

This book is printed on acid-free paper.

Manufactured in China

Library of Congress Cataloging-in-Publication Data

Witt, Michael.
   Jean-Luc Godard, cinema historian / Michael Witt.
   pages cm
   Includes bibliographical references and index.
   ISBN 978-0-253-00722-3 (cloth)–ISBN 978-
0-253-00728-5 (pbk.)–ISBN 978-0-253-00730-8
(e-book) 1. Godard, Jean-Luc, 1930– –Criticism and
interpretation. 2. Godard, Jean-Luc, 1930– Histoire(s)
du cinéma. 3. Motion pictures and history. I. Title.
   PN1998.3.G63W58 2013
   791.4302'33092–dc23
                                        2013005861

1 2 3 4 5   18 17 16 15 14 13

FOR ALEX, WITH LOVE

Contents

I WOULD LIKE TO THANK MICHAEL Lundell for commissioning this book, and Jane Behnken and Raina Polivka for seeing it through to completion with great care. I am also extremely grateful to Michael Temple and Nicole Brenez for their incisive feedback on the manuscript.

In addition, I am indebted to the following for their generosity, help, and support of various kinds: Derek Allan, Timothy Barnard, Nil Baskar, Raymond Bellour, Janet Bergstrom, Martine Beugnet, Christa Blümlinger, Nika Bohinc, Agnès Calatayud, Michael Chanan, Stuart Comer, Chris Darke, Gilles Delavaud, Bernard Eisenschitz, Dror Elkivity, Wendy Everett, Joël Farges, David Faroult, Laetitia Fieschi-Vivet, Monica Galer, Augustin Gimel, Jean-Luc Godard, Roman Gutek, Junji Hori, Youssef Ishaghpour, Nick James, Maja Krajnc, Roland-François Lack, Jae Cheol Lim, Catherine Lupton, Laurent Mannoni, Adrian Martin, Ewa Mazierska, Jurij Meden, Douglas Morrey, Laura Mulvey, Dalia Neis, Dominique Païni, Mark Rappaport, Keith Reader, Wilfried Reichart, Jonathan Rosenbaum, Brad Stevens, Olivier Thévenin, Muriel Tinel, Thomas Tode, Ysé Tran, Rob Tregenza, Michael Uwemedimo, James Williams, and Maxa Zoller. I am especially grateful to Paul Sutton, Head of the Department of Media, Culture and Language at the University of Roehampton, for the valuable support he has given this project. My sincere thanks, too, go to my other Roehampton colleagues, and to the archivists and librarians at the BFI National Library, Bibliothèque nationale de France, Bibliothèque de l'Arsenal, Inathèque de France, Bibliothèque du film, and Archives françaises du film.

Much of the initial research for this book was made possible by a grant from the Arts and

Acknowledgments

Humanities Research Board. I am grateful to the following for commissioning or publishing earlier versions of some of the material included in it, and for permitting me to draw on parts of that work here: Perry Anderson, Emilie Bickerton, Susan Watkins, and Tony Wood at *New Left Review*; John Caughie at *Screen*; Raymond Bellour at *Trafic*; Elizabeth Ezra and Sue Harris, editors of *France in Focus: Film and National Identity* (Berg, 2000); Michael Temple and James Williams, editors of *The Cinema Alone: Essays on the Work of Jean-Luc Godard, 1985–2000* (Amsterdam University Press, 2000); and Nicole Brenez, David Faroult, Michael Temple, and James Williams, with whom I co-edited *Jean-Luc Godard: Documents* (Éditions du Centre Pompidou, 2006).

I am profoundly indebted to my late parents, Julie and Nigel, for their love and unwavering support. John and Frank and their respective families have also been a vital source of strength. Above all, I would like to express my heartfelt gratitude to my family – Alex, Jack, Ella, and Violet Mo – whose love, patience, encouragement, and good humor made it possible for me to write this book.

Jean-Luc Godard,
Cinema Historian

FOR THE PAST FOUR DECADES, JEAN-LUC Godard has pursued a sustained investigation of the theory and practice of audiovisual history. At the heart of his project lies one of his most ambitious and significant achievements to date: the monumental, labyrinthine cinema history series *Histoire(s) du cinéma*. This is simultaneously a set of essays on the history of cinema and television; on Godard's life, and his place within that history; on the history of cinema in the context of the other arts; on the history of film thinking; on the history of the twentieth century; on the interpenetration of cinema and that century; and on the impact of films on subjectivity. It is also a critique of the longstanding neglect by historians of the value of films as historical documents, and a reflection on the narrow scope and limited ambition of the type of history often produced by professional film historians. "All I want to say," as he summed up this aspect of the series, "is that history is badly told."[1] In addition, it offers an exploration of the possibilities of audiovisual historiography generally, and of what Godard has described as a "theorem" regarding cinema and history in particular.[2] This theorem is premised on two main ideas: first, that the cinema, a product of the inventions and discoveries of the nineteenth century, assumed the role of historian of the twentieth, documenting it from beginning to end; and second, that every moment of the past remains potentially available to history. "The past is never dead. It's not even past," he says at one point in the series, citing William Faulkner's celebrated dictum.[3] If the fundamental challenge facing all historians is that of bringing the past to life, Godard's response to that challenge – the central tenet of his theorem – is the proposal and demonstration of a cinematically inspired

Godard's Theorem

method of fabricating history based on the principle of the montage of disparate phenomena in poetic imagery. "Bring together things that have as yet never been brought together and did not seem predisposed to be so," he suggests simply, citing Robert Bresson.[4]

The polysemic *histoire* (meaning both "history" and "story") and *du* in the title *Histoire(s) du cinéma* are central terms. Their combination suggests not only a project about both cinema and history, and about all the stories told by cinema, but also the principle of a form of history derived materially from, and composed out of, the very stuff of cinema. Godard's point of departure for the series was the idea of an audiovisual history of cinema based on the principle of reprojection or reproduction:

> The history of cinema appears to be easy to do, since it is after all made up of images; cinema appears to be the only medium where all one has to do is re-project these images so that one can see what has happened. In "normal" history, one can't project, because it's not projectable; one has to codify in one form or another, write, make manuscripts; whereas here it would seem that all one has to do is reproduce.[5]

In addition to this underlying emphasis on audiovisual form, Godard frequently stressed the centrality to his vision of visual and audiovisual history of montage as a key compositional tool. Video allowed him not only to copy and combine archival film clips, but also to incorporate all manner of extracinematic sounds and images and to make these speak cinematically through montage:

> In a striking manner, film was able to recount its own history in a way quite different from the other arts. And in montage alone, there was a story, or attempts at stories, told in film's own language. One can put a Goya after an El Greco, and the two images recount

something without the need for a caption. One doesn't see that anywhere else. Literature can't do it: I've never seen a history of literature that simply puts a Cervantes and a Sartre side by side. That's cinema. And for cinema, little by little, it could be done, and this principle would establish a cinematographic history.[6]

Besides editing, the full palette of cinema's expressive resources is at the disposal of the filmmaker-historian: light and shadow, color, shape, altered motion, angles, music, sound, and voice. Godard has long been a passionate advocate of cinema's ability to express the ineffable in a manner distinct from that of any other art-form (its capacity for articulating "the words that stay in the throat," as he puts it in the fourth episode, 2B).[7] This idea is represented visually in *Histoire(s) du cinéma* by a handful of emblematic clips: the dance scene from *Bande à part* (1964), which is used to illustrate this sequence in 2B; the shot of the anxious embracing couple from Aleksandr Dovzhenko's *Earth* (1930), which is cited in 1B; and a brief extract from Nicholas Ray's *They Live by Night* (1948), in which Catherine "Keechie" Mobley (Cathy O'Donnell) is shown rising and turning in the half-light, which Godard uses in 1A and 4A. In addition, he sees audiovisual history as offering not only a different means of articulating the past, but also a qualitatively different experience of the past for the viewer-listener to that produced through the reading of history books. The key thing, he stressed to historian Eric Hobsbawm in 2000, is that the meaning should emanate directly from the combination of images and sounds rather than from an explanatory or interpretative text written about or imposed on them.[8] The task of the spectator in this context, he emphasizes, is not necessarily that of understanding, but rather of hearing, receiving, and "seeing" the effects of his compression and concatenation of his disparate source materials in the intuitive, emotional, and visceral way one might experience a piece of music.[9] He has been reiterating the importance, for filmmakers and audiences alike, of learning the creative art of seeing for nearly four decades now: "one should see, and remain in the realm of vision," as he already summarized this central strand of his thinking in 1980.[10] It comes as no surprise, therefore, that he should position *Histoire(s) du cinéma,* in the opening episode, in the tradition of sensuous, rhythmic, visual communication – one exemplified here by the medieval image-based *Book of Kings.*[11] He also relates his project to the later innovatory practices of art historians such as Élie Faure and André Malraux. In addition, we should note in this context an example about which Godard has remained curiously silent: Aby Warburg's pioneering experiment in visual art history, the unfinished *Mnemosyne* "atlas in images" project, in which the latter sought to investigate and chart the memory and transmission of Antique iconography in the art of the Renaissance, via the symphonic arrangement of disparate photographic reproductions on large black panels.[12] If Warburg, as Giorgio Agamben has argued, can be considered the founder of a hitherto "unnamed science whose contours we are only today beginning to glimpse," Godard is his successor and has a word for that science: "cinema," or, better in the context of *Histoire(s) du cinéma,* "video" – literally "I see."[13]

WHAT IS *HISTOIRE(S) DU CINÉMA*?

Histoire(s) du cinéma was released by Gaumont in 1998 as a four-and-a-half-hour video series,

The cinema alone: *Earth* (Aleksandr Dovzhenko, 1930) in 1B, *Bande à part* (Godard, 1964) in 2B, and *They Live By Night* (Nicholas Ray, 1948) in 4A.

From the thirteenth-century picture
bible *Book of Kings*, cited in 1A.

and has been reissued since by a number of companies on DVD (by Imagica in Japan in 2001, by Intermedio in Spain in 2006, by Gaumont in France in 2007, by Artificial Eye in the United Kingdom in 2008, by Olive Films in the United States in 2011, and by Madman in Australia in 2011). Materially speaking, it is a labor of love, involving the painstaking orchestration of thousands of clips from films, television, and radio; details of drawings, paintings, photographs, cartoons, and texts; extracts of songs and music; and a number of recitations and staged sequences.[14] Through the weaving and layering of what are, for the most part, unprepossessing scraps of reproductions, Godard has produced an audiovisual tapestry of astonishing sumptuosity. The series is divided into eight parts:

1A *Toutes les histoires* (All the [hi] stories), 51 minutes;

1B *Une histoire seule* (A solitary [hi]story), 42 minutes;

2A *Seul le cinéma* (The cinema alone), 27 minutes;

2B *Fatale beauté* (Fatal beauty), 29 minutes;

3A *La monnaie de l'absolu* (Aftermath of the absolute), 27 minutes;

3B *Une vague nouvelle* (A new wave), 28 minutes;

4A *Le contrôle de l'univers* (The control of the universe), 28 minutes; and

4B *Les signes parmi nous* (The signs amongst us), 38 minutes.

The episodes bleed into and at times repeat one another, and a number of images and sounds recur in several different contexts, conveying distinct meanings each time. Despite their formal similarity and shared idiom, however, the episodes differ considerably from one another in theme, density, mood, and tone. The first two-part chapter, made up of episodes 1A and 1B, is the series' cornerstone. 1A, whose title derives from a comment made by André Malraux about the early achievements of photography (besides being an art historian, Malraux was a celebrated novelist, filmmaker, and politician), presents in condensed form the principal lines of thinking that run through the remainder of the series, especially in relation to Hollywood and World War II.[15] In 1B, Godard examines his own place within the history of cinema, and pursues a number of theoretical reflections – each of which he presents twice through reference to different examples – on what he considers some of cinema's defining characteristics. The subsequent six episodes are what he has termed "localized case studies."[16] 2A develops the metaphor of "projection," which he had already introduced in 1B; and 2B, whose title, *Fatale beauté*, recalls that of the French release version of Robert Siodmak's *The Great Sinner* (1949), *Passion fatale*, explores the relationship between cinema and the expression of beauty.[17] 3A, whose title *La monnaie de l'absolu* Godard borrowed from the third volume of Malraux's philosophy of painting, *Psychologie de l'art* (*Psychology of Art*, 1947–49), focuses on cinema and the representation of war in the context of the Western pictorial tradition, through particular reference to Italian Neo-realism;[18] and 3B offers a personal account of the French New Wave. 4A reflects on cinema as art through the example of Alfred Hitchcock; and 4B, which derives its title from a fable by the Swiss author Charles Ferdinand Ramuz, is less a further case study than a combination of somber, intimate self-portrait and meditative stocktaking in relation to the series as a whole.[19] Running throughout is a three-way tension among a bleak overarching narrative of

cinematic decline, the vitality of the crystalline forms through which that narrative is expressed, and a recurrent thematic emphasis on artistic metamorphosis and renewal.

It is important to recognize that the title *Histoire(s) du cinéma* does not just designate the videos or DVDs, but that it is also the title of two further artifacts derived from them: a four-volume set of art books published in 1998 in Gallimard's prestigious Blanche collection (republished in a single volume in 2006); and a box set of five audio CDs and multilingual books released by ECM Records in 1999. Godard had initially hoped that Gaumont would also release the series on CD, but when they declined, he turned to ECM Records, who had already issued the digitally remixed soundtrack of *Nouvelle vague* (1990) on CD in 1997.[20] Not solely an audiovisual series, *Histoire(s) du cinéma* is in fact a more complex integrated multiform work. The quotations from the series used in this book are generally my translations of the abbreviated poetic French-language text derived from the soundtrack, which Godard arranged for the Gallimard books.[21] In addition to the three main versions of the series, we should also note a number of further related projects realized, or sometimes simply imagined, by Godard following completion of the videos. Godard was particularly critical of the quality of the videos, especially the mono soundtrack, which had destroyed his creative investment in stereo. His original wish had been for the series to be shown initially on television, and for this television broadcast to be followed by publication of the books and then release on DVD (his preferred choice of format for domestic release from the outset, primarily because of the superior sound quality).[22] Almost exactly the opposite occurred: the books appeared first (on 9 October 1998), a month prior to the audiovisual version (which, contrary to his preference, was released on VHS), and a year before the release of the CDs and broadcast of the series on Canal Plus. Two years later saw the first screening of a 35 mm "best of" compilation of "selected moments" from the series commissioned by Gaumont for theatrical distribution, *Moments choisis des Histoire(s) du cinéma* (2001). This abbreviated 35 mm version, he suggested in 2001, was kept buried by the production company, "like everything Gaumont makes."[23] It was screened once at the Pompidou Center in November 2001, but then not distributed until December 2004, when it was shown for several weeks at the same venue. In it, Godard has reordered the source material significantly. Although there are few major textual changes, and the film is divided into eight numbered sections bearing the titles of the original episodes, these sections are of variable length, and do not follow the original order. Moreover, on several occasions the material included under a given heading derives from a different episode altogether, and 1B does not feature at all.[24] Once the series was finished, Godard also expressed an interest in pursuing the project in a number of further directions. He regretted, for instance, not having mounted an exhibition to accompany the release of the videos and books, as a means of demonstrating what he described as "the different modes of entering and leaving what one can call History."[25] He also talked of having considered staging *Histoire(s) du cinéma* as a play.[26] This, he suggested, would have had to have taken place in a cathedral square, and to have combined a recitation of the text of the series' soundtrack with the projection of its image track onto a vast

book, the pages of which would have had to have been turned by unknown actors. Moreover, inspired by Chris Marker's *Immemory* (1998), he apparently considered the possibility of making a CD-ROM.[27] And finally, although in some respects a separate project and fresh departure, the exhibition he staged at the Pompidou Center in 2006, *Voyage(s) en utopie: JLG, 1946–2006, À la recherche d'un théorème perdu* involved the redistribution of shards of many of the series' constituent ideas, arguments, sources, and references within the three-dimensional space of an art gallery.

THE AIMS AND ORGANIZATION OF THIS BOOK

This book examines the development, forms, themes, and concerns of *Histoire(s) du cinéma* in its various manifestations, and the historical propositions made within it, against the backdrop of three decades of related work by Godard. My understanding of this wider body of work, and of the centrality of *Histoire(s) du cinéma* to it, was shaped by my encounter with Godard's films and other output in the 1980s – when I discovered his early feature films alongside essayistic works such as *Le gai savoir* (1968), *Numéro deux* (1975), *France tour détour deux enfants* (co-dir. Anne-Marie Miéville, 1979), the three-hundredth issue of *Cahiers du cinéma* he edited in 1979, *Scénario du film Passion* (1982), and *Soft and Hard: Soft Talk on a Hard Subject between Two Friends* (co-dir. Miéville, 1985); together with the transcription of the film history lectures he had delivered in Montreal in 1978, *Introduction à une véritable histoire du cinéma* (Introduction to a true history of cinema), which appeared in 1980.[28] During my subsequent doctoral research on Godard and Miéville's collaborative work of the 1970s, I came to realize that the former's emerging *Histoire(s) du cinéma* formed part of a broader interest in history and audiovisual historiography that reached back, via films such as *Ici et ailleurs* (co-dir. Miéville, 1974) and *Moi je* (1973, unfinished), to the image-text "scenario" that he had proposed for an audiovisual history of cinema to Italian television in the early 1970s, and even beyond that to the late 1960s.[29] Living in Paris, I was fortunate to have the opportunity to view and review the virtual entirety of Godard's audiovisual output at the "Tout Godard" retrospective in 1989, including then recent video works such as *On s'est tous défilé* (1987), *Puissance de la parole* (1988), and *Le dernier mot* (1988). Fascinated by these, I obtained copies from the production companies and recorded *Soigne ta droite* (1987), *King Lear* (1987) and the initial versions of the first two episodes of *Histoire(s) du cinéma* from television. Thus, by 1990, I had already unknowingly gathered almost all the key initial traces of a vast work in progress – whose scale and scope would only come fully into focus almost a decade later.

My doctoral research afforded me two essential insights into Godard's work, which remain central to my understanding of it. The first was a realization of the extent and variety of Godard's work in different media and contexts: he was, and remains, less a conventional feature-film director than a multimedia poet, philosopher, critic, and essayist who, over the years, has produced a unique form of expanded cinema, comprising television programs, video scenarios, feature films, audiovisual pamphlets, found-footage poems, written and audiovisual self-reflective metacritical essays, critical articles, books, talks, and interviews. As I have

argued elsewhere, there is no significant difference in his practice between research, work in progress, and finished artwork, and the disparate manifestations of his varied output and interventions are best thought of as the interconnected components of a vast installation under continual development on multiple fronts.[30] In this perspective, considerations such as budget size or conventional hierarchical distinctions between major and minor works (e.g., feature films versus short commercial commissions) or media (e.g., 35 mm versus video or photocopier) are redundant. The second insight concerned the integrated nature of his project, and the flow and metamorphosis within it of references, ideas, motifs, and themes. Each of his works, as Jacques Doniol-Valcroze observed perspicaciously as early as 1965, is "to be continued" in the next[31] – or, as Jean-Louis Leutrat aptly put it, Godard's output as a whole constitutes a sort of infinite "protoplasmic œuvre," one characterized by the constant circulation of matter from one constituent work to the next.[32] Indeed, often the larger individual works can themselves be broken down into a series of separate but interrelated artifacts – all made by Godard – such as written documents, graphic collages, video scenarios, trailers, and pressbooks. This organic, transmedial model is reflected in the relationship between the different versions of *Histoire(s) du cinéma*, which are in turn indissociable from the cognate satellite works that Godard made alongside them, and with which they are in close conceptual and textual dialogue. With these two insights in mind, this book combines a diachronic approach to the series as it developed over time with a synchronic engagement with it in the context of his overall project. These approaches are complemented by three others:

source criticism; an engagement with selected sequences from the series in the context of its overall rhythms, flow, and different manifestations; and a concern for the broader lines of thinking that feed into and run through it. An important source of information regarding the latter is Godard's commentary on his project in interviews. Despite the contingent nature of these documents, the strategic posturing they sometimes contain, and the occasional divergence between what he says and the evidence of the work, they provide an invaluable record of the genesis and development of his thinking. Finally, the task of speaking about Godard is in my view considerably aided and enriched by the creative and critical use of images. I have, therefore, incorporated in this book a form of iconographic criticism, which seeks, variously, to complement and further my discussion of Godard's work, to extend or reinforce a line of argument developed in the text, and to suggest associations through the creation of visual rhymes between images situated in different parts of the book.

The first two chapters adopt a diachronic and synchronic approach, respectively, to the genesis of *Histoire(s) du cinéma*. Chapter 1 offers a history of the series from its inception, via Godard's film history lectures in Montreal and Rotterdam through his production of draft episodes in the 1980s and completion of the various versions in the late 1990s. It includes an analysis of his theorization of cinema as an intrinsically, ontologically historical medium and an examination of the significance to the series of his longstanding intellectual dialogue with the critic Serge Daney. Chapter 2 focuses on his overall output since the early 1970s in terms of its thematic and stylistic relationship with *Histoire(s) du cinéma,* and explores the emergence in his

work of the 1980s of a key metaphor, that of projection. Turning to Godard's role as historian, chapter 3 begins with a discussion of his use in the series of the myth of Orpheus, and goes on to relate the principal features of his historiographic method to a range of guides: historians such as Jules Michelet, Georges Duby, Fernand Braudel, Georges Canguilhem, and François Jacob; philosophers such as Emil Cioran; philosophers of history such as Charles Péguy, Walter Benjamin, and Alexandre Koyré; art historians such as Élie Faure and André Malraux; cinema historians such as Georges Sadoul and Jean Mitry; the film collector, curator, and co-founder of the Cinémathèque française, Henri Langlois; and a range of audiovisual essayists and historians of cinema – such as Santiago Álvarez, Guy Debord, Hollis Frampton, Chris Marker, Artavazd Peleshian, Mikhail Romm, Dziga Vertov, and Orson Welles. Chapters 4 through 6 focus on the substance of Godard's thinking about the history of cinema and television and explore the perspectives he adopts, the topics he covers, and the propositions he advances. Chapter 4 unravels his discourse on silent cinema and on the unrealized potential of the cinematograph as a revolutionary tool for the revelation of the world afresh to a mass audience. It concludes with an analysis of his theorization of the power of cinema to anticipate social upheaval and change, and of its failure to adequately confront and reflect what he considers to be the pivotal historical event of the twentieth century: the Holocaust. Chapter 5 explores his conceptualization of the interrelationship of cinema and nationhood and of filmmaking as a popular, collaborative art-form. It examines the reasoning behind his focus on a handful of national cinematic traditions (American, Russian, German,

Italian, and French) at the expense of virtually
all others, and pays particular attention to his
treatment of French cinema and the New Wave.
Chapter 6 analyzes his longstanding discourse
on the deleterious effects of television, and the
role played by television within the dramaturgy
of *Histoire(s) du cinéma*. It goes on to explore
the origins of his approach to the fabrication of
history through videographic montage, which
it relates to his development of a poetics of the
image in the televisual and digital ages, and to
the range of poetic, scientific and cinematic
models on which he draws. Chapter 7 returns
us to the various manifestations of the series and
the relationship between them. It focuses in particular on the books and CDs, which it considers through reference to Godard's antecedent
output as a graphic and sound artist and to his
recurrent concern in *Histoire(s) du cinéma* for
artistic metamorphosis.

1

Histoire(s) du cinéma: A History

Looking back on the early stages of his film history project from the perspective of 1979, Godard suggested that his desire to actively investigate cinema history had originated in a growing confusion he had experienced around 1967 or 1968 regarding how to proceed artistically. He realized that what he needed to sustain and renew his creative practice as a filmmaker was a deeper and more productive understanding of the relationship between his own work and the discoveries of his predecessors, and felt a thorough dissatisfaction in this regard with written histories of cinema:

> Little by little I became interested in cinema history. But as a filmmaker, not because I'd read Bardèche, Brasillach, Mitry, or Sadoul (in other words: Griffith was born in such and such a year, he invented such and such a thing, and four years later Eisenstein did this or that), but by ultimately asking myself how the forms that I'd used had been created, and how such knowledge might help me.[1]

His approach to the making of history through the bringing together of disparate phenomena as the basis for the creation of poetico-historical images can be traced back as far as the late 1960s. In the course of a 1967 televised discussion of the relationship between people and images, for instance, he was already starting to think about cinema from a historical perspective and to formulate the central principle of his later historiographic method:

> I'm discovering today that Griffith was the contemporary of mathematicians such as Russell or Cantor. At the same moment that Griffith was inventing the language of cinema, roughly the same year, Russell was publishing his principles of mathematical logic, or things like that. These are the sorts of things I like linking together.[2]

Moreover, even in his early work, he had in many ways been a conceptual montage artist. As early as 1965, Louis Aragon, we recall, had perspicaciously characterized him, as a "monteur" in the manner of Lautréamont: "What is certain is that there was no predecessor for [Delacroix's] *Nature morte aux homards,* that meeting of an umbrella and a sewing machine on a dissection table in a landscape, just as there is no predecessor other than Lautréamont to Godard."[3] His theorization of the task of the historian, his approach to cinema history, and his reflection on history more broadly, all flowed directly from this longstanding experimentation with montage.

The earliest trace of Godard's film history project dates from 1969, when he and Jean-Pierre Gorin sketched a brief history of cinema through a collage of images, quotations and handwritten text, as part of an abandoned book project entitled *Vive le cinéma!* or *À bas le cinéma!* (Long live cinema! / Down with cinema!).[4] This was also the year of *Vent d'est,* which, as Alberto Farassino has suggested, can be read not only as an experimental political film, but also as an historical interrogation of the Western, of the costume drama genre, of Hollywood, and of the birth of photography.[5] Godard's drive to investigate cinema history was fueled in the early years by an acute awareness of the profundity of the changes to cinema brought about by the spread and effects of television, coupled with a concern for what he considered growing amnesia in relation to cinema's past artistic achievements, and a loss of understanding regarding the methods and techniques that had made them possible. While shooting *Tout va bien* in 1972 with Gorin, for instance, the duo attempted to model a shot on the sequence depicting Vakoulintchuk's

death in Sergei Eisenstein's *Battleship Potemkin* (1925), and discovered that the secrets behind the insights of the great poet-filmmakers of the silent era, in areas such as framing, montage and rhythm, appeared to have been forgotten. Their attempts to reproduce them resulted in a sense of ungainly imitation: "[W]e realized something very simple: that we didn't know how to make an angle in the way that Eisenstein did; if we tried to film someone with their head bent slightly forward looking at a dead person, we had absolutely no idea how to do it. What we did was grotesque!"[6] By 1973, Godard's venture, known at that point under the working title *Histoire(s) du cinéma: Fragments inconnus d'une histoire du cinématographe* ([Hi]stories of cinema: Unknown fragments of a history of the cinematograph), already included a spread of themes – debated with Gorin over the preceding four years – that would recur throughout much of his ensuing work:

> How Griffith searched for montage and discovered the close-up; how Eisenstein searched for montage and discovered angles; how von Sternberg lit Marlene in the same way that Speer lit Hitler's appearances, and how this led to the first detective film; how Sartre made Astruc wield the camera like a pen so that it fell under the power of meaning and never recovered; true realism: Roberto Rossellini; how Brecht told the East Berlin workers to keep their distances; how Gorin left for elsewhere and didn't come back; how Godard turned himself into a tape recorder; how the conservation of images by the board of directors of the Cinémathèque française operates; the fight between Kodak and 3M; the invention of Secam.[7]

During the mid- to late 1970s, Godard pursued his plan – or at least an explicitly autobiographical variation thereon, which focused in particular on his incomplete projects – under the working title *Mes films,* commissioned by the Société française de production (SFP). However, while Godard grappled with this film for three years, he was ultimately overwhelmed; he refunded the development money and conceded defeat: "I was branching off in every direction, and it was turning into an impossible film: two hundred thousand hours, and I didn't even have enough of my life left to make it."[8] Throughout this decade, Godard made regular allusions to the embryonic *Histoire(s) du cinéma* in interviews and working documents, including the script of his major abandoned project of this period, *Moi je*, the closing five pages of which are presented as "a few as yet very incomplete fragments" of "a true history of cinema," and include what would become over the ensuing decades a central strand of reflection on Eisensteinian and Vertovian montage theory.[9]

The most important early document relating to *Histoire(s) du cinéma* to have come to light is a twenty-page English-language collage he made in the mid-1970s, in which he outlined his plans with Anne-Marie Miéville for a series of "Studies in art, economics, technics [*sic*], people" under the title "Histoire(s) du cinéma et de la télévision"/"Studies in Motion Pictures and Television." The document probably dates from between 1974 and 1976, since it employs a number of images also used in *Ici et ailleurs* and *Six fois deux (Sur et sous la communication)* (co-dir. Miéville, 1976). In any case, the final page suggests that it was produced while Godard and Miéville were still based in Grenoble, rather than in Rolle, Switzerland, to where they relocated their Sonimage company in 1977. The document gives a good deal of precise information not only about the organization and contents of the proposed series, but about the budget and technology they planned to use. It envisages ten one-hour videocassettes (masters to be produced in 2-inch NTSC), each one budgeted at $60,000–$100,000, with a proposed sale price of $250–$500 each. According to this document, the whole series was to be completed in two phases over two years: five cassettes were to be fabricated in the first year, and five in the second. The main organizing principle was that of a division between silent and sound cinema: (1) "Silent U.S.A.," (2) "Silent Europe," (3) "Silent Russia," (4) "Silent Others," (6) "Talking U.S.A.," (7) "Talking Europe," (8) "Talking Russia," (9) "Talking Others." Cassettes 5 and 10 are described not in thematic terms, but rather as an introduction and summing up. The outlines of the episodes given in this document point to significant continuity between this early prototype, Godard's ongoing concerns as the project developed, and the final version of *Histoire(s) du cinéma*. Cassette 7 ("Talking Europe"), for instance, proposes an unorthodox approach to the star system ("the west side story of the star system"), which is illustrated by a comparison of Albert Speer and Hitler on the one hand, and Joseph von Sternberg and Marlene Dietrich on the other. This juxtaposition recurs across Godard's work from the early 1970s to the 1980s and beyond (see the 1973 document cited above): "Bring together a close-up of Dietrich, lit by the man who loved her, with another close-up, organized by the minister for equipment, to light the face of the man he loved at the time: Adolf Hitler."[10] Similarly, cassette 2 ("Silent Russia") presents in synoptic form, through reference to the celebrated sequence depicting the apparent rising up of the stone lions in *Battleship Potemkin*, a line of thinking that culminates in 1A and 3B: Godard's thesis regarding Eisenstein's discovery not of montage, but rather of the effects that can be achieved through the combination of different angles in editing.

In December 1976, Henri Langlois and Godard announced a joint project for an audiovisual history of cinema, which they would cowrite and co-direct for release on film and videocassette.[11] It was to be financed and produced by Jean-Pierre Rassam, whose position at Gaumont in the early 1970s had already been instrumental in allowing Godard and Miéville to experiment extensively with video technology. In the late 1960s and early 1970s, Langlois had been lecturing widely, having first accepted an invitation from Serge Losique in April 1968 to commute to Montreal from Paris every three weeks for a period of three years, beginning in the autumn of that year. Born Srdjan Losic in the former Yugoslavia, Losique, who would go on to found and direct the Montreal World Film Festival, was at that point a professor in the French department at Sir George Williams University (one of two institutions that merged in 1974 to form Concordia University), where he taught French film.[12] In 1967, Losique had founded the Conservatoire d'art cinématographique as a film archive and repertory cinema under the auspices of the university. It was here that Langlois embarked on his now legendary Montreal "anti-lectures," during which he would project reels of films and deliver semi-improvised three-hour talks to students. These anti-lectures were followed in the early 1970s by similar engagements in Washington, D.C., Harvard, and Nanterre. The 1976 prototypical vision of *Histoire(s) du cinéma* conceived by Godard and Langlois was almost immediately abandoned, however, due to the latter's untimely death in January 1977. In March, Godard traveled to Montreal to present a season of twenty-two of his films at the

Cover page of an outline of *Histoire(s) du cinéma* by Godard from the mid-1970s.

Collection Wilfried Reichart.

Conservatoire.[13] During this visit, he pursued discussions with Losique, which were already underway, of the possibility of his picking up where Langlois had left off.[14] In August, at the time of the inaugural edition of Losique's festival, he returned again for further exploration of the idea of a series of unorthodox film history lectures, which he envisaged as investigative research for his true history of cinema and television:

> I'll soon be fifty, which is generally the time that people write their memoirs and recount what they've done. But rather than writing those memoirs, and saying where I come from, and how it is that I've happened to have taken the journey that I have in this profession of mine, the cinema, rather than doing that, I'd like to tell my stories, a little like tales about cinema. And that's what I'm intending to do. There will a dozen courses, which will lead to a dozen cassettes, and, perhaps later on they will produce some more elaborate works.[15]

So began Godard's film history experiment in Montreal.

Despite his deep admiration for Langlois, Godard was not always in full agreement with his mentor. As he stressed to Losique, it would therefore be less a question of him taking over from Langlois than of continuing the work in another way.[16] The original plan had been for Godard to begin delivering his talks in fall 1977. Although this slipped to spring 1978, he started commuting regularly from Rolle to Montreal in April, and delivered fourteen of a proposed twenty lectures on consecutive Fridays and Saturdays at various points throughout the year. The lectures took place on 14–15 April, 5–6 May, 9–10 June, 16–17 June, 6–7 October, 13–14 October, and 20–21 October; further visits were planned for December but did not take place. He envisaged the talks as the first concrete step

on an open-ended journey into what he termed the "completely unknown territory" of cinema history, and anticipated this exploratory voyage culminating in a visual study entitled *Aspect inconnu de l'histoire du cinéma* (The unknown aspect of cinema history), to which he was already planning to devote the remainder of his working life.[17] Although his principal inspiration for the screening/anti-lecture format was undoubtedly Langlois, we should also recall the three-day event that took place at the initiative of Antoine Bourseiller in February 1969, involving Jacques Rivette, Sylvie Pierre, and Jean Narboni, which was conceived around a combination of film screenings and discussion of the concept and practice of montage.[18] The intention of this experiment, as Rivette put it, was "to attempt, in a rather hazardous (indeed aleatory) manner, a 'montage of films': to interrelate, by means of these examples, different approaches to methods of structuring film, and to see what these connections and continuities might produce."[19] Like this event, which was itself clearly informed by Langlois's example, Godard's Montreal talks are best considered not merely as lectures, but as live, practical experiments in performative, visual history. These were part of a co-production deal – the costs of the ten voyages were shared equally between the Conservatoire and Sonimage – designed to lead in the first instance to an introduction to cinema history to be published in book form, and later to a video series, with the participation of the Conservatoire as co-producer. A transcription of the lectures appeared in 1980 as *Introduction à une véritable histoire du cinéma*, a book described retrospectively by Godard as "the beginning of a process," rather than an end in itself.[20] The lectures map many of the themes and methods he subsequently distilled into *Histoire(s) du cinéma,* especially the strong national cinema perspective, the guiding principles of thinking through images and of combining found footage to make history and generate thought, and the fundamental task of exploring what he described as "the history of the type of vision that cinema, which shows things, developed, and the history of the blindness to which it gave rise."[21]

The early autobiographical impetus to Godard's plan, which was explicit in the *Mes films* project, would remain a constant through his work on *Histoire(s) du cinéma.* As he made clear from the outset, his intention was to approach the task of recounting the history of cinema from the perspective his own experience as a filmmaker, and to "explore what was impersonal in this first-person novel, and personal to everybody."[22] He was motivated in his work, he suggested, by a need to express his gratitude towards an art-form that "has allowed me to exist, and given me the desire to do things, and to continue to exist."[23] Moreover, he also considered what he was doing – in the lineage of *Moi je* – as a kind of public "psychoanalysis of myself, of my work."[24] It was with these aims in mind that he approached his earlier films in Montreal as documentary glimpses of his past life – "as if I were going to see my younger self," as he put it.[25] The end result, *Histoire(s) du cinéma,* like Marcel Duchamp's portable museum, *Box in a Valise,* is a distilled summation of Godard's art and thought since he began writing about and making films. Indeed the series is explicitly informed not only by a reengagement with his own films, but also with his early critical texts: many of the clips he samples and treats videographically, until they glow with an almost radioactive intensity, are precisely the same sequences he had

described in his writings in the 1950s. While he was working on the series, he observed, these half-remembered images and sounds functioned in a manner analogous to that of the pebbles in the tale of Tom Thumb, providing a trail that enabled him to retrace his footsteps and piece together an account of his life, and of cinema, through fragments of the films he had loved.[26] Following the pebbles through the forest in the manner of Tom Thumb led him in turn to larger questions regarding both cinema history and history, such as "What forest are we in?" and "What is the history of the forest?"[27]

In April 1978, just before he delivered his first lecture in Montreal, Godard summarized the rationale of his project in terms of a quest to explore a unique historical period – essentially that of silent cinema – in which the liberating, democratizing power of the image momentarily threatened the hegemony of language:

> I want to make a history of cinema that will show that at a particular moment the visual almost took over, a moment when painting and the image had greater weight. In periods when people couldn't write, in the Middle Ages or during the reign of Louis XIV, there was an image of Louis XIV that everyone knew; it was the only one, but it was well known. And since people didn't know how to write, there was a different relationship with text and writing. Then, little by little, forms of communication gave precedence to text; and if cinema – especially silent cinema – was so popular at a given moment, it's because people saw, and there was montage and the association of ideas. There was no need to say "I've seen that"; one understood through seeing.[28]

In June, during his fourth trip to Montreal, he outlined plans for an eight-part series lasting a total of four hours, to be organized principally by national cinema and by a separation between the silent and sound periods (for example, one episode on silent America, one on talking America, and so on).[29] The following month he sketched out an alternative model, very close in structure to the ten-episode series discussed earlier, which envisaged five episodes on silent cinema and five on the sound period.[30] This, he anticipated, would be produced or co-produced – like his and Miéville's two television series, *Six fois deux* and *France tour détour deux enfants* – by the Institut national de l'audiovisuel (INA).[31] The working title of the project at this stage, *Introduction à une véritable histoire du cinéma et de la télévision* (Introduction to a true history of cinema and television), slightly adapted, would become the subtitle that opens the *Histoire(s) du cinéma* books: "Introduction to a true history of cinema, the only one, the true one." The principal outlet he envisaged at this point for the series was television, although he also foresaw a potentially vast videotape market among the burgeoning academic film studies community, especially in the United States. If nothing else, he suggested in a gentle jibe, it would give university lecturers something visual to show and discuss in their seminars, and perhaps have the effect of stimulating new ways of thinking about the investigation and communication of film history. One idea he advanced was that of giving video cameras to students and setting them the task of reproducing certain angles or scenes from classic films; another – which was inspired by one of the Montreal screenings, when a film arrived from the distributor with one of its reels missing – involved removing an entire reel from a feature film and challenging the director whose film it was to reconstruct the reel from memory with the assistance of the students.[32] At the time, the main drawback to such a use of remaking and pastiche in a cinematic

context, as Jean Mitry noted in 1979, in an otherwise enthusiastic response to Godard's advocacy of its potentially productive application in the field of cinema history, was that of cost.[33]

Godard's anti-lectures were organized around a morning projection of one or two films, or of selected extracts from several, which he recalled having helped him when he had made the example of his own work projected in the afternoon. The first film of the day was almost always from the silent era. This played a defining role in relation to the whole of the voyage in question, providing what he termed the "title" of the day's projections, and the overarching framework within which to consider those that followed, including his own.[34] By setting his films in tension with others from the history of cinema, he was not only situating and examining his practice historically, but also, as he made clear, seeking to chart the genealogy of the forms he had created. Thus the first lecture of his second visit combined reels from a variety of films featuring strong, doomed heroines, usually against a backdrop of poverty and social injustice. Those juxtaposed on this occasion were Renoir's *Nana* (1926), Dreyer's *La passion de Jeanne d'Arc* (*The Passion of Joan of Arc*, 1928), and Stroheim's *Greed* (1924), followed by his own *Vivre sa vie* (1962). Day two placed *Le mépris* (1963) alongside a selection of other films about filmmaking: Vertov's *Man with a Movie Camera* (1929), Minnelli's *The Bad and the Beautiful* (1952) and Truffaut's *Day for Night* (1973). At times, Godard toyed with historiographic methods that he would subsequently leave far behind, such as the systematic inclusion of the date of a film's production together with key contextual background information relating to the year in question.[35] For the most part, however, from the beginning of the first lecture onwards, he expressed little interest in chronology or in the ordering of "landmark" names, dates, and masterpieces, preferring instead to present his venture through reference to the disciplines of archaeology, biology, geology, and geography.[36] In an important passage toward the end of the second half of the fourth voyage, he suggested that a genuine history of cinema would need to include three interrelated aspects: contextual information about a given filmmaker and his or her work (he gives the example of Griffith); analysis of the film in question (in this case *Birth of a Nation*, 1915); and the history of a viewer who saw the film when it was first shown.[37] Although this might look initially like a conventional context/text/reception approach to cinema history, Godard's key point, which is clear from the wider discussion of which it is part, is that the majority of cinema histories seldom go far beyond context – and that even that, in his view, is generally poorly done. Contrary to this, his own approach is weighted heavily towards the second and third parts of this triumvirate, especially the last, which he conceives less in terms of empirical audience research or of quantitative reception studies than of a history of mentalities, of the emotional and imaginative investment of spectators in films, and of the effects of this investment on subjectivity.

Let us consider the relationship between Godard's reflections on this topic in Montreal and his later treatment of it in *Histoire(s) du cinéma*. In the series, his emphasis on the viewer, including himself, is even more powerfully felt. His concern lies not just with the emergence, technologies, and forms of cinema, but also – perhaps above all – with the impact of films on subjectivity and memory, what we might think of as the cinema "in us." It is in this sense that the series, as suggested via an on-screen title in 2B, is "Histoire(s) du cinémoi" ([Hi]stories of cineme). But Godard's concern is not only with his own life and self and with the films that have become part of him, but also with the broader idea of the absorption and internalization of films. This is a topic hitherto investigated most fully not by historians, but by artists, critics, and philosophers – such as André Breton, Jean Louis Schefer, Stanley Cavell, and Jonathan Rosenbaum. Breton, for instance, stressed the "incomparable, ever scintillating traces" left by films in the memory, and "how life's supreme moments are filtered through their beam."[38] Schefer, in his reflections on the same phenomenon, explored how films construct memories in the lives of ordinary cinemagoers, "annexing" a part of them in the process.[39] Cavell summarized the issue succinctly in his landmark study *The World Viewed*:

> The impact of the movies is too massive, too out of proportion with the individual worth of ordinary movies, to speak politely of involvement. We involve the movies in us. They become further fragments of what happens to me, further cards in the shuffle of my memory, with no telling what place in the future. Like childhood memories whose treasure no one else appreciates, whose content is nothing compared with their unspeakable importance for me.[40]

This idea of the inscription of films in the human psyche, and of the inhabitation and animation of individuals by half-remembered clips, is conveyed simply and effectively throughout *Histoire(s) du cinéma* via the superimposition of film imagery over the human face, including Godard's own. These sequences recall Rosenbaum's exploration in his autobiographical *Moving Places: A Life at the Movies* of the process whereby films leave arbitrary but indelible "memory-stains" in the psyche.[41] We know Godard to be a keen admirer of Rosenbaum's book, which he once suggested would make a beautiful film.[42] Indeed, the tale spun by the former in 3A around King Vidor's *Bird of Paradise* (1932) can be seen in part as a discrete homage to *Moving Places,* in which this film occupies an exemplary role. If *Histoire(s) du cinéma* is made up of Godard's personal filmic memory stains, any encounter with it is inevitably also highly personal: there is no correct reading, and all routes through it, as he has been at pains to emphasize, are equally valid. "Let every eye negotiate for itself," as the onscreen instruction – borrowed from *Much Ado about Nothing* – puts it in the opening moments of 1A. As the recurrent foregrounding of the "toi" in "histoire" suggests, the history ultimately constructed by Godard is the one produced at the juncture of memory, thought and emotion in the mind of the individual viewer-listener. In this perspective, the series is not only "Histoire(s) du cinémoi" (cineme), but also "Histoire(s) du cinétoi" (cine-you). "What counts above all," as James Williams aptly puts it, "is that an intersubjective critical space is created that actively encourages the processes of memory, and forces us to consider the import and value of *our* own filmic memories."[43]

Returning to Godard's developmental work on the series: in June 1979, at the invitation of Freddy Buache, he delivered an important address on the relationship of the film archives to cinema history at a symposium held at the Cinémathèque suisse in Lausanne.[44] This event formed part of the 1979 annual congress of the International Federation of Film Archives (FIAF). Buache justified Godard's presence at the symposium, which was ostensibly devoted to independent and avant-garde film at the end of the silent era, by arguing that such an event should look not only to the past but also to the future, and that Godard embodied the continuing spirit of avant-garde independence. Before an audience that included historians, critics, curators, filmmakers, and archivists – such as Jean Mitry, Claude Beylie, Robert Daudelin, and Ivor Montagu – Godard took stock of the Montreal experiment, pursued cherished themes such as the creative nature of seeing, and gave the most detailed account available of the state of his thinking up to that point about his film history project. He also made clear the difficulties he had encountered when attempting to generate interest in his idea among American universities, television production companies, and film archives – all of whom appear to have viewed his venture, with its absence of script and mind-boggling copyright implications, with arch skepticism:

> They always said to me, "The originality is that it will be visual!" And then they'd add, "Can you *tell* us how it will be visual?" So I'd say, "No! I can do it, but not tell it. Help me make a start, and then you'll have an idea!" And they'd say, "Can you tell me the start . . . ?" In other words, I was dealing with what I'd call scribes rather than photographers. And the only person I found was Losique.[45]

He proceeded on this occasion to signal the central role that Buache – co-founder of the Cinémathèque suisse in 1948, and its director from 1951 to 1996 – himself would come to play over the ensuing years: "The last times I saw him [Langlois], I was counting on him to guide me through cinema history. From now on, I'm counting on you."[46]

From the beginning of the Montreal venture, Godard had been acutely aware of the

HISTOIRE (S)
DU
CINÉMOI

Bird of Paradise (King Vidor, 1932),
the evocation of the film in 3A, and
intertitles from 1A and 2B.

difficulties his project faced: "I have the idea of the method, but not the means."[47] Although he had already formulated the idea of juxtaposing clips on two screens simultaneously, he realized even before starting that his plan was unrealizable, partly because of the layout of the Conservatoire (which made it impossible to project films simultaneously on adjacent screens in the same theater), and partly because Losique had been unable to raise sufficient funds to transfer the films to video so that they could be shown and compared simultaneously on monitors placed side by side.[48] This was a technique he had already explored extensively in *Ici et ailleurs* and, especially, the lengthy prologue of *Numéro deux,* in which he juxtaposed a wide range of materials in a rehearsal for the critical-historical method he would go on to hone over the ensuing decades. Montreal also allowed Godard to fine-tune his distinction between the act of watching a film and the art of seeing it: "Before producing a history of cinema, it will be necessary to produce the vision of films, and producing the vision of films – I suspected as much, but now I know for sure – is not just a question of viewing them, and talking about them afterwards; it's maybe a question of knowing how to see."[49] In Lausanne, he explicitly linked the possibility of seeing to the principle of comparison: "I'd put it as simply as this: there's no real history of cinema because there's only one screen, not two."[50] Nevertheless, he quickly resigned himself in Montreal to the fact that his conception of how the task might be approached differently could not be realized instantly, and he was therefore content to see the experiment through as agreed, with a view to pursuing it in another form at a later date. In Godard's view, the fact that the transfer of films to video for the purposes of comparative study was technically feasible in the late 1970s, but that there appeared to be an insurmountable array of legal, financial, and practical barriers to allowing it to happen was symptomatic of an underlying unconscious fear of the powers that might be unleashed by allowing films to be shown and seen in the manner he envisaged.[51] Paradoxically, of course, by this stage Godard had been working in video, and blending film and video for six years. What he needed above all to take his project forward was a telecine machine, which would enable him to transfer films (or film clips) onto video, and then combine and manipulate them videographically. He returned to this gap between what he believed was possible, and what he was ultimately constrained to do, during his fourth visit to Montreal, where he argued that the material limitations resulted in an overly conventional and ultimately unproductive screening/discussion format: "So we've been reduced to doing cine-club-style discussions: watching a film, and talking about it afterwards. In other words, obscuring. If by any chance something has been revealed during the projection, it is obscured again by language afterwards."[52]

By the time of the Lausanne event, Godard was convinced that the way forward was video, and that a true audiovisual investigation of cinema history could only come into being through a marriage of video, telecine equipment, and the collections of the film archives.[53] Specifically, he argued that archives should bring together projection and production, and that researchers attached to each archive should have access both to the collections and to appropriate technical facilities, so as to encourage the regular production of historical films using archival material.[54] The key problem of the cine-club model dismissed by Godard – the sequential projection of films or clips, followed by discussion – is that it entails a delay between seeing the material on the screen and the production of critical thought. Rather than allowing the viewer to sense and trace possible connections at the moment of projection, the historian-researcher is obliged to fall back on memory and language:

> What one termed seeing a film was simply projecting a film. And then, doing cinema history, or film criticism, consisted of reorganizing one's memories in a certain way, and saying what one had seen. . . . And films, in my opinion, are hardly seen any more, since for me "seeing" means the possibility of comparing. But comparing two things, not comparing an image and the memory that one has of it. Compare two images, and at the moment one sees them, trace certain relationships. But for this to be possible, the technical infrastructure that exists today needs to make it possible. Certainly, in the past, one could say, "OK, let's project!" If one says, "Eisenstein, in such and such a film, adopted the parallel editing theoretically inaugurated by Griffith," one would need to project Griffith on the left, and Eisenstein next to it. One would then see straight away, as in the judicial process, that something is true and something is false. And one would be able to have a discussion. But having two cinema theaters next to one another would be a bit difficult. Today, however, video exists. Films can be put on video and compared. One might think that this ought to be the first task of the cinematheques or film schools. Alas, it appears to be the last, and that precisely the only history that could be written, that of cinema, is not.[55]

What Godard could not know, as he uttered these words, was that he was speaking on the cusp of a technical and cultural revolution that would fundamentally alter both the situation and his method: the rapid proliferation of domestic video technology, the commercial release of many films on videotape, and the possibility of recording material off-air by anyone in possession of a VCR. As Dominique Païni later

Learn to see, not to read: *Ici et ailleurs* (Miéville and Godard, 1974) and *Numéro deux* (Godard, 1975).

observed, from this point on the relationship between film and spectator was irrevocably altered: copies of films were now at the mercy of the viewer, who was able to take control of them through interventions such as pausing, rewinding, fast-forwarding, copying, re-editing, and other forms of manipulation.[56]

The key initial hurdle facing the audiovisual historian seeking to work directly in images and sounds, rather than with pen and paper, is that of access to the films. The relatively low cost and ease of copying and manipulation opened up by video technology completely altered the situation, but at a high aesthetic cost: films on video (or television, or DVD), as Godard has consistently argued, are not the films themselves, but copies ("let's not / exaggerate / not even / copies / of / reproductions," as he describes films on television in 1A).[57] As a result, he suggests to Serge Daney in 2A, his project involves an unavoidable double compromise: he must work with poor quality, miniature copies of the original films; and the end result will be distributed for domestic consumption via the small screen, whether via television broadcast or on video or DVD. He was already fully aware in Montreal of the scale of the challenge facing him, and of the inevitable compromises he would have to make along the way as of the result of the unavailability of certain films, the scaled-down proportions of the image (assuming, that is, that the project was to come to fruition on video through television co-production in the way he then envisaged, rather than on 35 mm, which he considered unrealistic), and reduced image and sound quality: "The history that we'll make will be a trace, like a regret that it's not even possible to do cinema history, but we'll see a trace of it."[58] Reprising this point a decade later in

his conversation with Daney in 2A, he distills his regret into the distinction between cinema, which he associates with projection, and television, which he links to transmission: "My goal, therefore, alas (laughter), is like that little poem by Brecht: 'I examine my plan carefully; it is unrealizable.' Because it can only be done on TV, which reduces. . . . But we can make a memento of this projectable history. It's the only history that projects, and it's all we can do."[59] Ultimately, however, like comparable video-based film history essays, such as Mark Rappaport's *Rock Hudson's Home Movies* (1992) and Chris Petit's *Negative Space* (1999), *Histoire(s) du cinéma* ended up integrating the diminished, murky quality of the film image, mediated through electronic reproduction and repeated copying, into its discourse on technological change.

THE MUSEUM OF THE REAL

We shall now consider Godard's theorization of the relationship between cinema and history. By referring in 2B to Marcel Pagnol's speculative historical investigation into the mystery of the so-called man in the iron mask, who was apparently imprisoned for life during the reign of Louis XIV (and later immortalized by Alexandre Dumas), he lightheartedly suggests a natural affinity between the work of filmmakers and that of historians.[60] Underlying his suggestion, however, is a more serious proposition regarding cinema's historical function, which he outlined in detail during his talk in Lausanne. It is a view that had remained fundamentally unchanged since his early criticism, and would later feed into *Histoire(s) du cinéma*: all films carry an extremely high documentary charge, providing up-to-the-moment snapshots of an ever-changing present. This is how he presented his conceptualization of fiction films as news bulletins in 1966:

> Lumière, they say, is documentary, and Méliès is fantasy. But today, what do we see when we watch their films? We see Méliès filming the reception of the King of Yugoslavia by the president of the Republic. A newsreel, in other words. And at the same time we find Lumière filming a family card game in the Bouvard and Pécuchet manner. In other words, fiction.[61]

His model implies a number of different types of relationship between cinema and the world it represents. First, as chemical, electronic, or digital recordings, all films – irrespective of their nominal status as newsreels, documentaries, or fictional dramas – are intrinsically historical insofar as they capture and store time. Second, as a mimetic recording machine, cinema conserved the twentieth century on celluloid; as a result, all cinema's stories – as he suggested in 1989 – form part of, and recount, the same history.[62] All films, no matter how banal or trivial, and irrespective of ostensible intentions such as entertainment or information, serve to haphazardly document human attitudes, cultures, customs, behavior, clothing, and so on, thereby providing the historian with an incomparably rich audiovisual archive of the world from the late nineteenth century onward. "All one needs to do," as Godard has summarized this aspect of his thinking, "is watch fifteen films; one sees everything."[63] This is the main sense of the idea he advances in 3B of cinema as the "museum of the real." It is also one of the senses of the myth of Orpheus in *Histoire(s) du cinéma:* cinema seemingly allows us to miraculously bring back and survey the past at will. A succession of onscreen titles at the end of 2A, which are superimposed

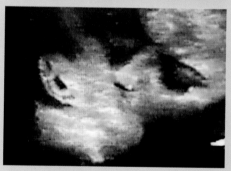

Rock Hudson's Home Movies (Mark Rappaport, 1992), *Broken Blossoms* (D. W. Griffith, 1919) in 1A, and *Negative Space* (Chris Petit, 1999).

over a still from Carl Theodor Dreyer's *The Bride of Glomdal* (1926) showing a man and a woman in a boat (the former is looking back over his shoulder at the latter), express this idea succinctly: "Cinema authorizes Orpheus to look back without causing Eurydice's death."[64] Although human memory is notoriously unpredictable and unreliable, cinema, Godard suggests in 1B, is "the only place / where memory is enslaved": the projector "remembers" the camera, which "remembers" the filmstock, which in turn "remembers" the real.[65] Godard is also alert, however, to what films have ignored, avoided, or distorted, and to the traces of rehearsal and control in documentary and newsreel footage. He is, after all, associated with influential epigrams such as "Fauxtographe" (*Week-end*, 1967), which he redeploys in an on-screen caption in 2B, and "This is not a just image, it is just an image" (*Vent d'est*, Dziga Vertov group, 1969), which he reuses in 1B (although it is important to note that the latter phrase, often wrongly attributed to him, originated with Jean-Pierre Gorin).[66] In *Histoire(s) du cinéma*, cinema's capacity to confuse or mislead is summarized through reference to Louis Feuillade's film *Une erreur tragique* (A tragic mistake, 1913, the title of which is used in 1B and 3B), in which the ostensible evidence of the image (that a woman is having an affair) is disproved by the context (the man with whom she is filmed turns out to be her brother), but only after her enraged husband has set out to punish her. Furthermore, in documentary, Godard suggested in 1998, it is the usually imperceptible processes of sociopolitical *mise en scène* that are recorded and revealed.[67] Thus caught in the Lumière brothers' celebrated film of workers leaving their factory, he has argued, are multiple layers of mediation and manipulation: not only

do those depicted, schooled in the workings of moving images, know they are being filmed and present themselves accordingly for the camera, but they are also enacting the gestures and stage directions mapped out for them by the factory management.

The third key aspect of the relationship between cinema, reality, and history insisted on by Godard, as he made clear in his conversation with Youssef Ishaghpour in 1999, is that at the level of theme and narrative, fictional films offer remarkably resonant metaphorical images of the periods in which they were made:

> [Cinema] is made from the same raw material as History. The fact is that even when it's recounting a slight Italian or French comedy, cinema is much more the image of the century in all its aspects than some little novel; it's the century's metaphor. In relation to History, the most trivial clinch or pistol shot in cinema is more metaphorical than anything literary. Its raw material is metaphorical in itself. Its reality is already metaphorical. It's an image on the scale of the man in the street, not the infinitely small atomic scale or the infinitely huge galactic one. What it has filmed most are men and women of average age. In a place where it is in the living present, it addresses them simply: it reports them, it's the registrar of History.[68]

Fourth, as he has argued through reference to films such as *The Battle of Algiers* (Gillo Pontecorvo, 1966), *L'aveu* (*The Confession*, Costa-Gavras, 1970) and *Time of the Gypsies* (Emir Kusturica, 1988), the fakery of bad cinema (or "cinematic falsification," as he has described it) is a precious indicator of "historical falsification."[69] Similarly, if the vitality of film language provides a concise echogram of social health, a reliance on the regurgitation of preexisting forms is a reliable sign of political oppression and social stagnation. Thus in the Soviet Union, for example, Godard has suggested that the rapid replacement of the innovatory experiments of filmmakers such as Vertov and Eisenstein by more conventional, conservative forms offers a clear cinematic record of the rise and abuses of Stalinism.[70]

To an extent, Godard's thinking on the relationship between cinema, reality, and history can be traced back to film critic and theorist André Bazin's influential definition of cinema in 1945, in his account of the ontology of the photographic image, in terms of the mummification of reality, and beyond it to the proto-realist film theory of the 1920s, notably the concepts of *photogénie* and mobile embalming developed by Louis Delluc and Jean Epstein, respectively. Although in many ways close to commentators such as these, Godard's thinking includes a significant additional step: in the process of representing the world, cinema drains the real of life, effectively killing it off before mourning and resurrecting it via the projected image. Thus every film, no matter how ordinary or mediocre, constitutes an "attempt at resurrection."[71] This is an idea enacted within the narrative of *Nouvelle vague*: sacrifice of Roger Lennox (Alain Delon), followed by his miraculous return, like that of the projected moving image in the theater, in the guise – remarkably similar, but not quite identical – of Richard Lennox (also played by Delon). This principle is played out and commented on in *Histoire(s) du cinéma* in a number of sequences. In a brief clip from Renoir's *La grande illusion* (*The Grand Illusion*, 1937) in 1A, for instance, Captain de Boïeldieu (Pierre Fresnay) – who, in the original film, has just been shot dead – is miraculously brought back to life through reverse motion. The same episode includes a glimpse of the resurrected dead in Browning's *Mark of the Vampire* (1935), and 1B

includes a still from Dreyer's *Ordet* (*The Word*, 1955) depicting Inger's (Birgitte Federspiel) return to life. This analogy between cinema and resurrection was explicit in a good deal of early writing on cinema. Here, for instance, is a 1911 account of the experience of the cinematograph by the poet and dramatist Jules Romains:

> The lights go down. A cry escapes from the crowd and immediately is taken back. . . . A bright circle abruptly illuminates the far wall. The whole room seems to sigh "Ah!" And through the surprise simulated by this cry, they welcome the resurrection they were certain would come.[72]

This, at its simplest level, is the sense of the phrase "the image will come at the time of the resurrection," which Godard has repeatedly attributed in interviews to St. Paul, and variations on which are given in 1B, 4A, and *Hélas pour moi* (1993). It is central to *Histoire(s) du cinéma,* and we shall return to it later. For the moment, let us simply note that although the theme of resurrection is important in St. Paul (as in his First Letter to the Corinthians), Godard's source, as Bamchade Pourvali has pointed out, in fact appears to be a 1984 article on his work by the author and art critic Jacques Henric, which drew an extended parallel between Godard and the Pauline notion of the madman, and indeed between Godard and St. Paul.[73] In his article, Henric attributed a variation on the phrase in question, "the image will only know fullness in the Resurrection," to St. Paul, and it is surely no accident that it was shortly after the appearance of the special issue of *Art press* in which Henric's article was published that Godard began citing this quasi-Pauline phrase.[74] Moreover, whether consciously or not, Henric was echoing an earlier comment by Langlois, in which the latter had also likened Godard to St. Paul.[75]

Where Godard parts company with writers such as Romains is in his insistence on the sacrifice on which the resurrection depends. Central to *Histoire(s) du cinéma,* and to Godard's thinking generally, is a model of the artistic process inspired by one of André Malraux's key propositions in his writings on art history: that the artist is the rival of reality, rather than its transcriber, and that the function of art is that of transfiguring and replacing reality, rather than of emulating or representing it.[76] For Godard, following Malraux, the function of cinema in *Histoire(s) du cinéma* and elsewhere is not just that of being true to life, but "truer than life" (1B).[77] His engagement with this key strand of Malrucian thought goes back a long way. He has made it his own, and consistently reformulated it in a manner that places particular emphasis on the sacrificial dimension of the creative process. In a 1957 article on Jean Renoir, for instance, he was already summarizing Malraux's model in terms of the idea of the inextricable interrelationship of destruction and creativity, which he presented through reference to fire: "Genius, Malraux wrote somewhere, is born of fire. *Of what it consumes.*"[78] This idea resonates across Godard's œuvre, in which it is almost always associated with fire imagery. Four decades later, he would repeat it in virtually identical terms in 2B (in a passage also used in *JLG/JLG: Autoportrait de décembre,* 1995): "art is like fire / it is born / out of what it consumes."[79] Throughout *Histoire(s) du cinéma,* he represents this idea through the recurrent use of vampire imagery, in which cinema itself is cast in the role of the vampire, feeding off the blood of the real as the basis for its poetic evocations of the world. This vampiric relationship is also conveyed in 2B through the combination of red, black, and white – as if the blood of the real, on which cinema feeds, were seeping out of the image. The same idea also haunts Godard's other work of the 1980s. "Is it true that cinema kills life?" asks the aptly named Eurydice (Marie Valéra) in *Grandeur et décadence d'un petit commerce de cinéma* (1985), the film in which Godard introduced the idea that photography, followed by cinema, were both born in black and white rather than color because (as Jean Almereyda [Jean-Pierre Mocky] puts it to Eurydice) they "had to take part in the mourning of life." This theorization of the film image is developed and presented towards the end of 1B, and reprised in 2B:

> because / here is what happened / in the early hours of the twentieth century / technologies decided / to reproduce life / so photography was invented / and cinema / but as morality / was still strong / and they were getting ready / to extract from life / even its identity / they mourned / this putting to death / and it was in the colors of mourning / in black / and white / that the cinematograph came into existence[80]

Godard goes on to suggest poetically that the mourning process at the heart of cinema also explains the proximity, following the widespread adoption of color, between the shades of Technicolor and those of funeral wreaths, a fact that cinema rapidly forgot as a result of its appetite for spectacle, stars, glamour, glory, and Oscars.

Thus far, Godard's theorization of the relationship between cinema, reality, and history is reasonably straightforward. It includes, however, another important dimension, which he has summarized in a deceptively simple formula: "the cinema is montage."[81] The term "montage" in this context does not just mean editing. Godard invests it with a range of connotations, which we need to unpack if we are to fully grasp his theorem regarding cinema's intrinsically historical nature. It is important first to recognize that his preoccupation with montage goes back a long way, and can be traced in particular to his 1956 critical article "Montage, mon beau souci" (Montage, my beautiful care), whose title he had long intended to reuse for a stand-alone episode of *Histoire(s) du cinéma*.[82] In "Montage, mon beau souci," Godard had confronted the anti-editing directive issued by Bazin, "Montage interdit" (Editing prohibited), and insisted instead on the taut interrelationship of montage (temporality, traditionally associated with poetry and music from the writings of critics such as Ricciotto Canudo onward) and *mise en scène* (spatial representation, usually allied to painting).[83] His argument in this article can be seen in part as an extension of the ideas of early theorists such as Jurij Tynjanov in the 1920s, who, like Eisenstein, used the term "montage" to designate not only the relationships between shots, but also intra-image relations.[84] In his later discourse, however, Godard goes much further, applying the term not only to the relationships internal to cinema, but also to a far broader set of social, political and even existential relations that are established and revealed through cinema (and art generally) between people, and between people and the world:

> Cinema was the true art of montage that began five or six centuries BCE, in the West. It's the entire history of the West. It's not the history of the East, nor that of Mexico and the Indians. That of black Africa, nobody knows what it is, and we're not even close to knowing. It's the history of the West, the history of a view of the world, of art coming to an end, and which can be seen today through cinema.

> Now we're entering another history. It was montage, the relationship between things, between people, by means of a relationship to things seen in the form of the reproduction of those things.[85]

Godard's thinking is reminiscent of that of the phenomenological philosopher Maurice Merleau-Ponty, whose reflections on cinema had in part inspired his filmmaking in the 1960s. In a lecture delivered in 1945, Merleau-Ponty argued that the medium's unprecedented power resided in its astonishing capacity for laying bare "the bond between subject and world, between subject and others."[86] We know Godard to have been very familiar with this text: when Raymond Bellour mentioned it to him during an interview in 1964, the former responded by quoting an extract of it from memory.[87] Merleau-Ponty's argument recalls Bazin's praise for the preservation and presentation of the "natural unity" between beings and things through the use of cinematic techniques such as deep focus and long uncut takes.[88] Moreover, Merleau-Ponty and Bazin were in turn very close on this issue to Malraux, who had defined art a few years earlier, in his "Esquisse d'une psychologie du cinéma" (written in 1939, first published in 1940, and translated as "Sketch for a Psychology of the Moving Pictures"), as "the expression of significant relations between human beings, or between minds and things."[89] Drawing and expanding on this key idea in Montreal, Godard suggested that cinema not only captures and reveals the relations between people and things, but also casts in relief human behavior and social relations, making them available for study and criticism.[90] He also began to identify, and to distinguish between, various different categories of "montage" at work in cinema (within the image, between images, between the viewer and the screen, and among the individual, society, and the phenomenal world):

> When people saw a film, there was something that was at least double, and since someone was watching, it became triple. In other words, there was something, something else, which in its technical form became gradually known as montage. It was something that filmed not things, but the relationships between things. In other words, people saw the relationships; and first of all they saw a relationship with themselves.[91]

This takes us to the heart of Godard's thinking regarding the profundity of the relationship between cinema, reality, and history. For him, the making of history depends on the juxtaposition, or montage, of apparently unrelated situations and periods. By recording the relations between disparate phenomena and between people and the world, and then revealing those relations to audiences at the moment of projection, cinema, for Godard, operated as a vast montage machine, which automatically and mechanically enacted the work of the historian as a monteur. Thus the age of cinema, he can claim, is "the only time in the past four hundred million years that a certain way of telling stories was 'history.'"[92]

DEVELOPMENT AND MORPHOGENESIS OF THE SERIES

We return now to Godard's developmental work on *Histoire(s) du cinéma*. In 1979, he approached Joël Farges, who at the time was co-editor with François Barat of the "Ça/cinéma" book series published by Éditions Albatros, which had established itself in this period as an important outlet for intelligent books on film history and theory. Godard gave Farges the audio recordings he had made of his Montreal talks, and the latter commissioned a transcription.[93] Once this was complete, the two met five or six times to go over and edit the manuscript of what would become *Introduction à une véritable histoire du cinéma*. Godard retained editorial control throughout, driving the project and making all the key decisions, including that of cutting the questions from Serge Losique and from the students. This had the effect of presenting his essentially dialogic lectures in the form of a monologue.[94] Godard also insisted that the book should contain a large number of images, so as to provide a dynamic pictorial evocation of the films projected during the original talks. With this in mind, he gave Farges a list of titles, and the latter sourced three or four relevant images per film, mainly from the Cinémathèque française photograph collection. From these, Godard in turn selected one image for each film, occasionally substituting a photograph of his own, and put them in the order in which he wished them to appear. He then gave Farges the green light to publish, and the book was printed in an initial run of two to three thousand copies. Within a week or so of the book's appearance in March 1980, however, Godard called to say that was not happy with it, and that he was particularly dissatisfied with the way in which the images had been reproduced. What he wanted, he insisted – and demonstrated using the photocopier in the Albatros office – were not illustrations reproduced in conventional grayscale on glossy paper, but graphically flat, high-contrast black-and-white photocopied images on matte paper. Moreover, he was also unhappy that the sections of images were integrated in each instance into the transcription of the first of the two lectures that make up each voyage, which had resulted in a mismatch throughout the book between the films discussed in the text and the accompanying images, together with corresponding lengthy passages of text where there are no images at all. He wanted the images redistributed more fully throughout the book, and, in particular, for the relevant images to be placed within the lecture to which they related. To demonstrate his precise wishes, Godard gave Farges a copy of the book, which he had physically taken to pieces and put back together exactly as he wanted it, adding in the process four handwritten poetic commentaries relating to the themes of some of the lectures. Thus two or three months after its original appearance, Albatros reprinted the book in accordance with Godard's wishes. Although the body of the text is identical in the two versions, the format of the table of contents and the manner in which the voyages and film titles are rendered at the beginning of each lecture were altered, and the book was repaginated. The publisher subsequently issued several further reprints of this second version. Godard was apparently content with the new version. Booksellers, however, were far less enthusiastic, finding the quality of the illustrations in it to be substandard, and indeed many of them complained; some even returned their copies to Albatros.

In the early 1980s, Godard occasionally mentioned in interviews that he was pursuing his film history project in the form of a two-year Dutch-backed venture in association with the Rotterdamse Kunststichting (Rotterdam Arts Foundation). The Foundation was closely linked to the Rotterdam film festival, Film International, which had been founded in 1972 by Huub Bals at the initiative of the Foundation's director, Adriaan van der Staay. In 1980, Bals's assistant, Monica Tegelaar, who by this

Illustration and critical commentary designed by Godard for the second print run of *Introduction à une véritable histoire du cinéma.*

point had come to occupy a key programming and acquisitional role at the festival, convinced the Foundation to make a substantial financial investment in Godard's project, with a view to enabling him to buy the telecine machine he had long coveted.[95] In exchange, Godard would deliver a further series of seminars on cinema history in Rotterdam. Prior to this, in 1978, Tegelaar had visited Godard in Rolle to discuss acquiring *France tour détour deux enfants* for Film International's distribution arm, and showing it at the festival itself (where it received its world premiere in January the following year, accompanied by a debate between Godard and the audience); she also subsequently prepurchased the distribution rights to *Sauve qui peut (la vie)* (1979) and *Passion* (1982).[96] As Jan Heijs and Frans Westra documented in their biography of Bals, following Godard's appearance at the 1979 event, he came again on the last day of the 1980 festival to announce that he would be giving a course on cinema history in Rotterdam over the following two years, starting in September 1980.[97] This plan was reported quite widely in the press.[98] The idea was that he should deliver eleven two-day sessions during 1980–81 to a select group of participants, made up mainly of Dutch filmmakers and critics, and that these should lead to the production of ten videotapes, which would be co-produced by Film International and Sonimage.[99] The conception of these videotapes appears to have been reasonably straightforward: a combination of Godard's recorded responses to the students with relevant archival film clips.[100] In September, the students were sent a letter, together with what Heijs and Westra described as "a sort of course pamphlet," which appears, on the basis of their description, to have been made up of a selection of the pages from the English-language collage outline of his project that he had produced in the 1970s. On 23 October 1980, Godard gave his first talk, which by all accounts was chaotic: it took place in the Faculty of Medicine at Erasmus University, where the participants found themselves joined by approximately forty other students, who had elected to attend the session as part of their general studies program; and he played them a recording in French – without translation – of a discussion between himself and Freddy Buache (doubtless a recording of his talk the previous June at the Cinémathèque suisse in Lausanne).[101] Moreover, he left the class half a day earlier than scheduled. "The people left behind," according to Heijs and Westra, "were flabbergasted and wrote to complain about the 'organizational chaos' that same afternoon."[102]

Godard postponed the next scheduled session (November 20) until 4–5 December, when he pursued a method he had already tried out in Montreal: the screening one after another of selected reels from different films, with a view to exploring the potential correspondences between them (on this occasion Resnais's *L'année dernière à Marienbad* [*Last Year at Marienbad*, 1961], Ozu's *Tokyo Story* [1953], and Renoir's *La règle du jeu* [*The Rules of the Game*, 1939]). The next class, which took place two months later, during the 1981 festival, was the most imaginative and interesting montage experiment he had attempted since embarking on the Montreal lectures three years before. For this occasion, he prepared a special edition of *Sauve qui peut (la vie)*, retitled *Sauve la vie (qui peut)*, which was made up of five ten-minute extracts from his own film interspersed with four ten-minute extracts from a selection of other films from the Film International collection (making ninety minutes in total).[103] The films he cut into his own were *The General Line* (Sergei Eisenstein, 1929), *Cops* (Edward Kline and Buster Keaton, 1922), *The Earth Trembles* (Luchino Visconti, 1948), and *Man of Marble* (Andrzej Wajda, 1977).[104] The result, which according to Jean-Claude Biette was apparently remarkable, nonetheless generated a degree of hostility on the part of some of the journalists present and confusion among the students, who remained unclear about their precise role in the production of the videotapes.[105] The next projection-discussion, chaired by Monica Tegelaar, took place on 19 June 1981. Godard juxtaposed extracts from three silent and three sound films, including *The General Line*, De Sica's *Umberto D.* (1952), Mizoguchi's *Ugetsu* (1953) and Antonioni's *The Cry* (1957). Unfortunately, the selection of films available had been severely limited due to the previous year's fire in the archive of the Dutch Film Museum.[106] The post-screening discussion was apparently rather fruitless, partly, one assumes, because of the language barrier (everything had to be mediated via an interpreter), but also because Godard had envisaged having access to basic video editing equipment to enable him to work practically with the students; it was not provided. At the end of the session, it was decided that for the next seminar, which was scheduled for September, the students would select and debate the films in advance, and so bring concrete points and questions to the discussion with Godard. It was also hoped that by this stage the video equipment requested by Godard would be in place. This proposed September slot was presumably canceled, since it is not mentioned again in any of the reports on the course, and there would be no further sessions. At the end of the following year, on 22 December 1982, Godard finally informed the Rotterdam Arts Foundation that he was unable to complete the project to his satisfaction, and offered to repay their investment of 150,000 guilders in monthly installments over six months.[107] The director of the Foundation, Paul Noorman, contested Godard's figures and demanded repayment of a much larger sum (321,760 guilders), which took into account both Godard's failure to honor the contract and the interest due on the original investment.[108] It is not clear how this dispute was resolved; what is certain is that the funds from the Foundation, and the equipment that Godard was able to purchase with them, were instrumental in enabling him to work in earnest on the series in the early 1980s. He did not forget the extent of his debt to the Foundation generally, and to Monica Tegelaar in particular: he thanked the former, along with Losique's Conservatoire d'art cinématographique, in each of the *Histoire(s) du cinéma* books; and he dedicated 1A to Tegelaar (jointly with Mary Meerson).

Asked following completion of the series how he had set about preparing for it, Godard replied that he had done two simple things: first, he had started recording lots of material from television and buying and classifying commercial videotapes; second, he had opened a dozen or so files – one per episode, and a series of subfolders devoted to topics such as men, women, couples, children, and war – in which to collate and categorize still images, such as photographs, pages from books and magazines, and book covers.[109] By the time *Histoire(s) du cinéma* was completed, Godard's audiovisual archive held approximately three thousand videos.[110] In the finished series, the televisual origin of some of this material is occasionally evident in the form of the logos of the channels on which it had been broadcast. Thus, one can clearly make out the word "Arte" over archival footage of an airplane dropping bombs in 1A, or the "Planète" logo over a clip from Alain Resnais's *Nuit et brouillard (Night and Fog,* 1955) in 1B. The presence of these indicators of the original source of the material is doubtless due in part to practical considerations, such as the availability of the films in question. In the latter instance, however, it is worth noting that the partial erasure of the logo, and the retention of a trace of the act of erasure, extends Godard's earlier critique (in a letter denouncing Antenne 2's superimposition of its logo over footage from the same film) of the manner in which television channels stamp marks of ownership over the material they broadcast – especially when this involves images of unspeakable human suffering, such as those in Resnais's film.[111] As for his paper archive, Godard presented and discussed some of his color-coded files in the course of a 1987 episode of the television program *Cinéma cinémas* devoted to his work.[112] Here he spread out a dozen or so files on his desk – including three entitled "Episode 5," "Shadow and Light," and "Montage" – from which he took various photographs and proceeded to suggest possible connections between them. In an exemplary demonstration of his historical montage method, he took a picture from the "Montage" folder depicting Anna (Lillian Gish) on the ice floe in Griffith's *Way Down East* (1920), and held it up next to a photograph of the director and his production team taken during the making of the film. He then went on to compare it with a photograph of a patient, Augustine (it is in fact the cover of Georges Didi-Huberman's study of Charcot's investigation of hysteria at the Salpêtrière Hospital in Paris in the nineteenth century, *Invention*

de l'hysterie [*Invention of Hysteria*]), and commented "close-up of one, followed by a close-up of the other: it's the same image." This comparison of the "symptoms" displayed by Anna and Augustine, respectively, can be read in part as an extension of Didi-Huberman's thesis regarding the theatricality of the hysterical body, and the transformation via photography of the doctor into an artist, and of the patient into an actor.[113]

In the 1980s, Godard referred at times to the emergent *Histoire(s) du cinéma* under the title *Splendeur et misère du cinéma* (The splendor and poverty of cinema), a reference to Balzac's *Splendeurs et misères des courtisanes* (*A Harlot High and Low*). This was doubtless in part a nod to the monumentality and panoramic ambition of the series to which this book belongs, *La comédie humaine* (*The Human Comedy*). A trace of this abandoned working title is visible in the onscreen announcement at the beginning of 1A: "Canal Plus présente *Histoire(s) du cinéma splendeur et misère.*" We also know from longstanding observers, such as Freddy Buache and Alain Bergala, that by the middle of the decade, Godard had already generated extensive exploratory drafts of certain episodes, which would ultimately bear little resemblance to the final versions. Bergala, for example, recalls having viewed highly developed early versions of parts of the series in 1985: "edited, completed episodes, very different in their conception from those of today, and which have never been shown. As if this initial form, while finished, was not yet the right one for this work."[114] In 1987, during the special edition of *Cinéma cinémas,* Godard also presented a carefully prepared display of the type of visual montage he had dreamed of in Montreal and Lausanne. His juxtaposition on adjacent monitors of clips from

Godard presenting his paper archive
on *Cinéma cinémas* in 1987, plus Lillian
Gish, Charcot, and Augustine in 1B.

Santiago Álvarez's *79 Springs* (1969) and Stanley Kubrick's *Full Metal Jacket* (1987) constituted a remarkable audiovisual critique of the filmmakers' respective uses of slow motion, and provided as eloquent a demonstration of comparative visual criticism as that to be found anywhere in his work since *Ici et ailleurs* and *Numéro deux*. He subsequently extended and reworked this experiment, using the same films, in a lengthy passage in *Les enfants jouent à la Russie* (1993).

Sections of early working versions of 1A and 1B were previewed out of competition at Cannes in 1988, where they were accompanied by Godard's first official press conference devoted to the series. Complete drafts of these episodes were broadcast on Canal Plus in May 1989, and projected at the Vidéothèque de Paris in October that year. However, the contents of these drafts would continue to change substantially over the ensuing years up to the time of the release of the video box set in 1998; Godard found them a little weaker than the others, having had the opportunity to hone his practice in the interim. Although the underlying structure and principal themes remained the same, and the soundtrack was left comparatively untouched, the quantity of black screen was increased. This has the effect of slowing the pace, and also brings these episodes in line formally, stylistically, and rhythmically with the remainder of the series. Visual effects and vision-mixing techniques deployed more fully in the later episodes were introduced. A proportion of the names of people and films given onscreen in the 1989 versions were erased. A significant number of still images were substituted or dropped. New still and moving images, sounds, and recitations were added. The type size, style, and color of the onscreen text was occasionally altered. 1A acquired a new ending.

And the closing credits of the 1989 version of 1A were removed.

The most striking change to 1B relates to the use of a production still depicting a scene from Ingmar Bergman's exploration of existence as living hell, *Prison* (1949, first distributed in the United States as *The Devil's Wanton*). Glimpsed in the 1989 version of 1B, this image, which in its original context represents a touching moment of human contact within an otherwise extremely bleak narrative, reappears throughout the final version, colorized and repeatedly reframed, as a central motif. It fulfills a rich polysemic function. Apart from signaling Godard's acknowledgment of the extent of Bergman's formative influence on his early work, it is emblematic of his historical project as a whole. In general terms, it conveys curiosity, fascination, and wide-eyed wonder at the magic of cinematic projection. From the perspective of the historian, it points to the process of excavation, scrutiny, and discovery that go into the fabrication of history, and evokes the historian's role as witness to the human condition. With the source narrative of *Prison* in mind (having rediscovered the projector in the attic of his aunt, who gave it to him when he was a child, the troubled Thomas [Birger Malmsten] enjoys a moment of tender communion with teenage prostitute Birgitta Carolina [Doris Svedlund]), it evokes the work undertaken by Godard in retracing the stages of his intellectual and artistic formation, as well as the tricks of memory more generally ("It's funny how things get lost, then suddenly turn up again," as Thomas says). In addition, in the context of Godard's filmmaking career, there is a direct link between *Prison* and his own work: Malmsten later went on to play the role of the man in the pornographic film-within-the-film in *Masculin féminin* (1966). And finally, in an autobiographical perspective, it underscores the centrality of his collaboration with Anne-Marie Miéville to his life and work since the early 1970s. Indeed, as if in recognition of this, the duo later restaged the scene depicted in this still, putting themselves in the place of Svedlund and Malmsten, in *The Old Place* (1998).

Over the ensuing years, the early versions of 1A and 1B were presented at numerous festivals and broadcast on German, Swiss, and British television. At this point, Godard was fully aware that he would require approximately another decade to bring the project to completion.[115] Looking back from the perspective of 1997, he emphasized the difference between the conception of 1A and 1B and that of the other episodes.[116] Although he had developed these two complementary halves of the foundational chapter as audiovisual illustrations of preexisting written texts, he suggested, he went on to compose the remainder of the series in a more exploratory, intuitive manner, using a handful of titles as more or less fixed conceptual and thematic armatures around which to weave and layer the fabric of the text. He has frequently drawn analogies between his compositional method and that of artists working in other media. Thus, he has likened the successive approaches he takes to his brute material to the work of a sculptor.[117] This sculptural dimension of his work is conveyed throughout *Histoire(s) du cinéma* via the motif of hands, and underscored through the onscreen use in 2B of the title of Denis de Rougemont's 1936 book *Penser avec les mains* (To think with one's hands), an important reference in the series to which we shall return.[118] Indeed, Godard has even gone so far as to suggest – in comments reminiscent of Diderot's reflections in *Lettre sur*

Prison (Ingmar Bergman, 1949) in 1B, and *The Old Place* (Miéville and Godard, 1998).

les aveugles (*Letter on the Blind*) – that given a choice between losing his sight or his hands, he would opt for sacrificing the former.[119] Furthermore, Godard has also often characterized his work in musical terms ("I make free cinema in the same way that others make free jazz."[120]). Moreover, he is not afraid to mix his models: in the image-text script for *Prénom Carmen* (1983), for instance, he combined extracts of Beethoven's diaries with photographs of musicians at work and sculptures by Rodin.[121] Godard has long compared his successive attempts to work in his own small film and video laboratory to the situation of painters in their studios, with their brushes and tubes of paint. One thinks in particular of Picasso's production of finished paintings from a lengthy process of layering, effacement, and metamorphosis, which was beautifully captured by Henri-Georges Clouzot in his cinematic study of the artist at work, *Le mystère Picasso* (*The Mystery of Picasso*, 1956). Godard has acknowledged that this film provides a concise representation of his own videographic working method, and that he included a clip from it in 4B for that very reason.[122]

Godard suggested in 1997 that the episode titles had been firmly established from the outset. This is partially true. In the late 1980s, however, he was still talking of a number of episodes that would ultimately fall by the wayside or end up spread across several others. These included an episode devoted to "all the films forgotten by history," and another that would explore "the story of the death of one of the greatest creators of forms in the modern era: Hitchcock," provisionally to be titled *L'industrie de la mort* (The industry of death).[123] Although he dropped these episodes, the latter title is used in the final version of 1B in a short passage on Hitchcock, and it plays an important role in 2B in the context of Godard's reflections on the centrality to the historical development of cinema of narratives concerning death. In fact, Godard had been nursing the idea for a long time of a sequence devoted to Hitchcock's ability to successfully combine popular filmmaking and genuine poetry, but could not decide where to place it.[124] In the end, it came to occupy a central position in the final version of 4A, in which Hitchcock is the subject of a lengthy study and homage. Although it is true, therefore, that the episode titles used in the definitive version had been in place since the late 1980s, several were dropped, and Godard's plan during the majority of the project's gestation had in fact been for a series not of ten (five times two) rather than eight (four times two) episodes. Another abandoned episode still apparently part of his overall plan as late as the early 1990s was called *La réponse des ténèbres* (The reply of the darkness), a title reminiscent of one of the chapters of Jean Louis Schefer's *L'homme ordinaire du cinéma*, "La leçon des ténèbres" (The lesson of the darkness). According to Godard, it was, like 3A (*La monnaie de l'absolu*), conceived under the direct influence of Malraux, and intended as that episode's complementary half. In his 1988 dialogue with Daney, he indicated that the long sequence devoted to cinema and national identity included in the final version of 3A was in fact originally designed for use in *La réponse des ténèbres*, and proceeded – in the most detailed discussion of this abandoned episode available – to summarize it as an exploration of the cinematic representation of war, which, broadly speaking, would have examined the proposition that cinema has essentially been a Western art-form made by white males.[125] Even in 1997, when the final version of the series was virtually complete, Godard still appeared to suggest that *La réponse des ténèbres* existed as a separate entity, whereas in fact it is clear that over time, he collapsed *La monnaie de l'absolu* and *La réponse des ténèbres* into a single episode, which, for the sake of the argument, we might say is titled *La monnaie de l'absolu,* and subtitled *La réponse des ténèbres.* As we have already noted, the other abandoned episode was to have been called *Montage, mon beau souci,* the title of one of his major early critical texts. This was provisionally planned as the second part of chapter 4, a complement to what he was then envisaging as episode 4A, *Une vague nouvelle* (which would ultimately become 3B). Its focus, as the title suggests, was to have been the history, theory, and practice of montage. In the final version of the series, an important sequence devoted to montage, introduced by the title "Montage, mon souci," appears in 3B. Confusingly, a residue of the planned ten-part structure is retained in the final series in the roll call of the episodes, including *La réponse des ténèbres* and *Montage, mon beau souci,* incorporated into the opening stages of the definitive version of each episode.[126] They also function as reference points – as virtual episodes, almost – in the images derived from the videos reproduced in the book version of the series. This is one of the ways in which the series is left open as a work-in-progress. Indeed Godard has often suggested that numerous other episodes could still be added to it, and that ideally it should be around a hundred (or even two hundred) hours long, and include a similar number of appendices, perhaps under

Cover page of an outline of *Histoire(s) du cinéma* by Godard from the early 1990s.

BFI Stills.

the generic title *Nouvelles histoire(s) du cinéma* (New [hi]stories of cinema).[127]

DIALOGUE WITH SERGE DANEY

The period between 1989 and 1993 saw a hiatus during which Godard channeled his energy elsewhere – notably into two feature films, which are in part allegorical tales inspired by his investigation of the theory and practice of audiovisual history, *Nouvelle vague* and *Hélas pour moi,* and into two medium-length essay films, *Allemagne année 90 neuf zéro* (1991) and *Les enfants jouent à la Russie.* These latter two works are both direct offshoots of *Histoire(s) du cinéma;* they explore the German and Russian contexts, respectively. Indeed *Les enfants jouent à la Russie,* as Godard suggested in 1998, is effectively an additional episode in the series devoted to Russian cinema.[128] Between 1993 and 1997, Godard focused primarily on completing the series, drawing inspiration in the early stages from the tapes of a lengthy discussion he had recorded in his Rolle studio with Serge Daney in 1988, which had originally been conceived as the basis for a possible pedagogical complement to *Histoire(s) du cinéma.* This conversation extended the dialogue between the two men that had continued throughout the 1980s. In particular, it picked up a wide-ranging discussion begun the previous year – cinema history and Godard's historical project had already been at the heart of their exchange – when Godard appeared for two consecutive weeks on the radio program hosted by Daney between 1985 and 1990, *Microfilms.*[129] In addition to what was actually said during these three important encounters, they are emblematic of the longstanding process of exchange between Godard's thought and practice and Daney's critical project, one that was elaborated in large part – as the latter was the first to recognize – in Godard's footsteps. Large portions of the conversation filmed by Godard with Daney in Rolle in 1988 were published in *Libération* in December of that year, and Godard subsequently integrated extracts of the recording into the fabric of 2A. The published version of the transcription, "Godard fait des histoires" ("Godard Makes [Hi]stories"), is one of the most frequently cited documents in discussions of *Histoire(s) du cinéma,* and it was republished in English translation in 1992. It is, however, incomplete, heavily edited, and at times extensively rewritten. Daney, who was himself apparently responsible for transcribing it, excised most of his own contribution. In 1997, *Cahiers du cinéma* sought to rectify this situation by publishing a fresh version.[130] This was a valuable exercise, since at times the initial version had omitted significant details. The new transcription reveals, for instance, that in his presentation of the logic underlying 3A, Godard had not only evoked the idea of visual criticism, and the example of Malraux (both of which are retained in both transcriptions), but had also defined the episode, in a passage missing from the first version, as "an analysis of criticism, since this had never been done."[131]

Reading the book version of the discussion between Godard and Daney in 2A is at first glance somewhat disconcerting, since the words of the two critics, in a manner emblematic of the symbiosis between their respective projects in the late 1980s and early 1990s, have merged into a soliloquy, in which the separate contribution of each is no longer identifiable. One could devote an entire book to a comparative study of Godard and Daney; it suffices to stress here that Daney's death in 1992 represented a significant loss for Godard, who experienced it not only in personal terms but also as a further blow to the perilous state of the relationship between cinema and its critical reception. As he put it simply in his short tribute to Daney, "The dialogue is over. The exchange between reality and ourselves is finished."[132] In 1988, he had proposed the idea in conversation with Daney (in a passage included in 2A) that art criticism had been a typically French activity, and that what was distinctive about the work of French critics was a combination of a genuine sense of critical agenda and a personal, literary style:

> Diderot, Baudelaire / Malraux / immediately after them I put / Truffaut / a direct line / Baudelaire talking about Edgar Allen Poe / is the same as Malraux / talking about Faulkner / is the same as Truffaut / talking about Edgar Ulmer / or about Hawks / it's only the French / who have made / history[133]

Godard had previously rehearsed this idea in the context of a tribute to François Truffaut.[134] In his eulogy to Daney, he added the latter's name to a variation on this list, omitting Truffaut on this occasion: "Denis, Charles, Élie, André, André again, Serge."[135] A few years later, he reiterated the same idea, and expressed again his view of the unusually strong link between Frenchness and the activity of criticism: "to me Daney was also the end of criticism, as I had known it, which I think started with Diderot: from D to D, Diderot to Daney, only the French make real critics. It's because they're so argumentative."[136]

Daney's death had a direct impact on the development and final shape of *Histoire(s) du cinéma,* especially 2A. This episode is permeated throughout with a profoundly elegiac quality,

us utile aux civilisations moder
i n'éveille en nous, dès que n
sir désintéressé de ses créati
sentiments les plus imprécis et
aisir. Il est singulier que cet ins
ne serve qu'aux plus matériels
appliqué à l'exploration du mo
us impuissant de tous à en péné

ou pour un mécène ayant a perdre quelq
urs films pourraient faire mourir des spe
te... Il suffit de songer un instant à ce
sercinement érotique pour s'en conva
néma et t un é l an enchaîné à ses huit
ses défenses, tamponné ses oreilles, mis
ne lui laisser que le minimum de force
s financiers américains concorde avec le p
rétiens, des sages arabes et orientaux et a
l est interdit au cinéma le montrer ce
viendrait n pas n plu dangereux que
lynamite, le cancer et les sauterelles.

MAURICE SCHÉRER

Le cinéma, art de l'espace

L'emploi systématique que des réalisateurs comme Orson Welles, Wyler
Hitchcock ont fait du plan fixe vient depuis peu nous rappeler que l'art du cinéma
se réduit pas à la seule technique du changement de point de vue, même aujourd'h
la valeur expressive des rapports de dimensions ou du déplacement des lignes
l'intérieur de la surface de l'écran peut faire l'objet d'un soin rigoureux.
On aurait pu, au contraire, caractériser l'évolution du cinéma jusqu'à ces derniers
années par l'affaiblissement d'un certain SENS DE L'ESPACE qu'il ne faut pas confondre
avec un sens de l'image ou une simple sensibilité visuelle. Il est remarquable que cet
évolution n'ait commencé d'être vraiment sensible que dix ans environ après
découverte du montage. Si la naissance du cinéma en tant qu'art date de l'époq
où « le découpeur imagina la division de son récit en plans », ce n'est pas, comm
l'affirme André Malraux (t), parce que la photo mobile est un moyen de reproduction d'expression, mais, bien plutôt par ce que la technique de la succession des pla
a contribué à renforcer le caractère expressif de chacun de ceux-ci : par exemple
rendant perceptibles des mouvements de très faible amplitude (battement d
paupières, crispation des doigts) ou en permettant de suivre ceux dont la trajecto

ou spécieuses.

d de voir : tout au long
rfaces blanches juste reh
si la maison est neuve e
s'attache d'abord aux ch
re cadre et de nos mœurs
surprendre de la part d'
ieu ? Réaliste, Matisse l'e
e, l'attrait de la page b

Qu'il y ait d'autres façons de filmer la
éricaine, qu'il y ait – c'est dur à dire
façon dont un vieux bonhomme p
mplexes camper sur un terrain qui se
in et qui, une fois son opération mené

Quoique... Est-ce bien ailleurs ? Par
liveira n'a-t-il pas les moyens de pos
estion que les Américains ne peuve

The French critical tradition in *Deux fois cinquante ans de cinéma français* (Miéville and Godard, 1995).

one announced by the principal opening music (Hindemith's 1936 *Trauermusik* [Funeral music] for solo viola and strings), and underscored by the ghostly reverb effect Godard applied to the extracts of his filmed conversation with Daney. Indeed, in many ways the episode functions as an extended homage to Daney, and is illustrated by a number of films closely associated with him, two of which feature young boys whom Daney had identified as his fictional cinematic "brothers," and selected as his "favorite alter egos."[137] The first is the film that dominates the episode visually, Charles Laughton's *The Night of the Hunter* (1955); the second is Fritz Lang's *Moonfleet* (1955), from which Godard inserts a still – depicting the young protagonist, John Mohune, gazing up at a hanged smuggler – early on into their dialogue. A recurrent phrase from *Moonfleet*, "the exercise was beneficial," was to have provided the title of the book about cinema which Daney had hoped one day to write, and which was ultimately used for his posthumously published notes written between 1988 and 1991.[138] In addition, besides these cinephilic references, Julie Delpy's reading of Baudelaire's meditation on death as a journey, "Le voyage" (she reads virtually the entire poem in a sequence lasting twelve minutes, making it the single longest recitation in the series), positions the themes of mortality and of literal and imaginative travel at the heart of the episode.[139] With its Baudelairian imagery of a child dreaming of the vastness of the world via maps and stamps, it is not only reminiscent of Joseph Cornell's found-footage ode to the power of the imagination, *Bookstalls* (c. late 1930s), but also constitutes a further tribute to Daney as an inveterate traveler and sender of postcards. Through his globetrotting, we recall, cans of films in his bags,

Daney often literally brought cinema to new audiences in other countries. For Godard, these trips – which are comparatively little discussed, and left few material traces – were as significant as his journalism.[140]

COMPLETION

Work on the remainder of the series fell roughly into two-year cycles for each pair of episodes: 2A and 2B, 1992–93; 3A and 3B, 1994–95; and 4A and 4B, 1996–97. Godard drew on several sequences involving actors (Sabine Azéma, Juliette Binoche, Alain Cuny, Julie Delpy, Maria Casarès, Denis Lavant, Mireille Perrier) reading texts; he had filmed these in 1988 and stockpiled them for later use. In August 1995, drafts of 1A, 1B, 2A, and 2B, together with *Les enfants jouent à la Russie* and *Deux fois cinquante ans de cinéma français* (co-dir. Miéville, 1995), were projected at the Locarno International Film Festival. Near-final drafts of 3A and 4A were screened in the "Un certain regard" section at Cannes in May 1997, where they were accompanied by an A4-format pressbook made by Godard, entitled *Histoire(s) du cinéma: Extraits*. This booklet featured images and texts extracted from these two episodes, some of which were presented in a different configuration to that used in the final book version. In September that year, the entire series was projected at the Ciné Lumière in London, although it would continue to change over the ensuing months. The version of 2A shown on this occasion, although very close to the final video release cut, acquired (like 1A and 1B) more black frames throughout, and numerous new still images. Its ending also underwent a significant reedit, which included the addition of a coda from the water taxi sequence in Rob

The voyage sequence in 2A, plus Joseph
Cornell's *Bookstalls* (c. late 1930s).

Tregenza's *Talking to Strangers* (1988) accompanied by Meredith Monk's *Walking Song* (1993). Above all, the version of 4B shown at the Ciné Lumière on this occasion, which was organized almost entirely around further lengthy extracts of Godard's conversation with Daney, had virtually nothing in common with the final release cut, on which Godard was evidently still working.[141] At twenty-seven minutes long, it was also a good deal shorter than the final version. In August 1998, the complete series was screened in the Château de Cerisy-la-Salle, during a conference entitled "Godard et le métier d'artiste" (Godard and the craft of the artist), and in November that year the videos and books were officially launched at a press screening at the Hôtel Montalembert in Paris.[142]

In practical terms, completion of the first versions of 1A and 1B became possible following the signing of an agreement for ten fifty-minute episodes with Canal Plus at the time of the launch of the new pay channel, which had begun broadcasting in 1984.[143] The project was also aided by the support of Georges Duby, chair of medieval history at the Collège de France, and a key member of the influential Annales School of history; Duby was one of the only leading historians of his generation in France to venture seriously into television. He took on the chairmanship, for instance, of the new cultural and educational channel, the Société d'édition de programmes de télévision (La SEPT), from 1986 to 1991. For Duby, television had the potential to be a "remarkably effective communication tool, which could multiply the audience for good history many times over."[144] His involvement with the medium went back to the early 1970s, and included adapting his own study of French art and society from 980 to 1420, *Le temps des cathédrales* (*The Age of the Cathedrals*), which has since become something of a classic of audiovisual history in its own right. As Christian Delage has noted, Godard's idea of an audiovisual history of cinema, combined with a history of the twentieth century through cinema, doubtless corresponded well with Duby's vision of an "audiovisual pleiad."[145] Ultimately, however, it was only when Gaumont, with the personal backing of its president, Nicolas Seydoux, agreed to produce, clear rights for, and distribute the series that completion of the project became possible. Godard thanked Seydoux publicly at the 1998 Césars ceremony, together with André Rousselet and Pierre Lescure, whose support at Canal Plus had allowed him to work in earnest on the series during the 1980s. On 3 April 1990, Godard signed an agreement with the French national film school (the Fémis), and the Centre national du cinéma (CNC), for the creation of a "Centre de recherches cinéma et vidéo," Périphéria, which was to be linked to the Fémis, and based in the Palais de Tokyo.[146] The idea behind Périphéria was that it should combine a research function with the provision of access for Fémis students to all stages and aspects of the filmmaking process. At this point, Godard envisaged 3A, 3B, 4A, 4B, 5A, and 5B (as noted above, he was still planning to make ten episodes at this point) as co-productions between JLG Films and the Fémis; integral to the 1990 agreement was a project described simply as *Histoire(s) du cinéma: Suite et fin* (that is, concluded). Although refurbishment of the Palais de Tokyo meant that Périphéria was unable to move physically into the building as planned, the deal was instrumental in allowing Godard to complete the project, and the final versions of 2A, 2B, 3A, 3B, 4A, and 4B are all billed as "presented by Gaumont and

Périphéria," and co-produced by Gaumont, the CNC, the Fémis and Périphéria.

Once the series was finally complete, Godard asked Bernard Eisenschitz to assume the Hitchcockian role of Mister Memory, and to draw up an inventory of all the visual materials he had used in the series. These lists provided the basis for those given at the end of each of the *Histoire(s) du cinéma* books, and were used by Gaumont as their point of departure for the task of clearing the rights for the voluminous quantity of items sampled in the series.[147] Godard had of course been fully aware of the potential scale of the copyright issue from the outset, and had argued as early as 1979 for a number of complementary approaches to the problem: the use of reenactment as an interesting alternative to the use of found footage, especially if the original material was lost or unavailable; the illegal pirating of prints ("albeit pretending that one isn't doing it"); and the granting of rights to film archives to make video copies of their holdings.[148] Once Gaumont had committed itself to the project, however, and agreed to take responsibility for the rights clearance process, Godard was ultimately able to use virtually everything he had selected, apart from a handful of paintings for which the rights holders withheld permission. He was therefore obliged to pursue the reenactment option, not, as he had originally anticipated, in relation to films, but in the case of a number of paintings by Henri Matisse and Nicolas de Staël, which he recreated himself for the purposes of the final version of the series.[149] With these pastiches, a project first imagined three decades earlier was brought to completion and launched into the public domain.

THE COMMON TENDENCY TO DIVIDE THE
Godardian corpus into successive discrete periods – the New Wave, the political work, the
video years, and so on – emphasizes discontinuity over the sense of a single developing artistic
project. It is clear that Godard's œuvre to date is
in fact characterized by a striking degree of continuity. The principle of recycling at the heart of
Histoire(s) du cinéma, for instance, can be traced
back to his earliest work. One of his first jobs
in cinema, we recall, was as a professional editor working with preexisting material on documentary films for Jean-Pierre Braunberger, and
on silent travel films for the Arthaud company.[1]
Similarly, one can trace a direct line from his ir-
reverent remix of material shot and abandoned
by François Truffaut, *Une histoire d'eau* (1958),
to his late found-footage practice. The only really significant break, as we look back over his
work as a whole, is the one resulting from the
dislocation to his working practices provoked
by his encounter with video. In this perspective,
the œuvre falls into two major movements: from
the postwar discovery of cinema and the early
New Wave, via the neo-Brechtian critique of the
society of the spectacle, to the political dead end
of the early 1970s; and from the beginning of
that decade – which marked the start of his sustained exploration of video technology, collaboration with Anne-Marie Miéville, development
of a resolutely subjective project, and quest to
resuscitate the simplicity and directness of early
cinema – to the present. Godard's output since
this time constitutes a single integrated project, with *Histoire(s) du cinéma* at its core. This
chapter examines key aspects of the organic
relationship between the series and Godard's
prior and parallel output, especially some of the
lesser-known and more experimental works,

2

The Prior and Parallel Work

where the emergence of his concerns and techniques is often at its most visible. It begins with an examination of the genealogy of some of the series' principal themes and stylistic characteristics, and goes on to explore the intertextual relationship between the series and the work he produced in parallel with it from the mid-1980s onward. It concludes with an analysis of a key metaphor in his project as a whole throughout this period, including in *Histoire(s) du cinéma*, that of "projection."

THINKING ONESELF HISTORICALLY

In many ways, the work made by Godard and Godard-Miéville between 1973 and 1984 functioned as preparatory research for *Histoire(s) du cinéma*. This body of work is dominated by four main concerns: self-interrogation and self-representation (announced in particular in *Caméra-œil* [1967], which is cited in 3B); an exploration of the potential of video as a means of combining home moviemaking with the processing of found images and sounds, as the basis of an investigation of the interpenetration of cinema, history, memory, and subjectivity; a reflection on the mutation of cinema in the age of television; and an increasingly explicit concern for the past, present, and future of cinema within the context of the history of art. The autobiographical dimension of the later work should be seen in the context of Brecht's call, relayed by Godard and Jean-Pierre Gorin in the concluding moments of *Tout va bien*, to "think oneself historically," and for each individual to become his or her own historian.[2] Video and thinking oneself historically are central to two key projects from the early 1970s, whose forms

and concerns underpin much of Godard and Miéville's subsequent work: the long-cherished but ultimately abandoned *Moi je*, the plans for which resonate across Godard's recurrent self-depiction in image and sound, from *Numéro deux* to his tribute to the late Éric Rohmer, *C'était quand* (2010); and *Ici et ailleurs*, their first completed project, which is a devastating indictment of the preceding Dziga Vertov group films and of the projection by Western intellectuals of their revolutionary zeal onto distant political struggles at the expense of the reality of their immediate environment and daily lives.

Ici et ailleurs developed out of a reworking of the ten hours of rushes shot by Godard and Gorin in Lebanon, Syria, and Jordan in 1969–70 at the invitation of Al Fatah for a project entitled *Jusqu'à la victoire*. This film – which was intended to be a record of the triumphant return of the Palestinians to their homeland – became, following King Hussein's offensive against the Palestinians in Amman in September 1970, a grim record of the dead. According to Gorin, by 1972 – well before Miéville and Godard subsequently revisited the rushes – he and Godard had already struggled long and hard with the material and produced several rough cuts.[3] Not content with any of these, they nevertheless envisaged using the material over time to produce a film that would be less about Palestinian revolution than a self-reflexive investigation into "how to film history," which would incorporate the rushes for *Jusqu'à la victoire* alongside fictional material, newsreels, and footage of the French Resistance during World War II.[4] Indeed, as late as 1974, Gorin was still talking of using the *Jusqu'à la victoire* material as the basis for a series of four or five ninety-minute films, in which he envisaged combining a consideration of the challenges of filming an historical process with a reflection on the difficulties that he and Godard had encountered editing what they had shot.[5] The final film, *Ici et ailleurs,* is in some ways an extension and distillation of these plans. Above all, however, it is the fruit of an extended dialogue with Miéville, who has claimed that she and Godard worked on editing it every day for eighteen months.[6] As the first of the Godard-Miéville films to blend film and video and to combine autobiography, a critique of television, and the composition of audiovisual history through the conjugation of preexisting footage and freshly shot material, it is also the blueprint, cornerstone, and in a sense the first chapter of *Histoire(s) du cinéma.* Given the film's programmatic quality in relation to Godard's historical project as a whole, it is not surprising that it should feature in the series (it is cited in 4B), and have become a key reference in his later work, including *Notre musique* (2004), *Voyage(s) en utopie,* and *Vrai faux passeport* (2006).

Many of the issues mapped out in *Ici et ailleurs* were pursued by Godard and Miéville during the 1970s in their collaborative Sonimage project, especially in *Six fois deux,* the three-hundredth issue of *Cahiers du cinéma* edited by Godard in 1979, and *France tour détour deux enfants.* It is not difficult, for instance, to see in the representation of amateur filmmaker Marcel Reymond, in episode 3b of *Six fois deux, Marcel,* not just an affectionate portrait of this particular individual, but also a concise self-portrait of Godard as passionate amateur filmmaker. Reymond is depicted as literally submerged in the images he has produced; as he works at his editing table these images are projected onto his body in a manner that directly anticipates Godard's self-presentation as historian in *Histoire(s) du cinéma.* The special issue of *Cahiers du cinéma* also resonates closely with the series. Made up in large part of critical studies in film history, it includes a stunning comparative image-text reflection on Wajda's *Man of Marble* and Eisenstein's *October* (1928), which is conducted through the prism of a critique of Krystyna Janda's acting style in the former. Moreover, there is a material connection between this issue of *Cahiers du cinéma* and *Histoire(s) du cinéma*: in 1B, Godard borrows from the former both imagery and text (notably a fragment of Brecht's 1933 poem "In Praise of Dialectics") that he had included in his report on Sonimage's abandoned collaborative plans with the Mozambican government for a series of "TV-cinema" programs, *Nord contre sud,* or *Naissance (de l'image) d'une nation* (1977–79 [unfinished]).[7] It is, however, the connections between *Histoire(s) du cinéma* and *France tour détour deux enfants* (cited in 2B) that are the most striking and substantial. The sections entitled "histoire" that close each episode look very much like draft (hi)stories to be refined and distilled in the later series, such as the reflection in the first movement on the image and the mystery of origins, or that in the second on the function of the image in the age of the mass media through reference to a blurred photograph of a prisoner in a Soviet gulag. More than this, *France tour détour deux enfants* introduces a number of important critical perspectives, which fed directly into *Histoire(s) du cinéma.* Underpinning the provocative presentation of Hitler in the eighth movement as the successor to Mozart, for example, are the ideas developed by French economist and scholar Jacques Attali

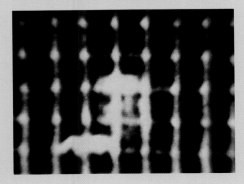

From the second movement of
France tour détour deux enfants
(Miéville and Godard, 1979).

in relation to music in his influential *Bruits: Essai sur l'économie politique de la musique* (*Noise: The Political Economy of Music*).[8] Attali argued that in Vienna, at the end of the nineteenth century, musical creation "rose to a fevered pitch, exploding prior to the political discontinuity for which it itself, to a certain extent, prepared the way."[9] Godard has long acknowledged the impact of this book on his thinking, and appropriated this thesis regarding the prophetic function of music in relation to social change and adapted it to cinema. Films, he suggests, operated in a similar way, notably *vis-à-vis* World War II. Likewise, in the eleventh movement, a two-minute montage on the subject of the impact of the twin concepts of sex and death on human behavior is accompanied on the soundtrack by a series of lightly adapted passages from the conclusion of François Jacob's history of biology, *La logique du vivant* (*The Logic of Life: A History of Heredity*).[10] In *Histoire(s) du cinéma*, Godard condenses the same passages previously used in *France tour détour deux enfants* into the notion, repeated twice on the soundtrack of 1B, that cinema all too quickly sacrificed the productive ambiguity inherent in moving images to "the two big stories," those of sex and death.

Godard's work of the early 1980s was characterized primarily by a reengagement with the Western artistic canon and religious tradition – especially painting (in *Passion*), music (in *Prénom Carmen*), and Catholicism (in *Je vous salue, Marie* [1985]). In hindsight, these films can be seen as a series of steps in his ongoing reflection in this period on the history of cinema in a broad artistic and religious context. All are sampled in the series: *Passion* in 1B and 3B; *Prénom Carmen* in 1B and 2B; and *Je vous salue, Marie* in 4B. The paintings reconstructed in the film-within-the-film in *Passion* marked an extension of his prior exploration of the worlds of a number of artists – El Greco, Rembrandt, Delacroix, and especially Goya – whose works would later punctuate *Histoire(s) du cinéma*. This exploration of cinema and painting in *Passion* was announced in the video *Passion, le travail et l'amour, introduction à un scénario* (1981 [made before the shooting of the film]), and dissected in *Scénario du film Passion* (made afterward). Both of these videos include material from Godard's only Hollywood studio work: a sequence photographed by Vittorio Storaro under Godard's direction in 1981 on one of the sound stages in Francis Ford Coppola's Zoetrope Studio during the making of the latter's *One from the Heart* (1982).[11] This material would provide the basis for one of Godard's most powerful late works, *Une bonne à tout faire* (2006). Comprising only eight shots, *Une bonne à tout faire* is structured around a cinematic reconstruction of Georges de La Tour's *The Newborn Child* (c. 1648), and includes a sequence depicting a camera operator on a crane, silhouetted against the bright white backdrop of a large reflector, swooping and gliding to the opening of Mozart's Requiem. When combined with Godard's ruminations on the soundtrack on the subject of light, painting, art, the creative act, television, and cinema, the film as a whole – and this sequence in particular – offers a potent evocation of the specificity and power of cinema as a technological art-form. Indeed, it has come to serve in his work as a sort of shorthand for the very idea of cinema as art: it recurs in 1A, 2B, and 4B – and in a sense came to represent *Histoire(s) du cinéma* in its entirety when Godard selected it for the front cover of the box sets of both the videos and books released in 1998.

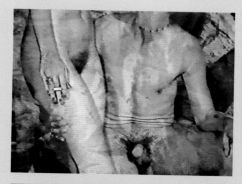

From the eleventh movement of *France tour détour deux enfants* (Miéville and Godard, 1979).

UNE
BONNE
NOUVELLE

Scénario du film Passion (Godard, 1982), 4B
and *Une bonne à tout faire* (Godard, 2006).

From the opening of 1A, Godard deploys a wide variety of forms of audiovisual manipulation and linkage, and uses these to interrogate, connect, and move between his disparate source materials, and to generate all manner of conceptual association. The techniques he uses include fades, dissolves, and rhythmic flashing; the layering of two or more still or moving images over one another; colorization and decolorization; the overlaying and fading in and out of onscreen text; simulation of flicker through the introduction of a rhythmic pulse of black or white frames; visual and sonic repetition; the reframing of still images; application of an iris or diamond-shaped mask effect (often combined with slow or rapid spotting, which produces the impression of one image emerging out of another); and the manipulation of any visual or aural fragment through slow, accelerated, saccadic, or reverse motion. Many of these techniques originated in the work that preceded the making of *Histoire(s) du cinéma*. We shall therefore now consider Godard's longstanding exploration of video, and the impact of that prior engagement on the series' forms and style. A glance at a filmography is sufficient to complicate straightforward identification of Godard with cinema, at least in the sense of feature films shot on celluloid and projected in darkened theaters. In the past three decades, he has made nearly twice as many works on video as on film, not counting the thirty-two constituent episodes of his three major video series (*Six fois deux, France tour détour deux enfants,* and *Histoire[s] du cinéma*). His interest in the medium goes back to the late 1960s, when he toyed with the idea of using one of the first Philips video camera/recorder outfits as a tool for auto-critical political analysis in *La Chinoise* (1967), having seen one displayed in the Philips shop window in Avenue Montaigne in Paris during preproduction on the film. (When he tried to buy it, he claims to have been told that he could not, since the technology was "a state secret."[12]) The earliest record of his having worked with video dates from 1968, when, alongside Alain Jacquier and Chris Marker, he used some of Sony's earliest ½" black-and-white equipment to make quick rough videotapes in the form of a video magazine called *Vidéo 5*, which was distributed in François Maspero's bookshop in Paris.[13] He finally acquired his first video camera, a Sony 2100, in spring 1970.[14] Thus, in 1999, he could legitimately characterize *Histoire(s) du cinéma* as the product of three decades' commitment to video, and stake a claim to having championed the medium from the outset as "paracinema" – an avatar of cinema ideally suited to relatively rapid and cheap research; experimentation; journalism; and the production of audiovisual notes, sketches, or *études* (studies, in both the intellectual and musical senses).[15] "Nobody," he suggested somewhat immodestly – but fairly accurately – the following year, "has worked as hard as I have to bring video into the pictorial tradition."[16] Certainly, since the late 1980s, which saw a marked intensification of his creative investment in video, with the production of three of his most tautly composed stand-alone video pieces – *On s'est tous défilé, Puissance de la parole* and *Le rapport Darty* (co-dir. Miéville, 1989) – alongside the initial versions of 1A and 1B, video has occupied a role as central and highly cherished in his work as 35 mm. If *Histoire(s) du cinéma* is in part a videographic elegy to cinema, it is also a hymn to the versatility and power of video itself, made just as the era of magnetic tape and electronic reproduction was drawing to a close.

Given the transition from chemical, via electronic, to digital reproduction in the postwar period, it is perhaps less surprising that Godard should have explored the possibilities of video so extensively than that most filmmakers of his generation should have opted not to. Schooled through exposure to film history, Godard's career has unfolded in close parallel with developments in video technology: under development from 1950 (the year of his first critical article); in commercial use from 1956 (the date of his initial foray into fiction, *Une femme coquette*); on sale for domestic use since 1963 (the launch date of the first Sony videotape recorder, and when he turned his sights on television for the first time in *Le grand escroc*); available in consumer format from 1965 (date of Sony's introduction of their 1" VCK-2000 Vidicon camera kits, and the year he shot the televisual *Masculin féminin*); used for rapid recorded broadcast playback from 1967 (year of Sony's introduction of their famous Video Rover, the DV-2400 portable black-and-white PortaPak, and the year he first sought to use video in one of his films, *La Chinoise*); developed by Philips in VCR videocassette format in 1970 (when he and Gorin first incorporated video into one of their films, *Vladimir et Rosa*); and made commercially available in the form of color VHS beginning in 1976 (the year of his and Miéville's first television series). The proliferation of domestic VCRs in the late 1970s, and the spread of camcorder culture from 1982, which we see reflected with interest in the saccadic motion of *France tour détour deux enfants* and *Sauve qui peut (la vie)*, but cast in an increasingly critical light in works from *Prénom Carmen* to *Meeting Woody Allen* (1986), was accompanied by Godard's steady accumulation of the videocassettes and other raw materials for use in *Histoire(s) du cinéma*.

Godard's early interest in video was due in part to the economic autonomy it afforded him in terms of production, the ideological challenge it posed to traditional filmmaking power structures (everyone, not just the director, can see and respond to the image during recording and playback), and the aesthetic control it offered over all aspects of a project's development, from conception to completion. These qualities, he noted enthusiastically in 1978, gave the videomaker some of the independence and flexibility long enjoyed by other artists, such as writers and painters.[17] Above all, video functioned for him from the outset as a quasi-scientific tool for the processing of found images and sounds, an instrument of thought that allowed him to combine and dissect material from disparate sources. As he put it succinctly in 1975, at a time when he was considering combining telecined extracts of *À bout de souffle* (1960) with fresh material shot on 16 mm as the basis for the project that would eventually become *Numéro deux* (the latter conceived at this stage as a remake of the former): "The interest of video is primarily that it permits me to reinject all the images I want, and allows all manner of transposition and manipulation. And above all it allows me to think in images, not in text."[18] *Comment ça va* (co-dir. Miéville, 1976) marked a particularly significant step in this exploration of videographic thinking, since Godard and Miéville used the medium here not just as a tool for processing and connecting images and sounds, but also as a means of reflecting on the linkage process and of presenting the process and effects of the comparison visually. For this reason, it, along with *Ici et ailleurs,* is a key film in the genealogy of *Histoire(s) du cinéma.* The simple technique that made this step possible was videographic superimposition. The early experiments with superimposition in *Comment ça va* revealed to Godard video's enormous potential not only as a tool for visual thinking, but also for the creation of composite images through montage *within* the frame. As such, they provide the blueprint for the wide variety of forms of vision-mixed imagery used throughout *Histoire(s) du cinéma,* including those that are technically more so-phisticated or conceptually denser. As the un-named Michel Marot character suggested in *Comment ça va* in response to Odette's (Anne-Marie Miéville) strategy of bringing together two apparently unrelated photographs, the guiding principle was that of the comparison of disparate phenomena as the basis for an explora-tion of the possible similarities and differences between them: "I was beginning to see why she was absolutely insisting on bringing these two photos together: simply to think. Simply bring together two simple images, simple because they show simple people, but who, because they dare to rebel, start something complex." Godard pursued this theoretical and practical explora-tion of superimposition in *Scénario de Sauve qui peut (la vie)* (1979), where he characterized the various photographs or clips that he brought together in this way not as images, but as "the beginnings of images, embryos." He went on to theorize his use of videographic superimposi-tion at length in *Scénario du film Passion,* and to put it into practice in virtually all his subse-quent video work. It allows one, as he later put it, to move "from one place to another without forgetting one's point of departure, and without

A Place in the Sun (George Stevens, 1951) and
Comment ça va (Miéville and Godard, 1976).

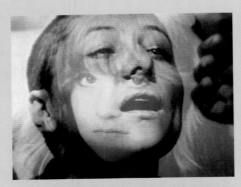

Scénario de Sauve qui peut (la vie) (Godard, 1979).

knowing exactly where one is going to arrive, nevertheless knowing that midway or three quarters of the way through, the unexpected might arise."[19] Moreover, in many ways, he has argued, video is a better medium than film for conducting comparative visual research of this sort, since it allows the fluid, quasi-musical passage to and fro between different moments in time, in a manner that is more difficult and time consuming to achieve in 35 mm.[20] In addition, as he has pointed out through reference to George Stevens's use of lengthy dissolves in *A Place in the Sun* (1951), the transition from one shot to the next in film always involves a slight loss of quality as a result of the need for an internegative, which produces a slight jump when the superimposition ends.[21] Video, by contrast, allows one to achieve the same result much more simply, and without this time-consuming and expensive intermediate stage, with its associated loss of quality.

In addition to superimposition, two features of Godard's antecedent practice are particularly crucial to the forms of *Histoire(s) du cinéma:* the orchestration of still images, and the use of on-screen text. In 1987, while working on the first two episodes of *Histoire(s) du cinéma,* and having already made a number of essayistic works in which still photographs from cinema history play a major role (*Soft and Hard, Grandeur et décadence d'un petit commerce de cinéma, Meeting Woody Allen,* and *King Lear*), Godard was explicit about the centrality of stills to his film history project, which he characterized in terms of "a chat, based mainly on photos, stilled moments, or the remnants left behind by stars."[22] Still images have featured strongly in his work from early on, becoming central in the latter half of the 1960s in a series of proto-videographic collage film essays: *Caméra-œil*, *Le gai savoir*, and the collaboratively made *Film-tracts* (1968). The *Film-tracts* made, or co-made, by Godard offer a particularly striking display – at this stage in 16 mm rather than video – of the centrality of the still image to his developing essayistic style, and of his capacity to achieve remarkable graphic and significant complexity through very modest means. *Film-tract 10*, for example, provides an exemplary demonstration of the association and dynamic orchestration of vast numbers of still images through rapid editing, and anticipates the centrality of stills to the innovative mode of critical visual thinking that he would subsequently pursue with Gorin in 16 mm works such as *Letter to Jane* (1972), and with Miéville from 1973 in video. Furthermore, at the level of content, among the barrage of still images dissected and combined in *Film-tract 12* we find a number of references to films that return in *Histoire(s) du cinéma*: the brutal execution sequence from the Magney section of Eisenstein's *¡Qué viva México!* (1931 [unfinished]); the appearance of the community of lepers in Lang's *The Indian Tomb* (1959); and the boy, Stepok, gazing at his mother's corpse in Eisenstein's *Bezhin Meadow* (1935–37 [unfinished]). A clip from *¡Qué viva México!* is used in 3B, and the film is evoked earlier in the same episode in relation to Jay Leyda, as well as in 2A; the image from *The Indian Tomb* is used in 1A; and *Bezhin Meadow*, a key reference in the series, is cited in the opening moments of both 1A and 1B, again later in 1A, and in 2B and 4A.

Godard also makes extensive use in *Histoire(s) du cinéma* of intertitles, subtitles, and overtitles. In his work he has consistently accorded on-screen text the same status as the other imagery. Indeed, he once suggestively described the

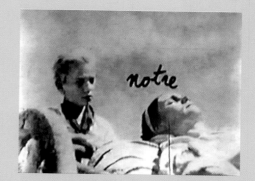

Bezhin Meadow (Sergei Eisenstein, 1935–37, unfinished), *The Indian Tomb* (Fritz Lang, 1959), and *¡Qué viva México!* (Sergei Eisenstein, 1931 [unfinished]) in *Film-tract 12* (1968).

Intertitles from *Vivre sa vie* (Godard, 1962) and *Greed* (Erich von Stroheim, 1924).

contrapuntal use of onscreen text as a form of vaccination, in which the combination of image and word (that is, body and serum) result in the production of valuable antibodies.[23] In Montreal, in a discussion of Erich von Stroheim's use of dialogue titles in *Greed* in relation to his own use of titles in *Vivre sa vie*, he pointed out that in the former, intertitles were integral to the conception of each sequence, and enjoyed the same status as any other shot. The result, he suggested, was that despite the absence of sound, Stroheim's silent films were often more expressive than those made in the era of the talkies: "at times, silent cinema spoke much more loudly than lots of sound films."[24] In the course of the same discussion, he went on to lament the abandonment by filmmakers of a technique used frequently in *Histoire(s) du cinéma:* that of the punctuation of the image-track by a descriptive sentence, or by a complementary line of argument, which is divided into fragments and presented in stages.[25] He identified this technique as a simple but effective device common at the time of silent cinema, which had helped to ensure that films contained a healthy mix and balance of images and words. In Montreal, he had explicitly set himself the task of reengaging with early cinema and of integrating the fruits of this reengagement into his ongoing work.[26] Miéville and Godard's extensive use of onscreen text in the Sonimage work, whether typed directly onto the screen or handwritten through use of a video pen, should be seen as part of a broader reclamation of the vanishing practices of the silent era, which Godard redeploys extensively in *Histoire(s) du cinéma*.

Finally, let us consider one of the comparatively little discussed areas of Godard's practice, which looks in hindsight like a particularly productive laboratory for the development of the forms of *Histoire(s) du cinéma:* his trailers. We should begin by noting that he has made virtually all his own trailers.[27] In Montreal, he had suggested in passing that in the future he might prefer to make trailers rather than films, but trailers that would last four or five hours.[28] In a sense, the four and a half hours of *Histoire(s) du cinéma* represent the realization of that ambition, not in relation to a single film, but rather to cinema in its entirety, or at least to the films that had fired his imagination in the 1940s and 1950s. His actual trailers have sometimes taken the form of prototypical pop videos (such as those for *Masculin féminin* and *La Chinoise*). Others, such as that for *Une femme est une femme* (1961), for which Godard playfully appropriated some reflections by Jean Renoir on the contingent nature of filmmaking, are brief self-reflexive essays. And others still, such as the trailer for *Deux ou trois choses que je sais d'elle* (1966), set out a number of ways of framing and thinking about the source film. On a stylistic level, there are striking links between these trailers and the series, notably in their use and combination of onscreen text, still photographs, magazine imagery, music, voiceover, rapid cutting, and superimposition. Trailers are unusual artifacts, in that they are typically made *after* the films to which they relate, using a handful of images and sounds extracted from them with a view to announcing them to potential audiences. In this perspective, *Histoire(s) du cinéma* might be said to announce the films that shaped Godard as an artist, and it is therefore highly appropriate that in constructing his densely packed megatrailer for them, he should have drawn so extensively

From Godard's trailer for *La Chinoise* (1967).

on the succinct textual strategies he had honed over the decades in the brief, compact found-footage films that are his actual trailers.

THE PARALLEL OUTPUT

Besides works such as *Allemagne année 90 neuf zéro, Les enfants jouent à la Russie, Deux fois cinquante ans de cinéma français* and *De l'origine du XXIe siècle* (2000), all of which explicitly extend *Histoire(s) du cinéma* in their use of found footage to explore cinema and history, the extent and complexity of the relationship between the series and Godard and Godard-Miéville's parallel (and subsequent) output has only become fully apparent with hindsight. In terms of their relationship with *Histoire(s) du cinéma*, the works made from 1985 onward can be categorized into five broad, overlapping clusters. First are those that anticipate or extend Godard's reflections in the series on the mutation of cinema in the televisual and digital ages (*Soft and Hard, Grandeur et décadence d'un petit commerce de cinéma, Meeting Woody Allen, King Lear, Deux fois cinquante ans de cinéma français, Une bonne à tout faire,* and *Film socialisme* [2010]). The second category comprises those that seek to use cinema as a means of responding quickly to unfolding events (German reunification in *Allemagne année 90 neuf zéro;* the spread of market capitalism to Russia in *Les enfants jouent à la Russie;* conflict in the Middle East in *Notre musique;* and the Balkan war in *Je vous salue, Sarajevo* [1993], *For ever Mozart* [1996], and *Notre musique*). The third category includes works that confront the injurious effects of the excesses of big business and the logic of market capitalism (*King Lear, Le rapport Darty, Nouvelle vague, Allemagne année 90 neuf zéro, Les enfants jouent à la Russie,* and

Film socialisme). A fourth category comprises those that are in part or in whole self-portraits (*King Lear, JLG/JLG, Liberté et patrie* [co-dir. Miéville, 2002], and *Notre musique*). Finally, the fifth category includes films that reflect philosophically on the challenge of knowing and representing the past (*Le dernier mot, Nouvelle vague, Hélas pour moi,* and *Éloge de l'amour* [2001]).

In the last of these categories, two films are of particular note in relation to *Histoire(s) du cinéma*, since both address the issue of the audio-visual representation of the past head on: *Hélas pour moi* and *Le dernier mot*. The former, whose narrative revolves explicitly around an investigation into the past, has already received extensive critical attention in this regard.[29] *Le dernier mot*, by contrast, has attracted comparatively little interest. In it Godard sought to imagine the last moments of the life of Valentin Feldman, a French philosopher of Jewish origin and member of the Resistance, who was executed by the Germans in July 1942 at the age of thirty-three. After several years of research, an unnamed character played by Hanns Zischler – the son of the German officer who ordered the execution four decades previously – is visiting the place in Haute-Savoie where the events took place. He is on the trail of a secret ("as if looking for a lost path," as the voice-off puts it), searching for a trace, or traces, which might enable him to picture what happened. Godard invents a fictitious son (played by Pierre Amoyal) for Feldman (André Marcon), a violinist whose music (by Bach) appears to facilitate the passage between present and past.[30] Overall, the film offers not only a tribute to Feldman and an attempt to represent the last moments of his life, but also the beginnings of a wider meditation on the question at the heart of both *Hélas pour moi* and *Histoire(s) du cinéma:* that of how to access the past and articulate a genuine sense of it.

The organicity of Godard's œuvre became increasingly pronounced and visible in the works he made from 1985 until the completion of *Histoire(s) du cinéma*. During this period, he consistently worked glimpses of the films he had recently completed, or on which he was still working, into the series' fabric: *Grandeur et décadence d'un petit commerce de cinéma* is sampled in 3B; *Armide* (1987) in 2B; *Soigne ta droite* in 1B, 2B, 3A, and 3B; *King Lear* in 1A, 2A, 2B, 3B, 4A, and 4B; *Nouvelle vague* in 3B and 4A; *Allemagne année 90 neuf zéro* in 2A, 2B, 3B, 4A, and 4B; *Hélas pour moi* in 3B and 4B; *JLG/JLG* in 3A, 4A and 4B; *Deux fois cinquante ans de cinéma français* in 3B; and *For ever Mozart* in 4A and 4B. In addition, he folded an extract from the soundtrack of *Adieu au TNS* (1996), made well after the release of the initial versions of the early episodes, into the final version of 1A. The same is true of the written documents he produced during this period, where we often encounter phrases, and at times lengthy passages, from episodes that were under development at the time.[31] Moreover, the flow of material also ran the other way – and certain clips, sequences, and still images from *Histoire(s) du cinéma* reappear in other contexts. *Puissance de la parole,* for instance, includes a sequence from 1A of a reel of 35 mm film on the editing table, complete with an extract of the soundtrack of Renoir's *Boudu sauvé des eaux* (*Boudu Saved from Drowning,* 1932), with which this image had already been combined in the context of *Histoire(s) du cinéma*. Likewise, *Les enfants jouent à la Russie, Deux fois cinquante ans de cinéma français,* and *For ever Mozart* all incorporate stills from the series.[32] Often, Godard

altered the material slightly when reusing it in the new context. Emblematic of this process is the sequence from a Russian pornographic film he used in 1B, which he recycled and stripped of its color, in *Les enfants jouent à la Russie,* reused again in 3B, and then used again without color in *De l'origine du XXIe siècle.*[33]

Besides these instances of direct citation, there is also a range of less explicit forms of exchange between *Histoire(s) du cinéma* and the films that Godard made from 1985 onward. One frequently senses, for instance, in the composition of a shot he has created in one of these films, an echo of a clip that he had previously manipulated in the series.[34] Occasionally, these echoes take the form of distant visual rhymes, as in the relationship between the scene depicting the galloping horse toward the end of *King Lear* (heralding the imminent birth of an image), and the sequence from Boris Barnet's *Alyonka* (1961) cited in 1B, which shows a young woman on horseback careering into a wide expanse of water to her death. Rather stronger is the similarity between the depiction of Letty (Lillian Gish) struggling in a sandstorm in Victor Sjöström's *The Wind* (1928; cited in 1B), and that of the unnamed actress (Bérangère Allaux) being filmed on a windswept beach in the film-within-the-film in *For ever Mozart* (a sequence itself subsequently reused in 4A). On other occasions, the process of reenactment is explicit: a shot in *JLG/JLG,* for instance, is clearly modeled on the corridor sequence from Cocteau's *La belle et la bête* (*Beauty and the Beast,* 1946), which is cited in 2B and 3B (in 2B, Godard has flipped Cocteau's image so that the windows and curtains are on the left of the corridor, rather than on the right); the sequence depicting Camille (Madeleine Assas) being encouraged to "Make an effort – fight!" in

For ever Mozart is based on the scene from Bresson's *Les dames du Bois de Boulogne* (*The Ladies of the Bois de Boulogne*, 1945) cited in 1A; and the shot of Zoya's (Galina Vodyanitskaya) bare feet descending steps in the snow in Lev Arnshtam's *Zoya* (1944, used in 4B) is reprised in the depiction of the native Americans descending the hotel staircase in *Notre musique*.[35]

There is also a steady two-way flow between *Histoire(s) du cinéma* and the parallel work of cinematic, literary, poetic, and philosophical references. *Le rapport Darty*, for instance, with its character Mademoiselle Clio (Anne-Marie Miéville), announces the significance of poet, essayist, and philosopher Charles Péguy's philosophy of history, *Clio: Dialogue de l'histoire et de l'âme païenne* (Clio: Dialogue of history and the pagan soul) to Godard's historical practice.[36] In a cinematic perspective, even a lightweight shaggy dog story such as *Détective* (1985; cited in 1B) continues Godard's exploration of cinema history, through its playful homage to film noir (it is dedicated to John Cassavetes, Edgar G. Ulmer, and Clint Eastwood), fleeting film references embedded in scenes and dialogue (such as to Bertrand Blier's *Notre histoire* [*Our Story*, 1984], which is cited in 1B), and the clips from films playing on television monitors in the hotel rooms, which return in *Histoire(s) du cinéma*. These include *La belle et la bête* (cited in 2B, 3B, and 4B) and a delirious Erich von Stroheim in his self-parodic role as Arthur von Furst in George Archainbaud's *The Lost Squadron* (1932, used in 3B). Similarly, in *Grandeur et décadence d'un petit commerce de cinéma*, Gaspard Bazin (Jean-Pierre Léaud) cites an extract from a discussion by Élie Faure of Rembrandt's use of light and shade, which Godard reprises at length in 4A (Alain Cuny reads a passage from Faure's

text lasting a little over eight minutes, in which Godard has systematically substituted the word "cinema" for "Rembrandt").[37] Furthermore, this text reminds us of the intricacy of the relationship between *Histoire(s) du cinéma*, Godard's parallel work, and his early film criticism: the rhetorical structure of the final paragraph of the article he had devoted in 1959 to Boris Barnet's *The Wrestler and the Clown* (1957) had already been modeled on a section from this same eulogy by Faure to Rembrandt.[38]

PROJECTION

Godard's work of the mid- to late 1980s was particularly significant in relation to *Histoire(s) du cinéma*, since it announced and underpinned the early versions of 1A and 1B, and ushered in many of the principal themes and concerns of the series as a whole. Two of his least favorably received feature films, *Soigne ta droite* and *King Lear*, are especially important in this regard, and require significant reappraisal in the light of the series. In terms of its relationship with cinema history, *Soigne ta droite* is in part an homage to the vestiges of the comic burlesque tradition, represented here by Jerry Lewis, from whose *Cracking Up* (1983) Godard borrows a number of situations and gags. In a literary perspective, the film draws on a range of authors – including Aragon, Baudelaire, Beckett, Koestler, and Malraux – whose work punctuates *Histoire(s) du cinéma*. However, the principal significance of *Soigne ta droite* in relation to *Histoire(s) du cinéma* lies in its *mise en scène* of a metaphor central to Godard's discourse of the 1980s and 1990s, that of projection. As he has reiterated since that time, projection lies at the heart of cinema's specificity and its difference from all

La belle et la bête (Jean Cocteau, 1946) in 3B,
JLG/JLG (Godard, 1993), *Zoya* (Lev Arnshtam,
1944) in 4B, and *Notre musique* (Godard, 2004).

Sherlock Junior (Buster Keaton, 1924)
and *Soigne ta droite* (Godard, 1987).

the other arts. The projection metaphor features especially strongly in 1B, 2B, 3A, and 3B, and is usually illustrated, at least in part, by a clip from *Soigne ta droite* (which is cited no less than seven times in these episodes). *Soigne ta droite* ends with a visual summary of his concept of projection, in which he cuts from a shot of a projector being adjusted to a recurrent figure of projection in his work, that of a door (or sometimes a window) opening, and then to the orb of the sun (he reprises this sequence in his presentation of the history of projection in 1B). In interviews accompanying the release of *Soigne ta droite*, Godard was absolutely clear about the subject of his film: "This time I'm speaking about projection, and I think that apart from Buster Keaton, nobody has spoken about it. The projection apparatus, the booth, and the human being who projects himself into the world. I like this idea of people projecting themselves rather than rejecting one another."[39] (The reference to Keaton relates to *Sherlock Junior* [1924]; cited in 4B, in which the eponymous hero, played by Keaton himself, is a cinema projectionist and wannabe detective.) When using the term "projection," Godard refers not only to the mechanical act – nor just to the scale, immateriality, and ephemerality of the projected moving image – but also to the mass distribution of films, to the resurrection of the world in the image-based stories they tell, to the projection by audiences of themselves into those stories (and, via them, into the world), and, conversely, to the projection of the stories into the human psyche. There was something unique, he argues, about the scale of the projected image and the mythical dimension of cinema's stories, which encouraged a form of identification and involvement quite different to that offered by literature or painting – or indeed by any other

art-form.[40] Many of these ideas are succinctly captured in Godard's Baudelairian evocation of the reader's self-propulsion through films on an imaginative journey. This connection is made explicit in 2A, in which a frontal shot of a projector starting up, together with the mechanical noise of the film passing through the gate, launches and punctuates Julie Delpy's performance of "Le voyage," which is illustrated by, among other things, some of the marvelous imagery of adventure, fear, and wide-eyed wonder from *The Night of the Hunter*.

To an extent, Godard's discourse on projection can be seen as an extension of André Bazin's distinction between theater, which he related to the "luminous, crystalline, circular, and symmetrical" forms of the chandelier, and cinema, which he characterized in terms of "the long prism of rigid light – agile comet or the ray of moonlight from the projectionist's booth."[41] Moreover, the idea of the cinema as a sort of out-of-body experience has a lengthy history within film criticism. As director and critic Roger Boussinot once put it, "cinema is the art of projecting the spectator onto the screen without his leaving his chair."[42] Godard rehearsed this same idea repeatedly in interviews during the 1980s, and developed it at length in his discussion with Miéville in the closing moments of *Soft and Hard*:

> Painting, the novel, and music were already projected in space, or in time, but the cinema was projected in a recognizable form, that of visual representation. Thus the I was projected and magnified; it could get lost, but the idea could be found again, there was a sort of metaphor. With television, on the contrary, television no longer projects anything; it projects us, it projects us, and so we no longer know where the subject is. In the cinema, in the idea of the screen, or in Plato's cave, there was an idea of project.

Le mépris (Godard, 1963) in *Soft and Hard* (Miéville and Godard, 1985).

Besides, projection (in other languages it's perhaps something else), but in French: project, projection, subject. One has the impression with television that, on the contrary, we receive it and are subjected to it, that we are the King's subjects, or something like that.

Godard's emphasis is on the invitation extended by cinema to viewers to project, lose, and rediscover themselves through films in a way that nurtured the development of a sense of individual and collective identity – "a place on earth," as the subtitle of *Soigne ta droite* puts it. It is against this backdrop that Godard has likened cinematic projection to the birth of a child, and drawn a series of analogies between the darkened theater, the birth canal, the beam of light from the projector, the image on the screen, and the newborn baby being projected into the world.[43] This equation of cinematic projection with birth is conveyed in the "Le voyage" section of 2B via a brief clip showing a hand emerging from a swirling pool of red liquid. The simultaneous evocation in this clip of childbirth and drowning offers a memorable image of the intensity of the filmgoing experience, and of the visceral effects of films on viewers.

The projection metaphor is introduced in *Histoire(s) du cinéma* midway through 1B, via the citation of lengthy extracts of *Soigne ta droite*. These include the closing scene depicting the man (François Périer) starting up the projector and, in a further echo of *Cracking Up*, projecting the film – *A Place on Earth* – on which the Prince/Idiot (Godard) has apparently been hard at work over the course of the fragmented narrative. This section of 1B is accompanied by a quotation, also borrowed from the soundtrack of the closing sequence of *Soigne ta droite*, which Godard had drawn originally from

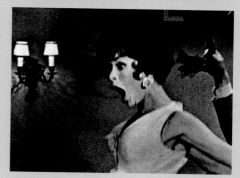

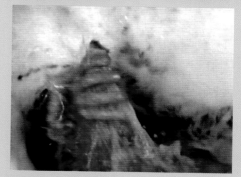

Projection in 2A.

a longstanding reference in his work: Hermann Broch's meditation on aging, memory, and the responsibility of the artist in the face of humanity's capacity for evil – *The Death of Virgil*.[44] This book has been a key reference in Godard's work since *Soft and Hard,* in which he and Miéville both read lengthy extracts. It reappears in *Deux fois cinquante ans de cinéma français,* 1B, 3B, and, especially, 2B, in which Sabine Azéma reads a selection of passages lasting over six minutes. The passage read by Périer in *Soigne ta droite,* and reused by Godard in 1B and 3B as another way of summarizing his theory of projection, evokes the overcoming of darkness via light projected from behind: "it's because one last time / the night is gathering its strength / to vanquish the light / but it's in the back / that the light / is going to stab the night."[45] Surprisingly, however, the principal presentation of the projection metaphor in *Histoire(s) du cinéma,* involves neither *Soigne ta droite* nor Broch. It comes in an exhilarating sequence in 2A, which is composed out of a combination of materials from an eclectic assortment of films, including a production still showing a silhouetted Jacques (Jean Gabin) leaping through the air in *La bête humaine* (*The Human Beast* [Jean Renoir, 1938]); Rose Alvarez (Janet Leigh) seemingly being propelled forward, a look of astonishment on her face, in *Bye Bye Birdie* (George Sidney, 1963); Disney's Goofy being blasted out of a cannon; and a lengthy sequence, which Godard extends and accentuates through slow motion, depicting Suzanne (Suzanne Grandais) recoiling from the cinema screen and collapsing backwards in *Le mystère des roches de Kador* (*The Mystery of the Kador Rocks* [Léonce Perret, 1912]), accompanied by the words "The cinema alone" etched in large red letters across the image. These visual fireworks lead into a sequence that he had already used in *Les enfants jouent à la Russie* (he merely adds here a superimposed image of himself typing, together with bursts of the mechanical sound of his electric typewriter): an anecdotal summary of the theory of projective geometry formulated by Jean-Victor Poncelet in the early nineteenth century, followed by the image and sound of the working projector mentioned above.[46] (This sequence precedes and ushers in the "Le voyage" section.) Crucially, suggests Godard, Poncelet's discoveries were a product of his incarceration in prison, from which his only means of escape was that of imaginative projection within the confines of his cell:

> The idea of projection comes from a prisoner shut up in front of a wall. So for me, one of the historical moments of the birth of cinema, that of projection, comes from a prisoner who imagines and projects, like all prisoners do, who project an escape, for instance; and since he was a mathematician, this is what he focused on.[47]

The projection metaphor is also central to *King Lear,* especially in the scene in the cinema theater, where Professor Pluggy (Godard) explains to Professor Kozintsev (Freddy Buache) the importance of the layout of the seats, and of the way in which the eyes of the audience are all aligned, and directed upward at a screen illuminated by light projected from behind. Godard presents his *Lear* successively as a "study," "approach," and "clearing" in relation to Shakespeare's play. It also functions in precisely these ways in relation to *Histoire(s) du cinéma,* where it is cited no less than ten times (in 2A, 2B, 3B, 4A, and 4B). It is exemplary of Godard's work of this period in that it functions as a sort of exploratory notebook, in which we see him selecting his interlocutors, developing his motifs, and testing

King Lear (Godard, 1987).

and refining the arguments that he will develop
in the series. In addition to its extended exploration of the themes of projection, cultural decay,
artistic amnesia, and creative renewal, the film
is infused with an opposition between seeing
and naming, and includes a reading by Godard
in (a sort of) English of a series of short texts,
all of which return in the series. These include
a comment on painting by the philosopher and
social activist Simone Weil from her reflections
on beauty in *La pesanteur et la grâce* (*Gravity and
Grace*), which he also uses in 1B ("A painting
such as one could place in the cell of a criminal
sentenced to solitary confinement for life without it being an atrocity, on the contrary.");[48]
two ruminations on the image, and on the importance of restraint and rigor in audiovisual
composition, from Robert Bresson's collected
notes on the cinematograph (both of which he
uses in 1B and 2B, the latter twice in 1B, which
it opens);[49] a description from Philippe Sollers's
Femmes (*Women*) of the vacuity of twentieth-
century life (used four times – in 1A, 1B, 2B, and
3A);[50] and the closing passage from a text by
Jean Genet on Giacometti about the solitude
of people and objects (used in 1A).[51] Although
these references clearly represent only a fraction
of those subsequently woven into the fabric of
Histoire(s) du cinéma, they nevertheless demonstrate the extent to which, by 1987, Godard had
not only thoroughly prepared his methods and
tools and established his principal themes, but
also gathered together many of the interlocutors with whom he would pursue his imaginary
dialogue about cinema over the course of the
next decade. The following chapter examines
the substance of these conversations.

GODARD'S HISTORIES ARE SUBJECTIVE, imaginative, sensuous, anecdotal, digressive, discontinuous, lacunary, rhythmic, repetitious, humorous, dramatic, and frequently contentious. Brimming with emotion, intuitions, insights, and provocations, they are made up in large part of resonant fables, tall tales, shaggy dog stories, quasi-mathematical riddles, and – above all – poetic images. Their dense texture and serpentine forms are closer to those one more readily associates with poets and musicians rather than historians, and recall in particular the traditions of serial and fugal composition of modernist authors such as André Gide, William Faulkner, Ezra Pound, Hermann Broch, and Virginia Woolf – all of whom are prominently cited in the series.[1] Moreover, Godard's self-depiction in his histories works against the conventional image of the historian as detached observer, coolly gathering facts and weighing evidence. In 3B, for instance, he presents himself as a conductor in the manner of Georges Méliès in *L'homme-orchestre* (*The One-Man Band,* 1900), manipulating and channeling the mass of images and sounds he has selected. Elsewhere he adopts the posture of a chair-bound dreamer, surrounded by books, submerged in his thoughts and memories, and disappearing into imaginative reverie in the manner of the mathematician Jean-Victor Poncelet; or of Darrell Standing, the protagonist of Jack London's *The Star Rover,* cited in 1A, who escaped the tedium and violence of prison by propelling himself on trance-like voyages into the world of the imagination. Contrary to the impression given by such imagery and references, Godard took the historical dimension of *Histoire(s) du cinéma* extremely seriously, and, despite the wave of enthusiastic reviews that met

3

Models and Guides

L'homme-orchestre (Georges Méliès, 1900), and Godard's self-depiction as historian in 1B and 3B.

the release of the series in 1998, he frequently expressed regret that it was consistently categorized as an audiovisual poem, and that commentators failed to engage with it as a piece of (or reflection on) history or as a contribution to audiovisual historiography. For Godard, history and poetry are inseparable, and the only way of bringing the former fleetingly to life in the mind's eye in the present is through art. This idea can be traced back to his early criticism. In his review of Léonard Keigel's short film *La vie et l'œuvre d'André Malraux* (The life and work of André Malraux, 1957), for instance, he pointed to the power of art – notably, already, the art of filmic montage – to conjure up the past: "Art, in its own way, makes history come back to life."[2] The principle features of his late historiographic method – plurality, lyrical extravagance, and the poetic use of montage – are all traceable to a select set of antecedent practices. This chapter begins by examining Godard's use in *Histoire(s) du cinéma* of a celebrated allegory of the creative process, the myth of Orpheus. It goes on to explore the affinities between the series and the work of the principal figures in the realms of history, the philosophy of history, art history, cinema history, and filmmaking respectively, whose example inspired and shaped his own approach, method and style.

THE ORPHIC CHALLENGE

The task of the historian is represented throughout Godard's historical work via the pervasive theme of the detection. For instance, the opening two episodes of *Histoire(s) du cinéma* are permeated with references to popular crime fiction, such as Gaston Leroux's *Le mystère de la chambre jaune* (The Mystery of the Yellow Room, 1907) and

Images of detection: *Alphaville* (Godard, 1965) in 3B, *L'avventura* (Michelangelo Antonioni, 1960) in 2A, *King Lear* (Godard, 1987) in 2A and 4B, and *Hélas pour moi* (Godard, 1993).

Le parfum de la dame en noir (*The Perfume of the Lady in Black,* 1909). Similarly, the numerous detectives in the series, and in Godard's related films, all function in part as historian figures: intergalactic special agent Lemmy Caution (Eddie Constantine), on his mission to locate and retrieve Natasha (Anna Karina) in *Alphaville, une étrange aventure de Lemmy Caution* (1965), a film sampled extensively in 3B; the unnamed character played by Hanns Zischler in *Le dernier mot,* who is attempting to unravel the truth surrounding his father's role in the murder of Valentin Feldman; Professor Pluggy (Godard) and Shakespeare Junior V (Peter Sellars) in *King Lear,* who are on the trail of the lost secrets of the image and of Shakespeare's play, respectively; and Abraham Klimt (Bernard Verlay) in *Hélas pour moi,* who is investigating a mysterious event in the past that may, in fact, not even have occurred.

The principal narrative through which Godard evokes the work of the probing of the past and the making of history in *Histoire(s) du cinéma,* however, is one on which we have already touched, and which we shall now consider in greater detail: the myth of Orpheus. Godard uses the Orphic myth in part as an allegory for the activity of the historian. The Orphic-like challenge facing the historian is announced at the start of 1A via the citation of a celebrated phrase from Virgil's *The Aeneid,* which signals from the outset the scale of the difficulty that confronts both the historical investigator and the viewer alike – who, in their respective positions, are faced with the task of constructing an image of the past. In response to Aeneas's declaration of his intention to visit the underworld, Sibyl observes that although the descent is easy, the real challenge lies in retracing one's

steps to daylight – that is, bringing the past to life: "Hoc opus, hic labor est" (That is the task, the hard thing).[3] The main story through which Godard pursues this theme is that of Orpheus himself, and in particular its articulation in Jean Cocteau's film *Orphée* (1949), with its celebrated depiction of the voyage made by Orphée (Jean Marais) through the mirror into the underworld. Orphée's task, which offers a clear parallel with that of the historian in relation to the past, is to retrieve his wife Eurydice (Marie Déa) from Death. Indeed, as Jacques Aumont has observed, in a valuable discussion of the Orphic myth in *Histoire(s) du cinéma,* a number of films by Godard – *Alphaville, Allemagne année 90 neuf zéro, Hélas pour moi* – might even be considered remakes of *Orphée.*[4] The various detective figures mentioned above can also all be seen as stand-ins for Orpheus, and numerous further evocations of the Orpheus-Eurydice couple punctuate *Histoire(s) du cinéma,* whether in the form of clips depicting men visiting women they have known in the past (Johnny [Sterling Hayden] and Vienna [Joan Crawford] in Nicholas Ray's *Johnny Guitar* [1954], for instance, which is cited in 1B and 3B), or of men saving women from mortal danger (the most obvious example of which is Scottie [James Stewart] saving Madeleine [Kim Novak] from drowning in Alfred Hitchcock's *Vertigo* [1958], which is cited in 1B, 3B, and 4A). Similarly, the numerous clips simply showing men picking women up in their arms also provide a succinct shorthand summary of the Orphic narrative, such as Eddie (Henry Fonda) and Joan (Sylvia Sydney) in the closing sequence of Fritz Lang's *You Only Live Once* (1937), cited in 3B; Godard's treatment of the same motif in one of his advertisements for Marithé et François Girbaud,

Orphic narratives: *La belle et la bête* (Jean
Cocteau, 1946), *Paisan* (Roberto Rossellini,
1946), *Johnny Guitar* (Nicholas Ray, 1954),
one of Godard's advertisements for Marithé
et François Girbaud (1988), *Alphaville*
(Godard, 1965), *Destiny* (Fritz Lang, 1921),
and *The Searchers* (John Ford, 1956).

which he samples in 2B; Count Torlato-Favrini (Rossano Brazzi) holding the dead Maria (Ava Gardner) in his arms in Joseph Mankiewicz's *The Barefoot Contessa* (1954) in 4A; and Ethan (John Wayne) lifting up his long lost niece Debbie (Natalie Wood), in John Ford's *The Searchers* (1956), which is cited in 1A, 2B, and 4A. However, the Orphic allegory is most prominent in 3B, the bewitching opening of which conveys the idea of the difficulty of visiting and animating the past through history via the interweaving of two highly evocative sequences: Belle's (Josette Day) tentative negotiation of the corridors of the Beast's castle in Cocteau's *La belle et la bête*; and Harriet (Harriet Medin) and Massimo's (Gigi Gori) dangerous attempt to reach "the other side" (in the original narrative, an area still under fire from the Germans and Italian fascists) via a secret passage in Rossellini's *Paisan* (1946). This is followed by a glimpse of Klimt in *Hélas pour moi,* and a lengthy sequence organized around the combination of, and passage to and fro between, two further Orphic narratives: Lemmy Caution attempting to retrieve Natasha from Alphaville; and the unnamed young woman (Lil Dagover) entering the land of the dead to negotiate with Death for the return of her dead lover in Lang's *Destiny* (1921).

As we saw in chapter 1, one of the senses of the Orphic myth in *Histoire(s) du cinéma* is simply that of turning around to face the past. Cinema for Godard allows Orpheus to look back, in the sense of allowing the historian to survey the twentieth century at will. As Alain Bergala noted, in an important early reflection on the series, Godard came to view the countless reels of film and other audiovisual media that make up cinema history as a place of limbo, in which the bodies, faces, and gestures of long-forgotten

stars, bit players, extras, and passers-by languish, "suspended in the emulsion."[5] The "waters of oblivion" of cinema history, as Bergala put it, are analogous to the intermediate Zone in *Orphée,* which Cocteau defined as "a no man's land between life and death."[6] Here Godard's thinking about cinema history opens onto a broader reflection on the relationship between past and present, and his discourse operates on two levels simultaneously: first in relation to the events of the twentieth century, which, as we have seen, cinema archived fairly comprehensively; and second in relation to the past as a whole. In both contexts, for Godard the past – as he puts it through use of a key phrase from Faulkner that we have already cited – is "never dead. It's not even past." This idea of the past not being completely dead, but being trapped in a sort of Zone, awaiting remembrance and resuscitation, is suggested in *Histoire(s) du cinéma* through the references to tales of the inhabitation or visitation of the present by ghosts, such as *Wuthering Heights* (in 1B) and *Hamlet* (in 3B). It is also evoked in the recurrent water imagery in *Histoire(s) du cinéma* and related works, especially that depicting the shoreline, people emerging from the water (as in *Hélas pour moi*), and characters being saved from drowning (as in *Nouvelle vague* and *Vertigo*). Moreover, the Orphic connotations associated with the imagery of shores and water in *Hélas pour moi* are underscored through simple technical means: the gradual bringing into focus of a blurred image. The same idea of the ghostly haunting of the present by the past is explicit in a lengthy sequence in 1B constructed around the theme not of water, but of the wind: "sometimes in the evening / somebody whispers in my bedroom / I turn off the television / but the whispering continues / is it the wind

Hélas pour moi (Godard, 1993), and
Vertigo (Alfred Hitchcock, 1958) in 1B.

/ or my ancestors."[7] In 1B, Godard relates this idea back to the story of Orpheus in general, and to Cocteau's *Orphée* in particular. This occurs in a sequence illustrated by a composite image showing the restless movement of Ingrid Bergman's head in *Stromboli* (Roberto Rossellini, 1950), where she is made to appear, as a result of Godard's manipulation of the material, as if her sleep is being disturbed by the characters from *Week-end,* who are shown in superimposition, seemingly strolling through her mind. He then riffs on a succession of wind-related clips, stills, and titles (*Vent d'est* [*Wind from the East*], *Une histoire de vent* [*A Tale of the Wind* (Joris Ivens and Marceline Loridan Ivens, 1988)], *The Wind, Written on the Wind* [Douglas Sirk, 1955–56], and *Gone with the Wind* [Victor Fleming, 1939]), before going on to underscore the Orphic dimension of the entire sequence by pointing out on the soundtrack that the source of the comment about the whispering of the dead is in fact a character from his own *Soigne ta droite:* the man, played by François Périer, who, as a young actor, had played none other than the role of Heurtebise in *Orphée,* the angel responsible for helping Orphée to bring Eurydice back to life.

HISTORIANS AND
PHILOSOPHERS OF HISTORY

Let us now turn to the philosophers and historians to whom Godard reached for inspiration and methodological guidance when preparing for and working on *Histoire(s) du cinéma.* Many of these are cited in his work or feature prominently in his related discourse. Following the release of the various versions of *Histoire(s) du cinéma,* he went to some lengths to pursue a discussion of cinema and history with historians

such as François Furet, Jean-Pierre Rioux, Pierre Vidal-Naquet, Jean-Pierre Vernant, and Eric Hobsbawm, but virtually always encountered considerable skepticism regarding his work as a genuine form of history.[8] Furet, the author of prominent studies of the French Revolution and of twentieth-century communism, admired Godard's compositional skills, but expressed strong reservations regarding his use of highly charged imagery.[9] Similarly, during the encounter staged by Marc Ferro in 2000 between Godard and Hobsbawm, the latter, who had recently published his *Age of Extremes: The Short Twentieth Century, 1914–1991,* treated the books of *Histoire(s) du cinéma* not as the work of a historian but of a poetic visionary. None of these dialogues proved particularly fruitful, and to better understand Godard's project, we need to look instead to his virtual dialogue with those historians, alive and dead, whose work reflects philosophically on epistemological issues. We have already noted in this context the importance of François Jacob's history of heredity, *La logique du vivant.* According to Godard, in this book and elsewhere Jacob was in fact working in the manner of a filmmaker and engaging in the practice of montage.[10] As we shall see, this is a common thread running through the work of all of his principal guides: the centrality of poetic imagery to the fabrication of history. Two of the figures to whom he has returned most frequently in the context of his ambitions in *Histoire(s) du cinéma* are philosophers and historians of science: Georges Canguilhem, author of the influential study of "normality" in biology, *Le normal et le pathologique* (*The Normal and the Pathological*); and philosopher of history Alexandre Koyré, author, among other things, of a seminal study of changing scientific perceptions of the world, *Du monde clos à l'univers infini* (*From the Closed World to the Infinite Universe*). It is undoubtedly the critical, interrogative nature of these books, and their epistemological implications, that Godard values as much as their subject matter, and with which he feels a kinship. Above all, as with Jacob, it is the manner in which Canguilhem and Koyré forge links and create imagery through their prose that Godard values, and which qualifies them as filmmaker-historians: "they're people I like a lot because they're making cinema."[11]

In addition to Jacob, Canguilhem, and Koyré, there are a number of other historians and philosophers of history with whose ideas Godard has engaged in depth, and whose thinking is central to *Histoire(s) du cinéma*. These include Walter Benjamin, Charles Péguy, André Malraux, Fernand Braudel, and Emil Cioran – all of whom, with the exception of Benjamin, he includes in a select list of thinkers in 4B, in which he credits them with having confronted the fundamental question "What is history?" in an innovative way. The odd person out on this list is Cioran, to whom Godard referred relatively infrequently during the making of the series. However, in the course of an interview with the literary magazine *Lire* regarding his relationship with literature, he clarified the value of Cioran for him; Godard claimed to be an avid, long-standing reader of the philosopher's work, and expressed particular admiration for Cioran's ability to distill complex ideas into compelling aphorisms, which he likened to scientific formulae.[12] The two philosophers of history whose work guided the development of *Histoire(s) du cinéma* most directly, however, are Péguy and Benjamin. Godard first cited Péguy's imagined dialogue between history and the pagan soul,

Clio: Dialogue de l'histoire et de l'âme païenne, in the late 1980s (in *Le rapport Darty*), and its significance to him is clearly signaled by the inclusion of a number of passages from the book in 4B, where we also glimpse parts of the cover. Péguy's book resonates closely with *Histoire(s) du cinéma* in a number of ways, including in its proposition of a proto-Godardian form of historical montage: if he were a history teacher, suggests Péguy, he would compare the form and content of plays written by Beaumarchais between 1775 and 1792 as the most effective way of communicating an historical sense of the period to his students.[13] Similarly, one might also point to Péguy's reflections on the responsibility on the part of the consumer of art to invest actively in the process of co-creation, which anticipate Godard's position in interviews since the 1960s.[14] On a stylistic level, the lyrical, repetitious, digressive forms of Péguy's prose – which he relates in the book to his own two principal guides, Victor Hugo and Jules Michelet – provides Godard with a key model of intuitive, poetic, anti-positivist historical writing. For Clio (and, one senses, for Péguy), Hugo's collection of polemical poems, *Les châtiments* (1853), provides a technical lesson in historical writing, whereas Michelet is simply the genius of history.[15] Moreover, as Annette Aronowicz has argued, *Clio* not only summarizes Péguy's voluminous philosophical musings on history, but also serves as "a polemic against modern historiography, a meditation on memory and aging, and the embodiment of a way of doing history the way Péguy thought it should be done."[16] If Péguy's derision is reserved for the nineteenth-century positivists, Godard's appropriation of *Clio* is in part a means of mounting a critique of their contemporary successors.

Godard has frequently reiterated his admiration for the book: "I was very influenced by Péguy's *Clio*. The muse speaks of two aspects of history: chronological history, which, in cinema, produces a film such as Loach's *Land and Freedom*, and what Clio calls memory, an example of which on the same theme would be *Espoir* by Malraux."[17] The distinction between history and memory in *Clio* to which Godard alludes arises out of a discussion by Péguy of Michelet, and of history as resurrection. It is echoed in Péguy's related distinction between "chroniclers" (exemplified by Michelet, who serves as Péguy's main model of an engaged, memory-based, intuitive, poetic historical writer, whom he places unhesitatingly alongside artists such as Corneille, Rembrandt, and Beethoven) and professional historians, who – by sticking to the facts, remaining at a distance, and risking little or nothing of themselves in their accounts – in his view, miss the essence and true significance of past periods, people, and events, and fail entirely to bring them to life.[18]

Although not explicitly mentioned in *Histoire(s) du cinéma*, Péguy's chronicler provides Godard with a crucial example of an alternative model of a historian, who advocates and produces a poetic, imaginative form of history. It is in this perspective that we might best situate the latter's casual attitude to factual accuracy, and his openness to the incorporation of invented facts into his composition, if these help to create resonant stories, which in turn breathe life into history. We should recall in this context that the French word *histoire* means not only "story" and "history," but that it can also imply fabrication, as in the expression *Ne raconte pas d'histoires!* ("Don't tell lies!"). Indeed, Godard at times foregrounds this dimension of his work, playfully signaling some of his creative errors in passing on the screen – thereby both poking fun at historical convention and underscoring the significance of a particular idea, or the moral of a given fable, over the specifics of names and dates. Péguy's chronicler is also an important reference for Godard for his embrace of fiction as a particularly fruitful means of articulating a sense of the essence (as opposed to the factual truth) of the past. To an extent, this aspect of his thinking recalls the identification by commentators such as Hayden White of the proximity of history to fiction in terms of their shared narrative, rhetorical, and poetic techniques.[19] More than this, however, imaginative fiction is for Godard a crucial component of the historian's toolkit, and may in his view be at times the most effective vehicle for evoking certain aspects of the past, such as desire and affect.[20] Since completing *Histoire(s) du cinéma,* he has made frequent reference in interviews to the paucity of the treatment of personal relations in much historical writing, arguing that these are more accurately portrayed in cinematic fiction.[21] The attempt to fathom and convey the emotional worlds of our ancestors would, he suggests, facilitate readers' and viewers' identification with the past and help them to relate that past to the pressing concerns of their own present.[22]

The lightly reworked passages from *Clio* read by Miéville in 4B are spread over a six-minute sequence toward the end of the episode, and address three key points in relation to the fabrication of history, which Godard is clearly keen to reemphasize as he draws the series to a close.[23] First comes a discussion by Péguy of the implications of the shift from the traditional appeal to the judgment of God to the modern secular appeal to the judgment of history. This change, suggests Péguy, effectively implies looking to future generations for judgment. However, faced with the pressures and demands of their own present, he argues, there is no reason to think that the latter will be any better placed to review and assess past pleas.

Next comes a crucial, dense passage devoted to the topic of the difficult and usually unsuccessful evocation of the past through history:

> I was given a name, History, and a first name, Clio. What would it have been if it had had nothing at all to do with a text, but with movement itself, with an idea, with reality, with life (and you know that I don't at all like misusing these words). Or simply if it had still had something to do with a text, but had had nothing to do with determining it on the basis of words, but on an idea, for example, or on an intention, or on a movement. On a usage. Or on a familial connection. . . . You see, Péguy, she says, nothing is as handy as a text. And nothing is as handy as a word in a text. We only had book to put into book. . . . What would it be like if one had to put reality into a book, into book? And on the next level, if one had to put reality into reality? What always happens, my friend. Night falls. The holidays come to an end.[24]

Godard's use of this passage serves to reiterate his distinction between written history, which interests him comparatively little, and audiovisual history, which he relates here to Péguy's ideal of a form of history made up of movement, and indeed of reality itself.

And third comes a key passage, which follows directly, in which Clio outlines the conundrum of the historian faced either, as in ancient history, with too few facts, or, as in modern history, with too many: "I need a day / to tell / the history of one second / I need a year / to tell the history / of one minute / I need / a lifetime / to tell / the history of one hour / I need an eternity / to tell / the history / of one day / one can do everything / apart from / the history / of what one does."[25]

Let us now turn to Godard's engagement with the philosopher and critic Walter Benjamin. While working on *Histoire(s) du cinéma*, he made relatively little reference to Benjamin in interviews, and the latter's writings are barely cited in the series. However, this relative absence of direct reference should not mislead us. As Alain Bergala and others have noted, Benjamin's work has been a longstanding point of reference for Godard, especially his eighteen brief "Theses on the Philosophy of History," which are cited in *Les enfants jouent à la Russie* and *Hélas pour moi*, and alluded to in *The Old Place*.[26] Bergala has argued convincingly that Godard's close identification with the angel of history as perceived by Benjamin (in Thesis IX) in Paul Klee's painting *Angelus Novus* (1920) is clear from a montage of clips towards the end of the initial version of 1B, which includes Klee's *Forgetful Angel* (1939–40). Given the predicament of the modern historian identified by Péguy, it is not hard to appreciate why Godard should identify so closely with the situation of Benjamin's angel:

> His eyes are staring, his mouth open, his wings are spread. This is how one pictures the angel of history. His face is turned toward the past. Where we perceive a chain of events, he sees one single catastrophe which keeps piling wreckage upon wreckage and hurls it in front of his feet. The angel would like to stay, awaken the dead, and make whole what has been smashed. But a storm is blowing from Paradise; it has got caught in his wings with such violence that the angel can no longer close them. This storm irresistibly propels him into the future to which his back is turned, while the pile of debris before him grows skyward. This storm is what we call progress.[27]

Moreover, as Monica Dall'Asta has noted, although *Forgetful Angel* was cut from the final version of 1B, the figure of the angel of history haunts the episode in its entirety, not only via the various images of angels and the recurrence of the word *ange*, but also, by metonymic association, through the photograph of the couple in Bergman's *Prison,* who gaze offscreen at unseen events. "This frame," she argues, "in short, stands in the place of the angel, or better – to take literally the message that appears in the caption – it is 'l'ange.'"[28]

The challenge facing the angel is overwhelming, and calls for a radically different approach to historiography from the one exemplified, for Benjamin and Péguy alike, by the totalizing aspirations of the nineteenth-century positivists. For Benjamin, as for Godard, no moment of the past is irrevocably lost. The former's philosophy of history is underpinned by a combination of secular theories of social revolution (notably Marxism), and a nonlinear, ruptural conception of time inspired by Jewish messianism. Drawing a distinction between "homogenous, empty time" on the one hand, and messianic time on the other (what he describes as the *Jetztzeit,* the "time filled with the presence of the now"), he suggests that the interruption of the former by the latter has the potential to momentarily reinscribe the past in the present in an image.[29] This idea of the evocation and redemption of the past through fleeting images offers a concise description of Godard's historical montage practice. Indeed, Godard's use of the quasi-Pauline phrase discussed in chapter 1 ("the image will come at the time of the resurrection") can be read in this context as a succinct summary of Benjamin's model. The interruption and subversion of ordinary time by messianic time, the

production of a transitory image, and the arrest of thought "in a configuration pregnant with tensions" has the potential, argues Benjamin, to produce "a revolutionary chance in the fight of the oppressed past."[30] In this context, the task of the historian is less that of narrating a sequence of events than of grasping the "constellation" formed between the present era and an earlier one.[31] The key practical example of the application by Benjamin of his model, which looms large over *Histoire(s) du cinéma,* is his pioneering unfinished experiment in constructivist historiography, *The Arcades Project,* which eschews any attempt at factual narrative or exhaustive coverage in favor of a monumental, quasi-cinematic literary collage.[32] As Dall'Asta put it succinctly, *Histoire(s) du cinéma* basically does with the twentieth century what *The Arcades Project* did with the nineteenth.[33]

In *Histoire(s) du cinéma,* the idea of the return of a fragment of the past in an image is generally articulated through the Orphic imagery discussed above. Emblematic in this respect is the clip of Ethan and Debbie in *The Searchers,* which is explicitly associated with this process in 2B, via an onscreen title announcing "time regained." The formation of a connection between present and past is also expressed through the recurrent motif of the outstretched hand, and the idea of the establishment of a physical link between two people. This process is particularly explicit in *Nouvelle vague,* which is structured around three such moments, including the climactic sequence in which Richard (Alain Delon) grabs Elena's (Domiziana Giordano) hand to prevent her from drowning. The same process is reenacted near the start of 1B in Godard's dramatic manipulation of the lengthy concluding section of King Vidor's *Duel in the Sun* (1946),

The image will come at the time of the resurrection: *Nouvelle vague* (Godard, 1990), plus *Duel in the Sun* (King Vidor, 1946) and *Ordet* (Carl Theodor Dreyer, 1955) in 1B.

in which the wounded Pearl Chavez (Jennifer Jones) claws her way up a rocky hillside, before dying in the arms of Lewt McCanles (Gregory Peck), who is also fatally injured (in the original film, Pearl and Lewt have just shot one another). Here Godard makes explicit the link between the iconography of hands reaching out to each another, and the idea of the return of a moment of the past in an image, through the use of a variation on the aforementioned Pauline phrase: "the image / will come / oh! Time / of the / oh! Time / oh! Time / of the / of the / resurrection." (Godard is playing here on the words *au temps* ["at the time"], which are rendered in the onscreen text as "oh! Temps" ["oh! time"].) The image, however, as in Benjamin's formulation, is fleeting: as soon as it has been created (in this instance, once Pearl and Lewt have successfully reached and embraced one another), it quickly fades (both die).

Godard is generally dismissive of other historians, reserving his principal admiration – like Péguy – for one figure: Jules Michelet, author of the monumental eighteen-part *Histoire de France*.[34] Michelet's work haunted Godard as he developed his historical project. In 1989, for example, at the time of the bicentennial of the French Revolution, he proposed filming Michelet's harrowing account (in his history of the French Revolution) of the murder of the Princesse de Lamballe.[35] Godard's Benjaminian conception of history, and the picture he paints in 1B of his ancestors whispering in his bedroom, resonates powerfully with Michelet's reflections on his own experience of researching and writing his vast history of France a little over a century earlier: "In the solitary galleries of the Archives where I wandered for twenty years, in that profound silence, murmurs nevertheless came to my ear. The distant suffering of so many souls suffocated in those ancient times was complaining in low voices."[36] Godard also values the concrete connection between Michelet and what he wrote about: when working on his history of the French Revolution in the mid-nineteenth century, he would have had access – as in the case of the New Wave in relation to early cinema – to the eyewitness accounts of those who had experienced the events in question, many of whom would still have been alive at the time.[37] Above all, however, Godard cherishes Michelet for his lyricism and powers as a prose stylist, which, as Michelet himself acknowledged, often made him as much an artist as a historian.[38] Godard has returned repeatedly in interviews to the quality of Michelet's prose, expressing great admiration for the latter's use of poetic imagery, the "incredibly visual" quality of his writing, his willingness to include strong displays of emotion, and the inseparability in his work of the making of history and the art of literature.[39] As he put it simply in 1999, "It seemed to me that history could be a work of art, something not generally accepted, except by Michelet."[40]

In the modern era, Godard has time only for methodological innovators – notably Foucault, Duby, and Braudel. Godard cites Foucault's *L'ordre du discours* (*The Discourse on Language*) at the beginning of 4B, and has occasionally evoked the latter's archaeological method in interviews.[41] We have already indicated the significance of Duby's material contribution to the development of the series. Let us also note Godard's suggestion that medievalists such as Duby (he has also referenced Justine Favrod in this regard), faced in their work with a comparative scarcity of archival materials, generally proved more willing to accept the ebb and flow of *Histoire(s) du cinéma* as a bona fide form of history.[42] In addition, Godard has consistently expressed admiration for Duby's work, doubtless partly because of the latter's status as a public intellectual willing to work in television, and his attempts to cultivate an interest in medieval history with a popular audience, but also because of his powers as an essayist and prose stylist.[43] For Godard, although a historian such as Furet conveys an impression of knowing everything, Duby declares from the outset that we know virtually nothing, but nevertheless ends up evoking a sense of the place and period under investigation.[44] Godard has expressed particular admiration in this regard for Duby's *Dames du XIIe siècle* (*Women of the Twelfth Century*), which he considers an interesting, successful example of historical writing where archival documentation is scarce or non-existent. As he does Jacob, Canguilhem, and Koyré, Godard characterizes Duby as a filmmaker, and this book as a film: "It's his best book, because one sees that there's nothing, but one ends up seeing things. It's a real film."[45]

The most prominent historian on display in *Histoire(s) du cinéma* is Braudel, who is referred to at some length in 3B, and again in 4A. In addition, the cover of his *L'identité de la France* (*The Identity of France*), which is mentioned in passing in 3B, is shown on the ground, covered in mud, in *For ever Mozart*. It is worth recalling, in the context of Godard's critique of the paucity of the engagement with cinema by the majority of historians, and of the evident esteem in which he holds Braudel, that the latter played a key role in casting a spotlight on the significance of films to the historian, and in legitimizing the historical study of cinema within the Academy.[46] More than this, however, *Histoire(s) du cinéma* chimes methodologically with Braudelian theory in a number of important respects, including its insistence on plurality and polyphony. In an influential article written in 1958, Braudel had issued a passionate plea for multiplicity in history: "For me, history is the total of all possible histories – an assemblage of declarations and points of view, from yesterday, today, and tomorrow. The only error, in my view, would be to choose one of these histories to the exclusion of all the others. That was, and always will be, the cardinal error of historicizing."[47] Godard has echoed Braudel on this topic on numerous occasions, criticizing history as it is often practiced as little more than an incomplete, biased, quasi-fictional narrative, which is usually constructed long after the events it describes have taken place.[48] The Braudelian principle of multiplicity is clearly reflected in the plural "histories" of the title of Godard's series, and in that of its first episode, "Toutes les histoires." It also resonates with the references in the series to books made up of large numbers of constituent tales, such as *One Thousand and One Nights* (cited in 1A and 2B), which in this context evoke not only "all the stories" told by cinema, but also history's limitless potential constituent histories. However, the sequence in which Godard enacts and reflects most explicitly on this Braudelian principle comes not in *Histoire(s) du cinéma,* but in an important passage in *Hélas pour moi,* in which a variety of approaches to the representation of a single event in the past are presented from a succession of slightly differing points of view, each one mediated through the process of subjective memory. The combination of these viewpoints, as is made explicit in an accompanying intertitle in the film, has the potential to evoke – however hesitantly or fleetingly – something of the truth of what might have happened: "And so, little by little, the past returns in the present through means of the imaginary *mise en scène* of a visual experience, which always requires several observers."

In 3B, Godard samples excerpts from the soundtrack of a television program devoted to Braudel, *La dernière leçon de Fernand Braudel* (Fernand Braudel's final lesson).[49] This program is based on a filmed recording of Braudel's last public lecture in October 1985, a month before his death. It also contains an indirect link to Godard, in that it was made by one of his principal collaborators of the late 1960s and 1970s, Gérard Martin. Godard foregrounds in particular those parts of Martin's film that stress Braudel's rejection of traditional approaches to the teaching of history through dates and events, and Braudel's disappointment at having failed in his efforts to have his methods adopted more widely within the state education system. Those responsible for institutionalizing his ideas within the school curriculum, suggests Braudel in one of the clips selected by Godard, ended up doing precisely the opposite of what he had intended: introduction of his so-called new history in primary schools, and retention of the old model in the final years of secondary school. Overall, through his choice and arrangement of selected extracts from Martin's film, Godard presents Braudel in 3B as a misunderstood outsider figure who combined intellectual ambition and methodological innovation with a highly poetic, accessible prose style.[50]

Godard has suggested that Braudel and Duby's principal contribution to history was to have introduced into it a sense of geography. He is referring here to the new history of the Annales School, and in particular to the Braudelian notion of the *longue durée,* which downplays the role of specific events and individuals in history in favor of a panoramic history, measured in centuries rather than decades, which is primarily concerned with the long-term effects of factors such as geography and climate on human behavior in the premodern world.[51] Braudel contrasted *longue durée* history with that of the more familiar history of instants and events (what he called, following François Simiand, *histoire événementielle*), which he characterized in terms of the "headlong, dramatic, breathless rush of its narrative."[52] Godard's appropriation of the distinction between *longue durée* history and *histoire événementielle* is explicit in a series of titles in 4A, in which the former is illustrated by the frantic running of the anguished murdering landowner Thomas (Pyotr Masakha) in Dovzhenko's *Earth,* and the latter by a reworking of the aforementioned shot from *The Searchers:* "One history advances towards us with precipitate steps. Another history accompanies us with slow steps."[53] It is not hard to appreciate why Braudel's emphasis on *longue durée* history should have appealed to a Godard eager to situate the history of cinema within the context of visual representation since Lascaux. However, we should not overlook the playful nature of his engagement with this aspect of Braudelian thought, and the fact that he has adapted and applied it in a highly unorthodox manner to distinguish the relationship to reality mediated through television and the mass media from that established by cinema and art:

There are two histories: a close history, which runs towards us with precipitate steps – and it's television and *Der Spiegel,* and soon Goya and Matisse on CD-ROM (Rom for Romans, doubtless, *pax romana, pax americana*) – and a distant history which accompanies us with slow steps, and it's Kafka, it's Pina Bausch, it's Fassbinder, to cite only artists from your country. . . . For me, all this slowly became clear when I noticed that I had been accompanied since birth by this second history that Braudel spoke of, the one that accompanies you with slow steps.[54]

ART HISTORIANS

In the field of art history, Godard has long relied on two principal sources of inspiration, Élie Faure and André Malraux. He has frequently acknowledged his debt to both of these figures, expressing particular admiration for their "impassioned, lyrical style."[55] The former, whose discussion of Velázquez he had cited prominently at the beginning of *Pierrot le fou* (1965), was among the first art historians to take cinema seriously, declaring it an original art-form, the natural successor to painting and sculpture in the age of industrialization.[56] The latter played a fundamental role in Godard's early artistic formation, and, as we have seen, his theory of art is central to Godard's conceptualization of the artistic process. Godard's first love, he has indicated, was literature, through which he discovered painting, essentially via Malraux, at roughly the same time he began seriously engaging with cinema, between the ages of twenty and twenty-two.[57] Indeed, Malraux has exerted a powerful influence on Godard throughout his career, and this despite his fury at the former's failure to intervene to stop the banning of Jacques Rivette's *Suzanne Simonin, la religieuse de Diderot* (1966), and his contempt for Malraux's role in the attempts to remove Henri Langlois from his position as director general of the Cinémathèque française in 1968 (events that have come to be known in postwar cultural history as the Langlois Affair). However,

the intensity of Godard's dislike for Malraux during these two periods notwithstanding, the latter reappeared with a vengeance in his thinking and work from the 1980s onward, notably in *Soigne ta droite*, in which *La condition humaine* (*Man's Fate*), *Antimémoires* (*Antimemoirs*) and *Lazarus* are all cited. Indeed, in the mid-1980s, he was seriously considering developing a film project about Malraux's work under the title *La métamorphose des dieux* (*The Metamorphosis of the Gods*), a reference to the latter's three-volume philosophical study of the visual arts published between 1957 and 1976.[58] Although this project was not pursued, *Histoire(s) du cinéma* is in many ways its partial realization.

Godard inherits from both Faure and Malraux an inclusive, global vision of art, one that is less concerned with chronology and factual accuracy, than – as Faure put it in *L'esprit des formes* (*The Spirit of the Forms*, 1927) – with the "grand circulation of energy" running through all creative human activity.[59] Malraux, in particular, ranges freely across time and place, moving from Europe, Asia, China, and Africa to Polynesia, sometimes in a single long, rich sentence. He also leaps across the centuries; at one point – in a pairing of images that anticipates one of the "exercises in artistic thought" in *The Old Place* – he juxtaposes photographs of a Picasso sculpture and an example of third century BCE Sumerian art.[60] Professional art historians frequently took Malraux to task for his lack of systematic research and factual inaccuracies. For Godard, however, the significance of his work lies not in its conventional scholarship, but rather in the ambition and scope of his thinking, in the types of connections he establishes, in the perspectives he opens up, in his style, and in the novelty of his method. As Michael Temple put it in an important discussion of Faure and Malraux in relation to *Histoire(s) du cinéma,* what is so valuable to Godard about their work is "the broad sweep and flux of the thinking, the philosophical dimension of cultural history, the preference for big ideas over linear exposition and material facts, and above all an uncompromisingly poetic approach to the actual fabrication of that history, its design, its composition, its rhythms."[61]

Let us look in more detail at the principal areas of overlap between these three art historical projects, especially those of Malraux and Godard. On a conceptual level, Godard adopts three key Malrucian ideas. The first is the latter's theorization of artistic creativity in terms of the sacrifice and transfiguration of the real, which, as we saw in chapter 1, Godard has tended to formulate in terms of fire-related metaphors. The second, as suggested by the Malrucian (and now Godardian) title *La monnaie de l'absolu,* is the idea of art as the aftermath of the absolute, in the sense of a by-product of humanity's never-ending struggle against the human condition, the passage of time, and death.[62] And third is the principle of metamorphosis, wherein the art of the past is remembered, destroyed, and reinvented in that of the present. Malraux's theory of metamorphosis is multifaceted and quite complex, evoking simultaneously the transformation of the idea of art from one culture to another; the expansion in the type and quantity of objects categorized as art; the alteration in status conferred on objects resulting from their display in museums; the physical changes to artworks that take place over time; and the remembrance and destruction of inherited forms, and the creation of new ones, in the art of the present. It is this latter aspect of Malraux's theory that is the most significant for Godard. In it,

we can again see traces of Godard's underlying sacrificial model of the creative process: when he likens art to fire and links it inextricably to destruction (it is, we recall, "born out of what it consumes"), he is not just evoking the idea of the sacrifice of reality, but also the Malrucian concept of the sacrifice of the art of the past in that of the present. In 1B, he illustrates this idea of sacrifice and rebirth through the combination of the closing sequence from *Le mépris,* in which classical art is represented by both Homer and Fritz Lang, with a shot of himself (filmed in the 1980s) lighting his cigar; as the flame from his lighter licks upwards into the clip from *Le mépris,* the camera in the latter pans to the horizon, and the phrase "birth of cinema" appears on the screen.

On a methodological level, Godard has long identified both Faure and Malraux's principal innovation, which in his view also underpinned their popularity, as lying simply in the fact that they used lots of images.[63] Although this is something of a simplification, it is true that Faure pioneered a novel approach to the comparative use of pictorial reproductions and details in the composition of art history, which would have a profound impact on subsequent art historians, including Malraux. "I do not comment upon the picture through the text," wrote Faure. "I justify the text through the picture or through a fragment of the picture."[64] Following Faure, Malraux pursued a remarkable experiment in iconographic history in his two three-volume studies *Psychologie de l'art* (1947–49) and *Le musée imaginaire de la sculpture mondiale* (1952–54), which were based not only on writing, but also on the juxtaposition of images, on the passage between reproductions of whole works and details, and on a shifting relationship between image and text. Malraux talked in this context, in vocabulary subsequently adopted by Godard, of the *rapprochement* of photographs, and of having discovered and demonstrated through the use of visual *rapprochements* "an intelligence of images, which is faster than that of ideas."[65] Moreover, we know from texts such as his preface to his study of Goya, that Malraux was fully conscious of the quasi-cinematic nature of his deployment of techniques such as montage, rhythm and reframing:

> They (the photographic plates) scarcely belong to what historical studies call illustration; they do not accompany the description of works but replace it and, like the shots in a film, are intended on occasion to convey a suggestion by their content or by the order in which they occur.[66]

Although the versions of the *Psychologie de l'art* books published in a reduced format retain a sense of the originality and power of Malraux's project, only the beautifully produced original outsize editions published by Skira, which were lavishly illustrated with large color plates and black-and-white reproductions throughout, convey the sense of poetic visual thinking that underpins the conception and method of both the videos and books of *Histoire(s) du cinéma*. The stunning first edition of the first volume of *Psychologie de l'art,* published by Skira in 1947, "showed me the way," Godard acknowledged in 2000.[67] In his later books on art, as Godard has also recognized, Malraux withdrew to a large extent from his earlier bold pictorial method. However, although the use of illustrations in the *La métamorphose des dieux* trilogy is more conventional, Godard observed that "the image is more in his text than in the photo."[68] Despite the shift in Malraux's approach, Godard continued to value the art historian's deployment

Cover of the first edition of André Malraux's *Psychologie de l'art: Le musée imaginaire* (Skira, 1947).

of rhetorical devices such as prosopopoeia, suggesting that his writing was "full of visions" that served to reveal sudden connections between disparate objects and traditions.[69] Like Michelet's prose, Malraux's methods – whether based on the juxtaposition of pictures, the combination of picture and text, or qualities inherent in the writing itself – afforded Godard a crucial glimpse of the possibility of a poetic, visual approach to the composition of history.

Malraux's books are rooted in a recognition of the profundity of the impact of museums and photographic reproduction on our relationship to art. Thanks to the metamorphosis in perception brought about by museums, and then by photography, all the world's art, he argued, is now "under review."[70] Museums and photographic reproduction both divorce items from their original (often religious) contexts and produce art-works from essentially functional objects. Moreover, the use of photographic techniques – such as angles, lighting, framing, color, and, above all, the magnification of details – served to draw attention to small-scale works and effectively created hitherto invisible traditions, which Malraux dubbed "fictitious arts."[71] At the same time, he argued that the proliferation of photographic reproductions of artworks had led to the establishment of an ever-expanding "museum without walls," which facilitated the task of visually charting the metamorphosis of forms and genealogy of styles over time, and encouraged a comparative, critical, and fundamentally intellectual (as opposed to contemplative) experience of art in books. And what photography made possible in relation to painting and sculpture, electronic (and later digital) technologies made possible in relation to cinema: the juxtaposition and comparison of fragments of works.[72] Ultimately, however, as Malraux emphasized in his tribute to Picasso, the museum without walls is "a place of the mind," which "lives in us" – the net result of the individual's voyage through the sea of reproductions.[73] And the most significant such inner museums, he went on to argue, are those of contemporary artists, whose activities ensure the continued metamorphosis of forms. *Histoire(s) du cinéma* is both a concrete example of an imaginary audiovisual museum, and a sustained investigation by Godard of his own inner museum, whose expanding contents have informed, and reappeared transfigured within, the work he has produced over the past six decades.

Toward the end of *Le musée imaginaire,* Malraux broaches the question of cinema, which he positions as the extension of painting's quest to render movement. He also argues that photography's liberation of painting from the strictures of naturalism can be seen as the prelude to the spectacular renaissance of descriptive art through cinema.[74] In fact, Malraux had already published "Esquisse d'une psychologie du cinéma," which was informed by his experiences of having shot *Espoir: Sierra de Teruel* (1939–45) on location during the Spanish Civil War. Godard adapted, read, and filmed eight passages from this essay for use in *Histoire(s) du cinéma,* but ultimately did not use them.[75] It is worth noting, however, that in 1996 Godard recalled having discovered the original version of this text among his mother's book collection after the war, and that he recognized this discovery – alongside that of the first edition of *Psychologie de l'art* – as having had a profound impact on him.[76] Malraux's primary concern in this early sketch had been to situate cinema within the history of the Christian tradition of dramatic

André Malraux selecting images
for his imaginary museum of
world sculpture in 1953.

© Maurice Jarnoux/*Paris Match*/Scoop.

representation; to outline the main differences between cinema, theater, and the novel; and to propose a reading of American cinema of the 1930s in terms of a potent cocktail of journalism and myth. Its main appeal to Godard, however, arguably lies elsewhere: in its practical demonstration of a mode of writing about cinema in Cioranesque aphorisms – a number of which he recycles in 1A, including "cinema addresses the masses, and, for good or evil, the masses love myth," "myth begins with Fantômas, but ends with Christ," and Malraux's celebrated closing words, "in addition, cinema is an industry."[77]

CINEMA HISTORIANS

We shall now consider the cinema historians whose work and methods most inspired and influenced *Histoire(s) du cinéma*. As we have already noted, on the whole Godard has little time for written histories of cinema. Among the numerous early examples of the genre, he has singled out in interviews – in spite of the authors' fascist politics – Maurice Bardèche and Robert Brasillach's 1935 *Histoire du cinéma* as a rare example of a subjective, emotional history rooted in personal experience, and unafraid to foreground its cinematic likes and dislikes.[78] What evidently appeals to him about this book is the authors' conception of it not as an erudite history, but rather as "a collection of impressions, the diary of what we loved."[79] In certain respects, Godard's advocacy of the potential of audiovisual history, and his quest to work with video copies of films as the basis for the composition of a so-called true history of cinema, can be seen as the conceptual extension and practical realization of the aspirations of many of the leading film historians of the postwar

period. Georges Sadoul and Jean Mitry, for instance, who wrote their major works before the widespread availability of video and telecine technology, were acutely aware of the need to get closer to their object of study, which they knew in turn would transform their discipline. Rereading their books today, it is very striking to note how frequently they bemoan the difficulty of producing accurate historical accounts without proper access to film prints or adequate tools for handling them. In 1952, for instance, Sadoul dreamed out loud about how such access and tools – holding the films in one's hands, analyzing them frame by frame, studying editing patterns, and so on – would undoubtedly revolutionize the understanding and practice of cinema history.[80] A little over a decade later, he issued a passionate call for research copies of archive prints, together with appropriate viewing facilities, to be made available to researchers in the same way that books and journals were accessible in libraries.[81] Similarly, during the 1979 symposium held at the Cinémathèque suisse in Lausanne, Jean Mitry enthused about Godard's vision of audiovisual film history:

> It's obvious that the history of painting is done above all in museums, with the preserved, painted works; the history of cinema ought to be done, if not with the totality of films, at least of course with sufficiently significant extracts. . . . The day that we can use certain cinematographic material in the same way that we use quotations in literature, on that day, Godard's project will indeed become realizable, and I wish it with all my heart.[82]

Indeed, as Mitry went on to note, he himself had made just such an audiovisual study in 1965 devoted to the history of montage. This was a clip-based collage film, *Film sur le montage* (Film about montage), made in collaboration with the Belgrade Cinematheque, which at the time of the Lausanne event had never been shown beyond the walls of that cinematheque due to copyright issues.[83] Seated at his desk, flanked by cans of film, Mitry's self-depiction in the opening moments of his film provides a striking image of the audiovisual cinema historian reprised by Godard in *Histoire(s) du cinéma.* Moreover, irrespective of whether Godard was familiar with Mitry's film, there is significant continuity between *Film sur le montage* and *Histoire(s) du cinéma,* not only in terms of underlying method, but also of the corpus of films on which they draw.

In his preface to the 1972 reedition of Sadoul's history of cinema, Henri Langlois pursued a similar line of thinking to that of Mitry and Sadoul, predicting the revolution in film historiography that would inevitably result from improved access to prints.[84] However, Langlois's influence on Godard runs much deeper than this. In the first instance, Godard's esteem is based on a recognition that Langlois, in collaboration with Georges Franju in the early years, saved and then made visible large numbers of neglected or forgotten films: "If there hadn't been Franju and Langlois, we would never have known that there had been silent films, that *Sunrise* existed and was perhaps the equal of certain old paintings."[85] For him, Langlois was a "discoverer" and "instigator" on a par with figures such as Gaston Gallimard and Bernard Grasset, but whose contribution to twentieth-century art and culture has been seriously and unjustly undervalued by comparison.[86] He considers Langlois an innovative visual thinker and poet-historian, for whom "showing was a form of thinking," and who had effectively pioneered an exploratory form of visual cinema history through the art

Film sur le montage (Jean Mitry, 1965).

of comparative projection.[87] Thus he has often described Langlois as a *filmmaker,* who composed great experimental macro-film collages through the juxtaposition of the works of others in his projectors.[88] As he put it when chairing a press conference in support of Langlois at the Cinémathèque in 1968: "Henri Langlois for me was one of the greatest French directors.... One might say that he was director and scriptwriter of a film called the 'Cinémathèque française,' the director of production being the Centre du cinéma, and the general producer being the French state."[89]

Godard's intervention at the 1979 Lausanne symposium is one of a succession of eulogies by him to Langlois. These began with the address he delivered at the Cinémathèque française in 1966 ("Grâce à Henri Langlois"), in which he declared his boundless admiration and friendship, acknowledged the extent of his personal debt to his mentor and stressed the significance of the latter's single-mindedness and "titanic efforts" in the realms of film collection and curation for future generations of filmmakers and filmgoers.[90] These tributes have continued in the interim (such as *Deux fois cinquante ans de cinéma français,* which ends on a close-up of Langlois's face), and have culminated to date in the extended homage in 3B, in which he characterizes Langlois as a magician, who revealed simultaneously an invisible art-form, and a new history of the world through it ("one evening / we went to see / Henri Langlois / and then / there was light").[91] Besides this key sequence, *Histoire(s) du cinéma* is informed throughout by a constant dialogue between Godard and Langlois, and not just on those occasions in which the latter is explicitly mentioned. The former's evocation in 1A and 3B of various categories of

absent or virtual films – such as those that have been banned, mutilated by studio interference, forgotten by history, not made at all, or simply hardly shown – recalls the lost films repeatedly lamented by Langlois in his writings and interviews, and his constant struggle against institutionalized indifference to the destruction of negatives.[92] One of the most striking precursors to the series are the films of Langlois's anti-lectures directed by Harry Fischbach for the TV Ontario series *Parlons cinéma* (Let's talk cinema) in 1976. As is true of Mitry's *Film sur le montage,* watching *Histoire(s) du cinéma* after *Parlons cinéma* generates a powerful sense of continuity, filiation, and intertextual dialogue – notably in areas such as the prominence of the historian's body and voice, the use of still imagery, and the topics selected for discussion. A special episode of *Parlons cinéma* devoted to Langlois following his death in 1977 includes a discussion of Soviet cinema in terms of engineering and chemistry, which resonates suggestively with Godard's positioning of Eisenstein in 2B in the context of the history of medicine and anatomy.[93]

A key point of convergence between Langlois and Godard relates to their shared conceptualization of cinematheques in terms not only of preservation, restoration, and projection, but also of production. What is the point, asked Godard in 1975 (in comments that anticipate his return to this topic in 2B), of stockpiling and preserving films, if not as a basis for making new ones?[94] Godard has long characterized Langlois not just as an experimental programmer-producer, but also as a "director of productions," who "produced production" by nurturing a curiosity and love for films and a desire to make them.[95] For Langlois, the role of the Cinémathèque française was not merely to show films, but to educate, inspire, and equip its members to contribute to the present and future of cinema – whether as filmmakers, critics, historians, and programmers, or as collectors, archivists, and viewers. As Laurent Mannoni has argued, Langlois's cultivation of a critical spirit among the Cinémathèque's audiences from the late 1940s onward, notably by exposing them to films from the silent era and from around the globe, was instrumental in revitalizing written criticism in the 1950s, which in turn paved the way for cinematic renewal in the shape of the New Wave.[96] This was entirely intentional on Langlois's part, since he had been talking as early as 1946 of facilitating the blossoming of a new avant-garde.[97] As he made clear in 1962, this productive dimension of programming was fundamental to the way he viewed his calling:

> What interests me is that new films are made. That cinema advances. For me, the broadcasting of culture through the cinematheques is a question of creating the future, because a cinematheque is the museum of a living art, a museum that isn't only one of the past, but of the future. For me, the victory of the Cinémathèque is to have made possible *Les quatre cent coups, Le beau Serge, Paris nous appartient, Le signe du lion, À bout de souffle, Le rideau cramoisi,* and *Paris 1900,* to have helped Resnais and Rouch, to have contributed in the past in Milan and Rome, in 1938 and 1939, to the genesis and sources of Neo-realism.[98]

There is also a more literal sense in which Langlois can be thought of as a producer. Not only did he welcome works by young filmmakers such as Philippe Garrel at the Cinémathèque, but he also contributed production funds to others such as Kenneth Anger (whom he helped financially to make *Rabbit Moon,* 1950), and gave filmstock to figures such as Raymond Queneau, Jean-Paul Sartre, Pablo Picasso, and Jean Genet.[99] It is in the context of this conceptualization of Langlois

Henri Langlois in 1B, Georges Franju in 3B, and *Parlons cinéma: Hommage à Henri Langlois* (Harry Fischbach, 1977).

**The Méliès and fairground cinema
rooms in Langlois's museum at the
Avenue de Messine in 1953.**

Courtesy Cinémathèque française.

as a producer that Godard's view of the role of cinematheques must be understood, including his provocative joke in a 1975 letter that Langlois should sell his collection of films and distribute the proceeds among his favorite filmmakers as a way of directly fueling the regeneration of contemporary cinema.[100]

Dominique Païni has persuasively positioned Langlois as the single most significant precursor to the Godard of *Histoire(s) du cinéma*, arguing that the former is best considered not only through reference to the history of cinephilia, but also to artists and thinkers such as Duchamp, Cage, Boulez, Barthes, and Godard, all of whom he describes as "programmers" who are in dialogue with the works of their predecessors, and who are concerned with the museal *mise en scène* of these works as a means of transcending their figurative and illusionist limits.[101] He has also argued that *Histoire(s) du cinéma* is indicative not only of the scale of the impact of Malraux on Godard, but of the extent to which the principles underlying Langlois's conception and use of the Cinémathèque française in the postwar period as a kind of laboratory for the projection and comparison of films, were themselves underpinned by Malrucian thought.[102] Mannoni has also emphasized the influence of Malraux's ideas and methodology on Langlois's comparative approach to the exhibition of films and display of documents in his museum, as well as on his use of metaphor, aphorism, and hyperbole.[103] Furthermore, Mannoni has shown that prior to the Langlois Affair, Langlois and Malraux had enjoyed a long relationship built on a high degree of mutual trust and respect, which reached back to at least 1945, and perhaps even to the mid-1930s if – as the former claimed – Malraux had been a regular attendee at the Cercle du cinéma cine-club co-founded by Langlois and Franju in 1935.[104] In a discussion of a document detailing six months of programming at the Cinémathèque between 1956 and 1957 devoted to "Twenty-five years of cinema," Païni has gone on to characterize Langlois as a conceptual collage writer, whose neo-Eisensteinian programming practice – he proposes the suggestive idea of "programming-attraction" – constituted a pioneering practical experiment in cinematographic figurability, which simultaneously invented "a veritable method of mnemo-technical 'conservation.'"[105] In a conversation with Freddy Buache about Langlois in 1990, Godard also compared the latter to Eisenstein: "[H]e [Langlois] evoked a history of cinema that much later made me want to learn . . . a history he edited in the way that Eisenstein edited his films, by hand, just with a pair of scissors and a splicer. It was surprising."[106] Langlois, Godard suggests in the course of this same conversation, "knew very well what he was doing with his 'disorderly' projections and his bizarre museum. It was full of nuances, of *sous-entendus*. Of unexpected comparisons that set off genuine reflection."[107] Not everyone, however, valued Langlois's contribution as a historian as highly as Godard – least of all Truffaut, who, dismayed at the channeling of funds into the museum at the expense of the other pressing activities of the Cinémathèque, made his dissent quite clear, arguing that just because Langlois stuck a couple of film stills on a wall, or put one of Greta Garbo's costumes next to the skull from Hitchcock's *Psycho* (1960), it certainly didn't make him a meaningful critic, let alone a historian.[108]

Païni also suggests that the numerous lists of film titles compiled by Langlois over the course of his lifetime constitute a form of poetry, or at least extended wordplay.[109] Langlois's play with titles anticipates Godard's subsequent deployment of book and film titles throughout *Histoire(s) du cinéma.* This was already a strong feature of pre–*Histoire(s) du cinéma* works such as *Grandeur et décadence d'un petit commerce de cinéma,* in which Godard incorporated not only photographs and video clips from cinema history, but also numerous inserts in the form of film titles. In the series itself, the titles sometimes serve merely to recall the source film. Usually their function is also to create a mood, to establish a tension with other titles or graphic elements, to provide a brief comment on the imagery, or to offer a broader commentary on an aspect of cinema history or Godard's life story. As Roland-François Lack has observed, the book titles – most of which are of course also the titles of films derived from the books – listed by Godard in 1A over a sequence depicting Anna Karina in *Bande à part,* provide a rapid summary of, and reflection on, their time together as a couple: Molière's *L'école des femmes* (*The School for Wives*), Laclos's *Les liaisons dangereuses* (*Dangerous Liaisons*), Musset's *On ne badine pas avec l'amour* (*There's No Trifling with Love*), Chandler's *Farewell, My Lovely,* Sagan's *Bonjour tristesse* (Hello, sadness), and Flaubert's *L'éducation sentimentale* (*Sentimental Education*).[110] We can trace this play with titles back to Godard's early critical articles, which frequently deployed a sort of cinephilic code based on their appropriation, combination and *détournement.* In a 1958 article on Bergman, for instance, in addition to a veiled reference to Dostoyevsky's *Insulted and Injured,* Godard managed to weave the French-language titles of Boris Barnet's *Bountiful Summer* (1950), Roger Leenhardt's *Les dernières vacances* (*The Last Vacation,* 1948), and Bergman's

A Ship to India (1947) into a single sentence.[111] He also carried the practice over into his early films. The trailer for *À bout de souffle,* for instance, ends on a woman's voice listing a series of film titles, which serve simultaneously to contextualize, frame, and offer a rapid commentary on the source film: *La peur* (*Fear* [Roberto Rossellini, 1954]), *Le diable au corps* (*Devil in the Flesh* [Claude Autant-Lara, 1947]), *Du rififi chez les hommes* (*Rififi* [Jules Dassin, 1956]), *Et dieu créa la femme* (*And God Created Woman* [Roger Vadim, 1956]), and *Scarface* (Howard Hawks, 1932). Like Langlois's lists, these titles also form a self-contained poem. In the same way, the lists of films given at the back of the *Histoire(s) du cinéma* books offer succinct poetic histories of cinema composed entirely from titles, and it is worth noting in this context that although the inventory of films drawn up by Bernard Eisenschitz for Gaumont used the original foreign-language titles, for the purposes of the lists at the back of the books, Godard generally opted for the more evocative French-language versions.[112]

This characterization of Langlois as a Malrucian/Eisensteinian montage artist not only provides a suggestive conceptual model, but is accurate at a literal level also. Apart from combining films through his projectors, Langlois pursued a comparatively little known career as a compilation filmmaker; he had new negatives struck from existing prints (or had new prints laboriously struck frame by frame from existing shrunken negatives), and used these as a means of reprinting selected clips, which he then edited together to produce montage films, at least half a dozen of which were made in the 1960s and 1970s. Here is an eyewitness account of the twelve-hour nonstop montage of clips from two hundred films devoted to "Paris through the

Grandeur et décadence d'un petit
commerce de cinéma (Godard, 1985).

cinema from Louis Lumière to Jean-Luc Godard" shown at the Palais des congrès in March 1974. Langlois, installed in the projection booth and armed with glue and scissors, was frantically composing the film about to be shown moments before it was projected: "He sticks, unsticks, resticks the film. Edits and dismantles. With his memories and scissors as his only tools. A phone call distracts him. Pity! On the screen, in a moment, the word DNE will appear instead of END. 'Damn, it's backward!'"[113] These compilation films include examples devoted to the Lumière brothers, early silent French cinema, the French avant-garde of the 1920s, experimental German cinema of the 1930s, and the work of Gloria Swanson. Informed by Langlois's deep knowledge of cinema history, and inspired by his quest to investigate that history through the creative use of found footage, they are – alongside Langlois's many other initiatives and activities – among the most significant forerunners to *Histoire(s) du cinéma.*

FOUND-FOOTAGE ESSAYISTS

Langlois's filmic output leads us to a consideration of the other principal filmmakers who paved the way for Godard's audiovisual historical method. We begin with a number of key found-footage essayists and historians. As Jay Leyda noted in his landmark study *Films Beget Films,* compilation filmmaking is almost as old as cinema itself.[114] The reediting of topicals and the composition of improvised narratives from preexisting material was commonplace from the 1890s onward, driven by public demand and by a commercial recognition that release of the same footage in different forms and combinations provided a simple but effective way

of maximizing profits. This commercial exploitation of the archive was accompanied by the emergence of a more personal, critical, and political use of found footage to construct alternative or oppositional histories, a tendency exemplified in the 1920s and 1930s by pioneering compilation work made by figures such as Esfir Shub, Dziga Vertov, Henri Storck, and Germaine Dulac. Godard samples material by both Shub and Vertov in *Histoire(s) du cinéma,* and the latter has of course been a major point of reference in Godard's work ever since the late 1960s, when he and his collaborators adopted the Dziga Vertov name for their filmmaking collective. This alignment with Vertov signaled an identification with a form of political cinema rooted in an engagement with the present and the everyday, and an engagement with some central strands of Vertovian theory, which continue to inform Godard's later practice. These include the dream of a quasi-scientific research laboratory in which to pursue audiovisual experiments; a deep-rooted mistrust of the application of a literary form of narrative to cinema, combined with contempt for the conventional written script, and a quest to develop an extralinguistic visual symphonic-cinematic form; expansion of the idea and practice of montage to include every stage of the filmmaking process; the theorization and application of interval theory, whereby film poems are composed around the movements and transitions between the visual stimuli carried by individual shots; and an unshakable faith in the camera as a scientific scope through which to penetrate the surface of reality and reveal the invisible.[115] This latter idea has been particularly important for Godard, who has frequently characterized the camera as sort of X-ray machine capable of revealing and

magnifying hitherto imperceptible physical realities and the injuries of social injustice.

Godard also pursues a dialogue in *Histoire(s)
du cinéma* with a number of other prominent
found-footage essayists and historians, such
as Santiago Álvarez, Mikhail Romm, Chris
Marker, Artavazd Peleshian, and Guy Debord.
We shall examine each figure's position within
Godard's schema. The prolific Cuban pamphle-
teer Álvarez, to whom 2A is jointly dedicated,
plays a particularly significant role in the series,
and occupies a prominent place in Godard's
later work. This can be partly ascribed to a recognition on Godard's part of Álvarez's skill in
the artisanal orchestration of still images, and
of the latter's sizable contribution to the art of
quasi-musical political compilation filmmaking.
More than this, however, Álvarez has come to
function in Godard's work as a shorthand for
the documentary dimension of all cinema. From
Álvarez's vast corpus, Godard has selected one
film, and one sequence within it, to represent
this important aspect of his conceptualization
of cinema. It is an astonishing passage from *79
Springs,* in which the film itself, in a reflection of
the danger and violence it seeks to represent, appears to lurch and jump in the projector, seemingly at times close to complete disintegration.
Godard first used this sequence in his televisual
demonstration of his concept of comparative
montage in 1987, and he went on to cite it in
3B (where it is equated with the documentary
aspect of the New Wave) and in essays such as
Les enfants jouent à la Russie and *De l'origine du
XXIe siècle.*

Mikhail Romm's influential but currently
neglected found-footage study of the rise and
legacy of Nazism, *Ordinary Fascism* (1965; cited
in 1B), combines historical ambition with formal

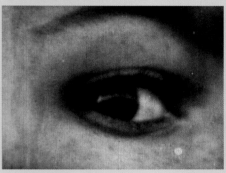

Kino-Eye (Dziga Vertov, 1924).

79 Springs (Santiago Álvarez, 1969) in
De l'origine du XXIe siècle (Godard, 2000),
and Godard's comparison of the film
with *Full Metal Jacket* (Stanley Kubrick,
1987) on *Cinéma cinémas* in 1987.

innovation, irreverence, humor, daring juxtapositions, and the use of tools such as intertitles, chapters, and voiceover commentary. As such, it preceded, and doubtless nourished, Godard's essayistic work from the late 1960s onward. Godard has discussed *Ordinary Fascism* in interviews on a number of occasions, indicating that it was the film he had in mind when considering developing a long-cherished project on the topic of the Holocaust, of which *Histoire(s) du cinéma* is in part the belated realization.[116] In addition to the formal and thematic connections between *Ordinary Fascism* and *Histoire(s) du cinéma*, especially the centrality of Nazism and the Holocaust to the two films' respective accounts of the twentieth century, there are a number of direct textual links between them. Romm, for instance, included a powerful montage of photographs, which have since become familiar through frequent reproduction, depicting the 1941 execution by the Nazis of three members of the Lithuanian resistance movement: Masha Bruskina, Volodia Shcherbatsevich, and Kiril Trus.[117] Fragments of one of these photographs (which Godard and Miéville had previously manipulated in both *Comment ça va* and *Photos et Cie*, episode 3a of *Six fois deux*) return near the end of 1A, where they are used twice, and again in 4A. In both the Romm and Godard films, this photograph evokes simultaneously the human capacity for evil, and the great bravery of those who confronted and resisted the Nazi occupation. In *Histoire(s) du cinéma* it also provides an image of resistance to tyranny in all its forms, including intellectual and artistic. In 1A, Godard pays tribute to Bruskina, Shcherbatsevich, and Trus via the insertion over a fragment of the photograph of the title of Hitchcock's Resistance-themed French-language wartime propaganda film, *Bon voyage* (1944), and links them to both Goya and Valentin Feldman, the young philosopher whose last moments Godard had sought to imagine in *Le dernier mot*.

When asked in interviews in recent years about the fact that he and Chris Marker often appeared to be working on parallel tracks, Godard suggested that in his view, Marker was fundamentally more literary, whereas he considers his own approach to be more painterly and rooted in the image.[118] Like Romm's work, all of the material from Marker used by Godard in *Histoire(s) du cinéma* had in fact already been borrowed by Marker from elsewhere. This includes the devastating sequence from Dovzhenko's *Arsenal* (1928) depicting a railway track littered with dead bodies, which Marker had incorporated into his tribute to Aleksandr Medvedkin, *Le tombeau d'Alexandre* (*The Last Bolshevik*, 1993), and which Godard recycles in 3B and 4A, and has gone on to reuse in works such as *De l'origine du XXIe siècle*. He also borrows a number of clips from Marker's vast experiment in audiovisual historiography, *Le fond de l'air est rouge* (*A Grin without a Cat*, 1977). Marker's stated aims – to restore the polyphony of history, to allow the images and sounds to speak for themselves, and to enable viewers to create their own commentaries – directly anticipate those of Godard.[119] *Histoire(s) du cinéma* and *Le fond de l'air est rouge* also share a number of cinematic reference points, such as the lion sequence from *Battleship Potemkin*, which Marker links through editing to the student movements in America and Europe in the 1960s. In addition, Godard cites a sequence from *Le fond de l'air est rouge* toward the end of 4A depicting a moment often interpreted as a turning point in the history of the Left in Europe: the sea of red flags flowing through the

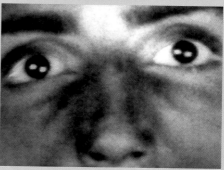

Ordinary Fascism (Mikhail Romm, 1965).

Godard's use of the photograph of the murder of Masha Bruskina and Volodia Shcherbatsevich in 1A and 4A.

streets on 5 March 1972 during the funeral procession for Pierre Overney, the young Maoist murdered by a guard outside a Renault factory the previous month (Godard has subsequently reused this sequence in *The Old Place* and *De l'origine du XXIe siècle*). However, perhaps the most crucial clip taken by Godard from *Le fond de l'air est rouge* derives from the film's closing sequence, which depicts the tracking and killing of wolves by helicopter. Fifteen years after the cull depicted, the voiceover suggests on the soundtrack, there were still wolves. By concluding 4A with this sequence, which is preceded by the Overney material, Godard not only pays warm tribute to Marker as a leading figure in the postwar left-wing filmmaking tradition in France, but also, following Marker, delivers through it an unequivocal statement of belief in the necessity of continued artistic and political resistance in the face of oppression in all its forms.

This theme of resistance is central to *Histoire(s) du cinéma,* and to Godard's related discourse, where it is rooted in a conception of authentic art and thought as intrinsic acts of resistance in the face of the homogenizing effects of the culture industry. Godard's point of departure as an artist is that of someone who resists.[120] Here he is close to, and probably influenced by, Gilles Deleuze – who, in a lecture delivered at the Fémis in 1987, offered a compelling definition of art in terms of resistance.[121] Godard's critique of mass culture and reflections on the social significance of art should also be situated in relation to the work of the comparatively neglected Swiss thinker Denis de Rougemont, and in particular to Rougemont's 1936 *Penser avec les mains,* lengthy extracts of which (the sequence lasts over five minutes) are read on the soundtrack of 4A.[122] In *Penser avec les mains,* Rougemont issued a passionate plea for individuals to assume their social responsibilities, through restoration of the link between society and engaged creative thought (in a key passage cited by Godard, Rougemont draws a causal link between the abandonment of thought and social ossification), and a renewed commitment to an ambitious mode of thinking and creativity that is both "dangerous for the thinker and transforms reality."[123] The film in which this conflation of political, philosophical and artistic resistance is most explicit in Godard's later work is the powerful short audiovisual pamphlet he made in 1993 in protest against the inaction of the European Parliament in the face of escalating humanitarian crisis in the Balkans, *Je vous salue, Sarajevo,* which was broadcast on Arte in January 1994 as part of an evening of programs devoted to the war in Bosnia:

> For there's a rule and an exception. Culture is the rule, and art is the exception. Everybody speaks the rule: cigarette, computer, T-shirt, TV, tourism, war. Nobody speaks the exception. It isn't spoken, it's written: Flaubert, Dostoyevsky. It's composed: Gershwin, Mozart. It's painted: Cézanne, Vermeer. It's filmed: Antonioni, Vigo. Or it's lived, and then it's the art of the living: Srebrenica, Mostar, Sarajevo. The rule is to want the death of the exception. So the rule for Cultural Europe is to organize the death of the art of living, which still flourishes.[124]

Godard recycles this definition of art in 4B. In the original film, the inhabitants of Sarajevo, like the Lithuanian resistance fighters, are emblematic not only of political resistance but also of artistic resistance and of artists and philosophers everywhere, who continue to think, write, and create – irrespective of the difficulties they are obliged to negotiate or of the reception of their work (whether they are unknown, forgotten, or

cursed, as Godard puts it in the closing moments of 4A). *Je vous salue, Sarajevo* also functions in this respect as a sort of trailer for 3A, and in particular for Godard's controlled but furious delivery of a text written by Victor Hugo in 1876 in response to the outbreak of violent conflict in the Balkans, prior to the Russo-Turkish War of 1877–78. Here he uses Hugo's text as a means of lambasting the governments of Europe for their collective failure to respond adequately to events in Bosnia in the 1990s, and the sequence prepares the ground for his presentation of Italian Neo-realism in terms of artistic resistance at the end of the same episode.[125]

Alongside Overney and Marker's wolves, we should place the Armenian audiovisual poet-philosopher Artavazd Peleshian. Godard included an extract from Peleshian's stunning *(In the) Beginning* (1967) – one that Peleshian had taken in turn from Pudovkin's *Mother* (1926) – in found-footage works such as *De l'origine du XXIe siècle.* For Godard, Peleshian was the inheritor of the cinematic secrets of Barnet, Eisenstein, Dovzhenko, and Vertov, and reassuring proof that the impact of their experiments continued to resonate.[126] Figures such as Peleshian, who continue to create against the odds, are represented in Anne-Marie Miéville's *Après la réconciliation* (*After the Reconciliation,* 2000) in the form of the weeds that somehow manage to survive in the cracks of the pavement in the heart of the city. Similarly, they are represented in the "Photos of Utopia" section in *The Old Place* by the poppies that flourish on the verges of motorways, where the poppies are explicitly equated visually (via the red flags) with political resistance, and verbally (via Miéville's commentary) with the notion of "the last artists." Let us also note that *Histoire(s) du cinéma* is peopled

Images of resistance: *Après la réconciliation* (Anne-Marie Miéville, 2000), *The New Babylon* (Grigori Kozintsev and Leonid Trauberg, 1929) in 1A, *Allemagne année 90 neuf zéro* (Godard, 1991), *Zoya* (Lev Arnshtam, 1944) in 4B, and *The Old Place* (Miéville and Godard, 1998).

by a sizable group of additional figures, many of them young women, who embody political, philosophical, critical, and artistic resistance: Michèle Firk, the young *Positif* critic (dedicatee of 2B), who abandoned writing for direct action with the Guatemalan resistance before shooting herself in 1968 to avoid capture by the police; Sophie and Hans Scholl, and the other members of the Munich-based White Rose group, who dared to resist the Third Reich by distributing tracts, and who paid for their courage with execution; Zoya Kosmodemyanskaya – the eighteen-year-old Russian resistance fighter tortured and executed by the Nazis in Petrischevo, near Moscow, in 1941 – who would become one of Russia's most celebrated wartime heroines (and whose story was recounted by Arnshtam in *Zoya*); and Grigori Kozintsev and Leonid Trauberg's fictional shop assistant Louise (Yelena Kuzmina) in *The New Babylon* (1929), who, politicized during the buildup to the establishment of the Paris Commune, joined the Communards and was executed for her commitment to her beliefs.

We shall conclude this discussion of found-footage essayists and historians with a consideration of the significance to Godard of one of the twentieth century's preeminent theorists of recycling and resistance, Guy Debord. In 3A, Godard stresses the magnitude of Debord's contribution as an artist and critic, and the latter's prescience in analyzing and resisting the rise of the society of the spectacle. The film version of Debord's *La société du spectacle* (*The Society of the Spectacle*, 1973), based on his eponymous 1967 book, provides a concise model of an oppositional form of found-footage audiovisual history, which, as Giorgio Agamben has noted, directly anticipates *Histoire(s) du cinéma*.[127] On a formal level, besides the manipulation and

détournement of preexisting images and sounds, *La société du spectacle* deploys a set of formal strategies very close to those refined by Godard since the 1960s: shock cuts, the establishment of visual connections and rhymes between fictional and documentary footage, use of a first-person critical voiceover, and a secondary reflection on the imagery through onscreen titles. Godard's dialogue in *Histoire(s) du cinéma* with *La société du spectacle* is perhaps clearest in the clips he uses from films previously sampled by Debord, such as *Johnny Guitar, Battleship Potemkin, Mr. Arkadin* (Orson Welles, 1955) and *For Whom the Bell Tolls* (Sam Wood, 1943). But his conversation with Debord runs deeper and predates the series. The latter's furious analysis of the circulation of images in capitalist societies that have entered what he terms their "spectacular phase," of the power structures represented and reproduced in such imagery, and of the fate of history in the age of spectacular capitalism was often remarkably close to Godard and Miéville's work of the 1970s. Like Debord they were ultimately concerned with dissecting and contesting the inequalities, violence, and homogenizing effects of the society of the spectacle, and simultaneously forging an oppositional mode of audiovisual criticism.

AUDIOVISUAL FILM CRITICS
AND HISTORIANS

The principle of applied visual criticism can be traced back at least as far as the reediting experiments conducted on imported American films such as Griffith's *Intolerance* (1916) in the young Lev Kuleshov's Workshop at the beginning of the 1920s, whose participants included future filmmakers such as Boris Barnet, Vsevolod

La société du spectacle (Guy Debord, 1973).

Pudovkin, and – briefly – Sergei Eisenstein. Among the most ambitious and exciting early examples of audiovisual criticism based on the principle of recycling is one that appears not to have progressed beyond the stage of a conceptual proposition: Left Front critic Viktor Pertsov's suggestion in 1926 of the development of a new type of visual film criticism – films about films, or "films-as-review" as he described them – that would draw on, quote, and combine preexisting material – and even turn films, through reediting, into "acerbic reviews" of themselves.[128] It was, however, above all in France that experimentation with film history through various means and media – books, lectures, and cineclub reprojections and debates – became a major focus in the 1920s, thanks largely to the activities of those associated with the cinematic impressionist movement, or First Wave. This decade also saw the proliferation in France of a number of didactic cinematic histories of cinema. The first of these was Julien Duvivier and Henry Lepage's chronological clip-based survey, *La machine à refaire la vie* (The machine for remaking life), a film first shown in March 1924. Christophe Gauthier has argued interestingly that this film provided the blueprint for subsequent histories of cinema through cinema, and had a formative influence on the foundation of cinema history as an academic discipline.[129] Immediately successful, it was projected over one hundred times in France between 1924 and 1927.[130] Moreover, as Duvivier and Lepage explained in an accompanying article, their film drew not only on material donated by Louis Lumière, but also on what they described as a "very interesting little film on the history of cinema" that had been made and kindly put at their disposal by none other than Léon Gaumont.[131]

Thus *Histoire(s) du cinéma* – made for "the heirs of Léon Gaumont," as Godard puts it in *JLG/JLG* – is the extension of a visual and audiovisual film history tradition that reaches back at least as far as Gaumont himself. The year 1926 saw the production of a rival film to that of Duvivier and Lepage, entitled simply *L'histoire du cinéma par le cinéma* (The history of cinema through cinema). Made by Raoul Grimoin-Sanson, with the assistance of Louis Forest, this film offered an alternative account of cinematic prehistory and history. However, rivalry and competing claims in the two films' respective accounts of early cinema history led to fierce exchanges in the press between their makers, driven primarily by Duvivier and Lepage's anger at what they considered Grimoin-Sanson's inflation of the importance of his own contribution, at the expense of that of Louis Lumière.[132]

Growth of the cinematic compilation and remix genres has been accompanied by a corresponding increase in the number of audiovisual essays in film criticism and audiovisual histories of cinema made by independent filmmakers. The proliferation of such essays has been fuelled in recent decades by easy access to copies of films, especially on VHS, DVD, and online, and of the availability of affordable, user-friendly electronic and digital editing technologies. In addition to *Histoire(s) du cinéma*, key examples include Al Razutis's *Visual Essays: Origins of Film* (1973–84); Hollis Frampton's *Magellan* (1971–84 [unfinished]); Orson Welles's *F for Fake* (1974); Noël Burch's *The Silent Revolution: What Do Those Old Films Mean?* (1987); Mark Rappaport's *Exterior Night* (1993), *From the Journals of Jean Seberg* (1995), and *The Silver Screen: Color Me Lavender* (1997); Martin Scorsese's *A Personal Journey with Martin Scorsese through*

American Cinema (1995) and *My Voyage to Italy* (1999); Michael Kuball's *Geliebtes Leben: Soul of a Century* (2003); and Gustav Deutsch's *Film Ist* (1998–2004).

This rich tradition lies beyond the scope of the current study, and we shall confine ourselves here to a discussion of Godard's engagement with two particularly significant figures in and around *Histoire(s) du cinéma*: Welles and Frampton. Let us begin with Welles, whom Godard adopted at the beginning of his career as one of his principal artistic guides. There were several reasons for this: the scale of Welles's contribution to cinema in his completed films; the force of his visual imagination; his formal inventiveness; his commitment to artistic independence; and, as Godard wrote in 1964, his astonishing versatility as a one-man band – "author, composer, actor, designer, producer, scholar, financier, gourmet, ventriloquist, poet."[133] Since Welles's death in 1985, his presence has been particularly strong in Godard's work. The photographs of him in *King Lear,* for instance, were intended (as Godard made clear in his synopsis of the film) to remind us of Welles's absence, and of our relative lack of passion by comparison.[134] Above all, Welles haunts *Histoire(s) du cinéma* from beginning to end, and at times the wealth of Wellesian references lends the series the air of an extended homage. He is the subject of a tribute in 1A, and a large number of his films and uncompleted projects are cited throughout, with a particular concentration in the opening and closing episodes: *Citizen Kane* (1941; in 1A and 4B), *The Magnificent Ambersons* (1942; in 1B), *It's All True* (1942; in 1A and 2A), *The Lady From Shanghai* (1948; in 1A, 4A, and 4B), *Macbeth* (1948; in 4A and 4B), *Othello* (1952; 1A, 3A, and 4B), *Mr. Arkadin* (in 1A, 2B, and 4B), *Don Quixote* (1955 onward [unfinished]; in 1A), *Touch of Evil* (1958; in 1B and 3B), *The Merchant of Venice* (1969 [unfinished]; in 1A), and *F for Fake* (in 1A). *Histoire(s) du cinéma* is in a sense Godard's *Don Quixote,* a highly personal project cherished and nurtured over several decades, and Welles's unfinished project recurs and resonates across the series as an emblem of unfulfilled cinematic potential.

Less visible in the series, or in Godard's other work, but undoubtedly just as significant to him, is Welles's pioneering work as an audiovisual essayist. Metafilms such as *Filming Othello* (1978) and the abandoned *Filming The Trial* (shot in 1981, but not edited) not only anticipated the structure and rationale of *Scénario du film Passion,* but also established a mode of self-representation that directly announced Godard's self-depiction at his editing desk, surrounded by books and submerged in films, in *Histoire(s) du cinéma.* In the opening sequence of *Filming Othello,* Welles embarked on a "conversation" about *Othello* with the presentation of his principal compositional tool, the movieola. His comments could equally well have come from Godard:

> This is a movieola. A machine for editing film. But you know, when we say we're editing or cutting a film, we're not saying enough.... The pictures have movement; the movies move. Then there's the movement from one picture to another. There's a rhythmic structuring to that; there's counterpoint, harmony and dissonance. A film is never right until it's right musically. And this movieola, this filmmaker's tool, is a kind of musical instrument. It's here that other film instruments are tuned or finely orchestrated, so if you find me winding up our conversation here, you'll understand that as a filmmaker I'm speaking to you from my home.

Above all, however, it is Welles's playful, philosophical exploration of deception and the art of forgery in his self-reflexive essay film, *F for Fake,* that anticipates *Histoire(s) du cinéma* most directly. Indeed Bernard Eisenschitz has gone as far as to suggest that *F for Fake* might almost be considered part of Godard's series.[135] While working on it, Welles succinctly summarized its mischievous blend of fiction, theory, autobiography, and tomfoolery as "a new kind of film."[136] It is one that in many ways provided Godard with a model of what a creative audiovisual film history essay might look like, and how it might function, not least as regards the central role accorded the editing table and the storyteller, the manipulation of found footage, and the use of techniques such as stop motion. Moreover, as Eisenschitz also noted, the section of 1A devoted to Howard Hughes can be read as a tribute to Welles generally, and an acknowledgment of the significance of *F for Fake* in particular: Godard's treatment of Hughes engages directly with Welles's prior evocation of him in *F for Fake,* and includes a number of the same reference points (such as the bra designed by Hughes for Jane Russell to wear in *The Outlaw* [1943]) and same footage (such as newsreel material of the celebrations in New York following Hughes's round-the-world flight in 1938).

Finally, we turn to Godard's relationship with Hollis Frampton, whose 1971 essay "For a Metahistory of Film: Commonplace Notes and Hypotheses" played a key role in contextualizing *Histoire(s) du cinéma* at the time of the series' launch at Cannes in 1997: at Godard's instigation, the essay was reproduced in its entirety in a special edition of *Trafic* circulated to the press at this event.[137] Frampton wrote the essay originally as a manifesto for the monumental historical project to which he would devote the final decade of his life: the thirty-six-hour film cycle *Magellan,* of which – at the time of his premature death in 1984 – he had completed eight hours. The idea of *Magellan* was inspired by Portuguese explorer Ferdinand Magellan's attempted circumnavigation of the world in the early sixteenth century. Godard includes an adapted passage about the definition and function of art from Frampton's early reflection on his project toward the end of 4B.[138] This text as a whole offers a valuable framework within which to think about *Histoire(s) du cinéma.* In it, Frampton conceptualized cinema as a single integrated machine made up of every camera, projector, and piece of film ever made. Every still and moving image and sound ever recorded, he argued, forms part of a gigantic, ever-expanding "infinite film."[139] Against this backdrop, he stressed the impossible nature of the historian's quest to provide a true history of cinema and its audiovisual derivatives, in the face of what Daney, in 2A, dubs its "monstrous heritage": not just every documentary and fiction film ever recorded, but also the countless hours of home movies and scientific, educational, promotional, and industrial films languishing in archives and attics around the globe. Such a task, Frampton and Godard agree, is unrealizable. In his attempt to imagine a way out of this impasse, Frampton drew a distinction, which reverberates across Godard's project, between the impossible task of the historian, and the creative calling of a figure he calls the metahistorian:

> The historian of cinema faces an appalling problem. Seeking in his subject some principle of intelligibility, he is obliged to make himself responsible for every frame of film in existence. For the history of cinema consists precisely of every film that has ever been made, for any purpose whatsoever.
>
> Of the whole corpus the likes of *Potemkin* make up a numbingly small fraction. The balance includes

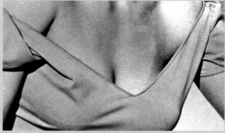

F for Fake (Orson Welles, 1974).

Lumière-inspired films made by Hollis Frampton for inclusion in *Magellan* (1971–84, unfinished).

instructional films, sing-alongs, endoscopic cinematography, and much, much more. The historian dares neither select nor ignore, for if he does, the treasure will surely escape him.

The metahistorian of cinema, on the other hand, is occupied with inventing a tradition, that is, a coherent wieldy set of discrete monuments, meant to inseminate resonant consistency into the growing body of his art.

Such works may not exist, and then it is his duty to make them. Or they may exist already, somewhere outside the intentional precincts of the art (for instance, in the prehistory of cinematic art, before 1943). And then he must remake them.[140]

Frampton opened his essay with an evocation of Clio, the muse of history, presiding over the production of "a class of verbal artifacts," or "an open set of rational fictions," which imaginatively address "what it felt like to reflect consciously upon the qualities of experience in the times they expound."[141] These fictions set aside "mere temporal chronology," and largely dispense with "the fairly recent inventions we call facts."[142] What interested Frampton was the possibility of an imaginative form of history, which reached back to before the nineteenth-century historiographic tradition, and the problem it had quickly encountered: the excess of facts. The solution he glimpsed involved the principle of the *rapprochement* of disparate phenomena, which Godard also had started to advocate in the late 1960s, and would subsequently hone as the basis of his historical montage method. In the example he gives of the type of metahistorical connections he envisages, Frampton sounds remarkably like Godard:

In the 1830s, George Büchner wrote *Woyzeck*. Évarist Galois died, a victim of political murder, leaving to a friend a last letter, which contains the foundations of group theory, or the metahistory of mathematics. Talbot and Niépce invented photography. The

Belgian physicist Plateau invented the phenakisti-scope, the first true cinema.

In the history of cinema these four facts are prob-ably unrelated. In the metahistory of cinema, these four events may ultimately be related.[143]

Thus, at almost exactly the same time that Go-dard was starting to formulate his plans for his audiovisual history of cinema, Frampton was outlining his own remarkable vision of a part-mathematical, part-poetic exploratory metahis-torical voyage through the "infinite film":

> The metahistorian of film generates for himself the problem of deriving a complete tradition from nothing more than the most obvious material limits of the total film machine. It should be possible, he speculates, to pass from *The Flicker* through *Unsere Afrikareise,* or *Tom, Tom, the Piper's Son,* or *La région centrale* and beyond, in finite steps (each step a film), by exercising only one perfectly rational option at each move. The problem is analogous to that of the Knight's Tour in chess.
>
> Understood literally, it is insoluble, hopelessly so. The paths open to the Knight fork often (to reconverge, who knows where). The board is a matrix of rows and columns beyond reckoning, whereupon no chosen starting point may be defended with confidence.
>
> Nevertheless I glimpse the possibility of constructing a film that will be a kind of synoptic conjugation of such a tour – a Tour of Tours, so to speak, of the infinite film, or of all knowledge, which amounts to the same thing. Rather, some such pos-sibility presents itself insistently to my imagination, disguised as the germ of a plan for execution.[144]

The ancient challenge of the Knight's Tour in chess involves moving a knight, starting from any square on the chess board, to every other square, landing only once on each one. Framp-ton's metahistorian is very close in conception and function to the figure of the chronicler in Péguy. Like the latter's *Clio,* Frampton's "Me-tahistory" essay provided Godard with an in-valuable example of a fundamentally poetic way of conceptualizing the role of the historian, and – in its proposition of a synoptic Tour of Tours – a succinct blueprint for how he might approach the task of investigating both his inner imaginary museum and the infinite film.

4

The Rise and Fall of the Cinematograph

WE SHALL NOW TURN OUR ATTENTION, IN the following two chapters, to the detail of Godard's account of cinema history and to the rationale underpinning it. We have already discussed his definition of cinema in terms of montage. In some respects, his thinking on this topic is in line with that of other commentators, who have approached montage as a composite idiom and radically new postindustrial kaleidoscopic form of vision.[1] But behind Godard's apparently simple equation of cinema with montage, and his treatment of the latter as a singularly potent expressive device, there also lies a historical narrative: the best of silent cinema, drawing on and combining aspects of all the other arts, began to develop a unique, popular, powerful, revelatory new means of expression, whose maturation was all too quickly curtailed as a result of commercial exploitation, the coming of sound, the catastrophes of the two world wars, and the emergence of television. His histories – as indicated in a shift in intertitles in 1A – are less "histoire(s) du cinéma" than "histoire(s) du cinématographe," and the story of what the cinematograph became in the age of the talkies.[2] Here is how he presented his overarching thesis in the course of an important talk in 1989, in which he equated the cinematograph with montage, and defined both in terms of the art of true vision:

The idea that I'm defending in the history of cinema that I'm preparing, *Quelques histoires à propos du cinéma* (Some stories about cinema) is that montage is what made cinema unique and different compared to painting and the novel. Cinema as it was originally conceived is going to disappear quite quickly, within a lifetime, and something else will take its place. But what made it original, and what will never really have existed, like a plant that has never really left the ground, is montage. The silent movie world felt it very strongly and talked about it a lot. No one found it. Griffith was looking for something like montage, he discovered the close-up. Eisenstein naturally thought that he had found montage. But, by montage, I mean something much more vast.... To return to what I said at the beginning: the idea of cinema as the art or technique of montage. Novels are something else, painting is something else, music is something else. Cinema was the art of montage, and that art was going to be born, it was popular. Mozart worked for princes, Michelangelo for the Pope. Some novelists sold in huge quantities, but even Malraux, even Proust didn't sell immediately in the same quantities as Sulitzer. Nor does Marguerite [Duras]. Suddenly, very quickly, cinema rose in popularity, much faster than Le Pen. In three years it went from thirty spectators to thirty million. Painting has never been popular. If Van Gogh were popular his paintings would go on tour. But cinema was popular, it developed a technique, a style or a way of doing things, something that I believe was essentially montage. Which for me means seeing, seeing life. You take life, you take power, but in order to revise it, and see it, and make a judgment. See two things, and choose between them in completely good faith.[3]

Godard went on to rehearse and refine this thesis repeatedly in subsequent interviews, sometimes adding the observation that the exploratory steps taken toward montage during the silent era have now been largely forgotten. This chapter examines the intricacies of his history of the power and specificity of cinema, or rather of the cinematograph, understood here both in relation to early cinema and – following Jean Cocteau's and Robert Bresson's use of the term – to a type of thoughtful cinema that lies beyond, and resists, the homogenous forms and homogenizing influence of the Hollywood-derived mainstream. It goes on to unravel his account of the successive failures of the cinematographic project in the first half of the twentieth century, and concludes with an examination of his accompanying discourse on artistic renewal.

THE INTELLIGENCE OF THE CINEMATOGRAPH

Godard's commentary on early cinema may appear to be insufficiently critical, and, conversely, his account of cinema's subsequent decline overstated. It is crucial, however, to recognize the magnitude of his conceptual investment in the cinematograph as a revolutionary tool, and in the silent era generally as a genuine moment of popular cultural revolution.[4] "The first revolution was Sumer," he has suggested. "We don't know about the East, but the history of the West started visibly with Sumer, with writing, and was followed five centuries later by something that looked like a sort of cultural explosion: the cinema."[5] His thinking resonates with that of commentators such as Annette Michelson, who has argued persuasively that the period following World War I saw a variety of theoretical and practical investigations of the cinematograph as a new cognitive instrument, whose common aim "was no less than the transformation of the human condition through a cinematic intensification of cognitive accuracy, analytic precision, and epistemological certitude."[6] Setting aside transitory factional infighting, political affiliation, or the divisions of national boundaries, Godard identifies widespread unanimity on the part of contemporaneous commentators and practitioners: the world had unexpectedly acquired an extraordinary new eye- and mind-opening vision machine, one capable of intensifying perception, jolting people out of their routine complacencies, and reinstating a sense of astonishment at a world still so poorly understood. This machine recorded, magnified and broadcast the physical world and social

Technologies of magnification in 1B and 2A.

relations; or, as Godard summarizes his idea in a simple refrain in 1B, "cinema projected / and people / saw / that the world / was there."[7] The foregrounding of the human eye, of the act of looking, and of technologies of vision throughout *Histoire(s) du cinéma* underscores the intrinsic pedagogical function of the cinematograph, and the process of visual education it set in motion. Inherently inclusive in its extra-linguistic mode of address, and drawing social classes together in the movie theater, the popular nascent art-form carried the promise, for Godard, of a contagious democratizing effect: by simply representing the physical and social world to vast numbers of individuals in an instantly accessible form, it facilitated a makeshift process of self-psychoanalysis on the part of the viewer, and a profound renegotiation of one's place in the world.

In an art historical perspective, Godard situates the cinematograph in a very broad Western artistic tradition. It was, he argues, the inheritor and direct extension of this tradition; or, as he puts it simply in 3B, it was art's "youngest child."[8] Its origins, he suggests, like that of the tradition to which he relates it, lie in the Church: "My working hypothesis in relation to the history of cinema is that the cinema is the last chapter in the history of the art of a certain type of Indo-European civilization. The other civilizations didn't have art (which doesn't mean that they didn't create), they didn't have this idea of art linked to Christianity, to a single god."[9] He pursued this line of thinking in an important dialogue with Régis Debray in 1995, in which he insisted in particular on the ethical function of art *vis-à-vis* the world in which it is made, and on cinema's function as an index of Western morality:

JEAN-LUC GODARD, CINEMA HISTORIAN

Godard: Besides, painting, the look, is Western. Buddhism, the Aztecs, and Islam don't have art in the sense that we understand that Giotto made works of art.... I would say that art was the morality of the West. Today art has disappeared, because this notion of art has disappeared....

Debray: So cinema was responsible for the morality of the image?

Godard: Yes, it was its last representative. But the most interesting thing from this point of view is that it disappeared very quickly.[10]

Godard sometimes goes even further than this, not only positioning the cinematograph as the continuation of the Christian iconophilic tradition, but also proposing that this tradition was itself rooted in pre-Christian attempts in the West to explore and make sense of the world through images.

Having situated the cinematograph within the Christian and pre-Christian tradition, Godard focuses his principal attention on the nineteenth century, and on pre-cinema and early cinema in particular. In response to Daney's suggestion in 2A that cinema was a twentieth-century affair, Godard counters that in his view it was essentially a nineteenth-century one, which was "resolved" in the twentieth. This idea runs throughout *Histoire(s) du cinéma;* early cinema is contextualized through reference to a variety of nineteenth-century phenomena, all of which Godard considers to have anticipated, paralleled, or fed directly into the emergent art-form. Some of his propositions are familiar from classical cinema histories, such as his positioning of the cinematograph as the extension of the nineteenth-century scientific project, one exemplified by the visual study of movement and of the natural world by figures such as Eadweard Muybridge, Étienne-Jules Marey, and Georges Demenÿ. Examples of motion studies by Marey are cited in 3B; others, by both Muybridge and Marey, are cited in 1B, in which the names of a number of other pre-cinematic pioneers are also cited onscreen: Charles Cros, Émile Reynaud, Pierre-Jules-César Janssen, and Thomas Edison. Some of Godard's other ideas are in line with recent research: investigation of the emergence of the cinematograph alongside psychoanalysis and the railway network (he links cinema to both of these in 1B); the identification of the development of a new mode of subjective vision, one reflected both in the fictional film character and in the cinema viewer (he presents this idea through reference to Manet's portraiture in 3A); and, following Stanley Cavell's discussion in *The World Viewed* of the way the nineteenth century anticipated cinema, exploration of the traces of "cinema" – the vocabulary and motifs of projection, the large screen, moving pictures, imaginary travel, and so on – in the pre-cinematic writings of authors such as Cros and Baudelaire.[11]

We have already considered the role played by Baudelaire's "Le voyage" *vis-à-vis* Serge Daney and the concept of projection. In addition to these associations, Godard's reflections on the announcement of cinema in nineteenth-century literature underpins the *mise en scène* of this poem in 2A. It is also central to *Deux fois cinquante ans de cinéma français,* which opens with a recitation by Anne-Marie Miéville of the beginning of Baudelaire's "L'invitation au voyage," followed by a discussion of "Le voyage," and of Cros's posthumously published collection of poetry and prose, *Le collier de griffes* (The necklace of claws).[12] Godard gives Baudelaire's and Cros's books to Michel Piccoli – who, in this film, plays himself in his role as president of the First Century of Cinema Association – to take home with him. Indeed the sequence also includes a short extract of Julie Delpy's reading of "Le voyage" (sound only) from 2A. In this film essay, Godard and Miéville emphasize both the concrete link between Cros and cinema (in addition to his writing, Cros experimented extensively with color photography, and in 1877 developed advanced plans for a pioneering sound recording device, the "paléophone") and the semantic connections. Although *collier* literally means "necklace," it is used in a photographic and cinematographic context to describe the adjustable circular clamps used for attaching lights, or for fixing telephoto lenses onto tripods. Similarly, as Godard has pointed out, the term *griffes* also has strong cinematic connotations:

> Charles Cros is not just anyone in connection to cinema. He invented or theorized things in relation to cinema; he was one of the inventors of cinema at that time, and later, to move film through the gate, the device used was called a claw. It could have been called "tooth," but the word used was claw, so *Le collier des griffes* corresponded to – announced – perforated film.[13]

For Godard, the cinematograph was a singularly fresh art-form, which generated a flood of highly charged images of the present. It also produced a sudden and unexpected period of artistic childhood – "the childhood of art," as he puts it in a Bernanos-influenced refrain in 1B, 2B, and 4A.[14] He has likened this notion of artistic childhood to the gaze of the infant:

> Anne-Marie told me how her little girl, when she was four or five months old, looked at a calendar on which there was a reproduction of a Cézanne. The little girl stayed for half an hour in front of the Cézanne: she probably saw things that only Cézanne had seen. When we say "cinema, the childhood of art," this is the gaze we mean. A gaze that people

accepted because cinema was silent, made no claims; and after watching the film, one could critique it.[15]

Elsewhere, he has illustrated this idea through reference to the childlike innocence and enthusiasm – the "mechanical naïveté," as he put it – with which cinema started again right from the beginning to tell afresh "all the stories," from the dinosaurs to Christ, and from ancient Greece to Shakespeare.[16] Moreover, fresh form and aesthetic innovation were matched by mass appeal, and art was suddenly in real demand. Cinema, as he puts it simply in 1A, is "the only art / that has been genuinely / popular."[17] This idea of the capacity of the cinematograph to reach out to and touch vast numbers of people as a community, irrespective of whether they understood everything they saw, lies behind the cryptic reference to Saint Bernard of Clairvaux in 1A. The sequence is based on the conclusion of Malraux's "Esquisse d'une psychologie du cinéma":

> what did the crowds understand / as they listened to / Saint Bernard preaching / something different from what he was saying / perhaps, without doubt / but how can we ignore / what we understand / at the moment that this unknown voice / strikes / into the deepest recesses / of our hearts[18]

Saint Bernard was a key figure in the Catholic Church in the twelfth century, a renowned orator, and one of the leading advocates of the Second Crusade. As Malraux noted in a later book, the knights listening to Saint Bernard's sermons could not possibly have heard everything he was saying (he was, after all, speaking without a microphone), but he nevertheless touched them sufficiently to inspire them to leave for the Crusade.[19] Here, of course, Saint Bernard is cinema.

If Godard's view of the potential of the cinematograph is characterized by reverence, his assessment of how it was subsequently relentlessly "insulted and injured," as he puts it in 1A through reference to Dostoyevsky's tale of a doomed relationship, is extremely bleak. He summarized his abiding view of the misuse, abandonment, humiliation, and failures of the cinematograph in a poetic elegy to the medium he published in 1991 in the first issue of *Trafic,* "La paroisse morte" (The dead parish).[20] At his darkest, he has even gone as far as to suggest that "the cinema was not used for anything, it did nothing, and there has been no film."[21] As he puts it in 1B, less than a hundred years after the Lumière brothers described the cinematograph as an invention without a future, we finally see that they were right. The stunted potential of the cinematograph is presented near the beginning of 1A via the title of Griffith's *Broken Blossoms* (*Le lys brysé* in French, literally "The broken blossom" [1919]). In one of the numerous instances in *Histoire(s) du cinéma* of cinema momentarily assuming the role of a fictional character within one of the clips sampled in the series, Godard pursues his line of thinking in this sequence through his manipulation of an extract from *Broken Blossoms,* which depicts the distressed, brutalized young Lucy (Lillian Gish), who has been whipped yet again by her drunken father, staggering through the streets of London's East End. Moreover, the theme in this sequence of the abandonment of the cinematograph is underscored visually by the degraded quality of the electronic video copy of the film. This theme is conveyed throughout *Histoire(s) du cinéma*

through two recurrent motifs: pornography and infanticide or child suicide. The former has long functioned in Godard's work as a shorthand for conventional or blocked communication ("Communication is what moves. When it doesn't move, it's pornography.").[22] Several montages in the series evoke the literal transformation of the cinematograph into pornography. A sequence near the end of 1B, for instance, presents the passage from the scientific analysis of movement ("splendor," represented here by collotype motion studies made by Muybridge in the 1880s) to "poverty," which is illustrated by two early pornographic films. Similarly, in a short sequence in 1A, Lillian and Dorothy Gish (in a still from Griffith's *An Unseen Enemy,* 1912) are made to appear as if they are recoiling in horror from the pornographic imagery laid over them. The sequences depicting infanticide and child suicide powerfully literalize the idea of the death of art's youngest child, as well as the end of the promise of artistic childhood it brought with it. This two-pronged argument is announced early in 1A via a photograph of Roberto Rossellini and his daughter Isabella, in which the former appears to be strangling his child.[23] This photograph is linked in this context to the idea of the death of the cinematograph, and of the promise of artistic renewal, via the Freudian phrase "Father, don't you see I'm burning?" a citation from a dream discussed by Freud in *The Interpretation of Dreams,* in which a father, following the death of his child, dreams that the child has come to his bed and whispered these words reproachfully to him.[24] Toward the end of the same episode, this dual argument is picked up in an horrific clip depicting Eric von Eberhard (Erich von Stroheim) hurling a child out

From pre-cinema to pornography in 1A and 1B.

of an upstairs window during the harrowing climactic rape scene in Allen Holubar's *The Heart of Humanity* (1919), which is combined with the suicide of the young boy Edmund (Edmund Moeschke) in Rossellini's *Germany Year Zero* (1948). Indeed Godard's use of this sequence in 1A carries a further veiled allusion to Griffith, who functions in the series as one of a handful of emblematic torchbearers of cinematographic art: the plot of *The Heart of Humanity* closely resembles that of Griffith's earlier *Hearts of the World* (1918), which had also featured Stroheim. The deaths depicted in the Holubar and Rossellini films are explicitly linked to the collapse of European cinema in the wake of the two world wars, to the rise of television, and to the general context of American economic might.

Godard's account of the cinematograph not only emphasizes its revelatory power, but also its wasted potential. The broad lines of his thesis are very close to those outlined in 1951 by André Breton, who, when casting his eye back over cinema's short history, had expressed a similar sense of loss, missed opportunity, and "a certain nostalgia for the idea of what the cinema might have become."[25] The "sordidness of the epoch" combined with commercial exploitation, suggested Breton, "were enough to clip its wings as soon as it flew the nest."[26] In 1A, Godard evokes the short lifespan of the cinematograph by combining the book and film titles *Farewell, My Lovely* and *Bonjour tristesse,* and repeats the same idea in 3B through his manipulation of the title of Epstein's *Bonjour cinéma* (Hello, cinema), which he alters to "Au revoir cinéma." Although not particularly complicated, Godard's discourse on the collapse and disintegration of the cinematograph, and of the promise of "montage" it had ushered in, contains multiple strands, and to engage with it fully we need to separate them. These strands are the early industrialization of cinema, the male domination of filmmaking, the coming of sound, World War II, and the impact of television (see chapter 6). We begin, therefore, with the question of industrialization. To some extent, suggests Godard, the brevity of the cinematograph's lifespan can be explained in material and economic terms: contrary to poetry (he offers the example of Soviet poet Osip Mandelstam's writing and circulating his poems on scraps of paper), it was always an expensive, technologically based art-form that required sophisticated machinery and dedicated spaces to keep it alive.[27] As such, obsolescence was inevitable, since it was built in from the outset (this is one of the senses of the extracts from Alfred van Vogt's tale of preprogrammed nuclear destruction, *Defence*, used in *Puissance de la parole*). Almost immediately, he suggests in 1B, the cinematograph sacrificed its most vital qualities – the ambivalence and openness of the image, with its dual appeal to the intellect and senses – to the profit motive, commercial exploitation, narrative, and trite scripts: "in place of uncertainty / establishing idea and sensation / the two big stories have been / sex and death."[28] The extract of Max's (Jean Gabin) dialogue from the soundtrack of Jacques Becker's *Touchez pas au grisbi* (*Grisbi*, 1954) in 1A, which is accompanied by the title of Zola's *J'accuse!* serves to present cinema (embodied momentarily here by Max) wistfully regretting the manner in which it had lost touch with its scientific origins and dreaming of what it might have become – had it not allowed itself to be seduced by the promise of glamour and riches and reduced, as a result, to the status of a subdivision of the cosmetics industry.

In the opening minutes of 1A, cinema is shown entering into a catastrophic Faustian pact with narrative, sex, and spectacle – thereby betraying almost immediately its scientific heritage, documentary power, and artistic calling in favor of high visibility, popularity, and cheap thrills. This critique is conveyed through the combination of a sequence depicting the appearance of the devil in F. W. Murnau's *Faust: A German Folk Legend* (1926), and another from Vincente Minnelli's *The Bandwagon* (1953), a film that includes within its narrative a failed attempt to stage an updated version of the Faust myth. As Jacques Rancière has noted, Mephisto is a double symbol here: "a figure for Hollywood grabbing this infant art with a mighty hand, and for this art itself, the art of Murnau, who became in turn the victim of the pact he brought to the screen."[29] Away from its original context, the clip from *The Bandwagon* – which depicts the hit show staged by the dance troupe in the film in the place of their abandoned attempt to mount a contemporary version of Faust – also evokes the seduction of cinema by color, spectacle, music, guns, and the formidable charms of Cyd Charisse. Rancière summarized this aspect of Godard's thinking succinctly:

> It [cinema] had already surrendered the power of its images to the huge industry of fiction, the industry of sex and death that substitutes for our gaze a world illusorily in accord with our desires. Already back then cinema had agreed to reduce the infinite murmuring and speaking forms of the world to these standardized dream stories that can so easily be aligned with the dreams of all men in the darkened rooms just by parading before their eyes those two great objects of desire, women and guns.[30]

American cinema is singled out for particularly caustic treatment in this regard: the foundation

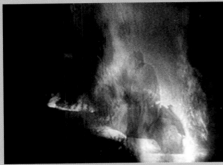

Cinema's Faustian pact: *Faust: A German Folk Legend* (F. W. Murnau, 1926) and *The Bandwagon* (Vincente Minnelli, 1953) in 1A.

of the Hollywood dream factories is equated in 1A with Babylon via films such as Griffith's *Intolerance* (part of which is devoted to the fall of Babylon), and Kozintsev and Trauberg's *The New Babylon* (the title of which refers, significantly, not to the legendary city, but to a nineteenth-century Parisian department store). It is also linked visually to a string of images of luxury, excess, superficial grandeur, artifice, and exploitation. Indeed the birth of Hollywood is illustrated at one point by a clip from Cecil B. DeMille's *The Ten Commandments* (1956) of an aging woman on the verge of being crushed to death. It is then associated with the plague when Godard spits out the title of Camus's eponymous book, after which he utters the words "the power of Hollywood," and then "the power of Babylon" – a transition illustrated dramatically by a photograph of a great mound of bodies.[31]

Godard suggests early in 1A, via a clip of Ann Darrow (Fay Wray) undergoing screen tests on board a ship in *King Kong* (Merian C. Cooper and Ernest B. Schoedsack, 1933), that throughout the majority of its history, film production has been dominated by stories made by men that feature women. The series' presentation of the humiliation and failures of the cinematograph places particular emphasis on the exploitation of women within the male-controlled Hollywood production system. "Cinema," he argued in 1989, "is an ideology based on men living out through their imaginations what they could not do with women."[32] Rather than seeking to confront and reflect the complexity and mystery of human experience, he argues in 1A, 1B, and especially 2B, the cinematograph, flattered by its popularity, was distracted and "fatally" sidetracked into the industrial exploitation of the female body. This feminist critique of the manipulation of women, both within the Hollywood filmmaking system and the narratives it produced, is conveyed in 1A and 1B through the contention that Hollywood was founded on the exploitation of countless anonymous aspiring female stars. The fine line between deification and demonization at the heart of the Hollywood star system is evoked brilliantly in a particularly disturbing and effective sequence in 1A, which is constructed out of clips depicting Gilda (Rita Hayworth – or Rita Cansino, as she is called here) in *Gilda* (Charles Vidor, 1946) and the burning of Herlof's Marte (Anna Svierkier) in *Day of Wrath* (Carl Theodor Dreyer, 1943). Godard pursues his argument in 1B through the use of composite imagery depicting male directors (such as Hitchcock, Lang, Renoir, and himself) inventing and filming stories of emotional and sexual relationships between men and women. Exemplary in this respect is the sequence in which Hitchcock is depicted, in an artificially created composite image, watching Henri (Mel Ferrer) attempting to kiss Eléna (Ingrid Bergman) in Renoir's *Eléna et les hommes* (*Paris Does Strange Things*, 1956), and observing Marnie (Tippi Hedren) being undressed in his own *Marnie* (1954), while Godard's superimposed face also looks on. Godard continues this exploration of the relationship between male power and desire – whether on the part of producers, directors, or audiences – and the female body in 1B via a combination of clips, stills and on-screen titles derived from films such as *The Bride of Glomdal*, *Prison sans barreaux* (*Prison without Bars*, Léonide Moguy, 1938), and *Child Bride* (Harry Revier, 1938, cited here under its French title *Esclaves du désir*, literally "Slaves of desire").

Perhaps the most successful sequence in which he pursues this argument is his playful presentation of the story of Howard Hughes in 1A. In a montage used in the book version of this episode (but not in the video), Godard mischievously summarizes Hughes's combined business and amorous exploits through the superimposition of the phrase "I'm going to write my name everywhere" over a photograph of four young women wearing swimming costumes.[33] In the video version, his manipulation of a short clip from James Kern's *Two Tickets to Broadway* (a 1951 RKO musical about a provincial girl aspiring to television stardom in New York) is especially effective: apparently imprisoned and panic-stricken, Nancy Peterson (Janet Leigh) emits an anguished cry as she attempts to open the door to leave her room. This sequence evokes not only the idea of the entrapment of female characters within Hollywood narrative structures, but also the manner in which Hughes aggressively courted Leigh during preproduction on this film – and indeed his notorious pursuit of women generally – and his tactic of "imprisoning" them with contracts at RKO.[34] This critique of Hughes is at times touching and funny, especially in the analogy that Godard draws between the producer and Robinson Crusoe. It is also more nuanced than it may at first appear. When Godard superimposes the title of Jean Genet's *Un captif amoureux* (*Prisoner of Love*) over a clip from *Criss Cross* (Robert Siodmak, 1949) depicting Anna (Yvonne De Carlo) leaving a room, in which we can see Steve (Burt Lancaster) sitting alone on the bed behind her, the implication is clear: whereas Anna recalls the numerous women pursued and snared by Hughes, the solitary, abandoned Steve is Hughes, the

The history of cinema as the story of
men filming women (1A, 1B, and 2B).

prisoner of conscious and unconscious desires he neither controls nor understands. As Jean-Louis Leutrat has pointed out in a close reading of this sequence, the clip from *Criss Cross* is particularly apt in this context, since Hughes had at one point been romantically involved with De Carlo.[35]

The next phase in Godard's account of the demise of the cinematograph relates to the coming of sound. Whereas he equates the cinematograph with the drawing of people together and social cohesion, he was already identifying the talkies in Montreal with a pre-televisual process of *démontage* – "collapse" or "dismantling."[36] Here is how he articulated his view of the normalizing impact of the arrival of sound on the cinematograph in an important interview following the death of Hitchcock in 1980:

> Montage, it's what had to be destroyed because it's what allowed people to *see*. The role of the talkies, supported by the printing houses and bad writers, was to prevent people from *seeing* what montage allowed them to *see*. Control over seeing had to be regained immediately. And besides, that's what television is. A great lost battle.[37]

This is a view that Godard has held consistently since the early 1970s: in *Letter to Jane,* for example, he and Jean-Pierre Gorin had already advanced the argument that the combination of economic recession and Roosevelt's New Deal had conspired with the coming of sound to produce an aesthetic mutation – and the beginning of the end of the cinematograph's status as a popular, documentary-based art. By the end of the decade, this had become a recurrent theme in interviews with Godard: "Walter Benjamin said the same thing to Adorno: the industry's unconscious took fright, and so the

The critique of Howard Hughes in 1A through *Two Tickets to Broadway* (James Kern, 1951), *Criss Cross* (Robert Siodmak, 1949), and Jean Genet's *Un captif amoureux.*

talkies were introduced."[38] In the context of a century marked by rapid technological and cultural change, the cinematograph's capacity for "montage" fell by the wayside. Taken in hand by the rhythms of mass production and the logic of capital, it was smothered by the script-based, dialogue-ridden talkies:

> The word "montage" has been much used. Today people say montage in Welles or in Eisenstein, or on the contrary the absence of montage in Rossellini. What fools, as Bernanos would say. Cinema never found montage. Tobis and RCA didn't allow it the time, and something was lost along the way, its speech. And it's language, words, that got the upper hand, but of course not the language or words of the Jeromine children, nor those of Narcissus and Goldmund.[39]

We turn now to the place of World War II in Godard's account of the history of cinema. If the cinematograph had sold out almost from the beginning, and its powers had been gradually eroded over the ensuing decades, he identifies its premature end in its failure to adequately confront or represent the Holocaust. His argument is rooted in an idiosyncratic theorization of cinema's documentary function, which he divides into two complementary stages: anticipation and bearing witness. In a line of argument reminiscent of Siegfried Kracauer's identification in *From Caligari to Hitler: A Psychological History of the German Film* of the premonitions of fascism in the German cinema of the 1920s, Godard ascribes cinema with the power to conduct a sort of visionary ethnology, or embryology, of imminent social mutation, *foreseeing* emergent patterns of political turbulence and social upheaval. In this perspective, as he suggests in 4B through reference to Ramuz's *Les signes parmi nous,* cinema is a kind of clairvoyant

gossipmonger, peddling rumors about what the future might hold. He had already arrived at this idea in Montreal:

> I've always thought that the cinema represents today what music was in the past a little bit: it communicates in advance, it communicates in advance the great shifts that are going to occur. And it's in this sense that it shows illnesses before they become visible. It's an external sign that shows things. It's a bit abnormal. It's something that's going to happen, like an eruption.[40]

Comments such as these are heavily indebted to Jacques Attali's thesis regarding the prophetic role of music. Indeed, Godard also considers arts other than music and cinema to have fulfilled a similar role at certain times. He has also referred in this context, for instance, to Impressionism, and to Georges Bataille's *Le bleu du ciel* (*Blue of Noon*), a book he deems to have "announced *everything* in its way."[41] But for Godard, in the twentieth century it is, above all, cinema that was endowed with this capacity for prophecy. He introduces his thesis in 1A via a film that was also important to Kracauer, and whose title alone provides a succinct summary of his argument: Arthur Robison's Expressionist thriller *Warning Shadows* (1922). He then develops it through reference to a range of films from the 1920s and 1930s, such as Renoir's *La règle du jeu* and Murnau's *Nosferatu* (1922). The former, he suggests, foresaw the disintegration of Europe into war, and the latter depicted a Berlin reduced to rubble in the aftermath of war from a vantage point long before the events took place. Godard makes his argument explicit in his treatment of *La règle du jeu,* by cutting to and fro between the dancing skeleton and ghostly figures at the costume performance in this film, and archival images of concentration

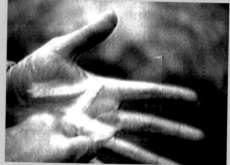

Warning shadows in 1A: Fritz Lang's
Siegfried (1924), *M* (1931), *The Testament of
Dr. Mabuse* (1933), and *Metropolis* (1927);
and Jean Renoir's *La règle du jeu* (1939).

camp prisoners. Moreover, this connection is re-inforced conceptually through our recollection of Renoir's exploration in his film of the themes of moral bankruptcy and antisemitism. Godard also deploys imagery from a host of other films, suggesting through their recontextualization the extent to which – with the benefit of hind-sight – they appear to have provided a striking premonition, and often chilling metaphorical representation, of the horrors to come: Max Ophüls's *Liebelei* (1933); Boris Barnet's *By the Bluest of Seas* (1936); Renoir's *La grande illusion;* and, above all, Fritz Lang's *Siegfried* (1924), *Metropolis* (1927), *M* (1931), and *The Testament of Dr. Mabuse* (1933).

Having announced the future, the comple-mentary aspect of cinema's documentary func-tion is – for Godard – that of confronting, and of broadcasting details of, the events it has proph-esied as they come to pass. This conception of the role of cinema as one of bearing faithful witness to an ever-changing present underpins his reading of films as the true news of the twen-tieth century: momentous moments of social instability and conflict are crystallized imme-diately in cinematic form, and made available for discussion. In this he is again in accord with Malraux, who identified the power of American cinema of the 1930s in its unique blend of myth and journalism. Indeed Malraux's *Espoir,* in its formally innovative attempt to construct an in-stant image worthy of the horrors of the Span-ish Civil War through a heady combination of documentary and melodrama, exemplifies this notion of cinema as news in 1A and 3B. It is also for this reason that Godard references the same film prominently at the beginning of *For ever Mozart,* in which, following Malraux's example, he sought to distill a reflection on unfolding events (in this instance, the war in Bosnia) into a cinematic story.

But within Godard's schema this image of the present must also be made available quickly for criticism and discussion. His reading of the ways Western societies have projected the world around them to themselves, and of the ensuing interpretative process (of negotiation, agree-ment, astonishment, or rejection) set in motion when audiences in turn project themselves into those images, feeds into a favored metaphor: the cinema theater as a popular courtroom, films as evidence, and the audience as judge and jury. This idea, which is reminiscent of Jean Epstein, has been central to Godard's thinking for many years. Godard remarked in 1981, "The image is like evidence in a courtroom. For me, making a movie is like bringing in evidence."[42] Consequently, to view films is to participate in a process of judicial review: "Cinema is made to spread out, to flatten. I always compare it to the court system. You open a file, that's cinema. (Godard opens a file). And then you weigh it."[43] Films representing pressing contemporary concerns are made, projected, viewed, and dis-cussed in the same way that evidence is brought into a courtroom and laid before a jury. The im-age can be accepted or refused, but it is there for discussion and it awaits a verdict. It invites the following question: Is this a just reality repre-sented on the screen, and does the image accord with one's personal experience? In this context, we should note that in *Histoire(s) du cinéma,* courtroom dramas and films in which ques-tions of guilt and innocence hang in the balance (such as those of Hitchcock), or which include significant courtroom scenes – such as Welles's *The Lady from Shanghai,* Stevens's *A Place in the Sun,* and Cukor's *Les Girls* (1957) – carry a high self-reflexive charge. Moreover, Godard relates his judicial metaphor to the syntactical basis of cinema:

> There's a shot before, and another one after. And between the two, there's a physical support. That's cinema. You see a rich person and a poor person and there's a comparison. And you say: it's not fair. Justice comes from a comparison. And from then weighing it in the scales. The very idea of montage is the scales of justice.[44]

This, incidentally, is precisely the principle enacted in *Vrai faux passeport:* faced with differing examples of approaches to the cinematic treatment of the same theme, the viewer is literally placed in the role of judge.

For Godard, World War II was the central cataclysmic event of the twentieth century, and it was cinema's failure to testify to the unbearable horrors of the Holocaust that resulted in the most damaging reduction yet in its powers: "Cinema 'stammered' history, and then at a given moment it no longer did it. The concentration camps weren't filmed; people didn't want to show them or see them. And that was the end: cinema stopped there."[45] As he summarizes this central strand of his argument poetically in 3A, "the flame was extinguished / for good / at Auschwitz."[46] Having announced the impending catastrophe, cinema failed to confront this atrocious reality, proved insubstantial in the face of such an onslaught, and so lost its honor, confidence, and future ability to fulfill its documentary duties:

> history of cinema / news of history / history of news / histories of cinema / with esses / SSes / thirty-nine forty / forty-one / betrayal by the radio / but the cinema keeps it word / because / from Siegfried and M / to the dictator / and to Lubitsch / the films had been made / hadn't they / forty / forty-one / even

> scratched to death / a simple thirty-five millimeter / rectangle / saves the honor / of all reality / forty-one / forty-two / and if the poor images / still strike / without anger and without hatred / like the butcher / it's because the cinema is there / silent cinema / with its humble / and formidable power / of transfiguration / forty-two / forty-three / forty-four . . . this is the lesson of the news / of birth of a nation / of man's hope / of Rome, open city / the cinematograph never wanted to make / an event / but primarily a vision . . . and if the death / of Puig and Negus / the death / of captain de Boïeldieu / the death / of the little rabbit / were inaudible / it's because life has never / given back to films / what it stole from them / and because forgetting / extermination / is part / of extermination / for nearly fifty years / in the dark / the people of the darkened theatres / have been burning the imaginary / to warm up / reality / now this is taking its revenge / and wants real tears / and real blood / but from Vienna to Madrid / from Siodmak to Capra / from Paris to Los Angeles and Moscow / from Renoir to Malraux and Dovzhenko / the great directors of fiction / were incapable / of controlling the vengeance / they had staged twenty times[47]

The reason that cinema missed its crucial rendezvous with history during World War II, suggests Godard, is that its documentary function had already been so anaesthetized that it found itself unable to react and respond – despite the fact that as early as 1932, the impending catastrophe had been clear from the testimony of German émigrés.[48] From this moment on, having lost its "documentary eye," cinema, he argues, has effectively been "unemployed."[49]

It is important to recognize, however, that Godard is not suggesting that no films attempted to represent the war generally, or the Holocaust in particular. On the contrary, he regularly cites two key films, which in his view fulfilled precisely the documentary role he so cherishes; thus both are alluded to in the above quotation, and sampled in 1A: Chaplin's *The Great Dictator* (1940), and Lubitsch's *To Be or Not to Be* (1942).

But other than these, he suggests, at this crucial moment cinema abdicated its documentary responsibilities, leaving the burden of historical witness to the comparatively insubstantial medium of the newsreel:

> it's the poor newsreel / cinema / that has to wash clean / of all suspicion / the blood and the tears / just as the pavement is swept clean / when it's too late / and the army / has already opened fire on the crowd / what there is of cinema / in the war newsreels / says nothing / it doesn't judge[50]

The principal material through which Godard develops this aspect of his argument is archival film of the concentration camps, notably some of the color 16 mm footage shot by George Stevens at Dachau in April and May 1945, and Andrzej Munk's unfinished story of a female concentration camp guard, *Passenger* (1963). In 3A, however, he dismisses *Passenger,* together with another Polish film devoted to the experiences of female inmates incarcerated in Auschwitz, *The Last Stage* (Wanda Jakubowska, 1948), as "expiation films," and has argued in interviews that the Poles were obliged to make these films to atone for their antisemitism and for the fact that Poland had been home to seven German-built extermination camps.[51] Besides, these two films were, in his view, essentially individual ventures rather than collective efforts on the part of the Polish nation to confront its past.[52] His key point is that the few films that addressed the topic of the Holocaust were very much the exception and generally came too late; cinema, in the sense of a buoyant, popular art-form providing a more or less instant, accurate image of contemporary reality simply fell to pieces. Literature, he suggests, did far better. He has cited in particular in this context the work of David Rousset, whose eyewitness account *L'univers concentrationnaire* (*The Other Kingdom,* first published in French in 1946) and novel *Les jours de notre mort* (The days of our death, 1947) he has described as "absolutely fantastic books."[53] Together with Robert Antelme's *L'espèce humaine* (*The Human Race,* first published in French in 1947; and cited onscreen in 4B), Rousset's books offer a remarkable example of the sort of immediate documentary testimony that cinema failed to provide. As regards later audiovisual attempts to address the topic, despite using a slowed-down clip in 1A from Claude Lanzmann's *Shoah* (1985), Godard has frequently been highly critical of this film. He dismissed it in 1989, for instance, as a scenario for a film rather than a finished work, the real research for which still remains to be conducted.[54] He has been equally critical of later cinematic attempts to treat the Holocaust, expressing contempt for Roberto Benigni's *Life Is Beautiful* (1997), and little short of loathing for Steven Spielberg's *Schindler's List* (1995), a film he has denounced in particularly strong terms for its factual inaccuracy in the sequence showing real water flowing from the showers in the gas chamber. This, he has argued, is "based on a lie," and makes the film akin to a "falsified document."[55]

In addition to the catastrophic hole in the cinematic representation of the twentieth century relating to the Holocaust, Godard points to the almost total absence of films addressing another wartime topic: "The other clue is the Resistance. In contrast to what is said and believed, there were no films in France about the Resistance. Once again there's a gap."[56] He dismisses the two most prominent and frequently cited Resistance films, René Clément's *La bataille du rail* (*The Battle of the Rails,* 1946) and Titus Vibe-Müller's *La bataille de l'eau lourde* (*Operation

Swallow: The Battle for Heavy Water, 1948), as "fakes," or "false films," reaching instead in 1A, 1B, and 3B for Henri Calef's lesser-known account of wartime resistance set in occupied Amiens, *Jéricho* (1945).[57] The films he gives the greatest prominence in this context, however, are two that are not usually considered in connection with the Resistance at all: Cocteau's *La belle et la bête,* which was made in the immediate aftermath of World War II, and whose production was dogged by delays and interruptions; and, in particular, Bresson's *Les dames du Bois de Boulogne.* Thus in 1A, he draws a link between the sequence from the end of *Les dames du Bois de Boulogne* depicting Agnès (Elina Labourdette) uttering the words "I'm fighting" and de Gaulle's wartime call to the French to resist. He fleshed out his argument in relation to this film during his presentation of *Histoire(s) du cinéma* at Cannes in 1997:

> I ask which character in a French film in 1942, at the time of de Gaulle, said, "I'm fighting." There's only one: Elina Labourdette in *Les dames du Bois de Boulogne*. And what was her role in the film? That of a demimondaine, or of a hussy or a prostitute. . . . At times, the story of *Les dames du Bois de Boulogne* as told by Bresson and Cocteau, is also a metaphor of France's situation at the time, which had behaved within the European alliance beforehand in exactly the way that Elina Labourdette behaves with men in *Les dames du Bois de Boulogne,* before she and Paul Bernard meet. And he turns out to be somebody who doesn't care, and who says, "I recognize you, but you must fight. You mustn't leave, and you mustn't be ashamed. Redeem yourself." And she says, "I'm fighting." And at the same moment this is what de Gaulle was asking the French. So I say, "There we are. If there's a moment of resistance in French cinema, it's not in *La bataille du rail* and later, and it's not in *Les visiteurs du soir*. It's earlier: it's here."[58]

In 1998, he also gave Sacha Guitry's *Donne-moi tes yeux* (*My Last Mistress,* 1943) short shrift, declaring that in his view, although it touches on issues such as the black market, the film is fundamentally weak.[59] Although poets such as René Char and Louis Aragon were active in the Resistance, as well as resisting through the production of sincere, angry poetry addressing their wartime experiences (see in particular Aragon's collected poems written between 1939 and 1940, two of which, "Les lilas et les roses" and "Elsa je t'aime," are cited in this context in 1A and 3A, respectively), the engaged voice of the cinema remained virtually silent.[60] In Godard's view, there nevertheless existed a genuine opportunity for the production of resistance films, in the sense of films either explicitly about the Resistance, or about the reality of the experience of life under German Occupation generally, which was not seized:

> The problem is that there's been no reflection on what happened. There were books, but no Resistance films were shot, even stupid ones, in London or Algiers. There was filmstock, cameras, actors, directors. But it wasn't done. If I'm told that in the Vercors in the snow, it would have been impossible to make a fiction film like that, okay. But that wasn't where it needed to be done.[61]

Following the same rationale, the final confirmation for Godard of cinema's capitulation in the face of key historical events is to be found in its failure to adequately reflect the events of May 1968. "There have never been any good films on that period," he has argued, including – in his view – his own work from that time, which he considers to be of little cinematic value.[62] It is due to this succession of gaps in cinema's representation of the twentieth century that Godard pulled back during the making of *Histoire(s) du cinéma* from his initial identification of cinema with Orpheus, and from the idea of the former's provision of unfettered access to the twentieth century. As he observed poetically in the concluding lines of a selection of extracts from the soundtrack of the series published in *Le monde* in 1994, when Orpheus turns around, sometimes he finds that there is nothing there.[63] Moreover, Godard suggested in this same document, in a passage not used in the series itself, that these gaps had important consequences for the subsequent development of cinema: "I, too, had believed for a moment that the cinema authorized / Orpheus to look back without causing Eurydice's death. / I was wrong. Orpheus will have to pay."[64]

RESURRECTION

Contrary to what one might surmise at first glance from *Histoire(s) du cinéma,* or from some of Godard's more trenchant statements in interviews, within the series' narrative cinema as a vital contemporary art-form does not entirely grind to a halt during World War II. Running alongside his account of the disintegration of its documentary eye is a competing story that emphasizes renewal. Here Godard's periodization echoes that of Gilles Deleuze's philosophy of cinema, and their respective models in turn anticipate those of subsequent commentators, such as Jean-Louis Comolli and Serge Daney, for whom the Holocaust also constituted the defining historical event of the twentieth century. For Comolli, cinema's response to the systematic dehumanization of the concentration camps and extermination of European Jews was to reply in a personal, subjective voice, by saying "I."[65] For Daney, and for a number of others after him, the shock of the camps was the founding trauma underpinning the self-conscious forms of modern cinema.[66] These forms are exemplified by the imagery of fictional characters looking directly at the camera, and questioningly or accusingly out of the screen at the audience, such as Irene (Ingrid Bergman) and Monika (Harriet Andersson) in Rossellini's *Europa 51* (1952) and Bergman's *Summer with Monika* (1953), respectively, or Cecile (Jean Seberg) in Preminger's *Bonjour tristesse* (1958).[67] The latter sequence, which is cited in 1B, of course anticipated the looks to camera by Seberg and others in Godard's own work. The link between the Holocaust and postwar cinema is articulated in *Histoire(s) du cinéma* through the motif of fire, which Godard has long associated with his reading of Malraux's model of the artistic process in terms of sacrifice, mourning, and resurrection. This motif became central in his work from *Grandeur et décadence d'un petit commerce de cinéma* onward, and is at the heart of *King Lear:* as Shakespeare Junior V puts it, "I was fired. I kept on thinking about the relationship of art and fire." In *Histoire(s) du cinéma,* Malraux's model, together with the fire motif, is at the heart of a key passage devoted to the process of cinematic rebirth toward the end of 1A; Godard suggests – via a composite image made up of a self-portrait by Rembrandt and an orchestra playing at Auschwitz (in a clip from *Passenger*) – that at this time and place, cinema rediscovered its true function as "that which is reborn / out of what has been burnt."[68] Shortly after this comes a sequence that has already attracted extensive critical attention, doubtless in part because it offers an eloquent summary and *mise-en-abîme* of Godard's Malrucian theorization of the cinematic process. Bringing together footage shot by George Stevens at Dachau in 1945 and material directed by him in Hollywood in 1951 (*A Place in the Sun*), Godard depicts the

Bonjour tristesse (Otto Preminger,
1958), *À bout de souffle* (Godard, 1960),
Adieu Philippine (Jacques Rozier, 1963),
and *Alphaville* (Godard, 1965).

young Angela Vickers (Elizabeth Taylor) in *A Place in the Sun* apparently rising up out of the documentary footage of the dead and dying at Dachau and into the embrace of Mary Magdalene, who is depicted here via a superimposed detail of Giotto's fresco *Noli me tangere* (1304–1306), which has been rotated by 90 degrees. Mary, we recall, was reputedly the first witness to the Resurrection. As Jacques Rancière has noted, 1A concludes with a further variation on this same idea, in the form of a manipulation of the scene from Rossellini's *Germany Year Zero* depicting Edmund's suicide, in which his sister, bending over Edmund's lifeless body, has now assumed the Mary Magdalene role.[69] Moreover, the connection between this sequence and the earlier montage based around the Stevens material is made explicit in the synoptic rendition of the same idea in the book version of 1A, where the two are juxtaposed.[70] In the context of Godard's history of cinema, both sequences evoke the partial resuscitation of cinema's documentary function in the postwar period in the form of Italian Neo-realism and, to a lesser degree, postwar Hollywood:

> and if George Stevens / hadn't been the first to use / the first / sixteen-millimeter color film / at Auschwitz / and Ravensbrück / there's no doubt that / Elizabeth Taylor's / happiness / would not have found / a place in the sun / thirty nine / forty-four / martyrdom and resurrection / of the documentary[71]

As noted above, the documentary footage referred to here was in fact filmed by Stevens at Dachau, not at Auschwitz or Ravensbrück. It is significant, Godard has argued, that Stevens was a mediocre filmmaker, and *A Place in the Sun* an average film; in the case of Stevens and De Sica (whom Godard has likened in this respect to Stevens), it was because of their very ordinariness that they were touched in this critical period by the "the grace of Art, if one can speak like that."[72]

An additional reason for the volume of critical attention attracted by the Stevens sequence is its recourse to Christian themes and iconography. The presence of large numbers of Christian references in *Histoire(s) du cinéma* can be somewhat disorientating initially; it quickly becomes clear, however, that their function is essentially allegorical or historical. Allegorically, cinema is presented in terms of a vision (1A), and the worship and practice of cinema at the time of the New Wave is recalled in terms of reverence, belief, and love (3B). Moreover, in interviews Godard has likened the process of the projection of the self into the unknown facilitated by cinema to the nature of religious belief, and has been explicit regarding the allegorical function of Christianity: the religion in question is cinema, its Apostles its cinephile advocates.[73] His clearest statement in this regard comes in 1B, where he cites a lightly adapted reflection by Ludwig Wittgenstein on the leap of faith required in religious (and, for Godard, cinematic) belief:

> cinema / like christianity / is not founded / on a historical truth / it gives us a narrative / a story / and tells us / now: believe / not / give this narrative / the faith appropriate to a story / but believe / whatever happens / and this can only be the result / of a whole life / you have there a narrative / don't take the same attitude to it / as you take towards / other historical narratives / wie zu einer anderen / historischen nachricht / give it / a quite different place / in your life / eine ganz andere stelle / in deinem leben / einnehmen[74]

In a historical perspective, Godard locates cinema's origins in the Church. He also argues that painting and cinema carry within them traces of their religious heritage in a way that is not true of literature, which remains rigorously secular, even when – as in the case of seminal texts such as the *Iliad* or the *Odyssey* – it explicitly involves the gods.[75] His thinking on this topic resonates with that of Raymond Bellour, who has also stressed the deep-rooted relationship between cinemas and churches, and between Christianity and the secular, mechanical art of film – both of which, he argues, derive their fundamental power from the image.[76] It also echoes that of Kerry Brougher, who has argued that cinema's use of science to create illusion met a profound human need for a form of secular mysticism, and that the intensity of the experience of vast projected moving images reconnected people with something that had been lost several centuries earlier.[77] Nevertheless, Rancière has expressed deep reservations regarding what he identifies in the Stevens sequence as a "spiritualism of the icon," a sort of neo-Christian process of "iconization," which he views as being underpinned by a religious faith in the miraculous, redemptive power of the image.[78] A number of commentators have, in turn, contested Rancière's reading. Douglas Morrey, for instance, has argued that what is at stake is ultimately that which remains unshown, but is nevertheless revealed through the combination of the 1945 and 1951 footage: the pervasive sense of deception and death that haunts *A Place in the Sun,* and, more broadly, the recording of time passing (and thus of death at work) in all cinema.[79] Rancière's argument is based partly on an interpretation of Giotto's Mary Magdalene and Edmund's sister in *Germany Year Zero* as angels of the Christian Resurrection.[80] Both figures, however, can equally well be interpreted, like Stevens and Rossellini in their roles as cinema's exemplary representatives, simply as witnesses.

1A, *D-Day to Berlin* (George Stevens/ George Stevens, Jr., 1945/1994), and *A Place in the Sun* (George Stevens, 1951).

As Myriam Heywood has argued in another
robust critique of Rancière, Godard's Mary
Magdalene can be viewed as one of a number
of secular or religiously unspecific angels in
Histoire(s) du cinéma, who function primarily
as go-betweens between the seen and unseen
worlds.[81] Heywood makes the persuasive case
that the theme of resurrection in the series, including in the Stevens sequence, is secularized
via the numerous non-Christian examples that
Godard uses to illustrate it – some of which, she
points out, involve *fake* resurrections (such as
those in *Mark of the Vampire* and *Vertigo*). As a
result, she concludes, Godard's treatment of the
theme is resolutely secular and contradictory,
and ultimately closer to the myth of Sisyphus
than to the Christian story of the Passion.[82]
Within the framework of Godard's theorization of the artistic process, the idea of secular
resurrection played out in these sequences in
1A points above all to cinematic renewal. In the
context of his account of the history of cinema, it
opens the series onto the postwar period generally, and in particular onto the two movements
that will be central to our examination of his discourse on national cinemas in the next chapter:
Italian Neo-realism and the French New Wave.

"THERE'S NO LONGER ANY CINEMA," Godard has often claimed.[1] Statements such as these refer in part to the effects of the successive humiliations and capitulations he identifies, and which we charted in the preceding chapter. However, they frequently also imply a very specific understanding of the term "cinema," and it is to this that we now turn. The corpus of films sampled in *Histoire(s) du cinéma* can for the most part be divided into four broad, partially overlapping categories: the silent cinema he discovered in the cine-clubs and at the Cinémathèque française in the 1940s and 1950s; the work of a handful of auteurs, such as Chaplin, Dreyer, Barnet, Bergman, Lang, Hitchcock, Renoir, Rossellini, and Welles (a list that has changed little since his early critical articles); postwar American, Italian, and French cinema, especially the films he wrote about as a critic in the 1950s; and his own output. Underlying the manner in which he treats this corpus, however, is a model of cinema that had been in gestation since the 1970s and found its fullest initial formulation in his Montreal talks. This model, which is perhaps somewhat surprising given his origins in a movement, the New Wave, that was inspired by films from all eras and from around the globe, is based on a conceptualization of cinema in terms of the interrelationship of films, national identity and the construction of nationhood. This chapter examines the rationale underpinning the "cinema(s)" in circulation in and around *Histoire(s) du cinéma,* and the development and logic of the discourse on cinema and nation that underpins it. It goes on to consider Godard's treatment of the principal national cinemas on which he focuses, and concludes with an analysis of his account of the New Wave.

5

Cinema, Nationhood, and the New Wave

Bearing in mind Godard's investment in the silent era, and his discourse on cinematographic montage and postwar cinematic decline, it should come as no surprise that the national cinemas that interest him most date from the prewar period – or, as we shall see in the case of Neo-realism and the New Wave, from the two decades directly following World War II. This is the reason for the dearth of post-1960s films in *Histoire(s) du cinéma*. The primary function of the few that are there – Souleymane Cissé's *Yeelen* (1987), Rob Tregenza's *Talking to Strangers,* and Šarūnas Bartas's *Three Days* (1991) and *Corridor* (1994), for example – is to provide evidential traces of the residue of prewar "montage" in the postwar period: flashes of invention, ingenuity, integrity, originality, and commitment on the part of a handful of figures, films, and movements in the face of widespread homogenization. Other later filmmakers, he suggests, may nevertheless carry within them a memory of montage, and still succeed in recalling and applying it semi-consciously from time to time. The principal context in which he has developed this strand of his argument was the protest movement spearheaded by filmmakers in France in 1997 against proposed new immigration legislation, the "Debré law," which was being debated in the National Assembly at that time. Introduction of this legislation would have had the effect, among other things, of requiring citizens to report immigrants whose papers were not in order (the so-called *sans-papiers*) to their town hall. The filmmakers galvanized opposition to the proposal (notably in a call for civil disobedience published in *Le monde* and

Libération), and produced a powerful short film-tract, *Nous, sans-papiers de France* (We, the *sans-papiers* of France, 1997), made collectively under the supervision of Nicolas Philibert.[2] Crucially for Godard, they also drew a direct connection between the aims and wording of the draft law, and those of strikingly similar antisemitic legislation introduced in 1941 by the collaborationist Vichy government. In 1997, although he considered the films of most contemporary filmmakers to display little genuine understanding of the workings and potential of montage, he suggested that faced with the "Debré law" they seemed to rediscover and apply it in a moment of crisis.[3]

The other principal manner in which Godard considers the traces of cinematographic montage to have been carried over into the postwar era is via the work of a handful of individual filmmakers, such as Cocteau, Hitchcock, Ray, and Welles, who had cut their teeth in the silent era, or, failing that, in the 1930s and 1940s. Thus he values Cocteau's work less for any consistent tone or style than for its ability to create productive, unforeseeable shocks through the combination of disparate ideas, and has summed Cocteau up accordingly as "someone who in his own way loved montage."[4] His esteem for Hitchcock – whom he has characterized as a visionary, and likened to everyone from Renaissance painters to Proust – is rooted in a recognition that this remarkable filmmaker achieved his immense popular success on the back of ambitious, technically difficult, formally inventive, non-formulaic, visually driven narratives: "Hitchcock is one of the century's great artists. He made difficult, sensitive, mysterious, and successful films that didn't follow a recipe.

That's extremely rare."[5] It is in this sense that Godard, in the section entitled "Introduction à la méthode d'Alfred Hitchcock" in 4A, can characterize Hitchcock as "the only / *poète maudit* / to have met with success," and "the greatest / creator of forms / of the twentieth century," who created imagery that cast a spell over audiences around the globe: "Alfred Hitchcock succeeded / where Alexander, Julius Caesar / Napoleon / failed / in taking control / of the universe."[6] Indeed, in the moving interview that Godard gave at the time of Hitchcock's death, the former went so far as to suggest that Hitchcock, uniquely, had actually *achieved* montage.[7] Paradoxically, therefore, it is Hitchcock's sound films, forever rooted in a resolutely visual logic intimately linked to the cinematograph and to painting, that serve as an illustrious, but all too solitary, example of what full-scale cinematographic montage might have become. In *Histoire(s) du cinéma* itself, however, it is Welles and Ray who are the most explicitly revered in the context of the idea of the preservation and transmission of the secret of montage. Although neither enjoyed the same level of popular success as Hitchcock, both kept alive the practice of montage through a bewitchingly fluid combination of motifs, movement with the frame, angles, and rhythmic cutting. In his dialogue with Youssef Ishaghpour, Godard explained the rationale underlying his use of certain material from Welles's *Mr. Arkadin* and Ray's *They Live By Night*. In the series, these two films exemplify the idea of the residual force of cinematographic montage in the sound era:

> In Nicholas Ray's first film *They Live By Night*, with Cathy O'Donnell, from which I took two or three shots that appear repeatedly in *Histoire(s) du cinéma*,

there's a sequence of four shots of Cathy O'Donnell standing up from a kneeling position. They're not quite centered frontal shots, and then they are, and you could say that this is a true beginning of artistic montage. Or as sometimes with Welles (although partly because he would shoot one half of a dialogue in Marrakech on a Tuesday, and the reverse shots a year later in Zurich on a Wednesday), in a simple conversation, there's a sequence of shots like the one in *Arkadin,* where it's more visible, where there's a sort of rhythm, which isn't just a shot/reverse shot, and isn't continuity editing either. There's a certain rhythm in the conversation that's just there, that's both a brilliant effect, and like a trace of what all those filmmakers were looking for, which is really montage for telling stories in a different way. There are people who talk glibly about montage, for example the girl using computers on a film by Téchiné says she's doing the montage on Téchiné's film, but she isn't doing montage any more than the girl who sells you an airline ticket.[8]

These ideas have their roots in Godard's early criticism: in the opening paragraph of "Montage, mon beau souci," he had already defined *Mr. Arkadin* – alongside what he considered another key film, Renoir's *Eléna et les hommes* – as "a model of montage."[9]

COLLABORATION AND POPULARITY

It is only a small step from Godard's discourse on montage – and the notion discussed in chapter 1 of the contribution of films to the revelation and formation of both social and existential relations – to the idea of the interconnectedness of cinema, community, and national cohesion. This is another sense of the imagery in *Histoire(s) du cinéma* of hands reaching out to one another – as, for example, in the clip from King Vidor's *Our Daily Bread* (1934) used in 1B (slowed down and flipped, so that it is back to front), in which members of the agricultural

Our Daily Bread (King Vidor, 1934), and Godard's use of the film in 1B.

collective, around whom the film's narrative revolves, realize that their crops are beginning to grow. Godard's thinking here flies in the face of auteur theory, and insists instead on filmmaking as a collaborative activity and popular art. The flourishing of cinema, then, depends on an adequate industrial infrastructure, a bedrock of creative desire among those involved in film production to ensure the provision of a sustained quota of average films, among which the occasional one will aspire to and attain artistic excellence, and a collective desire on the part of audiences to moderate and sustain the cycle. It is not sufficient simply to produce great numbers of films, nor for audiences to crave and consume large numbers of non-indigenously made films. For cinema to exist within the parameters established by Godard, there must be a wealth of more or less average films that engage with, rework, and reflect contemporary concerns of direct relevance to the nation in question – concerns that are in turn desired and engaged with by that national audience.

We shall look first at the question of collaboration. Godard has consistently argued since the 1970s that the Hollywood studio system provided the economic and industrial context that allowed filmmakers such as Lang, Hawks, Ray, and Ford to flourish, even if often essentially in opposition to institutional structures. He has also returned repeatedly to the idea that it was the collaborative nature of the filmmaking process in the Hollywood studios that constituted the strength of the American cinema, and that meant that even mediocre films were generally of a higher quality than those produced outside such an environment.[10] He has often claimed anecdotally that for cinema to exist, a film studio must have a cafeteria, and specifically a cafeteria where all those involved in the film-making process go, and where they are able to discuss the films they are working on. Nowadays, as he was already beginning to argue in Montreal, although directors and technicians may still share the same cafeteria, they spend their time talking about what was on television the previous night, rather than the challenges of the film they are currently working on:

> I realized quite recently that the strength of the New Wave, which allowed it to break through in France at a given moment in time, was simply due to there being three or four of us, who were discussing cinema among ourselves. The strength of the average prewar American cinema came from those who were together all day, talking in the morning, in the cafeteria, and in a space other than a factory; it was a factory, but a very specific type of factory where they were able to talk.[11]

Godard proceeded to link this idea of the importance of discussion and debate to the notion of schools or movements in painting, and to suggest that genuine collaboration of this sort underpins all moments of innovation in cinematic history. He concluded his remarks with the unequivocal statement that, without the presence and stimulus of the discussion and collaboration between the directors and technicians within national cinema industries, cinema is not only less good, but absent altogether: "Otherwise, you don't make cinema."[12]

Let us now consider the issue of popularity. As Richard Dyer and Ginette Vincendeau have observed, the term "popular" is fraught with multiple meanings in a cinematic context.[13] Godard uses the term in both its anthropological and economic senses: films should be made for popular consumption, and be desired and valued by their popular audience. Contrary to music and painting, he argues, cinema brought real art to the masses:

> Painting never experienced this: Goya was seen by very few people; Beethoven was little heard.... But cinema was immediately seen by one hundred people at the Grand Café. And then came phenomenal expansion. It took hold in a truly popular way, whether this was intentional or not, or for economic reasons or not.[14]

This is a crucial characteristic repeatedly emphasized by Godard (see the long quotation from his talk at the Fémis cited at the beginning of chapter 4). Cinema was widely distributed and immediately "popular": people loved it and wanted more. It was the only art to have found a massive popular audience, and to have been hugely popular with that audience: "Everyone can like a Van Gogh, but then someone invented a way of broadcasting Van Gogh's crows everywhere (albeit in a somewhat less terrifying form), so that everyone loved them and felt close to them."[15]

This model of a healthy cinematic environment for the production and consumption of films directly informed Godard's laments in the 1980s and 1990s that cinema no longer exists. It was not just that filmmaking had been taken over by television, but also that films had come to be conceived, made and distributed in a manner that no longer required or fostered cohesion, collaboration, or a sense of a community: "I come back to the idea that our films have lost the need to be cinema, that they're primarily films. Because we only have an individual reason for making something."[16] For Godard, although films were (and are) still being made, and often of a high quality, they are no longer "cinema," in so far as the context, upon which the use of the term depends for him, has disappeared. There emerged therefore in the 1980s a clear distinction in his discourse between cinema and films: "We make films, but not cinema."[17] Films may have constituted the individual units of cinema, but if we follow this line of thinking, we can no longer speak of the existence of cinema in a meaningful way, other than as a pale imitation of its earlier incarnation. As a result, we are left with a disjointed collection of films, isolated, encircled, and adrift among the electronic and digital media. This is the bleak scenario that provided the backdrop to his self-characterization throughout the 1980s, in films such as *Scénario du film Passion* and *Grandeur et décadence d'un petit commerce de cinéma,* as a dinosaur on the verge of extinction, alongside comparable aging survivors such as Jean-Pierre Mocky, Jacques Rivette, and Jean-Marie Straub, adrift, ill at ease, and reduced to reliance on television for survival.

CINEMA AND NATIONAL IDENTITY

The idea that for cinema to exist there must be a climate in which a filmmaking industry can flourish, and that the films produced by that industry should function in part as quasi-documentary news reports addressing the concerns and realities of their audience, may meet many of the expectations one might have of a vibrant, relevant contemporary art-form in relation to the epoch it inhabits. It informed the national cinema perspective underpinning the panoramic narratives produced by some of the major founding cinema historians, such as Sadoul, as well as many of Langlois's programs at the Cinémathèque française. Despite the recent growth in transcultural and transnational film studies, it also accounts in large part for the enduring centrality of approaches to film history through national cinemas. But Godard's version of the national cinema model is very specific. Besides meeting the general criteria outlined above, within his schema cinema must function as the privileged site for the quest for a national image, which is reflected back to the nation and outward to the rest of the world: "It's when nations lose their identity that they need something that's ineffable and ephemeral through which to provide an account of themselves: an image."[18] True cinema is deemed by Godard to have existed only when the collective thirst for a national self-image – always when this is absent, challenged, or under threat – has produced a simultaneous revolution in film language. It is not sufficient to appropriate wholesale the forms, technology, and genres of previous generations; the quest for national identity must itself throw into question and reinvent the means through which it is sought and articulated. Drawing on Jean Giraudoux's *Siegfried et le Limousin* (*Siegfried and the Limousin*), he has often (as in *Allemagne année 90 neuf zéro*) related the idea of nations being embroiled in such an internal struggle for a national identity through cinema to the process of civil war. In this context, films depicting internal national conflicts or actual civil wars occupy an exemplary position, and – like courtroom dramas – play a self-reflexive role in relation to his discourse as a whole: "[T]he great national cinemas, apart from Germany, have always been great war films, and particularly civil war films. In other words, a time at which the nation is fighting against itself and no longer knows what it is. It's *Birth of a Nation* in the United States, it's *Potemkin* in Russia, and it's *Rome, Open City* in Italy."[19]

Given the longstanding centrality of questions of individual and collective identity to Godard's concerns, he was a natural choice for guest interviewee at the 1991 conference at the National Film Theatre, London, "Image and Identity in Contemporary European Cinema." Let us begin by recalling in this context *Nord contre sud*, or *Naissance (de l'image) d'une nation*, his and Miéville's attempt to participate in the 1970s – at the invitation of the government of the People's Republic of Mozambique – in the nascent nation's project of constructing a national television infrastructure. His and Miéville's aim, as he put it in Montreal, had been to reflect audiovisually on the "birth of a nation through the image it constructs of itself, would like to construct, or succeeds in constructing, and then wants to pass on to others."[20] Their conceptualization of the infrastructure, as is evident from the project's title – "Birth (of the image) of a nation" – had explicitly taken into account television's potential role in the construction of Mozambican national identity.[21] At the London conference, the specificity of Godard's thinking was cast in relief: whereas his interlocutor, Colin MacCabe, suggested that cinema would undoubtedly be one of the key media through which new European identities would evolve in the face of the growing disparities between dominant cultural stereotypes and rapidly shifting socioeconomic realities, Godard refused to entertain the idea that it would be through cinema – his idea of cinema – that such emerging identities would take shape.[22] Although for him cinema has certainly performed this function in the past, it has always been when nations were seeking to construct or rebuild their self-image, and he was evidently not willing to entertain the possibility of the same model operating at a transnational or federal level.

The conclusion of Godard's reflections on the interrelationship of cinema and nationhood in the 1970s and 1980s, which fed directly into *Histoire(s) du cinéma*, is that cinema has truly existed only on a very limited number of occasions: in Russia in the 1920s; in Germany between the wars; in Italy after World War II; and in the United States in the 1940s and 1950s. All other nations, all other cinemas, have done something else, but it is not "cinema" in the highly specific sense formulated by Godard. Here is how he presented his argument when introducing *Histoire(s) du cinéma* at Cannes in 1997:

> Two or three nations made a personal use of cinema, if I can put it like that, and recognized themselves more than other nations in this form of relationship with reality invented by cinema. To put it in more concrete terms, I'd say that there was Italian cinema, German cinema, French cinema (a little), American cinema and Russian cinema. But if I say, for instance, that there was no Swedish cinema, I nevertheless recognize that there were Swedish filmmakers and films (and some very great Swedish filmmakers). But the Swedish people did not recognize themselves in the image of the world presented as an image of the world – as a *Swedish* image of the world – offered by Sjöström and Stiller. Whereas the French, Italians, and Germans did, albeit not all the time. As did the Russians, albeit not for long: from 1915 to 1925. The Russians recognized themselves, but it was at a time when Russia was thinking about changing its relationship with the world, or suddenly had another vision of the world, and cinema represented that change of vision. The Italians had it at the time of Neo-realism. The French had it in another way: there perhaps wasn't a French cinema, but there were *so*

many French filmmakers who loved cinema that it ended up providing a sense of cinema. And one could see this very clearly during the Occupation: occupied France recognized itself in these average films, and when the American cinema arrived, it recognized itself less, because this cinema was something of a cinema of forgetting, and wasn't really a genuine vision of the world.[23]

His thinking on this topic informs *Histoire(s) du cinéma* throughout, and is explicit in his presentation of Neo-realism in 3A:

> why is it / that in forty / forty-five / there was no resistance cinema / not that there weren't resistance films / on the right, on the left / here and there / but the only film / in the sense of cinema / that resisted the occupation of the cinema / by America / a certain uniform way / of making cinema / was an Italian film / it is not by accident / Italy was the country / that fought least / that suffered greatly / but that changed sides twice / and so suffered / from a loss of identity / and if it got it back / with Rome open city / it's because the film was made / by people out of uniform / it's the only time / the Russians made / films of martyrdom / the Americans made / advertising films / the British did what they always do / in the cinema / nothing / Germany had no cinema / no longer had a cinema / and the French made / Sylvie et le fantôme / the Poles made / two films of expiation / passenger and the last stage / and a film of memoirs / kanal / and they ended up by welcoming Spielberg / when, never again / has become / it's better than nothing / whereas with Rome open city / Italy simply / reconquered the right / of a nation / to look itself in the eye[24]

As Godard has made clear elsewhere, his suggestion here that Italy "changed sides twice" is a reference to the Second Italo-Abyssinian War of 1935–36, Mussolini's alignment with Hitler during World War II, and – following the removal of Mussolini – the signing of the secret armistice between the Italian Grand Council of Fascism and the Allies in 1943.[25] Overall, what we see in this sequence, which is entirely in line with

his earlier reflections, is a model of cinema that emphasizes immediacy, formal innovation, and popularity, and privileges those moments when cinema is itself being interrogated and reinvented as a vital cultural form. At the same time, of course, it sets to one side the overwhelming majority of national cinemas.

NATIONAL CINEMAS

We shall now consider the manner in which Godard characterizes the various national cinemas he champions or derides. It is important to note at the outset that the distinction he draws above between countries with a healthy number of films and good filmmakers (such as Sweden) and those caught up in a broader quest for national identity through cinema accounts for the lack of a significant engagement in *Histoire(s) du cinéma* with other major film-producing nations such as Japan and Denmark. This is despite his profound esteem for filmmakers such as Mizoguchi and Dreyer, clips from whose films are nevertheless prominently sampled. Indeed, there is an unresolved tension throughout the series between his overarching argument on national cinemas and the auteurist films of the past that he so cherishes – and through which he presents that argument. He has also suggested that part of the problem regarding countries such as Japan, as well as Britain, was not just their relatively weak filmmaking traditions, but also a lack of a self-conscious awareness of those traditions.[26] This is the context in which we should approach Godard's dismissal of British cinema in 3A, which is an extension of his longstanding refusal to accept the existence of a British cinema that was already evident in his early critical articles. Here, for instance, is

Woman in a Dressing Gown
(J. Lee Thompson, 1957).

BFI Stills.

how he savaged *Woman in a Dressing Gown* (J. Lee Thompson, 1957), shortly after it had been awarded two prizes at the Berlin Film Festival:

One really has to rack one's brains to find anything to say about a British film. One wonders why. But that's the way it is. And there isn't even an exception to prove the rule.... [M]ultiply the ugliness of *Death of a Cyclist* by the unfunniness of *Passport to Pimlico*, raise to the power of the worst of the bad taste of Carol Reed or David Lean, and you will get *Woman in a Dressing Gown*.... How have the descendents of Daniel Defoe, Thomas Hardy and George Meredith reached such a degree of incompetence in matters of art? Why, for instance, do English actors who are the best in the world (cf. Charles Laughton, Cary Grant) become absolutely commonplace as soon as they start work at Elstree or Pinewood? A mystery as aggravating as Agatha Christie's novels. Even the Cannes jury in its bad days would not have let itself be bowled over by Yvonne Mitchell's "Look at me!" performance as a virago half-way between an ostrich and Donald Duck, compared to whom Katharine Hepburn is a model of freshness and youth in *Summer Madness,* and Joanne Woodward a model of sensitivity and discretion in *The Three Faces of Eve.* No, it really is enough to make one despair. Except that to despair of the British cinema would be to admit that it exists.[27]

We find similar such statements in interviews with Godard, particularly in the 1960s. He once suggested, for instance, that British cinema was characterized less by any identifiable approach to *mise en scène,* than by a sort of clumsy "mise en place": "The British don't really create films – they just set them up."[28]

Godard is certainly partly suggesting on occasions such as these that British films are poorly made and lacking in creative flair. Underlying his provocations, however, is the model of cinema outlined above, which insists on a healthy relationship between a vibrant industry and a popular need and response to the products of that industry. And Britain, due largely to the linguistic proximity of Hollywood, has arguably lacked a meaningful indigenous cinema industry and culture in which the collective desires and anguishes of a nation could be worked through and played out in cinematic form. One could, of course, mount a defense of British cinema from within *Histoire(s) du cinéma,* by foregrounding the centrality of Laurence Olivier's *Hamlet* (1948) to his reflections on the poetics of the image (see chapter 6), or the presence of other key British-born talent such as Charles Chaplin, Alfred Hitchcock, Ida Lupino, and Moira Shearer. But Godard's response would doubtless be that sooner or later these figures invariably abandoned Britain for Hollywood. Indeed this line of argument was already present in his review of *Woman in a Dressing Gown,* in which he suggested that it had all been downhill for British cinema since "the departure of the filmmaker who knew too much" (that is, Hitchcock).[29] This damning view of British cinema was not uncommon among the New Wave, and can be traced back at least as far as Bardèche and Brasillach, whose interest lay primarily with the American, French, German, and Russian traditions. Bardèche and Brasillach pointed instead to the vitality of Britain's writerly heritage compared to what they considered the relative paucity of its painterly, musical, and cinematic output.[30] In a similar way, when Godard dismisses a given national cinema, it is important to note that he is fully aware that the nation in question may well be home to other strong artistic traditions:

The British have made a few films: the ones I prefer belong to the documentary school, with Thorold Dickinson and John Grierson. They had Chaplin and Hitchcock, who left for America, and that's it! By contrast, they have had great actors and, for the past thirty years, very great singers. These things need to be said! France had great painting, but not great music. Germany had great music, but not great painting. One can speak of Italian painting, but not of Spanish painting. There were painters, and they happened to live in Spain. But there has never been an invention of painting as there was in Italy and, for a time, in Holland.[31]

For Godard, Britain's contribution has been primarily through literature. Like Russia, and like the United States later accomplished through cinema, the small sea-bound nation projected its myths and values around the globe with remarkable success through literary fiction at a time of rapid colonial expansion.[32]

Let us now turn to Godard's argument in relation to the other national cinematic traditions he focuses on, and to the films and filmmakers he draws on to illustrate his case. He has tended to position the blossoming of German cinema in the interwar years less in relation to the musical, pictorial, or literary traditions than in a uniquely German philosophical perspective. He has suggested, for instance, that formal innovation and renewal in this period – contrary to what happened in the other national contexts – was driven by a pursuit of philosophical thought, and by a quest to articulate ideas through images.[33] Thus, he argued, Murnau's *Tartuffe* (1925) and *Faust* were nourished less by theater than by "German thought," and Emil Jannings, whom he has described as a "living Rodin," does not act in these films in the conventional sense so much as project a *presence* in the philosophical sense. Apart from this specificity, German cinema otherwise fits his model perfectly: in the wake of World War I, cinema – notably in the work of the Expressionists – functioned as a site of extended national self-scrutiny, as well as anticipated the rise of Nazism (see chapter 4).

Tartuffe (F. W. Murnau, 1925), and *People on Sunday: A Film without Actors* (Robert Siodmak and Edgar G. Ulmer, 1929).

Unsurprisingly, given his longstanding admiration for Fritz Lang, the latter enjoys particular prominence in the series. He has also signaled the important role played by others from the 1910s and 1920s – director Paul Leni, actor-director Lupu Pick, and Austrian director Karl Grune, for instance – in providing a resonant documentary snapshot of the mentalities of the time, and in forging an enduring cinematic image of Germany.[34] Of particular note in this context is Robert Siodmak and Edgar G. Ulmer's account of a day in the life of young Berliners, *People on Sunday: A Film without Actors* (1929), which features prominently near the beginning of 1A, and offers an exemplary model of the sort of fresh, understated documentary-based fiction that so inspired the New Wave.

For Godard, this period of artistic vitality in Germany drew to a close in 1932–33.[35] Much later, he sees the quest for a national self-image being played out again, albeit in a much more muted manner, in elements of the New German Cinema of the late 1960s and 1970s. Rainer Werner Fassbinder, in particular, is accorded a privileged position, and presented as a unique, wayward shooting star who attempted to singlehandedly reinvent a German cinema for the post–Marshall Plan generation, making "films for the two Germanys, all alone, for twenty years," and dying of "a kind of overdose of creative obligations" in the process:

> Fassbinder, who made almost exclusively very bad films, or at least not very good ones, was one of the last filmmakers to still make cinema. I didn't like his films much, but I so loved the fact that he was driven to make them, which was more important. He said, "I'm German, and I make films for German people." As soon as he made a Hollywood film like *Despair,* it really wasn't any good, it wasn't his thing. But while he was making *Maria Braun* and so on, five identical films with the same actors, etc., *that* was cinema and had no need to be films.[36]

Despite the backhanded nature of the compliment, Fassbinder is one of the very rare German filmmakers of the postwar generation to be cited in *Histoire(s) du cinéma,* both via his work (*Lili Marleen* [1981] is sampled in 1A) and as a person (his portrait ends the line of artists to whom Godard pays tribute in 4A, and a further photograph of him is used in the opening moments of 4B).

As we have already seen, Italian Neo-realism is absolutely central to Godard's thinking about film history. The movement represented, as he put it to Daney in 1988, the "last twitch" of cinema.[37] In *Histoire(s) du cinéma,* it exemplifies his thesis regarding cinema and national identity, and functions as a point of convergence for several interrelated strands of his discourse: biographically, it was at the heart of his cinematic formation; ethically, it embodies his idea of cinematic testimony; artistically, it exemplifies the concept of formal renewal; and politically, it encapsulates his idea of art as resistance. The majority of the sentimental homage to the movement in 3A is composed out of well-known clips from classic films of the 1940s to the 1970s, most of which are probably fairly instantly recognizable to cinephiles: *Stromboli, The Swindlers* (Federico Fellini, 1955), *Umberto D., The Earth Trembles, Bicycle Thieves* (De Sica, 1948), *Theorem* (Pier Paolo Pasolini, 1968), *Red Desert* (Michelangelo Antonioni, 1964), *Bitter Rice* (Giuseppe De Santis, 1949), *Zabriskie Point* (Antonioni, 1970), *Amarcord* (Fellini, 1973), *Senso* (Visconti, 1954), *The Road* (Fellini, 1954), *Garibaldi* (Rossellini, 1961), *The Flowers of St Francis* (Rossellini, 1950), and *Hawks and Sparrows* (Pasolini,

1966). This sequence is framed by a highly evocative suggestion: despite the artifice inherent in
Neo-realism's reliance on post-synchronized
sound, the movement achieved unprecedented
poetic heights through the absorption of the
language of Ovid, Virgil, Dante, and Leopardi
into the body of its imagery.[38] To underscore
this idea, Godard punctuates the sequence with
short quotations in Latin from Lucretius's *On
the Nature of Things*, Dante's *The Divine Comedy*, and Ovid's *Metamorphoses* and *The Art of
Love*, and reinforces it further through use on
the soundtrack of Riccardo Cocciante's song
celebrating the power of the Italian language,
"La nostra lingua italiana" (1983).

Among the Neo-realists, Godard cherishes
above all Visconti and Rossellini:

> I like Fellini less than Rossellini or Visconti. Fellini
> was Rossellini's assistant. He didn't innovate, he
> followed. I adore *Amarcord*. The ending of *The
> Swindlers* disturbs me so much I've only ever dared
> watch it once right to the end. It's culture that made
> Fellini great, but he didn't suffer enough. De Sica
> made nice films like *Shoe-Shine* and *Bicycle Thieves*.
> His masterpiece was obviously *Umberto D.,* which
> was a total flop.[39]

Visconti is in fact referred to relatively infrequently in the series. By contrast, Rossellini – whom Godard has described as a sort of
uncle – crops up everywhere, and this despite
the notoriously problematic nature of his early
so-called fascist trilogy (*The White Ship* [1941], *A
Pilot Returns* [1942], and *Man of the Cross* [1943]).
When confronted in an interview with a characterization of Rossellini as "a former director
of fascist propaganda films," Godard brushed it
aside, arguing that in terms of cinema history,
these early films are irrelevant compared to the
work of redemption carried out by Rossellini on

Lucretius, Dante and Rossellini's
Rome, Open City (1945) in 3A.

behalf of Italian cinema (and indeed of all cinema) in his war trilogy (*Rome, Open City* [1945], *Paisan,* and *Germany Year Zero*).[40] A number of clips from two films from this trilogy occupy a vital position in the series: the sequences depicting the suppression and murder of the partisans in *Paisan* (cited in 1B, 3A, and 3B); and those showing the activities of the Italian resistance in *Rome, Open City* (prominently cited in the opening of 3B), especially the torture of Giorgio (Marcello Pagliero) (which is returned to repeatedly in 2B, 3A, 4A, and 4B), and the murder of Pina (Anna Magnani) (which also recurs several times in 2B, 3A, and 4B). These latter two sequences from the film exemplify Godard's characterization of *Rome, Open City* as "the only resistance film" – one that is not only *about* resistance, but that also sought to resist any normalizing tendencies through a quest to forge "another cinema."[41]

It is clear from the discussion so far that the Russian and Soviet traditions are central to *Histoire(s) du cinéma* for a number of reasons. For instance, Russia produced some of cinema's most inventive found-footage filmmakers and provided Godard with a number of powerful symbols of political and artistic resistance. One filmmaker in particular enjoys special prominence: Sergei Eisenstein. Having resisted the widespread deification of Eisenstein as the paradigm of a revolutionary filmmaker in the late 1960s, Godard began to reengage with him from the late 1970s onward. By the time of the completion of the early versions of 1A and 1B, Eisenstein had again come to occupy a central position in Godard's schema: *Battleship Potemkin, Bezhin Meadow, Aleksandr Nevsky* (1938), and *Ivan the Terrible, Part I* (1944) are cited therein. These references are retained in the

final versions, and sampled alongside clips from *Strike* (1924), *October, The General Line, ¡Qué viva México!* and *Ivan the Terrible, Part II* (1958), all of which feature elsewhere in *Histoire(s) du cinéma.* Eisenstein's high visibility is undoubtedly due in large part to his towering contribution as a theorist and practitioner of montage. Like Godard after him, Eisenstein accorded cinematic montage a transcendent intensity rooted in filmic materiality: montage is integral to cinema, not just as the grammatical basis to filmic expression (the combination of shots), but at the micro level of the interstice separating the individual photograms on the celluloid. At the macro level, Eisenstein (again, like Godard later on) sets aside "the limited business of the gluing bits of film together" to focus on the larger issue of montage as a productive principle accompanying the combination of two or more phenomena in any art-form (architecture, music, painting, theater, the novel, poetry, and so on).[42] One of Eisenstein's most compelling ideas, which formed part of his theory of vertical montage and "ocular music," and which Godard has adopted and made his own, is that El Greco was one of the forefathers of film montage, whose approach to composition relied on the synthesis of multiple viewpoints within a single frame.[43] The significance of this idea for Godard lies, of course, in the way it neatly encapsulates his own use of intra-frame montage in his composite video imagery. We should note, however, that Godard holds back from crediting Eisenstein with having fully *achieved* montage in the sense discussed in the previous chapter. Pursuing a line of thinking that he had first developed through dialogue with Jean-Pierre Gorin in the 1970s, he suggests that in hindsight it is clear that while searching for montage, Eisenstein ended up instead inventing a novel mode of filmic enunciation based on a self-reflexive fusion of cinematic and political angles on events.[44] Thus despite his admiration for the scale and significance of Eisenstein's contribution, this argument allows Godard to position the latter as just one of the many pioneers who were feeling their way across the vast uncharted continent of montage in the 1920s and 1930s, none of whom – with the possible exception of Hitchcock – succeeded in grasping or exploiting its full potential.

In terms of cinema and nationhood, 1A includes a sequence devoted to Soviet cinema, a sort of compressed Russian episode, which is subsequently unpacked in *Les enfants jouent à la Russie*. This sequence in 1A is announced earlier in the same episode by a series of clips from films by Eisenstein (*Aleksandr Nevsky, Battleship Potemkin,* and *Strike*), and articulated through a collage of material from classic films by Shub, Vertov, Eisenstein, Pudovkin, and Kozintsev and Trauberg. Godard evokes through his montage a sense of the dynamism and vitality of postrevolutionary Russian filmmaking, which is encapsulated in the celebrated passage from Eisenstein's *The General Line* depicting the ecstatic faces of members of a small farming collective, who are shown marveling at the power and potential of their new butter-making machine (this, incidentally, is the clip from *The General Line* that Godard had previously cut into *Sauve qui peut [la vie]* in Rotterdam in 1981). But if it was the intensity of the need for sociopolitical montage in postrevolutionary Russia that gave Russian cinema its urgency and force, the latter came to an abrupt halt in 1929 with Stalin's accession to power, an event conveyed here by Godard through his references to Arthur Koestler's devastating fictionalized tale of

Soviet totalitarianism, *Darkness at Noon,* and Aleksandr Solzhenitsyn's firsthand account of the Soviet forced labor and concentration camp system, *The Gulag Archipelago*. In this context, the fate of *The General Line* is emblematic: begun in 1927, the film was reedited and released as *Old and New* in 1929, following a change in the party line on collectivization and direct intervention by Stalin. The end of the great early Soviet cinematic experiments of the pre-Stalinist period is also conveyed via urgent shots of galloping horses in close-up from the climactic sequence of Vsevolod Pudovkin's *Storm over Asia* (1928), the title of which appears onscreen at the same time, thus reinforcing the sense of breaking political, social, and artistic catastrophe. Godard draws a connection here between a variety of phenomena: political stagnation in Russia; the close of a unique period of cinematic invention; the coming of sound; and the decadence of Hollywood. Henceforth, he suggests, Soviet and Hollywood cinema would be more or less indistinguishable from one another; the only significant difference, he once joked, were the three-piece suits, which were a little more crudely tailored in Moscow than in Los Angeles.[45]

Although Godard's emphasis in *Histoire(s) du cinéma* is very much on the cinema of the pre-Stalinist era, a small number of later Soviet filmmakers also play a significant role. Some of these are the same figures mentioned above, who continued to produce remarkable work, often against the odds and in extremely challenging political circumstances, such as Eisenstein with *Aleksandr Nevsky* and Kozintsev with *Hamlet* (1964). The work of Paradjanov also occupies a prominent position. Above all, however, one thinks in this context of Boris Barnet, a filmmaker highly cherished by Langlois, who has

A brief history of Russian cinema: from
Kino-Pravda (Dziga Vertov, 1922–25) to
The General Line (Sergei Eisenstein, 1929),
Storm over Asia (Vsevolod Pudovkin, 1928),
and Arthur Koestler's *Darkness at Noon*.

long been a major reference for Godard. In his 1959 article on Barnet, Godard had expressed his admiration for the Russian as a supreme, apparently effortless stylist, even in his lesser works.[46] Barnet remains a significant presence in *Histoire(s) du cinéma,* and in other later films such as *Les enfants jouent à la Russie* and *De l'origine du XXIe siècle:* three separate sequences from his *Alyonka* are used in 1B, and clips from *By the Bluest of Seas* and *Bountiful Summer* are cited in 1A and 4B, respectively.

In view of its Russian focus, and its status almost as an additional episode of *Histoire(s) du cinéma,* we shall briefly consider *Les enfants jouent à la Russie.* Freely inspired by Jules Verne's *Michel Strogoff (Michael Strogoff: The Courier of the Czar),* this "investigative cinematographic essay" (as Godard presents the film, via a phrase adapted from Aleksandr Solzhenitsyn), is above all a loving tribute to Russia as the "homeland of fiction," and in particular a homage to Russian literature and to the many filmmakers whose work has so inspired Godard. Many of the Russian and Soviet films glimpsed in *Histoire(s) du cinéma* feature here at greater length, notably Barnet's *By the Bluest of Seas,* the two completed parts of Eisenstein's *Ivan The Terrible,* and the execution scene from *Zoya* – which Godard renders almost unbearable due to the way in which he reworks and extends it. This film-historical dimension of *Les enfants jouent à la Russie* is accompanied by a furious political critique of the contempt and greed with which the West eyed, and – in the manner of Napoleon and Hitler, Godard suggests dramatically – sought to "invade," Russia through images in the wake of the collapse of Communism. It also includes an important reflection on the image, which is conveyed

Boris Barnet's *By the Bluest of Seas* (1936), *Alyonka* (1961) and *Bountiful Summer* (1950) in 1A, 1B and 4B respectively.

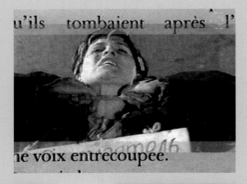

Zoya (Lev Arnshtam, 1944) in *Les enfants jouent à la Russie* (Godard, 1993).

in part via a mini-presentation by Harry Blount (Bernard Eisenschitz) to Alcide Jolivet (André S. Labarthe) regarding the relative absence of the shot–reverse shot figure in Russian cinema.

By the early 1980s, Godard had already identified Expressionism, Neo-realism, and postrevolutionary Soviet cinema as his principal examples of new relationships to reality being forged through cinema. At this stage in his thinking, two key issues remained unresolved: "that of American cinema, and that of the New Wave, which changed quite a few things."[47] We shall now, therefore, examine how he addressed these questions in the ensuing years.

In the American context, pioneers such as Chaplin, Griffith, and Sennett are treated with respectful awe throughout *Histoire(s) du cinéma*, as are exceptional outsiders such as Welles and Cassavetes (joint dedicatee of 1B). Above all, however, the history of American cinema presented in the series is essentially that of the foundation of the Hollywood studios by a handful of charismatic "hoodlum-poets" with a genuine love of cinema (he has expressed particular admiration in this regard for Harry Cohn and Howard Hughes), and the honing in the dream factories of an industrial mode of production, which he has dubbed "the cinema of good joinery."[48] Moreover, since the time of the film project he had hoped to make in America in the late 1970s devoted to the life of the gangster Bugsy Siegel, Godard has been fascinated by the relationship between Hollywood and organized crime: "The true history of Hollywood is that of the branch of the mafia that set up on the West Coast. All that was born at the same time."[49] As far as the films made within the studio system are concerned, the emphasis in *Histoire(s) du cinéma*, like that of his early criticism, is primarily on the period from the 1930s to the 1950s. The series accords particular prominence to B movies, to the work of many of the major émigrés (including Chaplin, Hitchcock, Lang, Lubitsch, Mamoulian, Murnau, Ophüls, Preminger, Renoir, Siodmak, Sirk, and Wilder), and to other longstanding Godardian reference points, such as Aldrich, Boetticher, Browning, Cukor, Dassin, Fleming, Ford, Hawks, Kazan, Lewis, Mankiewicz, Mann, Minnelli, Ray, Vidor, and Walsh. Although the filmmakers referred to in Histoire(s) du cinéma and his early criticism are largely the same, there are nevertheless significant differences at times in the manner in which they are treated. His damning critique of Kazan's stylistic shortcomings in one of his earliest articles, for instance, has given way in the series to a much more appreciative treatment of the complex issues this director tackled in films such as Splendor in the Grass (1961).[50]

As ever, Godard's relationship with American cinema is profoundly ambivalent. On the one hand, his cinephilic passion for the films is undimmed. On the other hand, his awareness of their ideological power and use also remains unaltered. In 1A, we recall, he attributes the ruin of the European film industries to the economic growth and global spread of American cinema in the wake of the two world wars. Since World War I, he argues, American cinema has functioned as a Trojan horse, a trailblazing showcase for American values and goods, whose potential was quickly identified and exploited by the nation's political leaders.[51] As regards the relationship in the United States between cinema and nationhood, Godard's position in Histoire(s) du cinéma is an extension of the well-rehearsed arguments of commentators such as Ricciotto Canudo: as a nation still in its

infancy, the United States badly needed a self-image, and Americans, unencumbered by the weight of European cultural history, were able to throw themselves into the new art-form and to simultaneously explore the world and invent a sense of national identity through the nascent medium.[52] Developing this line of thinking, Godard ascribes the intensity of the American desire to construct a national image, and to project this image to the outside world, to a relative lack of a national history and national identity. The inscription of this collective desire into the narratives of American films conquered the world; even if other nations did not necessarily recognize themselves in the narratives, they were nevertheless seduced by the passion and need that underpinned and shone through them.

As is clear from Godard's reservations cited above regarding France's automatic qualification for "cinema" status, French cinema generally, and the New Wave in particular, presented him with an awkward problem in relation to his model. If Neo-realism was cinema's last twitch, then the New Wave was what he called "the twitch of a twitch."[53] He argues in part that following the Liberation, French cinema became divorced from historical reality, and that against this backdrop, the New Wave constituted an attempt to recreate a fresher, more accurate image of France in the wake of the First Indochina War and in the face of the Algerian War.[54] Ultimately, however, he explains the novelty of the New Wave, and indeed the richness of French cinema as a whole, by referencing a different set of criteria than those informing his other selected national cinemas. Drawing on his distinction between "films" and "cinema," he argues that the French had lots of films and interesting filmmakers, but not a cinema in the sense of a nation and popular art-form undergoing a process of interaction and mutual realignment. However, he succeeds in devising a methodologically ingenious way of incorporating French cinema into his schema as an exceptional case. The first stage of his argument is simply that "the French had so many filmmakers that people ended up believing that they had a cinema."[55] More significantly, as indicated by his comments at Cannes in 1997, he suggests that it was not the mere number of filmmakers that was important, but their love of films, which served to produce, if not cinema, then at least "a sense of cinema." Here we see the traces of a line of thinking that originated with Langlois: the conceptualization of cinema as a country ("My country is cinema!" as Langlois famously put it).[56] Simply put, the combination of a deep appreciation of film history and passionate cinephilia on the part of significant numbers of French filmmaker-critics, notably those associated with the First and New Waves, created a new "country," that of cinema. "Cinema was a place, a territory," as Godard suggested in 1988.[57] Thus, although French cinema never functioned for Godard as a genuine site of national self-scrutiny, and notwithstanding the paradox of using a movement as profoundly transnational in origin as the New Wave in the context of an argument organized around national cinemas, this idea nevertheless allowed Godard to append France to his definitive roll call of cinematic nations, through the suggestion that the depth and extent of its cinephilia produced something equally distinctive: a unique new concept and practice of cinema.

Another distinctive category of filmmakers he singles out as typically French, and who he relates to the intellectual literary-cinematic tradition exemplified in the 1920s by Louis Delluc, is a select "gang of four" who began their careers as writers and only later gravitated toward cinema: Marcel Pagnol, Sacha Guitry, Jean Cocteau, and Marguerite Duras.[58] Godard suggested to Duras in 1987 that although these four filmmakers ultimately remained predominantly writers, their films demonstrated a certain "grandeur and power," which were enormously helpful in enabling the members of the emerging New Wave to believe in cinema as a true art-form.[59] Pagnol's *Angèle* (1932) enjoys particular prominence in *Histoire(s) du cinéma,* in which stills or clips are used in 1B, 2B, 3A, and 4B. Guitry also features strongly (in 1B and 3B), notably via Godard's recurrent use of a celebrated photograph of him by the photographer Willy Rizzo as an elderly man, sitting on the edge of his bed and editing a film. This photograph functions both as a touching tribute to Guitry and as a poignant self-portrait by Godard. It is fitting that the homage to Guitry in 3B, which includes both this photograph and a composite image depicting Duras and Guitry together, should be couched within the context of a sequence devoted to the "wild child," François Truffaut, who had been Guitry's staunchest champion at the time of the New Wave. Indeed Godard's use of this photograph of Guitry is also a way of continuing his dialogue with Truffaut, who, when invited by *Cahiers du cinéma* in 1981 to contribute to a special issue on French cinema, chose to reproduce this very image, together with a written reminder that the greatest challenge at the time of the New Wave had been to make the case for Pagnol and Guitry as "complete directors, strong personalities expressing themselves through cinema."[60] Whenever he felt tired, despondent, or discouraged, continued Truffaut, all he had to do was to look at this portrait of

Guitry, and he immediately rediscovered his energy, enthusiasm, and strength.

Godard's main French cinematic reference points in the series are largely the same as they have always been: Jean Vigo, Jean Cocteau, Robert Bresson, and Jean Renoir. Vigo is a gentle recurrent presence throughout, featuring in 1A, 1B, 3B, and 4B. Godard's treatment of Cocteau is particularly interesting, in that he has sought to reclaim him in recent years not only as a major poet-filmmaker and multimedia artist, but also as a formally innovative critic-filmmaker with an unshakable faith in cinema's capacity for articulating and conveying thought. He rates Cocteau's manner of theorizing cinema, and of generating critical insight through playful but piercing formulae, very highly indeed, and has placed the latter's critical project well above his own in his hierarchy of key film-thinkers, and indeed above that of comparable figures such as Marguerite Duras, above the New Wave critic-filmmakers generally, and perhaps even above André Bazin.[61] Similarly, he cherishes Bresson's poetic, aphoristic writings, and their capacity to subvert received wisdom and provoke thought: "They're sentences that I don't necessarily fully understand, but when one opens the book, they're like tunes one is happy to rediscover. A single phrase is enough for one to spend a pleasant hour reflecting on it."[62] In addition, and just as important, the example of formal rigor set by Bresson looms large over *Histoire(s) du cinéma,* especially in relation to compositional qualities such as framing, episodic structuring, the emphasis on details and fragments, and rhythmic editing. It is for all these reasons that Godard has described his series as "very Bressonian."[63]

Like figures such as Hitchcock and Rossellini, Jean Renoir recurs throughout the series as a constant touchstone, exemplifying the idea of the presence and importance of documentary within fiction, and of an approach to fictional composition based on what Godard has termed the "documentary method."[64] This, argues Godard, is quite different from any sort of documentary approach associated with the newsreel tradition, direct cinema, or on-the-spot filming.[65] In *Histoire(s) du cinéma,* he summarizes his "documentary method" idea through citation on the soundtrack of 1B of Jean Renoir outlining his views on the contingent nature of filmmaking, and insisting on the value of spontaneity and improvisation on the part of the director: "Everything depends on the circumstances, on the moment. I still belong to the old school of people, who believe in life's surprise, who believe in the documentary, and who believe that it would be wrong to ignore the sigh uttered by a young girl in spite of herself." When Alexandre Astruc mounted a defense of Renoir in 1948 as an inspired, misunderstood, pioneering prophet figure, he set in motion of critical reevaluation of the work of the filmmaker that would be picked up and pursued by Bazin and the New Wave.[66] Thus, in 1957, in a now celebrated formulation, Godard summarized Renoir's *Eléna et les hommes* in terms of a unique cocktail of intelligence, Frenchness, and self-reflexivity:

> To say that Renoir is the most intelligent of directors comes to the same thing as saying that he is French to his fingertips. And if *Eléna et les hommes* is "the" French film *par excellence,* it is because it is the most intelligent of films. Art and the theory of art, at one and the same time; beauty and the secret of beauty; cinema and apologia of cinema.[67]

This high esteem for Renoir has remained a constant: in the comic scene in *JLG/JLG,* in which inspectors from the "Centre du cinéma" (played by Bernard Eisenschitz, André S. Labarthe, and Louis Seguin) visit Godard in his home with a view to drawing up an inventory of the films in his video collection, most entire nations – with the exception of the United States – occupy only one or two shelves. Renoir, by contrast, has a whole shelf to himself.

There is a further French filmmaker, with whom Godard has engaged relatively little in the past, who enjoys particular prominence in *Histoire(s) du cinéma:* Jean Epstein. The latter's critical and creative project resonates closely with that of Godard in its theoretical and practical investigation of techniques such as altered motion and rhythm, its contempt for the swarms of "locust filmmakers . . . devoid of personality, whom God sent to plague the cinema," and its passionate advocacy of the powers of cinema to reveal reality afresh.[68] In 1950, in terms that directly anticipate Godard's subsequent position, Epstein identified cinema's principal power in its capacity for showing, informing, and communicating a savage reality "before names and before the law of words."[69] This key member of the First Wave features strongly in 1A, and is the subject of a powerful short tribute in 3B, where he appears as one of the filmmakers revealed by Langlois. The latter sequence is accompanied on the soundtrack by François Périer's recitation of the passage from *The Death of Virgil,* recycled from *Soigne ta droite,* regarding homecoming and cinema's luminous victory over darkness. Together with an onscreen reference to Epstein's 1921 book *Bonjour cinéma,* and an image-track comprising three still images, which are reframed and combined through superimposition (a photograph of Epstein as a young man, an image of Etna erupting from his *La montagne infidèle* (*The Unfaithful Mountain,* 1923), and Lady

Madeline [Marguerite Gance] in his *La chute de la maison Usher* [*The Fall of the House of Usher,* 1928]), the Broch citation serves to position Epstein as a key precursor to the New Wave, and as one of a handful of filmmakers who genuinely sought to use the cinematograph as a tool for investigating and illuminating the world.[70] For Jacques Aumont, Godard's use of the passage from Broch ("o return to the mother country / o return of the one / who no longer needs / an invitation") functions as a tribute to Epstein as someone who knew how to properly welcome cinema into the world.[71] In addition, it serves to recall the admonishment issued by Langlois to *Cahiers du cinéma,* at the time of Epstein's death in 1953, for having more or less ignored the latter while he was alive, and, as such, the sequence can also be seen as a rather humble admission of culpability on Godard's part at having not engaged more fully with Epstein previously.[72]

THE NEW WAVE

Godard's humorous self-depiction in 3B as the keeper of the New Wave museum functions in part to signal that this episode will make a number of critical points in relation to the movement that – in his view – have hitherto been inadequately noted. At the same time, of course, he is fully aware that it is, like *Histoire(s) du cinéma* generally, a highly personal account of the movement filtered through half-memories: "My memory's going, I no longer remember very well . . . ," as Jeanne Moreau sings on the soundtrack.[73] Although he samples many of his own films in the series, in his accompanying spoken discourse, he has consistently expressed strong views in relation to specific works from the 1960s: ambivalence towards *À bout de souffle;*

dislike for *Une femme est une femme, Bande à part,* and *Made in USA* (1966); a certain incomprehension regarding the widespread reverence for *Le mépris;* and comparatively high regard for *Deux ou trois choses que je sais d'elle* and *Weekend.* His interest in 3B, however, is less in these films, or in those of the other New Wave filmmakers, than in the movement's origins and genealogy. He situates the movement in relation to the French critic-filmmaker tradition associated with the First Wave, and has linked it in interviews to the German Romantic literature he discovered during his adolescence through his father: "The New Wave came from there. It's Novalis, or, if you prefer, *Werther,* who led me to Sartre."[74] Like most commentators, he has also related the movement to influences such as silent cinema, Neo-realism, documentary, postwar Hollywood, and selected key auteurs from Europe and elsewhere. The start date for the New Wave that he proposes in 3B, as is indicated via the combination of clips from *La belle et la bête* and *Paisan* that opens the episode, is the year in which these two films were released: 1946. (This, incidentally, is also the periodization he subsequently suggests in the title of *Voyage[s] en utopie: JLG, 1946–2006, À la recherche d'un théorème perdu.*) Besides its Orphic connotations, the clip from *La belle et la bête* also evokes the idea of the discovery of the world, of cinema, and of the world through cinema by the generation of children who grew up during the war, a period represented by brief extracts from Calef's *Jéricho.* 3B also contains a key sequence constructed around material from, among other things, newsreel footage of Marilyn Monroe, *Gigi* (Vincente Minnelli, 1958), and *The Beautiful Blond from Bashful Bend* (Preston Sturges, 1949). This sequence simultaneously offers a loving tribute to the energy, exuberance, and vitality of postwar Hollywood; a fond recollection by Godard of the New Wave's delight and excitement at its encounter with these films; and an acknowledgment of the extent of its impact on his early work, which is represented here by Angéla (Anna Karina) in *Une femme est une femme.* Complementing this sequence is an equally important one composed around extracts from Lang's *You Only Live Once* and Hitchcock's *Vertigo,* which are combined with clips from Rossellini's *Joan at the Stake* (1954), Álvarez's *79 Springs* and Truffaut's *Les quatre cents coups (The 400 Blows,* 1959). This second sequence provides a lyrical evocation of the Malrucian principle of artistic metamorphosis, in which Truffaut's film is presented as the product of the destruction and reinvention of the others (I say lyrical evocation rather than concrete visualization, since *79 Springs* postdates *Les quatre cents coups*). It is accompanied, as is usual when Godard references Malraux's theory of art, by the motif of fire, the source of which here is *Joan at the Stake.* In addition, this combination of films serves to illustrate the principle of the "equality and fraternity" of fiction and reality, which Godard identifies as lying at the very heart of the New Wave.[75]

Godard has consistently related the New Wave to the cine-club culture of the postwar era, and to the tradition of reviewing and discussing films: "The New Wave were the children of the Liberation and of the Cinémathèque, or of the Liberation and the Centre national du cinéma."[76] In this respect, the joint dedication of 3B to Eisenstein scholar Naum Kleiman, director of the Moscow State Central Cinema Museum, and to Frédéric C. Froeschel, who founded and ran the Ciné-club du Quartier

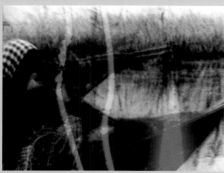

The equality and fraternity of fiction and reality in 3B: *You Only Live Once* (Fritz Lang, 1937), *Joan at the Stake* (Roberto Rossellini, 1954), *Vertigo* (Alfred Hitchcock, 1958), *79 Springs* (Santiago Álvarez, 1969) and *Les quatre cents coups* (François Truffaut, 1959).

Latin, which had led Godard to *Cahiers du ci-néma,* is entirely appropriate. The movement's distinctiveness, in his view, derived directly from the fact that its constituent directors had "grown up" in a place he has described variously as a museum, the "University of Cinema," or the "atelier of the great Masters," where they discovered the masterpieces of a near-invisible art-form: Langlois's Cinémathèque française.[77] "It was a unique moment," he suggested in 2000, "unique, not superior. In other words, it was a singular moment. The New Wave was the only child, the only daughters or sons of film."[78] In his portrait in 3B of the New Wave as a close-knit clan fanatically devoted to "the true cinema . . . that can't be seen," which had to be loved "blindly and by heart" (3B), Godard presents the encounter with Langlois, and the films he revealed, as absolutely decisive. This acknowl-edgment of the overriding importance of the role played by Langlois is illustrated by a clip from Abel Gance's *Napoléon* (1927), in which we see Napoléon heading off towards the horizon in a small sailing boat. In this context, the clip evokes not only Langlois's exploratory curato-rial project, but also the beginning of Godard's life in cinema, and – as is made explicit via the appearance in large blue letters of the words "Une vague nouvelle" – the start of the artistic adventure of the New Wave as a whole. Before the Cinémathèque, there was also for Godard the cine-club at the Musée de l'Homme run by Armand Cauliez (joint dedicatee of 2A) – "my first museum," as he has described it.[79] Prior to this, even, there were the film journals. As he has constantly stressed in recent years, his real initiation into cinema was not through films at all, but through the secondary means of articles and, above all, photographs in magazines:

Perhaps my interest in pictures comes from the fact that it was pictures that awakened my interest in cinema. Even before I had seen any films I would look at the pictures in art and film magazines. And it was a photo from a film by Murnau, whom I'd never heard of, that made me want to make a film. I wanted to get more closely involved with the cinema; up to then all I knew of it was a printed extract.[80]

It would be hard to overemphasize the formative role played by the second series of *La revue du cinéma* edited by Jean George Auriol between 1946 and 1948, which had given Godard a cru-cial glimpse of a new artistic continent, about which – in spite of the richness of his cultural up-bringing – no one had spoken to him.[81] "The real New Wave," as he put it unequivocally in 1998, "was *La revue du cinéma.*"[82] As he has repeat-edly stressed, his first experience of the films he would come to love, but whose qualities were confirmed to him only later when he came to see them at the Cinémathèque française, or in other cine-clubs, was through the photographs and articles in the pages of Auriol's magazine.[83] Engaging with the combination of text and im-age in *La revue du cinéma,* like watching films at the Cinémathèque, and writing about them in the pages of *Arts* and *Cahiers du cinéma,* was for him already equivalent to *making* cinema: "For me and for Rivette, it was what was writ-ten about cinema that mattered most. We saw the films much later. The good cinema was the one that wasn't seen because we couldn't see it, so we imagined it. We imagined *The River, Ivan the Terrible . . .*"[84] Furthermore, he has claimed that he has yet to see many of the films that he first encountered and fell in love with via the pages of the magazine: "I haven't seen four fifths of the films I talk about, and which I neverthe-less know as a result of having seen snatches of them. There are still loads of films that I believe

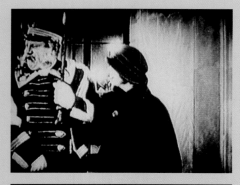

The Last Laugh (F. W. Murnau, 1924) in
Allemagne année 90 neuf zéro (Godard, 1991),
and *Napoléon* (Abel Gance, 1927) in 3B.

I've seen, and that I know due to the desire to see them that came from the old *Revue du cinéma,* which I discovered at the age of twenty or twenty-two."[85]

Godard has not been alone in foregrounding the significance of Auriol's contribution, and in pointing out the extent to which this has been obscured by the scale and unquestionable importance of the work of André Bazin. One of the co-founders of *Cahiers du cinéma,* Jacques Doniol-Valcroze, argued in the context of a discussion of the origins of the New Wave in 1987, for instance, that notwithstanding his deep admiration for Bazin and his recognition of the enormity of the latter's contribution, "in the beginning of everything, there is Auriol."[86] In the genealogy of Godard's formative intellectual influences and affinities presented in *Histoire(s) du cinéma,* Auriol is accorded a key place alongside Langlois and other Cinémathèque-related figures such as Georges Franju, Lotte Eisner, and Mary Meerson (joint dedicatee of 1A). By contrast, he treats Bazin respectfully, but with much greater detachment, as a senior authority figure, whose critical project he situates in the realm of knowledge rather than of love.[87] It is worth noting, however, given the scale of Malraux's influence on Godard, the extent to which both Langlois and Bazin were themselves conduits for Malrucian ideas – the former, as we have seen, in his programming at the Cinémathèque, and the latter, as Dudley Andrew has observed, in his adoption of Malraux's broad, interdisciplinary approach to art history, and in his transmission of the latter's "cult of genius" to the critic-filmmakers of the New Wave.[88] As Andrew has stressed, although this cult of genius was an aspect of Malrucian thought about which Bazin in fact felt profoundly ambivalent, it nevertheless provided one of the core ingredients of the concept forged collectively at *Cahiers du cinéma* in the 1950s, the *politique des auteurs* (auteur theory).

Godard's revisionist account of the New Wave includes a virulent critique of the *politique des auteurs*. This is exemplified by the discussion between the two visitors to his museum in 3B, and his insistence, following Langlois, in response to a complaint by one of them (Audrey, played by Domiziana Giordano), on prioritizing films over the names of directors. The *politique des auteurs,* he suggests here, was above all a question of the *works*. In other words, it was a historically specific strategic tool for the recuperation of unjustly overlooked contemporary artists, which allowed critics to identify artistic ambition and achievement, and stylistic and thematic continuity, in a body of work directed by the same person in the context of the industrially produced "cinema of good joinery." "What interested us in the notion of *auteur,*" as he later argued, "was the *politique* – we didn't give a damn about the *auteur.*"[89] The other strategic use of the *politique,* as he has also recognized, was as a tool for the self-propulsion by the New Wave critics into the notoriously closed French film industry of the 1950s.[90] For several decades, however, he has sought to distance himself from the *politique des auteurs,* and indeed was already suggesting in Montreal that "it was a really stupid thing to have done."[91] He has been particularly critical of the adoption of the term *auteur* in French law ("someone who wants to become a filmmaker is declared an *auteur* and protected by the law even before they've made a film"), and decried the pervasive effects of a devalued, mediatized version of the *politique,* wherein any sense of critical strategy is overlooked.[92] At the same time, the understanding and practice of cinema as a fundamentally collaborative art-form, he argues, has been neglected, and the basis of *auteur* filmmaking in the creative dialogue between directors, producers, technicians, and scriptwriters lost.[93] Moreover, he deems genuine film criticism to have been superseded by a culture of reviewing, one typified by excessive reverence for the persona of the director, and for what the latter says about their work and intentions, at the expense of the intrinsic qualities of their films. Against this backdrop, Godard is conceptually closer nowadays to the late Jean-Claude Biette, who came to insist on the principle of the equal treatment of every individual film on its own merits, irrespective of budget (what we might term a *politique des films*).[94] In many respects, he might also be said to have belatedly come round to the pre–*politique des auteurs* notion advocated by Alexandre Astruc in the late 1940s that "the real auteurs are the producers."[95] This sort of *politique des producteurs* lies behind Godard's paean to Irving Thalberg in 1A, and his recognition of the centrality of Hollywood's "hoodlum-poets" to many of cinema's key works. It is also evident in interviews, in which he has often emphasized the significance of the role played by figures such as John Houseman in relation to Welles; that of European producers, such as Carlo Ponti, Dino de Laurentiis, Georges de Beauregard, Raymond and Robert Hakim, Jean-Pierre Braunberger, Jean-Pierre Rassam, and Alain Sarde; and of the filmmaker-producer tradition from Chaplin and Pagnol to Melville and Coppola. He has also stressed that his admiration for Thalberg and Hughes is genuine: the former, he has suggested, invented a mode of industrial production that is essentially still with us today, and the latter pioneered a less orderly, more individualistic approach. Both were responsible, however indirectly, for some major films, such as (in Hughes's case) *Stromboli*.[96]

Let us look now at Godard's treatment of the constitution of, and dynamics within, the New Wave. First, he considers the Left Bank group (including Chris Marker, Alain Resnais, Agnès Varda) to be an interesting but separate phenomenon. Having considered his dialogue in *Histoire(s) du cinéma* with Marker in chapter 3, we shall focus here on the significance he attaches to Resnais's early work. He has often recounted how, when Resnais's *Hiroshima mon amour* (*Hiroshima, My Love,* 1959) first appeared, he and his New Wave colleagues – who believed they held "the copyright on novelty," as he put it in 2005 – immediately organized and published a roundtable discussion in an attempt to seize back the initiative by debating in their own terms what they perceived to be new and important about the film.[97] Moreover, Godard has frequently expressed his deep admiration for Resnais's early short films: not just *Nuit et brouillard,* which is cited in 1B, but also the latter's filmic studies of painters such as Van Gogh (to whom he devoted two short films in 1947 and 1948), and his remarkable exploration of the archive and memory, *Toute la mémoire du monde* (*All the Memory in the World,* 1956). Collectively, Godard has described these shorts as "absolutely decisive."[98] On a formal level, Resnais's early films on art (he also devoted shorts to Gauguin, and to Picasso's *Guernica*) provided Godard with an enduring lesson in the art of rhythmic montage, the tight reframing of details of paintings and documents, and the power to be derived from making sudden transitions from one detail to the next. His *Guernica* (co-dir. Robert Hessens, 1950), in particular, which is narrated by Maria Casarès (whose presence toward the close of 1B serves to recall both her role therein, as well as that of Death in *Orphée*), contains a catalog of formal strategies – superimposition, textual inserts, the animation of details of paintings and sculptures, and a dramatic use of music – that Godard reprises and extends through video in *Histoire(s) du cinéma*.

As for other filmmakers associated with the New Wave, Godard acknowledges a handful of key satellite figures, such as Jacques Rozier, Louis Malle, and Jacques Demy, and positions Éric Rohmer (or rather Maurice Schérer, to use his real name) as an inspirational older uncle figure and initiator. He dismisses Claude Chabrol as kindly but irrelevant, and treats François Truffaut, as he has done for several decades now, as a seminal critic but – after *Les quatre cents coups* – a distinctly mediocre filmmaker:

> The real problem with Truffaut is that little by little I realized that I didn't like his films much, and that by saying I liked them I was lying. I liked his cinematic drive, and I didn't differentiate much between the two. I liked him, but I felt he shouldn't have made films. And if you tell writers they shouldn't write, they take it badly.[99]

Although Godard's position regarding the poor quality of the majority of Truffaut's films has remained constant since the 1970s, and he has regularly suggested that the latter stepped straight into the shoes vacated by directors such as Claude Autant-Lara (whom Truffaut had of course attacked aggressively and effectively in his criticism), 3B nevertheless ends with a revival and continuation of the dialogue between the two of them. In response to Audrey's observation that Godard had known Becker, Rossellini, Melville, Franju, and Demy, he responds with a lightly adapted version of a phrase delivered by

Julien Davenne, played by Truffaut himself, in *La chambre verte* (*The Green Room*, 1978): "Yes, they were my friends." Ultimately, however, Godard locates the driving force of the movement in the passionate dialogue between himself and Rivette, whom he has acknowledged as a formidable theoretician, and the representative of a sort of "cinematic terrorism": "it was above all Jacques and me, François was on the outside."[100]

The New Wave, according to Godard, was fueled by passionate debate about films between two or three people, and by a cultural hatred for what they disliked, which he has compared to the attitude of the Surrealists.[101] It was, he argues, as we saw in our discussion of cinema as a collaborative art-form, the process of constant debate that gave the movement its energy and intensity, and made the critic-filmmakers fearless in their attacks on others.[102] He has also come to characterize the movement, in line with his broader discourse on art versus culture, in terms of artistic resistance.[103] He articulates this idea in 3B via the theme of money, and in particular through the suggestion that the New Wave put art first, and money at its service, rather than seek to maximize financial returns from the outset. Nowadays, by contrast, he suggests that the moneymaking principle has come to dominate all aspects of the production process.[104] He conveys these ideas through his use of the Sermon on the Mount scene from Pasolini's *The Gospel According to St. Matthew* (1964), in which Jesus (Enrique Irazoqui) declares angrily that one cannot serve both God – here, art and cinema – and money. The title of the other film intercut with Pasolini's account of the life of Christ sums up his argument concisely: Becker's proto–New Wave *Touchez pas au grisbi* – literally "Don't touch the loot."

Guernica (Alain Resnais and Robert Hessens, 1950).

The New Wave has often been presented in terms of amnesia *vis-à-vis* the recent past, especially World War II, and taken to task for its failure to address the pressing social and political issues of the time. As we have seen, Godard does not entirely accept this. He acknowledges that the movement was predominantly made up of middle-class intellectual white men from the regions, whose films – especially his own – were primarily self-reflexive essays about cinema, which "sought less to tell stories than to reflect on how to tell a story."[105] Nevertheless, historically speaking, he still considers the New Wave to have been "in touch with the basics," even if its principal concern was less with the recent or immediate historical real (World War II, Indochina, and Algeria), than with an imaginary world inspired by films and books, which he and his fellow directors staged in an authentic present.[106] Godard insists above all on the significance of the sense of freshness and authenticity that came from the filming of a new generation of actors in real locations. "All we wanted," as he puts it in a series of onscreen titles in 3B, "was to have the right to film boys and girls in a real world, and who, when seeing the film, are astonished to be themselves, and a part of the world." This statement is illustrated, among other things, by a clip from the casting scene in *Grandeur et décadence d'un petit commerce du cinéma*, which exemplifies the quest for new faces, gestures, and voices. In line with his genealogical approach, the New Wave's introduction into their films of a range of uninhibited personalities, fresh bodies, and spontaneous gestures is illustrated in 3B not by an actor or clip from the movement itself, but, in passing, by Marilyn Monroe and, at some length, by Monika (Harriet Andersson) and Harry (Lars Ekborg) in Bergman's *Summer with Monika*. The camera's presentation of Monika's exploration of her naked body, as she and Harry begin to make love, ushers in once again the words "Une vague nouvelle" on the screen.

Implicit in 3B, but explicit elsewhere in Godard's reflections on the New Wave, is a recognition of the coincidence of the movement with the rapid growth of television in France, and a reflection on the implications of this historical conjunction for cinema. Bazin, we recall, had also looked enthusiastically to the example of television in the 1950s:

> Television is reteaching cinema the advantages, which it has long since forgotten, of semi-improvisation and on-the-spot working. There can exist between television and cinema something greater than collaboration: a real symbiosis. While seeking to egotistically take from cinema what it finds most useful, television can inject cinema with a new lease of life.[107]

Alexandre Astruc, too, had enthusiastically anticipated the creation of a more intelligent form of cinema resulting from its encounter with television, and *Cahiers du cinéma* was conceived from the outset as a "Revue du cinéma et du télécinéma."[108] Furthermore, for *Les quatre cents coups* Truffaut drew on the talent of dialogue writers such as Marcel Moussy, whose work he had encountered via the live television drama series *Si c'était vous*; Renoir advocated, and explored in films such as *Le testament du Docteur Cordelier* (*Experiment in Evil*, 1959), cinema's potentially fruitful adoption of the techniques of live television drama, such as multi-camera filming; and Rivette developed his major theoretical idea of a form of post-televisual "live" (*direct*) cinema.[109] Godard, too, was fully alert to the potentially beneficial influence of television on

Gigi (Vincente Minnelli, 1958) +
Marilyn Monroe + *Summer With Monika*
(Ingmar Bergman, 1953) + *The Beautiful
Blond from Bashful Bend* (Preston
Sturges, 1949) = the New Wave.

Adieu Philippine (Jacques Rozier, 1963), and Godard's treatment of the film in 3B.

cinema at the time of the New Wave: his 1959 invented interview with Jean Renoir for *Cahiers du cinéma* was entitled "Television revealed a new cinema to me."[110] Thus, in a variation on the formula cited above, he has characterized the New Wave as "the children of the Liberation and of the Museum, of the advance on receipts, and of *hope in television*."[111] One could argue that a significant part of the novelty of the New Wave, the first explicitly post-televisual film movement, was a product of the filmmakers' familiarity with live broadcast television, which offered a window onto new talent, techniques, and forms. The emblematic film of the movement in this regard is Rozier's *Adieu Philippine* (*Good-bye Philippine*, 1962), which Godard had himself been instrumental in nurturing, not least by introducing Rozier to producer Georges de Beauregard in the first place, and then fulfilling the nominal legal role of technical advisor on the film.[112] *Adieu Philippine* tackled the television-cinema relationship head on, in both its subject matter and its form. Rozier, we recall, had firsthand experience of his subject matter: having graduated from the Idhec, he worked on Renoir's *French Cancan* (1954), before gaining extensive experience as an assistant director on live television drama. His first feature also exemplified the principle of showcasing young untutored actors and attitudes, explored the possibilities and difficulties of capturing the cadences of real speech recorded in synch on location, and addressed the key political event of the period: the Algerian War. It is for all these reasons that in 2A Godard uses a detail of a photograph from the film, which depicts Liliane (Yveline Céry) and Juliette (Stefania Sabatini) standing on a boat waving, to represent the New Wave. This photograph also carries an allusion to Rohmer, who, in his role as editor of *Cahiers du cinéma* at the time, had selected it to adorn the cover of the 1962 special issue of the magazine devoted to the New Wave (from which Godard doubtless recycles it). The film also occupies a prominent position in 3B, in which a shot of Liliane and Horatio (David Tonelli) dancing on a Corsican cliff-top is played in superimposition over imagery of Godard conducting his composition. In the enthusiastic "written 'improvisation'" he used to present the film during the inaugural International Critics' Week at Cannes in May 1962, Godard described *Adieu Philippine* as a sociological report composed by an artist, highlighted Rozier's moving use of landscape, and singled out for particular praise the latter's success in capturing the authentic cadences of real speech and in conveying a genuine sense of the relationship between the characters and the world they inhabit.[113] For Godard it was – and remains – a key film of the period:

> The Association of French Critics presents *Adieu Philippine,* which is quite simply the best French film of recent years.... *Adieu Philippine,* and I write this without jealousy, is the youngest film of the New Wave. Whoever hasn't seen and loved Yveline Céry dance a five-minute cha-cha in a static shot, her eyes riveted on the lens, no longer has the right to talk about cinema on the Croisette at Cannes. Like all the great poets, like Flaherty, Rouch, or Dovzhenko, Jacques Rozier knows how to recompose nature on the basis of the imagination. Because he knows that in the cinema it's a question of one thing alone: stalking the real behind the fictional, and then stalking the imaginary behind the truth.... And Carlton regulars be warned: *Adieu Philippine* is designed for the public at large – which is to say, for the television public.[114]

It was only later, following the rapid spread of television in the 1960s and 1970s, that Godard came to see the New Wave less as a revolutionary

Godard introducing *Adieu Philippine* alongside Jacques Rozier and Henri Sadoul at the 1962 Cannes Film Festival. From *Supplément au voyage en terre "Philippine"* (Jacques Rozier, 2008).

fresh start than as the endpoint of the cinemato-graphic project: "I thought the New Wave, at the time, was a beginning and that everything was going to continue. Now I think it was the door closing. And we didn't realize."[115] More than this, given his positioning of the cinematograph as art's youngest child, he has on numerous oc-casions gone as far as to treat the residual force of the New Wave as the waning of the Western artistic tradition in its entirety.[116] The secret of *seeing* inherited by the New Wave via Langlois from silent cinema, he suggests towards the be-ginning of 3B, is not transmissible. In the next chapter, we shall examine his account of the mutation and continuing decline of cinema in the age of television, and the theory and practice of image making that he developed during the same period.

IF GODARD'S FILMS OF THE LATE 1950S
and early 1960s were nourished in part by a
faith in the potential of television to reinvigorate cinema, his work since the late 1960s has
been infused with a sustained – and often virulent – critique of the younger medium. Within
the overarching narrative of *Histoire(s) du cinéma,* television's role is clear-cut and larger
than life: that of the nefarious Beast – the site
of "absolute evil," or "power in its pure state," as
he has characterized it – destined to vanquish
and devour Beauty (cinema).[1] It is important
to recognize, however, that Godard's actual
relationship with television has been far more
complex than this caricature might suggest. His
work as a whole does not indicate a rejection of
the medium per se, but rather a deep suspicion
of the superficiality, uniformity, and deleterious
effects arising from the manner in which it has
habitually been organized and used. Indeed, he
has often argued that television has enormous
untapped potential and could be extraordinary
if used imaginatively.[2] Furthermore, he has consistently sought to carve out a critical, oppositional space within the framework of broadcast
television, simultaneously foregrounding the
limitations and distortions arising from what
he considers its widespread misuse. It is, after
all, a sort of second home to him, as he likes to
joke: he was born in the Rue Cognacq-Jay in
Paris, a street that would subsequently come to
house the offices and studios of the French public broadcasting organization.[3] Indeed, few major filmmakers have worked so extensively for
television – whether in essays, such as *Changer
d'image* (1982), *Soft and Hard,* or *Pour Thomas
Wainggai* (1991); in made-for-television films,
such as *Le dernier mot, Grandeur et décadence
d'un petit commerce de cinéma,* and *Allemagne*

6

Making Images in the Age of Spectacle

année 90 neuf zéro; or in major theoretical reflections on the medium, such as *Six fois deux, France tour détour deux enfants* and *Histoire(s) du cinéma.* There is an additional sense in which television has been integral to his creative project: in its role as negative exemplar, it has provided the quasi-mythological destructive force against which he has reacted and struggled in the creation of his work, and in opposition to which he has defined cinema as art. This chapter examines the detail of Godard's case against television, and teases out the specificities of his position in relation to it in *Histoire(s) du cinéma.* It then proceeds to investigate his discourse on, and experimentation with, the creation of meaningful poetico-historical images in the age of the mass media.

BEAUTY AND THE BEAST

Let us begin by exploring Godard's treatment of television in *Histoire(s) du cinéma.* Whereas he equates the cinematograph with montage, projection, and revelation, he associates television in 3A with "unlearning" how to see.[4] Since the 1970s he has returned repeatedly to the distinction between cinema as the art of projection and television as the practice of programming: whereas cinema assumed the challenge of constructing an image worthy of life, one through which the injuries of the world might be evoked and momentarily redeemed, television merely broadcasts programs, which do not invite the same type or intensity of identification, nor offer the same promise or degree of discovery and self-discovery.[5] This highly critical assessment of television is evident in *Histoire(s) du cinéma* in the juxtaposition in 1B of Chaplin's composition "Oh! That Cello" (used in *Limelight* [1952])

with a clip from a television music show in which Chaplin is made to appear as if he is mourning the triteness and banality of the medium. The sequence is accompanied by the suggestion on the soundtrack that whereas the cinematograph had promised the childhood of art, television offers merely childishness:

> next one or two world wars / will suffice / to pervert / this state of childhood / and for television / to become / this idiotic and sad / adult / who refuses to see / the hole from which it came / and so restricting itself / to childishness[6]

Godard argues that television turned its back on cinema's discoveries *vis-à-vis* the power of seeing, revelation, and audiovisual communication, and associated itself instead with the traditions of journalism, radio, and the mass media.[7] Thus in 2B and *The Old Place,* the end of cinema is equated with the elderly Major Amberson, (Richard Bennett) in Welles's *The Magnificent Ambersons,* looking back over his life and ahead to death, unsure as to whether he (cinema) will even be recognized in the afterlife (the post-cinematic cultural landscape). Indeed, following André S. Labarthe, Godard has come to characterize cinema in its entirety, in the sense of collectively viewed projected moving images, as a brief but wonderful parenthesis between Edison's kinetoscope (the prototype, in Labarthe's schema, of television) and the subsequent widespread distribution of electronic and digital images – and their reception and consumption by individuals and families on a variety of small screens within the context of the home.[8]

Godard's main lines of attack in relation to television involve scale and language. Thus, in 1B he presents television's "dark victory" over cinema (through reference to Edmund Goulding's

1939 eponymous tearjerker) in terms of a huge reduction in the size of the image. This smaller scale, he suggests, is emblematic of the medium's reduced ambitions and communicative power:

> and if television achieved / Léon Gaumont's dream / of bringing spectacle from all over the world / into the shabbiest / of bedrooms / it was by reducing / the shepherds' giant sky / to the height / of Tom Thumb[9]

Accompanying this line of argument is a critique of the infiltration of both cinema and television by language: if the intrinsically visual medium of the cinematograph had already been invaded by language with the birth of the talkies, the televisual image was not only tiny, but also often literally obscured by onscreen text.[10] He formulated this aspect of his argument succinctly in 1980, when he observed that Hitchcock's death coincided with the invention of teletext, a technological development he considered symptomatic of the creeping suppression of the power of the image.[11] The combination of these two events, he suggested, marked the irreversible passage from one era to another. As the 1980s progressed, he began to argue that any residual expressive visual or audiovisual power that might once have been associated with television had disappeared altogether, and that the manner in which it subordinated image to text was starting to feed back into cinema, weakening the latter still further:

> Anyway, soon there will be no more images on television, but only text ... it has already begun ... you will no longer see an image of carrots which you can buy in a supermarket and the price you may have to pay, because it would take a Flaherty or a Rouch or a Godard to film them, and if they took me I would get interested in the cashier and start to tell a story ... but you will just be told in words, "The carrots are

cooked." That is the cinema of tomorrow, and already that of today.[12]

The other main target of Godard's critique of television in *Histoire(s) du cinéma* is its structural organization. This aspect of his argument is encapsulated in his polemical presentation in 3A of "the triumph of American television / and of its groupies" referencing the history of Universal Pictures, and, by extension, the idea of universality. In interviews, he has provocatively characterized television in terms of a "mild cultural Nazism," and throughout the series he equates its power and uniformity with fascism generally, and Nazism in particular.[13] His critique also brings in sound cinema, which he has described in this context as the "embryo of television."[14] Moreover, he has argued in a historical perspective that there was a direct connection between the talkies and the rise of Nazism in the 1930s:

> The talkies, as if by chance, came at a very precise time. They were invented by the two industrial brothers, America and Germany, by RCA and Tobis. And Tobis is Hitler. Cinema spoke, and Tobis took power on the radio. Sound cinema was invented at that moment, whereas it could have been invented before.[15]

This point, together with the idea of the connection between sound cinema and television, is articulated and illustrated in the sequence in 1B devoted to television's rejection of the legacy of cinema discussed above, notably in the section of that sequence devoted to the development and use of one of the early television camera tubes, the iconoscope. The inference in this passage – when the word "iconoscope" is juxtaposed with an image of Hitler – is that this technological development not only took

Against television: *Deux fois cinquante ans de cinéma français* (Miéville and Godard, 1995), 1A, 1B, and 3A.

place alongside the rise of Nazism, but also, crucially, that it ended up being perverted through misuse into another form of fascism.[16] Godard presents a similarly provocative idea in the closing stages of 1A, in which World War II, the birth of television, Nazism, and the ensuing postwar collapse of European cinema are all linked together through use of the logo of "Fernsehsender Paris" (or Paris-Télévision, as it was also known), the television channel established and run by the Nazis – using a transmitter on the Eiffel Tower – between 1943 and 1944.

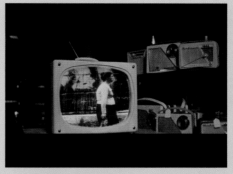

THE TELEVISUAL MUTATION

We shall now take a step back, with a view to contextualizing Godard's depiction of television in *Histoire(s) du cinéma* through reference to his treatment of the medium in his earlier films. His work as a whole offers a concise record of the rise of television, and of its impact on cinema and society. The visibility of the television set, which had already featured onscreen in *Une femme est une femme,* became more prominent in his work from films such as *Une femme mariée* (1964), *Alphaville,* and *Masculin féminin* onward. This increased visibility reflected a growing concern for television in his films' narratives, and coincided with his acquisition – on the recommendation of François Truffaut – of a television set of his own for the first time; he purchased it initially as a tool for identifying new acting talent, and for scrutinizing the performance of established actors in a fresh light.[17] His critique of the wide-ranging effects of television began in earnest in the late 1960s with *Le gai savoir,* and took center stage in Dziga Vertov group films such as *British Sounds* (1969), *Pravda* (1969), *Lotte in Italia* (1970), and *Vladimir et Rosa,* all of

Godard's *Une femme est une femme* (1961), *Vivre sa vie* (1962), and *Alphaville* (1965).

which interrogated its functioning and impact at length. Godard pursued this investigation through dialogue with Anne-Marie Miéville in the Sonimage work. It was particularly central to their first film, *Ici et ailleurs,* which sought to examine the emergence of a debilitating new system – governed by television – determining the production, circulation, and consumption of images and sounds in developed Western societies. Their aim in this film was nothing less than to chart and resist the impact of the "explosion" of television on filmmaking, daily life, and subjectivity.

Godard's work of the following two decades was pervaded by the idea of the "death" of cinema. This concept had already been in circulation since the early 1950s, via the pronouncements of figures such as Debord (in 1952), Welles (in 1953), and Rossellini (in 1963).[18] It quickly became an important notion for Godard as well: in 1965, he humorously responded to a *Cahiers du cinéma* questionnaire regarding the future of cinema with the suggestion that he was optimistically looking forward to its end.[19] It subsequently became central to his thinking; by the mid-1990s, the notion that the cinema was somehow "mortal" (*Deux fois cinquante ans de cinéma français*), and unlikely to survive much longer had been a refrain in his work for over a decade. Here is how he put it in 1987, when, as he often did in interviews and in his self-representation in his work, he drew a direct correlation between his own aging body and the winding down of cinema:

> To my eyes, twilight is the bearer of hope rather than of despair. I'm beginning to find something beautiful and very human in the cinema, which makes me want to go on making films until I die. And I think that I'll probably die at the same time as the cinema,

such as it was invented. . . . The existence of the cinema can't exceed, roughly, the length of a human life: between eighty and a hundred and twenty years. It's something that will have been transitory, ephemeral.[20]

Godard's work of the 1980s returned constantly to this idea of the decline of cinema in the age of television. In *Changer d'image,* for instance, he argued that the former had been usurped, and economically and aesthetically *occupied,* by the latter. Similarly, in *Lettre à Freddy Buache* (1981), he illustrated his observation that cinema was on the verge of dying, its potential unfulfilled, with a playful scene in which we see him and his crew trying to film on the emergency hard shoulder of a motorway, and protesting to a police officer that there is indeed an emergency: the light is fading, and cinema is about to disappear. His conviction that cinema was steadily deteriorating can be charted through each of his subsequent films: *Prénom Carmen* was "in memoriam small movies"; *Soft and Hard* was situated in the "era of the last cinema screenings"; in *Grandeur et décadence d'un petit commerce de cinéma* – which explicitly addressed the question of whether it was possible any longer to make cinema in the context of the omnipotence of television – Godard, playing himself, declared that cinema had now started to go backward; and following the making of *Détective,* he returned to the metaphor of occupation, suggesting that he had shot the film "under the Occupation – of cinema by television and all types of magazines."[21] And lest we be fooled by the number of films that continued to be made during and after the 1980s, Godard had an answer ready: bad cinema flourishes when occupied – whether by the Germans during World War II, or by television since the 1960s.[22]

One of the principal conclusions that Godard drew from the Sonimage work was that as audiences started devoting more and more time to the consumption of television than to other leisure activities, human perception had dulled. As the Michel Marot character put it in his summary of the findings of the videotape made by Odette (Miéville) in *Comment ça va,* the media were responsible for a contagious debilitation of our ability to *see:*

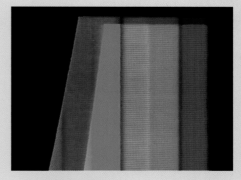

> What was Odette ultimately saying with this little video? That television and the press were rotten. And since we watched and read them, that the look was also rotten, as were our mouths and hands. In short that we had cancer, us first of all, but we didn't say so. And we didn't say so because we didn't know, and we didn't know because we didn't want to know, and we didn't want to know because we couldn't, and we couldn't because we didn't show it, and we didn't show it because we didn't want to.

Much of the imagery of the Sonimage films is peppered with shots of television monitors, which might be interpreted in this context as a visualization of the idea of cinema being eaten away from within by electronic televisual "tumors." Godard pursued this provocative hypothesis regarding the "cancerous" or "radio-active" effects of the media on subjectivity and creativity in the 1980s in works such as *Meeting Woody Allen:*

> Godard: Have you the feeling that something has really changed?
> Woody Allen: In terms of television?
> Godard: In terms of maybe making movies because of TV, of the way TV's accepting movies, or showing movies....
> Allen: It's a much smaller, petty experience. I don't think it's got any size to it, and I think it's badly hurt the cinema, certainly in the United States. I don't know about you, but it certainly has hurt the cinema here....

The omnipotence of television: *Grandeur et décadence d'un petit commerce de cinéma* (Godard, 1985).

Godard: Do you have the feeling that I have a bit, or maybe even a lot, that this TV power affects your creation? Exactly like radioactivity can have a harmful effect on your health.

Allen: You mean the actual . . .

Godard: The explosion of TV. Maybe you can look at it as radioactivity. So how many rems, cultural rems. . . . I think I receive too many cultural rems from TV.

Allen: Too much intake of . . .

Godard: Yes. And that it affects, it has affected my creative potential. Do you have any of this feeling at all? . . .

For example, the shots – the idea of which I like very much in *Hannah and Her Sisters* – of the New York buildings that you love. I like the idea very much, but I have the feeling that if you lived in a country where people had never heard of television, including yourself, you would *not* have done the shots like that.

Allen: This I don't know. It's too difficult to question. It's too hypothetical.

In a similar vein, Godard has evoked the insidious effects of television by referencing the title of Jacques Rivette's first critical article, "Nous ne sommes plus innocents" (We are no longer innocent).[23] Whereas Rivette referred to his generation's relationship to cinema history, Godard appropriated the phrase in the 1980s as a way of suggesting that all filmmaking had now come to be intrinsically tainted a priori by televisual "radiation."[24] An "irreversible mutation," he argued, had taken place, sparing no one, and affecting the ambition and quality of all films.[25] As a result, he went on, the desire and energy of all those involved in filmmaking had decreased, and television's ultimate effect had been that of lowering the standards and results for everyone involved in film production, even those alert to the dangers. The inevitable result, he argued throughout the 1980s, was a situation in which the average mainstream film was invariably less good than its equivalent before the televisual

era: "We don't make the films we're capable of making. Mocky doesn't make the films that he's capable of making. Verneuil does, and even he, at his level, is starting to go downhill."[26]

Godard identified in particular three main effects of the impact of television on cinema: a decline in the art of framing; a disappearance of the idea of a film as a succession of self-contained shots, each with their own internal logic and coherence; and a rapidly growing amnesia in relation to cinema history. He was already developing his critique of the lack of attention to framing in contemporary cinema in 1980: "I think that today people no longer know how to frame, and confuse the frame with the viewfinder."[27] His reflection on the centrality of the individual shot (*plan* in French, which means not only "shot," but also "plan" and "blueprint") can be traced to around the same period. It is visible, for instance, in *Lettre à Freddy Buache,* which is premised – through reference to Bonnard and Picasso – on the idea of a quest to construct just three shots, whose combination might offer an adequate evocation of the town of Lausanne. His lamenting of growing cultural amnesia, and, specifically, of a loss of memory regarding the history of the cinema, goes back even further. As noted in chapter 1, he and Jean-Pierre Gorin had already been conscious, when working on *Tout va bien,* of their inability to replicate some of the discoveries of their predecessors. By the time of *King Lear,* which is situated "after Chernobyl" – that is, after the catastrophic mutation engendered by television – the themes of amnesia, forgetting, and loss had come to constitute the film's very subject matter. After Chernobyl, everything (electricity, houses, cars, and so on) disappeared, then gradually started to come back – everything, that is, apart from culture. By the late 1980s, therefore, as television had started to impose itself as a garrulous but critically indiscriminate electronic cinematheque, it was no longer, for Godard, just a question of filmmakers losing touch with their heritage, and so forgetting how to film, but also one of audiences, for whom the cinema and art of the past were rapidly becoming an increasingly blurred memory. The history of cinema, as he suggested in works such as *Deux fois cinquante ans de cinéma français,* has faded remarkably rapidly, leaving only a homogeneous morass of old films lodged in the popular imagination. As Serge Daney put it in conversation with Godard in 1988, all sense of chronology seemed to be dissolving, but at the same time, films from the past had started to acquire a similar look, their differences less marked than their shared features as "cinema films."[28] At the same time, even mediocre or frankly bad films had started to look extraordinary.[29] As a result, Daney found to his surprise that his role as a critic had shifted noticeably during the 1980s – from that of analyzing and comparing individual films and filmmakers to that of defending and advocating the merits of cinema as a totality.

Daney's thinking was heavily indebted to Godard. The influence, however, flowed both ways, and in the 1980s and early 1990s, the two were often working on parallel tracks. The sense of flicking from film to film in the early episodes of *Histoire(s) du cinéma,* for instance, can be seen in part as an illustration of Daney's advocacy of the use of the remote control to deprogram the television schedules and to create a more personal form of television through the playful art of "zapping" (channel surfing).[30] Daney and Godard also echoed one another on other issues, such as the televisualization of film form; the

The quest for a shot in *Lettre à Freddy Buache* (Godard, 1981).

The fading memory of cinema in 3B and *Deux fois cinquante ans de cinéma français* (Miéville and Godard, 1995).

desertion of the cinemas by the public (a major concern in France in the 1980s); the waning of projection; the marginalization of cinema to the status of one of a range of proliferating electronic distractions; and the generalized absorption of cinema's residual power into the homogenous mass of what Daney dubbed the "visual."[31] A particularly significant shared concern was the contamination of the film image by advertising. In a powerful article on the "incest" between cinema and advertising written in 1988, Daney demonstrated how *Out of Africa* (Sydney Pollack, 1985), despite giving the superficial appearance of cinema, was in fact impregnated throughout with the logic of advertising.[32] Godard formulated a similar idea a few years later, when he recounted that he had gone to see *The Sheltering Sky* (Bernardo Bertolucci, 1990) at the cinema, dozed off during the opening advertisements, and woken up once the film had started, but found no significant difference in what he saw.[33] Perhaps their most important area of shared interest and concern, however, was the significance of the differing contexts in which cinema and television are consumed: the fundamental difference between experiencing films with strangers in the darkened theater, away from one's family (and the transgressive promise of this experience), and watching television at home (including films on television), was central to Godard's discourse of the 1970s and 1980s, and to Daney's of the 1980s and 1990s.

MAKING IMAGES, MAKING HISTORY

Godard's critique of television provides the backdrop not only to his repeated attempts to work in television, but also to his theorization of what might constitute a real image in the age of the mass media, and to his sustained efforts to make them. This brings us to a key aspect of his historical theorem: if cinema, thanks to its natural capacity for montage, effortlessly performed the work of a historian, the task of the historian is, in turn, to make history through the creation of poetico-historical imagery. As we saw in chapter 1, he was moving intuitively toward formulating this idea as early as 1968, and it is clear in hindsight that his theory and practice of historical image making grew out of his antecedent conceptualization and practical exploration of filmmaking in terms of the montage (or what he came to call, following Malraux, the *rapprochement*) of disparate objects, people, or events. We shall now examine, therefore, the development of his image-making practice, the models that inspired him, and the type of historical imagery he creates in *Histoire(s) du cinéma*.

In the 1980s, Godard consistently drew a distinction between the superficiality of the copies and reproductions proliferating in the print and audiovisual media and the depth and power of true poetic images: "People use the word 'image,' even though that's not what they are anymore."[34] To help him distinguish between reproductions (or pictures) and images, he has drawn on the Eisensteinian distinction between *izobrazhenie* (usually translated as "representation," and related to the individual shot) and *obraz* ("image").[35] He has, in turn, equated Eisenstein's terms with the words "picture" and "image" in English, and mapped them onto the Braudelian distinction between the measured profundity of *longue durée* history, and the breathless superficiality of the *histoire événementielle* discussed in chapter 3. He

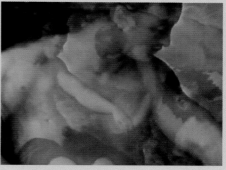

Tintoretto in *Grandeur et décadence d'un petit commerce de cinéma* (Godard, 1985).

explored this opposition – between *izobrazhenie* ("picture") on the one hand, and *obraz* ("image") on the other hand – in the scene in *Grandeur et décadence d'un petit commerce de cinéma,* in which independent film producer Gaspard Bazin (Jean-Pierre Léaud) evaluates his colleagues' and employees' artistic sensibility by showing them various classic paintings, notably Tintoretto's *The Origin of the Milky Way* (c. 1575) and *Ariadne, Venus, and Bacchus* (1576), and asking them how many characters each contains. Most see only the pictures (the literal number of characters); almost nobody sees the images (the subjects of the paintings).

A true image, Godard has long argued, is always the result of the combination, tension, and dynamic interplay among a number of component elements. He has rehearsed this idea repeatedly in his work and in interviews, and related it a number of models. He explored it in particular in his video work through the use of superimposition as a means of bringing together two or more visual sources within the same frame. In a modular perspective, Claude Shannon's information theory, which Godard and Miéville explored in some detail in *Comment ça va* (and where they also, significantly, first used superimposition extensively), constituted a particularly important early source of inspiration.[36] Information theory offered a model based on the principle of the separation of elements, each of which carries a potential communicative charge, and whose combination expresses a measurable quantity of information once that potential is resolved. A little later, Raymond Queneau's poem "L'explication des métaphores" (Explanation of metaphors) became another key reference.[37] In the course of a televised discussion of *Les enfants jouent à la*

Russie in 1993, Godard took a piece of paper out of his pocket and read the following extract from the poem: "The image is a relationship. It's either two distant things that we bring together, or two things that are close together that we separate. 'As thin as a hair, as vast as the dawn.' A hair is not an image; dawn is not an image; it's their relationship that creates the image."[38] This particular line from Queneau functions in the poem as an exemplary metaphor, whose meaning and operation is interrogated throughout. The principal reference, however, through which Godard has elaborated his theory of the image since the beginning of the 1980s – it is cited or adapted in *Passion, Grandeur et décadence d'un petit commerce du cinéma, King Lear,* one of his advertisements for Marithé and François Girbaud, *Hélas pour moi, JLG/JLG,* and *4B* (in which it is recycled from *JLG/JLG*) – is that provided by Pierre Reverdy's short poetic text *L'image* (1918). The opening lines of this text, which in fact originally developed out of a discussion between Reverdy and André Breton, were subsequently used by Breton to frame his first Surrealist manifesto. Here is the English-language version recited by Professor Pluggy (Godard) in *King Lear,* in which it plays a central role in establishing the film's intertwined themes of showing, seeing, projection, and image creation. It is reasonably faithful to the original:

The image is a pure creation of the soul.

It cannot be born of a comparison, but of a reconciliation of two realities that are more or less far apart.

The more the connections between these two realities are distant and true, the stronger the image will be, and the more it will have emotive power.

Two realities that have no connection cannot be drawn together usefully. There is no creation of an image.

Two contrary realities will not be drawn together. They oppose one another.

One rarely obtains forces and power from this opposition.

An image is not strong because it is *brutal* or *fantastic* – but because the association of ideas is distant and true.

The result that is obtained immediately controls the truth of the association.

Analogy is a medium of creation – It is a *resemblance of connections; and* the power or virtue of the created image depends on the nature of these connections.

What is great is not the image – but the emotion it provokes; if the latter is great, one esteems the image at its measure.

The emotion thus provoked is true because it is born outside of all imitation, all evocation, and all resemblance.[39]

This text, and its extended *mise en scène* in *King Lear,* offers a succinct distillation of the other models on which Godard had drawn previously. It also provides a concise summary of his theory and practice of historical image making in *Histoire(s) du cinéma.* He has illustrated the idea of "the reconciliation of two realities that are more or less far apart" in a variety of ways. For example, it is an additional sense – alongside the connotations discussed earlier of the idea of the establishment of community, and of the formation of a connection between past and present – of the recurrent motif in the series of hands reaching out to and clasping one another. It also offers a way of interpreting one of the key figures in his work generally, and in *Histoire(s) du cinéma* in particular: that of the heterosexual couple. Clips depicting emotional or sexual attraction within male-female couples always carry a self-reflexive charge in the series *vis-à-vis* his discourse on the poetic image. So, too, does the related motif of the kiss, which has been central to Godard's work for many years (at

one point he was considering making a film entitled simply *The Kiss*).[40] Thus, his use in 4A of the spectacular firework display from Hitchcock's *To Catch a Thief* (1955) – which in the source film accompanied John (Cary Grant) and Frances's (Grace Kelly) explosive first kiss (which we see briefly, together with another slow-motion kiss, between Scottie [James Stewart] and Judy/Madeleine [Kim Novak] in *Vertigo*) – offers a concise evocation of the idea of the successful formation of a poetic image.

The *rapprochement* of the constituent components of the image in Godard's work often leads to the creation of productive puzzles or riddles. It is worth noting in this context that he has explicitly characterized himself in interviews in recent years as a maker of jigsaws, and in 1B he foregrounds the idea of the riddle-like structure of much of the imagery of *Histoire(s) du cinéma* by incorporating an extract from the soundtrack of his own *Week-end* of a reading of one of Lewis Carroll's logic brainteasers.[41] As he has been at pains to point out, his technique of *rapprochement* in no way implies a direct equivalence between the various elements that he brings together, but rather a process of dynamic interactivity, and the production of critical thought, resulting from the effects of what Vertov termed the *interval* between them.[42] As Gilles Deleuze put it in a perceptive early discussion of Godard's poetics in terms of differentiation in mathematics, and of disappearance in physics, given one element, another has to be selected, "which will induce an interstice between the two."[43] Thus, the Godardian image does not offer or constitute a judgment in and of itself; on the contrary, like cinema when it is functioning healthily along the lines of the judicial model discussed in chapter 4, it invites interest, contemplation,

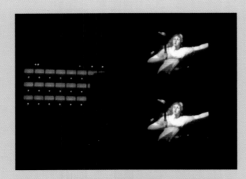

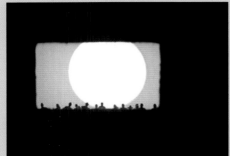

King Lear (Godard, 1987).

critical reflection, and – only then – judgment on the part of the viewer.

Besides the longstanding significance to Godard of Reverdy's *L'image,* we should also recall the importance to him of the practical example of historical image making by the various artist-historians discussed in chapter 3, such as Michelet, Péguy, Malraux, and Langlois. Above all, however, we should reemphasize the centrality to his thought and practice of Walter Benjamin's theory of the historical image. Although Benjamin's "Theses on the Philosophy of History" are an important reference in *Les enfants jouent à la Russie* and *Hélas pour moi,* his writings are barely cited in *Histoire(s) du cinéma* itself. By contrast, in the work that Godard has made since completing the series, he has related his thinking on the image to Benjamin in increasingly explicit terms, adopting in particular the latter's proposition – in both the "Theses" and *The Arcades Project* – of the idea of a poetic "constellation" linking past and present.[44] In *The Old Place,* for instance, he and Miéville present a succession of simple *rapprochements* under the heading "Logic of Images" (a sequence that is highly reminiscent of *Comment ça va*) and relate their practice directly to the Benjaminian idea of the fleeting resurrection of the past in an image. In this sequence, Godard summarizes on the soundtrack a key reflection on the image from *The Arcades Project:* "It is not that what is past casts its light on what is present, or what is present casts its light on what is past; rather, the image is the place wherein that which has been, comes together in a flash in the now, to form a constellation."[45] Godard had already visualized this flash, together with the concept of the successful creation of an image, in the form of burning sparklers, which he used to illustrate

the Reverdy sequence in *King Lear.* In *The Old Place,* which reprises the kiss sequence from *To Catch a Thief* previously used in 4A, the idea of the momentary connection between past and present through the formation of a poetic constellation is illustrated by the same shot of fireworks from Hitchcock's film, and is followed shortly afterward by Godard's summary of his model on the soundtrack: "The concept is that of *rapprochement.* Just as stars approach one another even as they are moving away from one another, driven by the laws of physics, for example, to form a constellation, so, too, certain things and thoughts approach one another to form one or more images." It is, simultaneously, an optimistic and bleak vision of history: optimistic because the past is not entirely dead; pessimistic because resurrecting the past is a difficult, haphazard affair, and the flashes of it that we are able to glimpse in the present in the form of images also serve to remind us of the extent of the surrounding void, where the remainder of it lies dormant and forgotten.

Godard devotes a good deal of *Histoire(s) du cinéma* and related works to presenting and experimenting with his theory of the historical image. It is important to note, however, that the series is far from being made up entirely of the type of imagery he advocates; on the contrary, much of it comprises more prosaic expository passages, which are based less on the principle of *rapprochement* than on a compositional method that uses the simple technique of placing one picture after (or on top of) another to further the narrative, develop a theme, or present a specific idea. Nevertheless, his later work generally – and the series in particular – is peppered with thought-provoking Benjaminian historical image-riddles, which are rooted in the principle of the *rapprochement* of unrelated objects, people, and events. Sometimes he brings together two past phenomena, whether from the same or from different eras; elsewhere he sets a past event in tension with the present. His imagery often appears to rely on simple, exploratory, and seemingly off-the-cuff juxtapositions; elsewhere, it takes the form of more considered, polished set pieces. In the former category, we might situate his *rapprochement* in *Hélas pour moi* of the *Communist Manifesto* and *Alice's Adventures in Wonderland* (which, he observes, were written at roughly the same time). Among the many examples in *Histoire(s) du cinéma*, we might point to his *rapprochement* of Georges Méliès and Howard Hughes in 1A; the wars in the Balkans in the 1870s and 1990s in 3A; and *La belle et la bête* and *Paisan* in 3B. In the "Logic of Images" section of *The Old Place*, he and Miéville showcase a number of similar basic *rapprochements* to illustrate their model, such as that of a photograph of Brigitte Bardot and another of Marceau (Julien Carette) in *La règle du jeu* – both of whom are holding rabbits. Although the examples in this sequence are all very simple, they have the potential – as Odette (Miéville) had observed long ago in *Comment ça va* – to set in motion a train of thought that can lead to a more complex set of reflections or questions. In the latter category (that of the carefully conceived set pieces), we would situate, for instance, the montage based on the George Stevens material discussed in chapter 4. We would also include in this category the powerful sequence in 3A constructed around the *rapprochement* of two very different, unrelated train journeys: the first taken by a number of celebrated French actors in 1942 on a tour of

German film studios; and a second made by Jewish writer Irène Nemirovsky, who was deported to Auschwitz from the same station the same year. This montage, as Godard put it succinctly, offers simultaneously a story, a thought, and the possibility for the viewer to formulate a judgment.[46]

Godard's most extended reflection on historical image making in *Histoire(s) du cinéma* comes in 4B. Having suggested a range of responses to his own question regarding the true nature of history, through reference to some of the figures he most cherishes (Péguy, Malraux, Braudel, and Cioran), he brings together a barrage of self-reflexive images of images: an extract from Reverdy (recycled from *JLG/JLG*); the Bresson quotation on the combination of elements ("Bring together things that have as yet never been brought together"); Mr. Alien (Woody Allen) stitching together strips of celluloid in his editing suite at the end of *King Lear*; a fragment from Beckett's short text *L'image* (used in 1B, and later in *Film socialisme*);[47] stills of Eisenstein and Stroheim at work editing, and of Buster Keaton tangled up in lengths of film in *Sherlock Junior*; a variety of stills or clips depicting couples from films such as Max Ophüls's *Madame de . . . (The Earrings of Madame de . . . , 1953)*, Marcel Carné's *La Marie du port (Marie of the Port, 1950)*, and Howard Hawks's *His Girl Friday* (1940); and a key image, which has a lengthy history in his work, based on the *rapprochement* of the terms "Jew" and "Muslim." This latter image has its origins in a specific time and place: the use of the term "Muselmann" in the concentration camps to designate prisoners in the final stages of starvation, exhaustion, and despair. According to Godard, he first encountered the use of this word in this context in anthropologist and resistance fighter Germaine Tillion's account of her incarceration in Ravensbrück.[48] Tillion's book was published in 1973, and Godard and Miéville immediately incorporated her observation into *Ici et ailleurs,* a film also sampled in this important sequence devoted to the image in 4B. After *Ici et ailleurs,* Godard returned to the combination of the terms "Jew" and "Muslim" several times, notably in a letter to the Palestinian writer and historian Elias Sanbar (who had acted as his and Gorin's translator during the shooting of *Jusqu'à la victoire* in 1969–70) in the special issue of *Cahiers du cinéma* he edited in 1979, and later in both *Notre musique* and *Film socialisme.*[49] Their significance for him lies in part in their embodiment of his idea of cinema's predictive function, in so far as the appearance of the word "Muselmann" in the concentration camps might be interpreted in hindsight as an anticipatory indicator of the subsequent turbulent history of the Middle East. However, his use of the two terms also constitutes an engagement with ethical debates surrounding the origins and significance of the use of the word "Muselmann" in the concentration camps, which runs from Tillion and Primo Levi (in *The Drowned and the Saved*), to Zdzislaw Ryn and Stanislaw Klodzinski (who co-authored a study of its appearance in the camps), and to Giorgio Agamben's theorization of the "Muselmann" as the exemplary, privileged "complete witness" to the Holocaust.[50] In a passage that resonates closely with Godard's use of the term in *Histoire(s) du cinéma* and elsewhere, Agamben, drawing on Foucault, has traced the successive stages in the process of the degradation of the Jews at the hands of the Nazis: transformation of the Jew

The Old Place (Miéville and Godard, 1998).

into a deportee; of the deportee into a prisoner; and of the prisoner into a "Muselmann." "Beyond the 'Muselmann,'" concludes Agamben, "lies only the gas chamber."[51] In the context of Godard's discourse on cinema and history, the Jew, reduced to a "Muselmann," is the ultimate witness to the atrocities of the Holocaust that cinema failed to be.

In his post–*Histoires(s) du cinéma* work, Godard proceeded to identify yet further models, through reference to which he has continued to redefine his theory and practice of image making. In *Notre musique,* for instance, he relates it to Baudelaire's "Correspondences," an extract of which is read by a woman who picks up a copy of *Les fleurs du mal* by chance from a pile of books in the burnt-out shell of the National and University Library of Bosnia and Herzegovina in Sarajevo.[52] In view of Benjamin's well-known fascination for Baudelaire's model, it is perhaps not surprising that Godard should have come to engage with it as well. Baudelaire's evocative vision of artistic expression in terms of the creation of correspondences between colors, smells, and sounds from among the "forest of symbols," which communicate lived experience to us via "prolonged echoes," provides one of the most suggestive models for Godard's later image-making practice. When I suggested to him during an 2005 interview that Baudelaire's poem provides a concise summary of the theme of his lecture in *Notre musique,* Godard agreed entirely. In addition to this engagement with Baudelaire, he has also proposed another simple variation on his idea of *rapprochement:* the concept of the image as the product of the combination of a shot (*champ*) and reverse shot (*contre-champ*).[53] This is the model he proposes in his staged lecture in *Notre musique,* which he presents by referencing Elsinore Castle. He has explained this reference as follows:

> A good example of a real shot/reverse shot is one I took from a book by German physicist Werner Heisenberg, who, on visiting his friend Niels Bohr before the war, arrived at Elsinore Castle. Here the shot is the castle, the reverse shot the description "Hamlet's Castle." In this case the image is created by the text. It's what poetry does – like two stars whose *rapprochement* creates a constellation.[54]

This story of Heisenberg's recollection of his discovery of Elsinore Castle is one of the recurrent examples of the workings of the image offered by Godard in his later work. Prior to its reference in *Notre musique,* Godard had used it in *Les enfants jouent à la Russie, For ever Mozart,* and *3B.* In *Les enfants jouent à la Russie,* in a sequence largely illustrated by material from the Reverdy image sequence from *King Lear,* in which it is combined with footage from Olivier's *Hamlet,* Elsinore Castle is explicitly equated with *izobrazhenie,* and the description "Hamlet's Castle" with *obraz.* In his synoptic presentation of the same idea in *3B,* in which he reuses the same *Hamlet* material, he distills his model into a brief, cryptic onscreen formulation: "when one says Elsinore / one says nothing / when one says Hamlet / that says it all." To emphasize his point, these words are followed immediately by the title "Montage, mon beau souci," which is superimposed over one of Eisenstein's lions. In both sequences, the idea of the successful formation of an image is illustrated by a slow-motion shot of Hamlet (Olivier) apparently soaring like a bird through the air (in the original narrative, he has just launched himself from the balcony onto his murderous uncle below).

Against the backdrop of the flood of reproductions in circulation on television, in the mass

The formation of an image: *Hamlet* (Laurence
Olivier, 1948) and *Battleship Potemkin* (Sergei
Eisenstein, 1925) in 3B, and Hitchcock's *To
Catch a Thief* (1955) and *Vertigo* (1958) in 4A.

media, and on the internet, Godard set himself the task long ago, in his capacity as a poet, of tirelessly exploring the possibility of genuine communication. This self-appointed mission was already explicit in the subtitle of *Six fois deux: on and under communication.* Guided by figures as diverse as Bresson, Shannon and Weaver, Queneau, Reverdy, Baudelaire, and Benjamin, Godard has tirelessly pursued his quest to communicate through poetry, and *Histoire(s) du cinéma* is the theoretical and material culmination of that quest in relation to history. However, his latest feature film, *Film socialisme,* suggests that something new may be stirring in his work, and that he may now be moving away from his longstanding investigation of history and audiovisual historiography. In a scene in this film, Otto Goldberg (Jean-Marc Stehlé), in response to the Moscow police detective's (Olga Riazanova) allusion to Godard's image making in terms of the comparison of "the incomparable from the non-comparable," replies a little wearily, "No, no. That's all over." If indeed it is "all over," it will be extremely interesting to observe how his thinking and practice evolve over the coming years, where this apparent move away from poetic historiography might lead, and whether such a move includes a reevaluation of his underlying theory of the image.

This closing chapter focuses on the Gallimard books and ECM CDs of *Histoire(s) du cinéma,* and on their relationship with the source videos. These two versions of the series, which have attracted little critical attention to date, are considered here through reference to Godard's prior work as a graphic and sound artist. As we have already noted, in the context of the organic nature of Godard's multifaceted œuvre, and given the principle of metamorphosis that runs through it, *Moments choisis des Histoire(s) du cinéma* and *Voyage(s) en utopie* can also be thought of as further variations on the series. To do justice to Godard's exhibition would require a separate study, so we shall set it aside here. We begin, however, with a brief discussion of *Moments choisis des Histoire(s) du cinéma* before turning in greater detail to the books and CDs. The rationale behind the making of the abbreviated 35 mm version of the series appear to have been relatively straightforward: financial considerations; a homecoming, in the sense of a reentry into the space of projection, the cinema theater; and, as Nicole Brenez has suggested, the return of selected fragments of the series to 35 mm film following their passage through video.[1] The difference in look and feel between the imagery of *Moments choisis des Histoire(s) du cinéma* and that of the DVD version of *Histoire(s) du cinéma* is noticeable straight away, and will only increase over time as the prints of the former acquire the familiar signs of wear and tear associated with celluloid. As Jean-Louis Leutrat has observed, in the distilled 35 mm version of selected "moments" from the videos, Godard has cut much of the comparatively conventional expository material used in 1A and 1B

The Metamorphoses

Room 1 (Today) in *Voyage(s) en utopie* (2006).

Photo: M. Witt.

relating to the foundation of Hollywood, and foregrounded instead the mythical dimension of the genealogy of cinema.[2] He has also rightly noted that the reordering of material in *Moments choisis des Histoire(s) du cinéma* includes a significant reduction in the prominence of the Orphic narrative, a change that is in line with Godard's retreat from his initial investment in the idea of cinema as Orpheus, discussed in chapter 4.[3] Finally, although there are few major textual changes, the synoptic 35 mm version allowed Godard to incorporate one or two significant additional elements, including an extract from a text about cameras written by James Agee (joint dedicatee of 3A), which he has long admired (he had previously cited it in the pressbook for *Sauve qui peut [la vie]*, and in *For ever Mozart*), and which he had recorded for use in the series but did not use.[4]

GLUE AND SCISSORS

Let us begin with the books of *Histoire(s) du cinéma*, which we shall situate within the context of Godard's earlier output as a graphic artist and in relation to his longstanding critique of the conventional illustrative use of film stills and other images by critics and historians in cinema-related magazines and books. He has long argued that in such publications, the image is virtually always redundant, the choice of imagery arbitrary, and its use banal: "[F]ilm criticism is done by literary people; criticizing a film involves writing 'this is good,' 'so-and-so acts well,' 'so-and-so acts badly,' 'extraordinary spectacle, beautiful colors,' things like that; and then they put a photo so that the reader of the journal can be certain that this is indeed the film

under discussion."[5] As he put it in 1979 in a letter to the editors of *Cahiers du cinéma*, in a critique of their "Photo special" edition of the magazine: "[P]eople only need a photo to use as a deposit or alibi for their page of writing."[6] The result of this bias toward writing, he has consistently argued, is that the critical, revelatory, and communicative potential of the imagery is undervalued, if not neglected altogether:

> I'm always surprised by the way photos are arranged and laid out in film history books. The photos are generally used as illustrations of theses already articulated in the text. A photo of Griffith is put next to the page on which Griffith is talked about, which is a bit simplistic, and we don't learn much. The author may well have seen something, but in my opinion, reading their books afterward, the things that Sadoul or Bazin saw, I have no way of seeing what they saw; that's what bothers me.[7]

Godard's aim in the *Histoire(s) du cinéma* books was to use image and text to create an historical work, which, like the videos, is both creative and critical in the manner in which it is conceived and organized. His intention, as he made clear, was to provide a concrete example of an alternative method of doing history in book form, which makes equal use of image and text.[8] The books are not, he has emphasized, the original archaeological investigation, but a sort of memorial résumé: "I filmed the Trojan War, then lost it, but I filed a report, and this is it."[9]

This defense of the role of the image in film books and journals should be understood in the context of Godard's graphic art practice of the 1970s and 1980s, and indeed of the late 1960s, when, as part of his exploration of modes of expression untainted by what he was already beginning to decry as the tyranny of the word, he attended drawing lessons with the artist Gérard Fromanger over a six-month period.[10] The idea of drawing as a more direct, less prescriptive means of expression than writing was a recurrent theme in interviews with Godard in the 1970s. The fruits of his experiences with Fromanger are visible in the storyboards of projects such as *Moi je* and *Comment ça va* and in his use of the video pen to write and sketch over the image in *Six fois deux*. In Montreal, he recalled with regret that he had once been able to draw well, but had since lost the ability to do so, and suggested that the use of drawing rather than writing as a means of taking visual "notes" might provide an alternative – and potentially more productive – means of communication to writing.[11] Traces of Godard's defense of the power of drawing, which forms part of his wider discourse on "seeing," also fed into some of his finished works of the 1970s: *Comment ça va* where it is a central concern; the long sequence in *Pas d'histoire*, episode 4a of *Six fois deux*, which pursues a humorous critique of the logic of market capitalism through the drawing of cartoons; and the reflections of the prisoner in episode 5a of the same series, *Nous trois*, who attempts to evade the repetitive memories in which he finds his imagination trapped when attempting to communicate via language, by expressing his thoughts through drawing instead.

The turning point in Godard's activities as a graphic artist coincided with that in his audiovisual work, and resulted from his acquisition in the early 1970s of an ostensibly banal piece of equipment: a good quality photocopier. Cherished along with his new video equipment, this machine was put to use as a creative tool for composing quickly and cheaply in reproductions of reasonably good quality, without the expense and time delay of professional offset printing. Crucially, it allowed him to "think with his hands," and to generate image-text propositions for film projects to send to producers and potential collaborators:

> I have a very good Xerox machine, and sometimes, instead of writing letters, I use an image, which gives me an idea. I put some words on it – "Why don't we make something on that?" – and send it to someone. It's more like painting and sculpture. And when you receive the money you start to think, "What the hell can I do?" like having paintings commissioned.[12]

This method led to the production of a string of large-scale collage works at the end of the 1970s, and established a way of working that would later culminate in the *Histoire(s) du cinéma* books. In this context, the published image-text outline of his unrealized American project on the life of Bugsy Siegel, which was ostensibly work in progress for a forthcoming film, is of particular note. In fact, like Jean Epstein's *Bonjour cinéma* and Chris Marker's "L'Amérique rêve" (America dreams, 1959), it is better considered a finished "film," imagined and expressed on paper, than a conventional script.[13] As Godard himself observed, by the time he eventually abandoned the project, he felt that he had effectively made the film three times: "[E]ach time I did the photocopied photos, my pleasure in composing images was satisfied."[14] We should also note in particular the pressbook he made for *Sauve qui peut (la vie)* and the special issue of *Cahiers du cinéma* he edited in 1979. The latter, which is one of his major works in any medium, incorporates a humorous critique of the conventional illustrative use of imagery in film magazines in the form of two blank rectangles in the middle of the text of

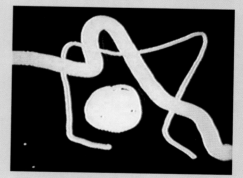

Film-tract no 1968 (dir. Gérard Fromanger, technician Jean-Luc Godard, 1968), *Leçons de choses* and *Pas d'histoire* (episodes 2a and 4a of Miéville and Godard's *Six fois deux,* 1976), and Godard's copy of Nicolas de Staël's *Nu couché bleu* (1955) in 1A.

an interview, accompanied by the caption "standard illustrations."[15] More importantly, Godard formulated in this volume his central idea of approaching the blank page not necessarily as a space to be filled with writing, but as a *screen:* "an example, which isn't unique, but solitary, of a piece of film criticism, which takes vision as its point of departure, which doesn't start by lavishing adjectives across the celebrated white page, but which uses this page as a screen to ... SEE."[16]

Godard pursued his graphic work in 1979–80 in the form of the sixty or so pages of images he selected, reframed, and juxtaposed for inclusion in *Introduction à une véritable histoire du cinéma.* As discussed in chapter 1, he was unhappy with the way in which these were reproduced initially. One of the effects of the photocopier, which he exploited extensively during this period, was the reduction of grayscale photographs to high contrast, graphically striking black-and-white forms, which verge at times on pure abstraction. Such imagery, as Jacques Aumont has observed, evokes a sense of the intensity of recollected images mediated through memory.[17] Since this period, Godard has gone on to produce a large, varied body of graphic collage work, which is best considered a form of expanded cinema realized through materials other than celluloid, and is certainly no less significant than his videos or films. This includes a two-page collage, "La 9ème symphonie," which he contributed to a special issue of *Cahiers du cinéma* edited by Wim Wenders in October 1987; a six-page collage published in *Cahiers du cinéma* that December, at the time of the release of *Soigne ta droite;* and a fourteen-page image-text letter to *Cahiers du cinéma* published in December 1996, at the time of the release of *For ever Mozart.*[18] Numerous other examples are showcased in the two volumes of

his collected writings, and might be loosely categorized as follows: production documents and scenarios, usually conceived in part, like their video counterparts, with a view to securing funding; poems, such as the seven-page "Deuxième lettre à Freddy Buache: Oh! Temps de l'utopie" (Second letter to Freddy Buache: Oh! Time of utopia), which is presented in explicitly filmic terms as a *métrage cinématographique;* and unpublished works such as the image-text book derived from *Deux fois cinquante ans de cinéma français,* which, like the *Histoire(s) du cinéma* volumes, extends and offers a fresh perspective on the source work.

As noted in the introduction, Godard's insistence on communicating through a balanced mix of images and words should be situated in the lineage of antecedent examples such as the *Book of Kings* and Aby Warburg's *Mnemosyne.* In addition, the *Histoire(s) du cinéma* books extend the tradition of the popular pictorial film history book genre and of alternative, imaginative histories of cinema, such as Kenneth Anger's *Hollywood Babylon.*[19] A particularly significant precursor in this regard is Nicole Vedrès's wonderful experiment in visual cinema history, *Images du cinéma français* (Images of French cinema).[20] This book had originally been intended as an accompaniment to Henri Langlois's landmark exhibition of the same name, and indeed the latter considered his exhibition and Vedrès's book as closely related companion pieces. As Laurent Mannoni has shown, the exhibition, which opened in December 1944, contained the seeds of all Langlois's subsequent shows, in which the latter deployed a host of quasi-cinematic techniques to bring film history poetically to life.[21] Organized into a series of themes ("The Burlesque and Comic," "Terror," "Adventure,"

"The Human Condition," etc.), each of which is framed by a brief text, the book presents and juxtaposes hundreds of beautifully reproduced images from the Cinémathèque française photo collection.

We should also bear in mind a number of other important precursors, such as *Documents,* the journal founded by Georges Bataille in the late 1920s; the Surrealist review *Minotaure* (1933–38, published by Skira); Auriol's *La revue du cinéma*; and, of course, the various books by Malraux and Faure discussed in chapter 3. In addition, Bataille's book *Manet* (1955), which includes over fifty photographic plates, constitutes a major reference point in 3A.[22] In *Manet,* Bataille was in close intellectual dialogue with Malraux and inspired by the latter's example of "cutting" from one page to the next, especially from the reproduction of a whole painting to a magnified detail from the same work. Indeed, the high-quality plates used in Bataille's study appear to have provided Godard with the source of much of the Manet imagery used in 3A, in which he also engages with Bataille's overarching thesis that this painter embodies a radical break in the history of painting, and pursues in particular Bataille's lengthy discussion of Berthe Morisot's eyes and face.[23] Moreover, the tight reframing by Godard of a series of faces painted by Manet extends the work of quasi-cinematic editing applied to the same corpus by both Malraux and Bataille. The latter, for example, moves from a reproduction of *The Balcony* (1868–69) to a detail of Morisot in the same painting on the following page; in 3A, Godard prolongs the "zoom," ending on a dark close-up of her face, eyes, and necklace, thereby emphasizing what Bataille describes as the "stormy weight" of the expression on her face.[24]

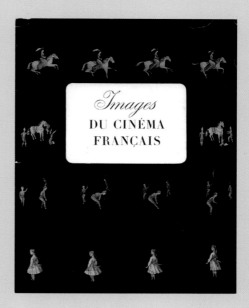

Nicole Vedrès's *Images du cinéma français* (Éditions du Chêne, 1945).

Collage by Godard based on an image from *Inside/Out* (Rob Tregenza, 1997).

Collection Rob Tregenza.

In the 1990s, a new type of still imagery started to proliferate in Godard's work, as he set aside the photocopier in favor of a printer capable of producing high-quality photographs directly from video. These photographs were often presented in conjunction with onscreen text, which was added through means of a basic video special effects generator. Although the means employed to produce this imagery is clearly more sophisticated than that used in his earlier graphic work, its use in the *Histoire(s) du cinéma* books and elsewhere (such as the press-books for *For ever Mozart* and *Éloge de l'amour*) is a direct extension of his previously artisanal photocopier-based glue-and-scissors art. It is worth noting in passing here Godard's belief that pressbooks should be self-contained works that give people a sense of the films to which they relate, and stimulate a desire to go and see them.[25] Like these handcrafted pressbooks – together with the seven slim volumes of "phrases" derived from his films, which Godard has published since 1996 in the form of continuous prose poems – the *Histoire(s) du cinéma* books are a product of the videos. Unlike all but one of the "phrases" books (the one derived from *Film socialisme*, which incorporates a number of images), the *Histoire(s) du cinéma* books differ insofar as they offer a record of the videos not just through text, but through the combination of image and text on the "screen" of the page.

Godard was closely involved with all stages of the books' production: "In the same way that I had made the films, I composed the pages line by line, each paragraph, the presence or absence of punctuation, the use of capitals."[26] Choices along the way ranged from the books' physical dimensions (several alternative formats were discussed, from large art book to Gallimard's smaller Folio and Tel collections) to final presentation. In particular, he was very keen that each volume should have an image on the cover, which he considered an important symbol of the cultural acceptance of a filmmaker, and thus of cinema, into Gallimard's writerly pantheon. By June 1995, Godard had already produced A4 mock-ups of the first three volumes, which were based on the six episodes of the video series then completed in draft form.[27] The artistic director of Gallimard, Jacques Maillot, who worked closely with Godard on the production of the books, was particularly struck by Godard's rejection of a conventional template to guide the placement of image and text, in favor of composition by eye: Godard stuck the various elements by hand onto the blank sheets exactly where he wanted them, with the result that there is considerable variation from page to page, and from volume to volume, in the scale and number of images used, and in the length and position of the textual elements.[28] Working documents for the Gallimard books, and the photocopies of the near-final versions of the books sent by Gallimard as samples to foreign publishers, retain clear traces of the outlines of the images and fragments of texts where Godard has glued them onto the pages, and of his handwritten textual alterations (such as spelling corrections, amendments to capital letters, and the insertion of commas). This emphasis on craft and manual composition lends the books a sculptural physicality and an unpredictable, uneven quality. It comes as no surprise in this context to learn that Godard chose the Bookman typeface not for

technical reasons, but for the symbolic fusion of "man" and "book" in the word itself.[29]

The careful attention to color throughout the books, where it is for the most part used very sparingly, has resulted, as Stéphane Bouquet has observed, in a strong sense of painting: virtually every image, once treated videographically, stilled, and printed, is ultimately as close to painting as it is to photography or cinema.[30] Godard insisted on the best possible quality reproduction, and he and Maillot opted in the end for an image frame of 200, considerably higher than the usual high quality standard of 175; this led to a long, expensive photocomposition process.[31] A sizable grant from the CNC meant that the books could be produced on high-quality paper, with lavish color throughout, but still sold – in line with one of the conditions laid down by Godard from the outset, along with those of size and portability – at a very reasonable price.[32] But high quality by no means implies the sort of clean imagery one might expect from a conventional art book, nor the decorative beauty associated with the coffee-table genre. Indeed, Godard explicitly characterized his work as "a book against art books," and high quality in this case meant the best rendition possible of the effects of repeated transmedial copying and reproduction, which would more usually be considered defects or indicators of poor production, such as loss of definition, color separation, image breakup, pixilation, and faint lettering.[33]

Although much is absent in the books in the form of music, voice and noise, their provision of a concrete trace of two of the most ephemeral means of representation – recorded sound and moving images – makes them intrinsically empowering for the reader, who is accorded considerable control over the manner in which he or she is able to negotiate each volume. However, they do retain a surprising amount of the videos' original energy and dynamism, thanks to the way in which the composite imagery and fragments of accompanying written text are arranged and presented. The organization of the visual and textual elements serves to establish a network of correspondences on each double page and a unique rhythm across each book. Whereas in the videos these connections are articulated through the shifting relationship between image, sound, and onscreen text, in the books the potential meanings are no less rich, and indeed may at times be even more densely and intricately layered, since each composite image carries within it the trace of preexisting connections between two or more sources, and each double page can contain as many as four such images, plus additional fragments of text. There are, of course, marked differences between the contents of the videos and the books: the transcription of the soundtrack is highly selective; the order in which the material is presented is sometimes altered; large swathes of the image-track are omitted; the images that are retained are often combined with different elements from those with which they were originally associated in the videos; fresh meanings are suggested through new juxtapositions and through the establishment of color-based continuities and rhymes from one image or page to the next; and, occasionally, further text, which does not feature onscreen in the videos, has been added over or between the imagery in the books. The overall effect is the most fully achieved realization in Godard's work to date of

the Malrucian principle of "the confrontation of metamorphoses."[34]

GODARD AS SOUND ARTIST

In 1990, midway between the release of a collective musical tribute to him in recognition of his contribution in the field of sound, *Godard ça vous chante?* (1985), and that of the digitally remixed soundtracks on CD of *Nouvelle vague* (1997) and *Histoire(s) du cinéma* by ECM Records, Thierry Jousse argued persuasively that Godard's work was henceforth more profitably considered through reference to contemporary music and musicians – notably the electroacoustic, contemporary, rock, and rap traditions – than to cinema and other filmmakers.[35] This is a line of thinking later pursued by a number of specialist music critics, including the panel that awarded the *Histoire(s) du cinéma* CDs the German Record Critics' Special Jury Prize in 2000. Before considering the CDs in more detail, we shall situate them in the context of Godard's frequently neglected status as a pioneering and influential sonic innovator, whose approach to sound recording and mixing has been characterized throughout his career by the openness to experimentation of the amateur and the precision of the professional. He has long used music, as he suggested as early as 1968, "like another image which isn't an image."[36] Ironically, the pervasiveness of the cultural influence of his sound work on others has made it difficult to pin down and easy to forget. In 1962, at the time of the release of *Vivre sa vie*, Jean Collet published an enthusiastic review of the film's soundtrack, emphasizing the ambition and novelty of a film shot entirely on location using synchronized sound, with noise and voice recorded directly onto a single track at the moment of filming. Ten years later, when his article was republished in English, Collet noted that much of what he had written had become virtually meaningless, so completely had Godard's innovations been absorbed into mainstream film and television practice.[37] By refusing the classical primacy of dialogue, and placing voice, noise, music, and ambient sound on an equal footing, Godard's exploration of the expressive possibilities of the soundtrack in the 1960s – with engineers such as Guy Villette (responsible for *Vivre sa vie*), René Levert, Antoine Bonfanti, and Jacques Maumont – was at least as fruitful as that of any other filmmaker during that decade. His subsequent political interrogation of sound-image relations with Jean-Pierre Gorin and the Dziga Vertov group, notably through intensive investment in the soundtrack, would have an enduring impact on his later practice: his new camera, as he suggested humorously in his role as Uncle Jean in *Prénom Carmen*, was a ghetto blaster. Since the end of the 1970s, music has played an increasingly central role for Godard, inspiring images, guiding the creative act, and – as in *Prénom Carmen*, in which the Prat Quartet's rehearsals of Beethoven's late string quartets repeatedly reinvigorate the faltering B-movie plot – driving forward narrative. Subsequent experiments in stereo sound collage – such as *Détective, Soigne ta droite,* and *King Lear* – were followed by increasingly ambitious sonic compositions, such as *Nouvelle vague*. All of these were products of Godard's collaboration with François Musy, who has been responsible, either alone or with Pierre-Alain Besse and a handful of others, for the sound of virtually all of his work since 1982.

Apart from anything, the *Histoire(s) du cinéma* CDs provide an eloquent practical demonstration of the scale of the hitherto untapped expressive potential of the soundtrack. Following the release of *Nouvelle vague* as a film, Godard explained to an astonished Wim Wenders that while working on the film he had used twenty-four tracks, all of which he had had access to from the start of the editing process. He went on in the course of this conversation to draw an explicit analogy between his practice and that of a composer:

> Wenders: When I'm editing, it's very hard for me to imagine any sound other than the one that is linked to the moment of creating the image.
> Godard: Yet that connection is not the only one possible. At the editing table, I first look at the image without any sound. Then I let the sound run without any images. It's only after that that I put the two together, the way it was shot. Sometimes I have a feeling that something isn't right in a scene – but perhaps it would work with different sound. Then, for instance, I'll replace the dialogue with the sound of a dog barking. Or I'll try it with a sonata. I'll fiddle around with it until I'm satisfied.
> Wenders: I'm shocked. I can see I'm a slave to sound.
> Godard: It's like a composer. The whole orchestra is at the composer's disposal, not just the piano. And yet the composer must have the discipline to use only the piano at first, and to imagine the rest. It's a discipline that leads to creativity. I have the whole orchestra in my head while I'm editing. And when I've chosen one particular sound, then I cut the scene accordingly, and throw the rest in the bin.[38]

To facilitate this orchestral work, Musy helped Godard set up a system for sound recording, mixing, and editing in his Rolle studio, which afforded him the creative autonomy he required when working on the sonic dimension of *Histoire(s) du cinéma*.[39]

In the age of DVD, which has ushered in the possibility of listening to films at home in high-quality digital stereo with or without the image-track, Godard has charted the parameters of "sound cinema" – in the sense both of sound-image relationships and of stand-alone image-less soundscapes – as thoroughly and daringly as anyone. Asked by a disbelieving Laure Adler in 1996, at the time of the release of For ever Mozart, whether he was seriously suggesting that his recent work could be experienced equally well with one's eyes closed, "Yes," replied Godard, "it's possible."[40] Indeed, he has gone as far as to suggest that the ideal way of presenting Éloge de l'amour would be to first show the image-track, then play just the soundtrack – and only then, for those who had already seen either or both of these versions, to project image and sound together.[41] In fact, such ideas are not as odd as they may at first sound: recent years have witnessed significant growth in the production of sound works conceived specifically for release and presentation to the mind's eye in darkened cinemas, such as those made under the umbrella of Matt Hulse's "Audible Picture Show" project.[42] Moreover, as Laurent Jullier has noted, the concept of "imageless cinema" has been with us a long time, and can be traced to early examples such as Walter Ruttmann's "sound film without images," Weekend (1930), a pioneering experiment in what would come to be known as musique concrète.[43] Comparable precedents within Godard's own œuvre include the promotional record for Une femme est une femme, which combined Godard's extensive commentary with excerpts from the soundtrack; the audio tape he included in the package he submitted to the CNC with a view to raising production funds for Passion; and the audio "cassette-montage" he sent to the editors of Cinématographe at the time of the release of Prénom Carmen, which was made up mainly of silence – broken sporadically by Godard's voice and combined with an eclectic assortment of sounds (a Red Guard march, a sound test, and the hubbub of a busy restaurant) and music (snatches of Bizet's Carmen and a Jacques Dutronc song).[44] If anything, given the extent and depth of his experimentation and innovation in the realm of sound, the most surprising thing is that more of Godard's films still have not been issued on CD, and that he has not been tempted to move into the field of pure sonic composition (as opposed to the production of sound works derived from preexisting audiovisual ones).

Cultivating a familiarity with Godard and Godard-Miéville's later work through sound on DVD or CD is one of the most accessible and immediately rewarding ways of engaging with its at times forbidding density. Not everything, of course, is of equal sonic complexity or interest. Conversation pieces such as Deux fois cinquante ans de cinéma français and The Old Place are less aurally rich or seductive than more complex essayistic compositions such as JLG/JLG and Histoire(s) du cinéma, or fictional soundscapes such as Nouvelle vague and Éloge de l'amour. What is so striking in the more intensely worked pieces is the coherence of the polyphonic aural universes produced through the sampling and orchestration of disparate source materials. The effect of Nouvelle vague or Histoire(s) du cinéma, for instance, is anything but dissonant or cacophonous. Part of Godard's achievement, and one of the distinguishing characteristics of his audio work, is his ability to marshal and present a wealth and diversity of sounds, while allowing the listener to savor each one individually. As

Mark Swed put it in a discussion of the *Histoire(s) du cinéma* CDs, "the texture is so transparently achieved that what we hear are contrapuntal layers rather than cacophony."[45]

One way of thinking about *Histoire(s) du cinéma*, as Thierry Jousse and Paul Griffiths observed at the time of the release of the CDs, is as *Histoire(s) de la musique*.[46] In other words, the series offers not only a history of cinema, but also a partial history of popular and classical music, song, and film music. Music is at the heart of Godard's later work, not only because of the sheer amount he uses, but also, more significantly, due to the special place he accords it. "Music is beyond," he suggested in conversation with Marguerite Duras in 1987, "whereas literature and cinema are on earth."[47] In interviews, he has refrained from discussing music in any detail, preferring instead to adopt the position of the naïve but enthusiastic amateur. This is particularly evident in his important dialogue with Jousse on the topic of sound, in which he insists that he is musically illiterate and has only a basic knowledge of most composers and musical traditions, and little or none of jazz or opera.[48] As James Williams has observed, however, by drawing a veil over his relationship with music in this way, Godard is effectively protecting it as an enigmatic, instinctive force beyond analysis: "Music *is* a mystery for him, and part of its unique power is that he feels unable to define or decipher it. It is ineffable; it simply *is*."[49] Furthermore, Williams has gone on to argue convincingly that the large number of *beginnings* of musical movements used in *Histoire(s) du cinéma*, which, he suggests, serve to perpetually relaunch and drive the series forward, are the logical extension of Godard's approach to music as an inexplicable and seemingly unstoppable source of creative promise: "By taking a movement of music not at its climax but at its very beginning, and sometimes just the opening snippets or the prelude before the theme or leitmotif succumbs to variation, Godard maintains music invariably in its proleptic and revelatory mode, in a continual state of becoming. Which is to say, it will never run the risk of staleness or complication because it remains forever 'open,' like an eternal hope or promise."[50]

In the late 1980s, Manfred Eicher, founder and director of ECM Records and a longstanding admirer of Godard's work, had started sending the latter CDs of music by ECM artists such as Arvo Pärt and David Darling. For Godard, this music revealed, as he later put it, the presence of a friend, brother, or sister working in similar or adjacent aesthetic territory, who was creating sound in musical form that "showed us, for whom the principal point of departure is the image, a direction in which to go."[51] Although Godard has described the ECM material as being sometimes too elaborate for his taste, he has also stressed, crucially, that it contains "sounds that speak to you, and that are in synchronization with what we are searching for."[52] Since *Nouvelle vague,* Godard and Godard-Miéville's work has been decisively colored by the sounds of the composers and musicians produced by "the indefatigable and devoted Manfred," including Ketil Bjørnstad, Anouar Brahem, Gavin Bryars, David Darling, Paul Giger, Heinz Holliger, Keith Jarrett, Giya Kancheli, Alexander Knaifel, György Kurtág, Meredith Monk, Arvo Pärt, Werner Pirchner, Dino Saluzzi, Trygve Seim, Valentin Silvestrov, and Tomasz Stanko,

Abii ne viderem (Giya Kancheli, 1995)
in 4A, and *Aleksandr Nevsky* (Sergei
Eisenstein, 1938) in 1A and 4B.

as well as by the works of other composers (such as Bach, Hindemith, Honegger, Mompou, Otte, and Scelsi) interpreted by ECM artists.[53] The music of Pärt, Bjørnstad, and Kancheli is particularly central to *Histoire(s) du cinéma:* Pärt's compositions recur throughout, Bjørnstad's *The Sea* (1995) dominates the soundtrack of 4B, and Kancheli's *Abii ne viderem* (I turned away so as not to see, 1995) provided Godard with the structuring armature for 4A. Characterizing the music he had used earlier in the series as conventional "film music," he has drawn a parallel between his use of *Abii ne viderem* in 4A and Eisenstein's collaboration with Sergei Prokofiev on *Aleksandr Nevsky:* "I'd listened to this record by Kancheli, and little by little I said to myself: 'I know, the episode will be constructed using this.' So then I really did like Eisenstein and Prokofiev, noting second by second so that there would be synchronisms and so on. And then afterwards one diverges somewhat, but the idea remained of a piece of music that was already there."[54]

Godard also samples works by numerous other composers in the series, such as Bartók, Beethoven, Liszt, Mahler, Mozart, Puccini, Schumann, Stravinsky, and Webern. Three play a particularly prominent role: Arthur Honegger, whose Symphony no. 3 ("Liturgique," 1945–46) punctuates 1A, in which we also hear his Symphony no. 5 ("Di tre re," 1950), followed by his *Pacific 231* (1923) in 1B; Franz Schubert, whose dramatic Symphony no. 8 in B Minor (the so-called Unfinished Symphony, 1822) provides the rhythm and dynamic impetus to much of the first half of 1A; and, above all, the omnipresent Johann Sebastian Bach ("Johann Sebastian the eternal," as Godard has described him[55]), whose *Violin Concerto* in E Major (BWV 1042, 1717–23) is used in 1A, *The Well-Tempered Clavier I* (BWV 846–869, 1722) in 2A, and whose Chorale Prelude for Organ (BWV 721, 1703) punctuates the series throughout (in 1A, 2B, 3A, and 4B). Another group of composers enjoys particular prominence due to their close connections with cinema: Camille Saint-Saëns, whose symphonic poem *La danse macabre* (1874) (used by Renoir in *La règle du jeu*), is put to haunting effect in 1A; Chaplin, a major reference throughout the series, provides a key example of an antecedent filmmaker-composer; Prokofiev, whose collaboration with Eisenstein provides an exemplary instance of creative dialogue between artists, and, at a formal level, between music and image; Bernard Herrmann, whose score for *Psycho* plays a major role in 1B and 2A, and returns in 4B (Herrmann, we recall, was one of the first composers to insist that film scores could be appreciated as stand-alone works); Dmitri Shostakovich, whose dramatic score for Kozintsev's *Hamlet* is used in 2A, and plays a significant role during the opening section of 3B; and George Gershwin, whose *American in Paris* (1928) provided the basis for Minnelli's 1951 film of the same name (cited in 1A, 2A, and 4B), which used numerous Gershwin tunes.

In addition to the special treatment of *Abii ne viderem*, pre-recorded music is put to a wide variety of uses. It often plays a fairly conventional supporting role, underscoring an emotion articulated through the imagery, onscreen text or other sounds; elsewhere, it is used in counterpoint. The shift from one function to the other can be rapid and disconcerting, as in the jump during Godard's deathly delivery of the text by Victor Hugo at the beginning of 3A, from the subdued mood and rhythm of Bach's Chorale Prelude for Organ (BWV 721) to the much lighter tones of Schumann's *Kinderzenen* (opus 15). On occasion, the music, like some of the films and books, has clearly been partly (perhaps primarily) selected on the basis of its title, as in the case of Liszt's *A Faust Symphony* (1857) in 1A, which resonates with and reinforces the Faustian theme of this episode. At other times, as Godard has insisted, the function of the music is primarily historical, in that it serves to provide a documentary record of the type of music that was made and heard in a given time and place.[56] One thinks especially in this context of the strong presence in the series of the work of Paul Hindemith, whose life coincided with the rise of Nazism, and whose work of the 1930s grappled with the predicament of the artist in an age of great violence and oppression. Godard uses Hindemith's *Mathis der Maler* (1934–35) in 1B and 3A. In this opera, the composer explored the dilemmas faced by the artist Matthias Grünewald in the early years of the Reformation as a way of wrestling with the issues of the role and responsibility of the artist in his own turbulent era. As Laurent Jullier has suggested, Godard, like Hindemith, is doubtless identifying here in part with Grünewald.[57] Moreover, Hindemith's *Trauermusik* for solo viola and string orchestra (1936; cited in 1B and 2A), which the composer wrote as an instant response to the news of the death of George V (it premiered the same day), serves as a concise illustration of Godard's theory of the testimonial function of art generally, and of cinema in particular. Godard also uses the music of Béla Bartók in a similar, albeit more eccentric, documentary fashion. His incorporation of numerous pieces by Bartók in 1B, for instance, was apparently partly guided by the strong sense of fiction it introduces.[58] Above all, however, he claims to have used it as

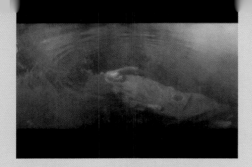

In praise of film composers:
Shostakovich, Saint-Saëns, Chaplin,
Herrmann, and Gershwin.

a substitute for the films that should have been made in Hungary in the first half of the twentieth century, but were not:

> I said to myself, "It's true, there's no Hungarian cinema, but there's Bartók." And Hungarian cinema is Bartók, more so than others. So one has to put him for historical reasons. But those who see or listen to it fail to see it historically, whereas I nevertheless went to some lengths to ensure that it was seen historically, if I can put it like that.[59]

Finally, Godard employs music at times as a means of exploring historical connections between cinema and the other arts. He has been particularly keen to point out, for instance, that certain key stages in the development of modern music were contemporaneous with those in cinema, and sought to demonstrate this relationship in *Histoire(s) du cinéma* through the combination of image and sound rather than by simply stating it. Exemplary in this regard is his *rapprochement* of Stravinsky (whose *The Rite of Spring* [1913] plays a significant role in 1A) with early cinema, especially the films of Louis Feuillade.

Histoire(s) du cinéma is also brimming with song. Episode 1A alone brings together classical singing (e.g. Mahler's song cycle *Lieder eines fahrenden Gesellen* [1884–85]), opera (such as Puccini's *Tosca* [1900]), and songs ranging in tone and sophistication from Ton Steine Scherben's proto-punk "Macht kaputt, was euch kaputt macht!" (Destroy what destroys you! 1971) to Leonard Cohen's "Came So Far for Beauty" (1979). The same episode includes a wide range of songs from films, including Rita Hayworth's "Put the Blame on Mame" from *Gilda*, Anna Karina's rendition (from *Bande à part*) of a song based on Aragon's poem "Les poètes" (1960), Taina Elga's interpretation of "Ça c'est l'amour"

in *Les Girls*, Hannah Schygulla's version of "Lili Marleen" in *Lili Marleen*, and Lucienne Delyle's delivery of the eponymous title song from Gance's *Le paradis perdu* (*Paradise Lost*, 1939). One of the effects of this emphasis on song in the series is a foregrounding of the modulations, tones, colors, rhythms, timbre and inherent musicality of the human voice. Indeed, in its capacity as a hymn to the range and beauty of the voice, *Histoire(s) du cinéma* is, among other things, the culmination of what Louis Aragon termed Godard's "spoken collages."[60] This close attention to the expressive possibilities of the voice can be traced to Godard's work with actors, and to his success over the years in producing often remarkable readings and dialogue delivery from them. The vocal dimension of *Histoire(s) du cinéma* is foregrounded at the beginning of 4A via a reading from Paul Valéry's poem in praise of the musicality and expressive force of the voice, "Psaume sur une voix" (Psalm on a voice); to illustrate Valéry's theme, Godard combines, and moves between, two very different renditions of the same text.[61] His exploration of the power of the human voice as an instrument is also strongly in evidence in the attention to accent, intonation, diction, vocal color, and even to the sound of human breath, in the numerous readings that punctuate the series, whether by actors (such as Maria Casarès, Julie Delpy, and Sabine Azéma), or in recordings of authors such as Charles Ferdinand Ramuz, Ezra Pound, and Paul Celan. Of particular note in this regard is the reading of a text by Cesare Pavese from Danièle Huillet and Jean-Marie Straub's *From the Clouds to the Resistance* (1979), which Godard uses at the end of 2A. This citation functions in part as a tribute to Huillet and Straub's meticulous attention to rehearsal, filming, sound recording, and – especially – to their audiovisual interpretation of written texts, which Godard values particularly highly.[62] Although rendered in the original Italian (and, as such, not necessarily comprehensible to all viewers), the meaning of this extract – as elsewhere in Godard's polyglot histories – lies as much in its rhythms and color as in what the words literally signify.

One's initial assumption as a potential listener to the CDs of *Histoire(s) du cinéma* is that they will be incomplete, since they lack the visual dimension of the composition as originally conceived. When one begins to listen, however, as Paul Griffiths observed, any sense that something is missing quickly disappears, "for there is so much that is not."[63] In a philosophical perspective, the CDs redirect the listener's attention towards the ontology of recorded sound, and to the historical charge of the sounds contained in the countless soundtracks that are an equal part of cinema's legacy – not just the sociological or linguistic interest of song and speech, but the historical detail caught in the everyday sounds of the countryside and city, home, and workplace recorded on disc, tape, or film – especially since the commercialization of synchronized sound. Could one not imagine, as Godard put it to Jousse, in addition to informational and pedagogical materials made up of still or moving archival imagery, sonic history "books" composed of archive sounds?[64] As an aesthetic experience for the listener already familiar with the audiovisual version of the series, listening to the CDs brings relief from sensory overload, and pleasure at the rediscovery of the work anew through different means. Without the visual dimension, the directness of the relationship of the series to cinema history recedes, especially in those episodes that make comparatively little

use of archival film soundtracks. At the same time, the thematic threads running through the series become less pronounced, and it demands increased imaginative input on the part of the listener. As Claire Bartoli put it in her account of her experience as a blind cinemagoer consuming films through sound alone, really listening to films – especially those by directors who invest equally in sound and image, such as Godard – allows one not just to follow their narratives, but also to appropriate, dream, imagine, personalize, and ultimately to reinvent and remake them.[65]

At the mixing desk, Godard is free to pursue his longstanding exploration of rhythm, counterpoint, harmony, layering, overlap, repetition, abrupt interruptions, unannounced sonic eruptions, sudden starts and stops, dissonance, auditory confusion, pauses, jumps in volume, silence, and of the dialogue or confrontation between the sounds, voices, noises, or fragments of pre-recorded music juxtaposed on the two stereo tracks. Stereo is central to Godard's compositional method, in that it provides him with an invaluable means of pursuing his technique of *rapprochement* through sound. Indeed, stereo offers a resonant metaphor for his historical image-making practice in general. On a practical level, it facilitates the simultaneous presentation of two sounds while ensuring that both remain audible, even when played at high volume. Contrary to Huillet and Straub's predilection for mono direct sound, he suggested to Jousse, he uses stereo as an additional tool – along with vertical layering and contiguous juxtaposition – for orchestrating various noises, sounds, and voices (including his own) as discrete elements within his composition. At times, the two tracks are in harmony, or complement one another; at others they compete and clash – sometimes playfully, but often dramatically and angrily. A good example of the establishment of a dialogue between the stereo tracks is Godard's treatment of the conversation between himself and Daney in 2A, in which the latter's voice dominates the right channel, while the former's is weighted heavily to the left.

One of the most striking compositional strategies used in *Histoire(s) du cinéma* involves the interweaving of two or more archival film soundtracks, and their combination with other sounds. This process is introduced from the opening of 1A via the combination of extracts from Resnais's *L'année dernière à Marienbad* (mainly on the left channel), Lang's *Rancho Notorious* (1952; mainly on the right), and Visconti's *The Leopard* (1963; on both channels, including an extract of the mazurka composed by Nino Rota for the film's celebrated ball sequence). This passage is punctuated by a Beethoven string quartet, and both preceded and followed by typewriter noise, Godard's voice, and extracts of Honegger's Symphony no. 3. Elsewhere in the series, pre-recorded music segues into archival film soundtracks, film music from different sources is combined, orchestral music is announced by mechanical noise, music and recitations vie with one another, and contrasting musical genres intermingle. Godard subsequently pursued these experiments, in *Voyage(s) en utopie,* in his use of extracts of film soundtracks (his own and those of others), which clashed and merged with one another as the films playing on the various screens in the gallery started and stopped, and as the visitor moved through the gallery space. Another key technique with which Godard composes his soundscapes is that of the rapid jump in sound

level, from extremely loud to barely audible. Among the more unnerving effects of listening to the CDs of *Histoire(s) du cinéma* is the sudden and often very loud eruption of blasts of mechanical noise, natural sounds, music, or voices – for which the viewer is often better prepared when watching the videos, thanks to the warning signs implicit in the imagery. In addition, Godard's presentation of his own voice – at varying volume levels, and in a range of rhythms and tones, and saying different things through the two speakers at the same time, as if there two (or three, or four) of him – is at times highly disconcerting, and produces a strong sense of someone who is not only in dialogue with the listener, and with the other material in the mix, but also with himself. Finally, among the most striking sonic features of *Histoire(s) du cinéma* are undoubtedly the strange, disquieting effects produced as a result of the manipulation of sound through altered motion. Jean Epstein succinctly outlined the potential of this type of sonic experimentation in an article in 1948, which was based on his own groundbreaking foray into this field, *Le tempestaire* (The storm-tamer, 1947). The application of slow motion to sound, he suggested, resulted in the breaking up and magnification of complex everyday sounds, and the revelation within them of "an apocalypse of shouts, cooings, rumblings, squealings, boomings, tones, and notes for most of which no name exists."[66] His description provides a succinct summary of the effects of Godard's videographic play with sound through altered motion five decades later.

It is against the backdrop of this extensive experimentation with sound that Eicher has argued that Godard is not just a filmmaker, but a composer at the vanguard of sound remix art, whose audiovisual and sound work holds its own alongside that of any other major contemporary musician.[67] Similarly, as Mark Swed suggested in his review of the *Histoire(s) du cinéma* CDs, it is now possible to think of Godard as "one of the world's most important sound artists."[68] In line with the model of the interrelationship of destruction and creativity at the heart of Godard's Malrucian theory of artistic metamorphosis, wherein cinema killed off the real so as to redeem and resurrect it though its imagery, the videos of *Histoire(s) du cinéma* can be thought of as a great videographic bonfire, fueled by the shards and memories of the art-works he has loved. Following the same principle, the subsequent versions of the series, which themselves depend in a sense on the "sacrifice" of the videos, repeat the process.[69] Given the privileged place of music within Godard's schema, it is the sounds of *Histoire(s) du cinéma* – extracted from their original sources and contexts, freed from the images to which they were linked in the videos, and resurrected in the CDs in the form of *musique concrète* – that constitute the purest and most fully achieved manifestation of his theoretical and practical investigation of the art of cinema to date.

IN THE YEARS SINCE THE RELEASE OF THE various versions of *Histoire(s) du cinéma,* Godard has gone on to produce an astonishing quantity and variety of work in different media and contexts, thereby confounding those critics who had assumed the series to be some sort of testament. This includes books; graphic image-text works; video sketches, essays, pamphlets, and poems; feature films; trailers; pressbooks; and a major exhibition. Two of his larger-scale post–*Histoire(s) du cinéma* ventures are of particular note in relation to his wider historiographic project: *Voyage(s) en utopie* and *Film socialisme.* The numerous models he prepared for the abandoned early incarnation of *Voyage(s) en utopie,* under the working title *Collage(s) de France,* and which he included in the final exhibition, are perhaps the freshest forms in which he has pursued his Langloisian investigation of autobiography, cinema, and history into the twenty-first century. It is too early to say for certain, but *Voyage(s) en utopie* may also turn out to mark the conclusion of his audiovisual and multimedia historiographic project, since *Film socialisme* hints at the turning of a page in this regard. Having disposed of his book and video archive, Godard has been working on two film projects: a short entitled *Les trois désastres* (The three disasters) and a feature-length film entitled *Adieu au langage* (Goodbye to language), which he is reportedly filming in 3-D. Whether these projects confirm this sense of a new departure remains to be seen. What is certain is that his recent output displays abundant evidence of formal vitality, of a continuing belief in the potential of new technologies – if used imaginatively – to produce potent poetic imagery, and of a deep curiosity for the digital image economy and contemporary world. Together these

Envoi

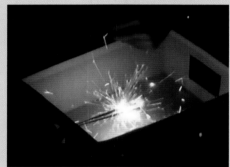

qualities give every reason for optimism, and remind us, as Rohmer once wrote of late Renoir, of Godard's remarkable artistic youthfulness as he traverses his ninth decade.[1]

Besides being a manifesto for further experimentation in iconographic, sonic, and audiovisual history, *Histoire(s) du cinéma* in its various manifestations is a milestone in multimedia film thinking and historiography. Whether professional historians will take note of Godard's montage theorem, or of his advocacy of a more imaginative approach to historiography in general, remains an open question, although some signs of his influence are starting to emerge.[2] In addition to a fuller consideration of some of the major topics investigated by Godard in the series, such as the sheer scale, significance and impact of the cinematograph, this study leaves us with a number of further tasks: an in-depth reassessment of Henri Langlois as a historian; a critical retrieval of Jean George Auriol; comparative studies of Godard and Jean Epstein, and of *Histoire(s) du cinéma* and Hollis Frampton's *Magellan*; an extended investigation of the audiovisual cinema history tradition; an exploration of the relationship between German Romantic literature and the New Wave (Godard in particular); systematic research into the influence of television on the New Wave; a reconsideration of Godard's œuvre in its entirety through reference to the thought of André Malraux; and,

above all, a thorough reappraisal of Godard as a multidisciplinary transmedial artist. Godard's own ultimate concern regarding *Histoire(s) du cinéma* appears to lie with the long-term future. He has talked of his desire, in the absence of children of his own, to "transmit" the series.[3] Like Langlois's Cinémathèque française, *Histoire(s) du cinéma* is fundamentally inspirational and productive: it is not only a bonfire of the art of the past, but also a time capsule filled with traces of films, evidence of a lifelong passion for cinema, and a record of the secret of cinematographic montage. Ultimately, it is an incendiary device designed to be projected into the future to nourish art-forms as yet undreamed of, and to ignite an artistic renaissance at some distant, unforeseeable moment in time: the image will come at the time of the resurrection. In the opening tale of their marvelous collection of sketches set in and around the world of cinema published in 1923, *Quelques histoires de cinéma*, Charles-Félix Tavano and Marcel Yonnet recounted the tale of the discovery by a group of construction workers, in the year 3024, of a tightly sealed chest buried deep in the ground, containing five reels of ancient film. Once restored and projected before an astonished, rapt audience, these fragments spark a thirty-first-century artistic revolution, inspiring a group of young directors, the "Primitives."[4] *Histoire(s) du cinéma* is that chest.

This list covers known works made by Jean-Luc Godard for various forms of public circulation and consumption, including scripts, films, videos, pressbooks, trailers, books, invented interviews with other filmmakers, and metacritical texts relating to his own practice. Building on the filmography-bibliography-discography compiled by Nicole Brenez, Bapiste Coutureau, David Faroult, Marina Lewisch, Sylvie Pras, Judith Revault d'Allonnes, and myself for *Jean-Luc Godard: Documents*, it presents Godard as a multimedia artist, and his audiovisual work (rendered here in **bold**) as part of a much larger, organically integrated transmedial project. It excludes private letters and interviews, and should be read in conjunction with a list of his theoretical texts and written criticism devoted to the work of other filmmakers.

Abbreviations

Godard on Godard: Jean-Luc Godard, *Godard on Godard,* ed. Jean Narboni and Tom Milne, trans. Tom Milne (London: Secker and Warburg, 1972).

Godard par Godard, vol. 1: Jean-Luc Godard, *Jean-Luc Godard par Jean-Luc Godard,* vol. 1, ed. Alain Bergala (Paris: Cahiers du cinéma/Éditions de l'Étoile, 1985).

Son + Image: Raymond Bellour and Mary Lea Bandy, eds., *Jean-Luc Godard: Son + Image, 1974–1991* (New York: Museum of Modern Art, 1992).

Godard par Godard, vol. 2: Jean-Luc Godard, *Jean-Luc Godard par Jean-Luc Godard,* vol. 2, ed. Alain Bergala (Paris: Cahiers du cinéma, 1998).

Jean-Luc Godard: Documents: Nicole Brenez, David Faroult, Michael Temple, James Williams, and Michael Witt, eds., *Jean-Luc Godard: Documents* (Paris: Éditions du Centre Pompidou, 2006).

In the Poem about Love: Tanya Leighton, ed., *"In the Poem about Love You Don't Write the Word Love"* (Berlin and New York: Sternberg Press, 2006).

Godard au travail: Alain Bergala with Mélanie Gérin and Núria Aidelman, *Godard au travail: Les années 60* (Paris: Cahiers du cinéma, 2006).

Godard: Biographie: Antoine de Baecque, *Godard: Biographie* (Paris: Grasset, 2010).

Works

Opération "béton" (Operation "concrete"), 1955, 20 min., 35 mm, b/w.

Une femme coquette (A flirtatious woman), 1956, 10 min., 16 mm, b/w.

Contribution to a collective film entitled *Sexual Rhapsody,* attributed to "Anthony Barrier." Cited in *Godard: Biographie,* 83.

Documentaries edited for Jean-Pierre Braunberger and

Works by Godard

travel films edited for Arthaud, 1956–57. See *Godard par Godard,* vol. 1, 14.

Contribution as a dialogue writer to projects by directors such as Edouard Molinaro, Jean-Pierre Mocky, and Pierre Schoendoerffer, 1956–58. See *Godard par Godard,* vol. 1, 14.

Pressbooks for Twentieth-Century Fox, Paris, 1956–58.

***Tous les garçons s'appellent Patrick,* or *Charlotte et Véronique (All the Boys Are Called Patrick),* 1957, 21 min., 35 mm, b/w.**

***Une histoire d'eau (A Story of Water),* co-dir. François Truffaut, 1958, 18 min., 35 mm, b/w.**

***Charlotte et son Jules (Charlotte and Her Boyfriend),* 1958, 20 min., 35 mm, b/w.**

Charlotte et son Jules: Sketch de Jean-Luc Godard, 1959. Record (Éditions Jacques Canetti Polydor), 11 min.

"Sur les traces du Quichotte" (In Don Quixote's footsteps), text by Juan Buñuel and Claude Pierson, adapted by Jean-Luc Godard, *Cahiers du cinéma,* no. 92, February 1959, 42–43.

"Un cinéaste c'est aussi un missionaire: Jean-Luc Godard fait parler Roberto Rossellini" (A filmmaker is also a missionary: Jean-Luc Godard interviews Roberto Rossellini), *Arts,* no. 717, 8 April 1959. Invented interview. In *Godard on Godard,* 140–42.

"Jean Renoir: 'La télévision m'a révélé un nouveau cinéma'" (Jean Renoir: "Television revealed a new cinema to me"), *Arts,* no. 718, 15 April 1959. Invented interview. In *Godard on Godard,* 143–46.

Script of *À bout de souffle* (written by François Truffaut, reworked by Godard), in *Godard au travail,* 23–25.

Script of *Une femme est une femme* (based on an idea by Geneviève Cluny), *Cahiers du cinéma,* no. 98, August 1959. In *Godard on Godard,* 155–60.

***À bout de souffle (Breathless),* 1960, 90 min., 35 mm, b/w.**

Trailer for *À bout de souffle,* 1960, 1 min. 50 sec., 35 mm, b/w.

Script of *Le petit soldat,* in *Godard au travail,* 76–77.

"La photo du mois" (Photo of the month), *Cahiers du cinéma,* no. 109, July 1960. Short text accompanying a photograph depicting the shooting of *Le petit soldat.* In *Godard on Godard,* 164–65, and (in facsimile) in *Godard au travail,* 43.

***Le petit soldat (The Little Soldier),* 1960, 88 min., 35 mm, b/w.**

Trailer for *Le petit soldat,* 1960, 57 sec., 35 mm, b/w.

"Les dix (10) meilleurs films de l'année" (The ten best films of the year), *Cahiers du cinéma,* no. 116, February 1961, 1. Handwritten text accompanied by a line drawing by Godard of a woman's head.

***Une femme est une femme (A Woman Is a Woman),* 1961, 84 min., 35 mm, color.**

Trailer for *Une femme est une femme,* 1961, 1 min. 50 sec., 35 mm, color.

Promotional record for *Une femme est une femme,* 1961, 34 min. 10 sec. Available on the Criterion DVD of the film. Transcribed in *Godard on Godard,* 165–71.

***La paresse (Sloth,* episode in *Les sept péchés capitaux [The Seven Capital Sins]),* 1961, 15 min., 35 mm, b/w.**

"Dans *Adieu Philippine* Rozier a trouvé le rapport des hommes et des choses" (In *Adieu Philippine* Rozier has found the relationship between people and things), *Les lettres françaises,* no. 928, 24 May 1962, 12. Text of a talk delivered during the inaugural International Critics' Week at the 1962 Cannes Film Festival.

Script of *Vivre sa vie,* n.d., in *Godard au travail,* 105–106.

***Vivre sa vie: Film en douze tableaux (My Life to Live),* 1962, 85 min., 35 mm, b/w.**

Trailer for *Vivre sa vie,* 1962, 2 min., 35 mm, b/w.

"*Vivre sa vie*" (promotional poem), *L'avant-scène cinéma,* no. 19, 15 October 1962. In *Jean-Luc Godard: Documents,* 25.

***Le nouveau monde (The New World,* episode in *RoGoPaG [Let's Have a Brainwash]),* 1962, 20 min., 35 mm, b/w.**

"Les carabiniers jouent 4 actes de Benjamino Joppolo" (The riflemen play four acts by Benjamino Joppolo), *L'avant-scène cinéma,* nos. 171/172, July/August 1976, 6–9. Early version of the script for *Les carabiniers,* which includes extracts of the original text by Roberto Rossellini and Jean Gruault, together with Godard's additions.

Introduction to *Les carabiniers* (Collection Bifi/Cinémathèque française). Cited in *Godard: Biographie,* 836n214.

Script of *Les carabiniers,* n.d., in *Godard au travail,* 128–30.

***Les carabiniers (The riflemen),* 1963, 80 min., 35 mm, b/w.**

Trailer for *Les carabiniers,* 1963, 2 min. 10 sec., 35 mm, b/w.

"Les carabiniers: synopsis," *L'avant-scène cinéma,* no. 46, 1 March 1965.

"Mon film, un apologue" (My film, an apologue), *L'avant-scène cinéma,* no. 46, 1 March 1965. In *Godard par Godard,* vol. 1, 237–38.

"Feu sur *Les carabiniers*" (*Les carabiniers* under fire), *Cahiers du cinéma,* no. 146, August 1963. In *Godard on Godard,* 196–200.

***Le grand escroc (The Great Swindle,* episode in *Les plus belles escroqueries du monde [World's Greatest Swindles]),* 1963, 25 min., 35 mm, b/w.**

"Scénario du *Mépris:* Ouverture" (Script of *Le mépris:* opening), n.d., in *Godard par Godard,* vol. 1, 241–48.

Script of *Le mépris,* n.d., in *Godard au travail,* 149–54.

"Le mépris," *Cahiers du cinéma*, no. 146, August 1963. In *Godard on Godard*, 200–201.

Le mépris (Contempt), 1963, 105 min., 35 mm, color.

Trailer for Le mépris, 1963, 2 min. 15 sec., 35 mm, color.

Script of *Bande à part*, n.d., in *Godard au travail*, 184–87.

Bande à part (Band of Outsiders), 1964, 95 min., 35 mm, b/w.

Trailer for Bande à part, 1964, 1 min. 50 sec., 35 mm, b/w.

Treatment for *La femme mariée* (Collection Bifi/Cinémathèque française). Cited in *Godard: Biographie*, 842n160.

Script of *La femme mariée*, n.d., in *Godard au travail*, 206–208.

"La femme mariée" ("The Married Woman"), *Cahiers du cinéma*, no. 159, October 1964. In *Godard on Godard*, 208.

Une femme mariée: Fragments d'un film tourné en 1964 (A married woman: Fragments of a film shot in 1964), 1964, 98 min., 35 mm, b/w. Formerly La femme mariée (The married woman).

Trailer for Une femme mariée, 1964, 1 min. 50 sec., 35 mm, b/w. Handwritten notes for another version of the trailer are available in *Godard au travail*, 207.

"Montparnasse-Levallois," *Cahiers du cinéma*, no. 171, October 1965. In *Godard par Godard*, vol. 1, 258–59.

Montparnasse-Levallois: Un action film (episode in Paris vu par . . . [Six in Paris]), 1965, 18 min., 16 mm, color.

Original treatment for "A New Adventure of Lemmy Caution," n.d., collection Michael Chanan.

Script of *Alphaville*, n.d., in *Godard au travail*, 231–32.

Alphaville, une étrange aventure de Lemmy Caution (Alphaville, a Strange Adventure of Lemmy Caution), 1965, 98 min., 35 mm, b/w.

"Lemmy Caution erre dans le futur comme dans le 'labyrinthe' de Borges" (Lemmy Caution roams in the future like in Borges's "labyrinth"), *Les lettres françaises*, no. 1077 (22 April 1965).

"Apprenez le François" (Studying François), *L'avant-scène du cinéma*, no. 48, May 1965. Prefatory note to the published script of Truffaut's *La peau douce* (1964). In *Godard on Godard*, 211.

Trailer for Alphaville, une étrange aventure de Lemmy Caution, 1965, 1 min., 35 mm, b/w.

Figaropravda, pressbook for *Alphaville*, 1965. Front page reproduced in facsimile in *Godard au travail*, 248.

Treatment for *Pierrot le fou* (Collection Bifi/Cinémathèque française). Cited in *Godard: Biographie*, 844n249.

Script of *Pierrot le fou*, n.d., in *Godard au travail*, 260–65.

Pierrot le fou (Pierrot Goes Wild, aka Crazy Pete), 1965, 110 min., 35 mm, color.

"Pierrot mon ami" (Pierrot my friend), *Cahiers du cinéma*, no. 171, October 1965. In *Godard on Godard*, 213–15.

Trailer for Pierrot le fou, 1965, 1 min. 40 sec., 35 mm, color.

Promotional poem for *Pierrot le fou*, included in the pressbook for the film. In *Godard au travail*, 254.

"Hier, j'ai rêvé . . ." (Yesterday, I dreamt . . .), *La cinématographie française*, 16 November 1965. Double-page handwritten open letter. In *Jean-Luc Godard: Documents*, 67.

"Grâce à Henri Langlois" (Thanks to Henri Langlois), *Le nouvel observateur*, no. 61, 12 January 1966. Text of a speech delivered at the Cinémathèque française in January 1966. In *Godard on Godard*, 234–37.

"Avec le sourire" (With a smile). Early script for the project that would become *Masculin féminin*. In *Godard au travail*, 290.

Treatment for *Masculin féminin* (Bibliothèque de l'Institut Lumière). Cited in *Godard: Biographie*, 846n10.

"Masculin et féminin: Scénario de travail" (Masculine and feminine: working script), n.d., in *Godard au travail*, 300.

Masculin féminin: Quinze faits précis (Masculine, Feminine: In 15 Acts), 1966, 110 min., 35 mm, b/w.

Trailer for Masculin féminin, 1966, 1 min. 58 sec., 35 mm, b/w.

"Mots qui se croisent + rebus = cinéma, donc": (Words that cross one another + rebus = cinema, so . . .".:), in Michel Vianey, *En attendant Godard* (Paris: Grasset, 1966). In *Godard par Godard*, vol. 1, 284–85.

"Lettre au Ministre de la 'Kultur'" (Letter to the Minister of "Kultur"), *Le nouvel observateur*, 6 April 1966. In *Godard on Godard*, 237–38.

"Le testament de Balthazar" (Balthazar's legacy), *Cahiers du cinéma*, no. 177, April 1966, 58–59. Signed "M. Merleau-Ponty and J.-L. Godard."

"Trois mille heures de cinéma" (Three thousand hours of cinema), *Cahiers du cinéma*, no. 184, November 1966. In *Godard par Godard*, vol. 1, 291–95.

Script of *Made in USA*, n.d., in *Godard au travail*, 312.

Made in USA, 1966, 90 min., 35 mm, color.

Trailer for Made in USA, 1966, 1 min. 30 sec., 35 mm, color.

"Les étoiles filantes" (The shooting stars). Early version of the script for *Deux ou trois choses que je sais d'elle*. In *Godard au travail*, 329.

"Deux ou trois choses que je sais d'elle: Scénario," 1966, included in the pressbook for *Deux ou trois choses que je sais d'elle*. In *Jean-Luc Godard: Documents*, 78–79.

Script of *Deux ou trois choses que je sais d'elle*. In *Godard au travail*, 329–31.

"Choses à filmer" (Things to film), n.d., in *Godard au travail*, 333.

Deux ou trois choses que je sais d'elle (Two or Three Things I Know About Her), 1966, 90 min., 35 mm, color.

Trailer for Deux ou trois choses que je sais d'elle, 1966, 1 min. 30 sec., 35 mm, color.

"On doit tout mettre dans un film" (One should put everything in a film), *L'avant-scène cinéma*, no. 70, May 1967. In *Godard on Godard*, 238–39.

"Ma demarche en quatre mouvements" (My approach in four movements), *L'avant-scène cinéma*, no. 70, May 1967. In *Godard on Godard*, 239–42. A longer version of this text, which was first published in Marie Cardinal, *Cet été-là* (Paris: Nouvelles Éditions Oswald, 1979), is anthologized in *Jean-Luc Godard: Documents*, 80–82.

"Lettre à mes amis pour apprendre à faire du cinéma ensemble" (Letter to my friends to learn how to make films together), *L'avant-scène cinéma*, no. 70, May 1967. In *Godard on Godard*, 242–43.

Anticipation (L'amour en l'an 2000) (Love through the Centuries, episode in Le plus vieux métier du monde [The Oldest Profession]), 1967, 20 min., 35 mm, color.

Trailer for Mouchette by Robert Bresson, 1967, 2 min., 35 mm, b/w.

Script of *La Chinoise*, n.d., in *Godard au travail*, 348.

La Chinoise (The Chinese woman), 1967, 95 min., 35 mm, color.

Trailer for La Chinoise, 1967, 2 min. 40 sec., 35 mm, color.

Caméra-œil (Camera-Eye, episode in Loin du Vietnam [Far From Vietnam]), 1967, 15 min., 16 mm, color.

"Manifeste" (Manifesto), *L'avant-scène cinéma*, no. 114, May 1971. Reproduced in facsimile in *Jean-Luc Godard: Documents*, 88. Text written to accompany the release of *La Chinoise* at the Avignon Festival in July 1967.

"La Chinoise, ou plutôt 'À la chinoise'" (La Chinoise, or rather "À la chinoise"), 1967. Synopsis included in the pressbook for *La Chinoise*. In *Jean-Luc Godard: Documents*, 92–93.

L'amour (Love, episode in Vangelo 70, or La contestation, or Amore et rabbia [Love and Anger]), 1967, 26 min., 35 mm, color.

Week-end (Weekend), 1967, 95 min., 35 mm, color.

Trailer for Week-end, 1967, 48 sec., 35 mm, color.

Jean-Luc Godard et François Truffaut vous parlent (Jean-Luc Godard and François Truffaut talk to you), March 1968, 57 sec., 35 min., b/w. Short film made in support of Henri Langlois.

Le gai savoir (The Joy of Knowledge), 1968, 95 min., 35 mm, color.

Film-tracts, 1968, 2–4 min. each, 16 mm, b/w.

Film-tract no 1968 (dir. Gérard Fromanger, technician Jean-Luc Godard), 1968, 2 min., 16 mm, color.

"Les rois les rois les rois" (The kings the kings the kings). Eight-page graphic reproduction of a film-tract. In *Art et contestation* (Brussels: La Connaissance, 1968), 190–97.

Un film comme les autres (A Film Like Any Other), 1968, 100 min., 16 mm, color and b/w.

Vidéo 5, 1968, video, b/w. Contribution of videotapes, alongside Alain Jacquier and Chris Marker, to the Vidéo 5 video magazine distributed in François Maspero's Paris bookshop.

One American Movie (aka *One A.M.*), 1968, 16 mm, abandoned.

One Plus One, 1968, 99 min., 35 mm, color.

Jean-Luc Godard par Jean-Luc Godard: Articles, essais, entretiens. Edited by Jean Narboni. Paris: Éditions Pierre Belfond, 1968.

Le gai savoir (mot-à-mot d'un film encore trop réviso). Paris: Union des écrivains, 1969.

British Sounds (aka See You at Mao), co-dir. Jean-Henri Roger, 1969, 52 min., 16 mm, color.

"Premiers 'sons anglais'" (First "British sounds"), *Cinéthique*, no. 5, September–October 1969. In *Godard par Godard*, vol. 1, 337–38.

Pravda, co-dir. Jean-Henri Roger, 1969, 58 min., 16 mm, color.

Vent d'est (Wind From the East), Dziga Vertov group, 1969, 100 min., 16 mm, color.

Vive le cinéma! or *À bas le cinéma!* (Long live cinema! or Down with cinema!). Abandoned book project for Les Éditions du Seuil. Co-authored with Jean-Pierre Gorin. A description of this book is given in *Godard: Biographie*, 484–85.

"Pravda." Text distributed at a screening of *Pravda* at the Musée d'art moderne de Paris, February 1970. In *Godard par Godard*, vol. 1, 338–40.

Breakdown of and remarks on *British Sounds*, February 1970. Text written to accompany a screening of the film at the Musée d'art moderne de Paris. In *Jean-Luc Godard: Documents*, 130–31.

Videotapes shot by the Dziga Vertov group, spring 1970. Shown on a monitor in François Maspero's bookshop. See *Godard: Biographie*, 482–83.

Lotte in Italia (Struggles in Italy), Dziga Vertov group, 1970, 60 min., 16 mm, color.

"Que faire?" (What is to be done?), *Afterimage*, no. 1, April 1970. The original handwritten version of this text is reproduced in facsimile in *Jean-Luc Godard: Documents*, 145–51.

"Schéma d'un film palestinien commandé par l'organisation El Fatah" (Outline of a Palestinian film commissioned by Al Fatah). Co-authored with Jean-Pierre Gorin and Armand Marco. Cited in *Godard: Biographie*, 860n80.

Storyboard for *Jusqu'à la victoire*. Co-authored with Jean-Pierre Gorin. Partially reproduced in facsimile in *Jean-Luc Godard: Documents*, 141–43.

List of images shot for *Jusqu'à la victoire*. Co-authored with Jean-Pierre Gorin. Cited in *Godard: Biographie*, 860n94.

Jusqu'à la victoire (Méthodes de pensée et de travail de la révolution palestinienne) (Until victory: Thinking and working methods of the Palestinian revolution), Dziga Vertov group, 1970, 16 mm, color, abandoned.

"Manifeste" (Manifesto), *El Fatah*, July 1970. In *Jean-Luc Godard: Documents*, 138–40.

Vladimir et Rosa (Vladimir and Rosa), Dziga Vertov group, 1970, 96 min., 16 mm, color.

"À propos de *Vladimir et Rosa*" (About *Vladimir et Rosa*). Shooting script for the film, co-authored with Jean-Pierre Gorin. In *Jean-Luc Godard: Documents*, 160–65.

"Que faire dans le cinéma?" (What is to be done in the cinema?), *Politique Hebdo*, no. 23, 11 March, 1971. Collage by the Dziga Vertov group. In *Godard par Godard*, vol. 1, 344–45.

"Pas de vrai plaisir sans Perrier" (No true pleasure without Perrier), *J'accuse*, no. 1, 15 January 1971. In *Jean-Luc Godard: Documents*, 174.

"Nantes-Batignolles: Un bond en avant" (Nantes-Batignolles: A leap ahead), *J'accuse*, no. 2, 15 February 1971. In *Jean-Luc Godard: Documents*, 176.

"Monsieur Robain, vous êtes un escroc, vous méritez la prison!" (Monsieur Robain, you are a crook, you deserve prison!), *J'accuse*, no. 3, 15 March 1971. Text by Catherine Humblot, photographs by Jean-Luc Godard. In *Jean-Luc Godard: Documents*, 177.

Schick (co-dir. Jean-Pierre Gorin), 1971, 45 sec., 16 mm, color.

"*Tout va bien*: Un projet de film de Jean-Luc Godard et Jean-Pierre Gorin." Synopsis of *Tout va bien*. In *Jean-Luc Godard: Documents*, 185–86.

Tout va bien (All's Well), co-dir. Jean-Pierre Gorin, 1972, 95 min., 35 mm, color.

Trailer for Tout va bien, co-dir. Jean-Pierre Gorin, 1972, 5 min., 35 mm, color.

Letter to Jane: An Investigation about a Still, co-dir. Jean-Pierre Gorin, 1972, 52 min., 16 mm, color.

"Enquête sur une image" (Investigation about a still), *Tel quel*, no. 52, winter 1972. Text of the soundtrack of *Letter to Jane*. Co-authored with Jean-Pierre Gorin. In *Godard par Godard*, vol. 1, 350–62.

Moi je, 1973. Abandoned film script. Reproduced in facsimile in *Jean-Luc Godard: Documents*, 195–243.

Two collages by Godard relating to *Moi je*. Used to illustrate an interview with Godard published in *Cinéma pratique*, nos. 124/125, June 1973. In *Jean-Luc Godard: Documents*, 192–93.

Ici et ailleurs (Here and Elsewhere), co-dir. Anne-Marie Miéville (co-dir. Jean-Pierre Gorin for Jusqu'à la victoire material), 1974, 53 min., 16 mm and video, color.

Numéro deux (Number Two), 1975, 88 min., 35 mm and video, color.

"Penser la maison en termes d'usine" (Think home in terms of the factory), *Libération*, no. 2, 15 September, 1975. In *Godard par Godard*, vol. 1, 380–82.

Comment ça va (How Is It Going?), co-dir. Anne-Marie Miéville, 1976, 78 min., 16 mm and video, color.

"Six fois deux: Sur et sous la communication," 1976. Thirteen-page image/text script. In *Godard par Godard*, vol. 1, 387–99.

Six fois deux (Sur et sous la communication) (Six times two [On and under communication]), co-dir. Anne-Marie Miéville, 1976, 610 min., video, color (12 episodes: 1a Y'a personne [Nobody's there]; 2a Leçons de choses [Lessons about things]; 2b Jean-Luc; 3a Photos et Cie [Photos and company]; 3b Marcel; 4a Pas d'histoire [No (hi)story]; 4b Nanas [Chicks]; 5a Nous trois [We three]; 5b René(e)s; 6a Avant et après [Before and after]; 6b Jacqueline et Ludovic.)

A transcription of an additional seventeen-minute abandoned sequence is available in *Jean-Luc Godard: Documents*, 262–65.

"Histoire(s) du cinéma et de la télévision" ("Studies in Motion Pictures and Television"), twenty-page image/text script, n.d., in *Jean-Luc Godard: Documents*, 281–85.

Faut pas rêver (Dream on), 1977, 3 min. 34 sec., video, color.

Open letter to Jean-Pierre Rassam, *Libération*, 24 November 1977. Reprinted in *Cahiers du cinéma*, no. 300, May 1979, 21–23.

Document produced for the Mozambique government relating to the abandoned *Nord contre sud/Naissance (de l'image) d'une nation* project, 1978. Partially reproduced in Colin MacCabe with Laura Mulvey and Mick Eaton, *Godard: Images, Sounds, Politics* (Bloomington: Indiana University Press, 1980), 138–40.

"From the Workshop of Jean-Luc Godard: An Open Letter to ZDF Television from Jean-Luc Godard," in Jan Dawson, ed., *The Films of Hellmuth Costard* (London: Riverside Studios, 1979), 20–21. Reproduced in facsimile in *Jean-Luc Godard: Documents*, 296–97.

"France tour détour deux enfants" (*France tour détour deux enfants*: Declaration à l'intention des héritiers" (*France tour détour deux enfants*: Declaration intended for the heirs), c. 1979, *Caméra/stylo*, September 1983. In *Jean-Luc Godard: Documents*, 302.

France tour détour deux enfants **(France tour detour two children), co-dir. Anne-Marie Miéville, 1979, 12 × 25 min., video, color. (12 episodes: 1 "Obscur/Chimie" [Obscure/Chemistry]; 2 "Lumière/Physique" [Light/Physics]; 3 "Connu/Géométrie/Géographie" [Known/Geometry/Geography]; 4 "Inconnu/Technique" [Unknown/Technique]; 5 "Impression/Dictée" [Impression/Dictation]; 6 "Expression/Français" [Expression/French]; 7 "Violence/Grammaire" [Violence/Grammar]; 8 "Désordre/Calcul" [Disorder/Calculation]; 9 "Pouvoir/Musique" [Power/Music]; 10 "Roman/Économie" [Novel/Economy]; 11 "Réalité/Logique" [Reality/Logic]; 12 "Rêve/Morale" [Dream/Morality].)**

Outline of *France tour détour deux enfants*, n.d., in *Godard par Godard*, vol. 1, 387–99.

Scénario de Sauve qui peut (la vie): Quelques remarques sur la réalisation et la production du film **(Scenario for *Sauve qui peut [la vie]*: A few remarks on the making and production of the film), 1979, 21 min., video, color.**

Bugsy/The Picture/The Story, 1979. Successive versions of an abandoned image/text script. The majority of one version of this script is reproduced in *Godard par Godard*, vol. 1, 418–41.

"*Sauve qui peut (la vie)*: Scénario," 11 April 1979. In *Godard par Godard*, vol. 1, 447–48.

"Lettre numéro un aux membres de la commission d'avance sur recettes" (Letter number one to the members of the advance on receipts committee), 12 April 1979. Preliminary remarks on the production and making of *Sauve qui peut (la vie)*. In *Jean-Luc Godard: Documents*, 307.

Cahiers du cinéma, no. 300, May 1979. Includes letters to Anne-Marie Miéville, Claude Jaget, Jean-Pierre Gorin, Elias Sanbar, Jean-Pierre Rassam, Wim Wenders, Jean-Pierre Beauviala, Carole Roussopoulos, and Alain Tanner; and four substantial image/text collages: "Voir avec ses mains: Comment joue Krystyna Janda," "Les dernières leçons du donneur: Fragments d'un entretien avec Jean-Luc Godard," "Le dernier rêve d'un producteur," and "Rapport sur le voyage No. 2A de la société Sonimage au Mozambique." The latter two documents are reproduced in facsimile (with English translation) in *In the Poem about Love*, 56–88.

"Lettre numéro deux aux membres de la commission d'avance sur recettes" (Letter number two to the members of the advance on receipts committee), n.d., in *Jean-Luc Godard: Documents*, 307.

"Lettre numéro trois aux membres de la commission d'avance sur recettes" (Letter number three to the members of the advance on receipts committee), n.d., in *Jean-Luc Godard: Documents*, 307.

Sauve qui peut (la vie) **(*Every Man for Himself*, aka *Slow Motion*), 1979, 87 min., 35 mm, color.**

Trailer for *Sauve qui peut (la vie)*, 1979, 2 min., 35 mm, color.

Pressbook for *Sauve qui peut (la vie)*, 1980. Reproduced in facsimile in *Jean-Luc Godard: Documents*, 308–15.

Une bonne à tout faire **(A general dogsbody), 1979–82, 5–6 min., color, not released.**

Drawing by Godard of a kiss. Used to illustrate a discussion of a film project entitled "The Kiss" in an interview with Jonathan Cott: "Godard: Born-Again Filmmaker," *Rolling Stone*, 27 November 1980, 32–36.

Introduction à une véritable histoire du cinéma. Paris: Albatros, 1980.

Lettre à Freddy Buache: À propos d'un court-métrage sur la ville de Lausanne **(Letter to Freddy Buache: About a short film on the town of Lausanne), 1981, 11 min., video transferred to 35 mm, color.**

"*Passion*: Premiers elements" (*Passion*: first elements), January 1981. In *Godard par Godard*, vol. 1, 484–85.

***Sauve la vie (qui peut)*. Special edition of *Sauve qui peut (la vie)*, made up of nine ten-minute extracts: five from *Sauve qui peut (la vie)*, and four from other films (Eisenstein's *The General Line*, 1929; Kline and Keaton's *Cops*, 1922; Visconti's *The Earth Trembles*, 1948, and Wajda's *Man of Marble*, 1977).** Screened during the Rotterdam film festival in February 1981.

"*Passion*: Introduction à un scénario" (*Passion*: introduction to a script), twelve-page image/text script for *Passion*, 1981. In *Godard par Godard*, vol. 1, 486–97. A slightly different version of the text of this document (dated 15 March 1981) was published in English translation in *Camera Obscura*, nos. 8/9/10 (fall 1982): 125–29.

"Là où c'était, je serai. Là où je serai, j'ai déjà été. Là où ça ira, on sera mieux" (Where it was, I shall be. Where I shall be, I have already been. When it's OK, we shall be better.), *Cahiers du cinéma* (Special issue: *Situation du cinéma français I*), nos. 323/324, May 1981. Two-page collage.

"*Lettre à Freddy Buache*." Short outline of the film, distributed at the Cannes Film Festival, May 1982.

Audio cassette of sound recordings relating to *Passion* submitted to the Centre national du cinéma with a view to raising production funds for the film.

Passion, le travail et l'amour: Introduction à un scénario*, or *Troisième état du scénario du film Passion **(*Passion*, the work and the love: Introduction to a script), 1982, 30 min., video, color.**

***Passion*, 1982, 87 min., 35 mm, color.**

Trailer for *Passion*, 1982, 2 min., 35 mm, color.

Pressbook for *Passion*, 1982.

Scénario du film Passion (Scenario of the film Passion), 1982, 53 min., video, color.

Changer d'image, or Lettre à la bien-aimée (Change of image), 1982, 9 min. 50 sec., video, color.

Image/text script and breakdown of sequences of *Prénom Carmen*, July–December 1982. In *Godard par Godard*, vol. 1, 557–73.

Prénom Carmen (First Name: Carmen), 1983, 83 min., 35 mm, color.

Trailer for Prénom Carmen, 1983, 2 min., 35 mm, color.

"Prénom Carmen," 1983. Poem included in the pressbook for the film. (The pressbook also includes extracts of the script.)

Audio "cassette-montage" sent to the editors of *Cinématographe* at the time of the release of *Prénom Carmen*. Transcribed as "Dernière minute" in *Cinématographe*, no. 95, 1983. In *Jean-Luc Godard: Documents*, 325–26.

Double-page collage illustrating the relationship between the camera, technicians and actors (through reference to *Prénom Carmen*). In *Godard par Godard*, vol. 1, 532–3.

Collage illustrating the potential of a lightweight ("8–35") camera. In *Godard par Godard*, vol. 1, 538.

Petites notes à propos du film Je vous salue, Marie (Little notes about the film Je vous salue, Marie), 1983, 20 min., video, color.

"Epilogue" (two-page collage), *Cahiers du cinéma*, no. 350, August 1983, 60–61.

Double-page homage to Georges de Beauregard, *Le film français*, 21 September 1984. In *Godard par Godard*, vol. 1, 610–11.

"Vu par le bœuf et l'âne," *Le nouvel observateur*, 6 January 1984. In *Godard par Godard*, vol. 1, 588. Part of this text was read by Godard on the soundtrack of *Une bonne à tout faire* (2006).

"*Je vous salue, Marie*: Scénario," n.d., in *Godard par Godard*, vol. 1, 590–92.

"*Je vous salue, Marie*: Continuité pour le montage" (*Je vous salue, Marie*: Editing continuity script), January 1984. In *Godard par Godard*, vol. 1, 592–97.

"Images of Britain," 1984. Synopsis of the project that would become *Soft and Hard*. In *Jean-Luc Godard: Documents*, 320.

"Tout seul" (All alone), *Cahiers du cinéma*, December 1984 (special out-of-series issue: *Le roman de François Truffaut*). In *Godard par Godard*, vol. 1, 612–13.

Homage to Jean-Pierre Rassam, *Libération*, 1 February 1985.

Je vous salue, Marie (Hail Mary), 1985, 78 min., 35 mm, color.

Trailer for Je vous salue, Marie and Le livre de Marie (co-dir. Anne-Marie Miéville), 1985, 1 min. 55 sec., 35 mm, color.

Pressbook for *Je vous salue, Marie* and *Le livre de Marie*, 1985. Published by Gaumont.

Détective, 1985, 95 min., 35 mm, color.

Outline of *Soft and Hard*, 1985. In *Jean-Luc Godard: Documents*, 321.

Soft and Hard: Soft Talk on a Hard Subject between Two Friends (co-dir. Anne-Marie Miéville), 1985, 52 min., video, color.

Jean-Luc Godard par Jean-Luc Godard. Edited by Alain Bergala. Paris: Cahiers du cinéma/Éditions de l'Étoile, 1985.

Grandeur et décadence d'un petit commerce de cinéma (Grandeur and decadence of a small-time filmmaker), 1985, 91 min., video and 35 mm, color.

Meeting Woody Allen or Meetin' WA, 1986, 26 min., video, color.

"Notes parmi d'autres" (Notes among others), *Le monde* (Radio-Télévision supplement), 22–23 June 1986. In *Jean-Luc Godard: Documents*, 327–28.

Armide (episode in Aria), 1987, 12 min., 35 mm, color.

Soigne ta droite: Une place sur la terre (Keep Your Right Up: A Place on Earth), 1987, 81 min., 35 mm, color.

Trailer for Soigne ta droite, 1987, 2 min., 35 mm, color.

Pressbook for *Soigne ta droite*, 1987.

King Lear, 1987, 90 min., 35 mm, color.

"No Synopsis," 1987. Synopsis of *King Lear*, included in the pressbook for the film published by Cannon.

Preface to *Cinémamémoire*, by Pierre Braunberger (Paris: Centre Pompidou, 1987). In *Godard par Godard*, vol. 2, 208–10.

On s'est tous défilé (We all ran away), 1987, 13 min., video, color.

"La 9ème symphonie." Two-page collage, published in *Cahiers du cinéma*, ed. Wim Wenders, special supplement to *Cahiers du cinéma*, no. 400, October 1987, 28–29.

"Colles et Ciseaux" (Glue and scissors). Six-page collage, published in *Cahiers du cinéma*, no. 402, December 1987. Anthologized as "Non-réponses" in *Godard par Godard*, vol. 2, 116–21.

Closed (series one), 1987. Ten advertisements for Marithé et François Girbaud, 20–30 seconds each, video, color.

Closed (series two), 1988. Seven advertisements for Marithé et François Girbaud, 20–30 seconds each, video, color.

Puissance de la parole (The power of words), 1988, 25 min., video, color.

Le dernier mot (The last word, episode in the series Les

Français vus par . . . [The French seen by . . .]), 1988, 12 min., video, color.

"*Le dernier mot: Les Français vus par JLG.*" Synopsis and commentary. In *Godard par Godard*, vol. 2, 156–57.

Early drafts of *Toutes les histoires* (All the [hi]stories) and *Une histoire seule* (A Solitary [hi]story), episodes 1A and 1B of *Histoire(s) du cinéma*, 1988, 51 min. and 42 min., video, color. Sections of these versions were previewed out of competition at the 1988 Cannes Film Festival.

"À propos de la coupure publicitaire à la télévision: Jean-Luc Godard, ses films, sa plume et ses ciseaux," *Le monde*, 3–4 July 1988. Available in English as "Regarding the Advertisement Cut on Television," in *In the Poem about Love*, 89–92.

Foreword to François Truffaut, *Correspondance*, ed. Gilles Jacob and Claude de Givray (Paris: Hatier, 1988). In *Godard par Godard*, vol. 2, 210–11.

"Chaque art a son verbe" (Each art has its verb). Short text and selected images accompanying Godard's conversation with Serge Daney: "Godard fait des histoires," *Libération*, 26 December 1988. Reproduced in English translation in *Son + Image*, 158.

"Trois scénarios refusés par Gaumont" (Three scripts rejected by Gaumont), 1988. In *Godard par Godard*, vol. 2, 220–22.

Le rapport Darty (The Darty report), co-dir. Anne-Marie Miéville, 1989, 50 min., video, color.

Initial versions of *Toutes les histoires* (All the [hi]stories) and *Une histoire seule* (A solitary [hi]story), episodes 1A and 1B of *Histoire(s) du cinéma*, 1989, 51 min. and 42 min., video, color. Broadcast on Canal Plus, 22/24 and 29/31 May 1989 respectively, and screened at the Vidéothèque de Paris, 20 October 1989.

"Textes à servir au(x) histoire(s) du cinéma" (Texts for use in *Histoire[s] du cinéma*), *Cahiers du cinéma* (special out-of-series issue: *Spécial Godard: 30 ans depuis*, ed. Thierry Jousse and Serge Toubiana), supplement to no. 437, November 1990. In *Godard par Godard*, vol. 1, 183–84.

"Nouvelle vague: Genèse" (*Nouvelle vague*: Genesis). Three versions of the script of *Nouvelle vague*. In *Godard par Godard*, vol. 1, 189–94.

Nouvelle vague (New Wave), 1990, 89 min., 35 mm, color.
Trailer for *Nouvelle vague*, 1990, 58 sec., 35 mm, color.

Synopsis of *Nouvelle vague* in the form of a short poetic text. Included in the pressbook for the film, and reproduced in *L'avant-scène cinéma*, nos. 396/397, November/December 1990.

Métamorphojean, 1990. Five advertisements for Marithé et François Girbaud, 20–30 seconds each, video, color.

Pue Lulla, 1990. Advertisement for Nike, 45 sec., 35 mm, color.

Preface to *Le cinéma français des années 70*, by Freddy Buache (Paris: Hatier, 1990).

Letter to Freddy Buache regarding a collective audiovisual project devoted to the history of Swiss cinema, 21 October 1990. In *Jean-Luc Godard: Documents*, 344–57.

"Projets" (three film projects), *Cahiers du cinéma* (special out-of-series issue: *Spécial Godard: 30 ans depuis*, ed. Thierry Jousse and Serge Toubiana), supplement to no. 437, November 1990. In *Godard par Godard*, vol. 2, 219–20.

"C'est la nuit qui parle" (It's the night that speaks), 1990. Preface to *Une caméra à la place du cœur*, by Philippe Garrel and Thomas Lescure (Aix-en-Provence: Admiranda/Institut de l'image, 1992).

"Histoire(s) du cinéma," c. 1990. Eight-page image-text collage script. In *Son + Image*, 122–29.

L'enfance de l'art (The Childhood of Art, episode in the series *Comment vont les enfants?* [How Are the Kids?]), co-dir. Anne-Marie Miéville, 1991, 8 min., 35 mm, color.

"Allemagne année 90 neuf zéro: Note d'intention" (*Allemagne année 90 neuf zéro*: Note of intention), n.d., in *Jean-Luc Godard: Documents*, 339–40.

Allemagne année 90 neuf zéro (Germany Year 90 Nine Zero), 1991, 62 min., 35 mm, color.

"Lettre à Louis Seguin sur *Allemagne neuf zéro*" (Letter to Louis Seguin about *Allemagne neuf zéro*), *La quinzaine littéraire*, no. 591, 16 December 1991. Response to an article by Seguin. In *Jean-Luc Godard: Documents*, 339–40.

Pour Thomas Wainggai (For Thomas Wainggai, episode in the series *Écrire contre l'oubli* [Against oblivion]), co-dir. Anne-Marie Miéville, 1991, 3 min., 35 mm, color.

"Préface: Entretien entre Jean-Luc Godard et Freddy Buache," in Marianne de Fleury, Dominique Lebrun, and Olivier Meston, eds., *Musée du cinéma Henri Langlois* (Paris: Maeght Éditeur, 1991).

"Rapport d'inactivité: Les mésaventures du centre de recherche sur les métiers de l'image et du son" (Inactivity report: The misadventures of the research center for professions relating to image and sound), *Le monde*, 8 October 1991. In *Godard par Godard*, vol. 2, 249–51.

"La paroisse morte" (The dead parish), *Trafic*, no. 1, winter 1991. In *Godard par Godard*, vol. 2, 254.

"Le ciné-fils" (The cine-son), *Libération*, 13–14 June 1992. In *Godard par Godard*, vol. 2, 252.

Parisienne People, co-dir. Anne-Marie Miéville, 1992.

Advertisement for Parisienne People cigarettes, 45 sec., 35 mm, color.

"Hélas pour moi: Proposition de cinéma d'après une légende" (Hélas pour moi: cinema proposal based on a legend), January–February 1992. In Jean-Luc Godard: Documents, 364–66.

Initial version of Seul le cinéma (The cinema alone), episode 2A of Histoire(s) du cinéma, 1993, 27 min., video. Screened at Museum of Modern Art, January 1994, and at the Locarno International Film Festival, August 1995.

Les enfants jouent à la Russie (The Kids Play Russian), 1993, 58 min., video, color.

Hélas pour moi (Oh, Woe Is Me), 1993, 84 min., 35 mm, color.

Trailer for Hélas pour moi, 1993, 46 sec., 35 mm, color.

"Hélas pour moi," synopsis of the film included in the pressbook. In Godard par Godard, vol. 2, 271.

Handmade image/text book based on Hélas pour moi. Presented by Godard to Bernard Pivot on Bouillon de culture, France 2, 10 September, 1993.

Je vous salue, Sarajevo (Hail, Sarajevo), 1993, 2 min. 24 sec., video, color.

Two scripts of JLG/JLG: Autoportrait de décembre, 1993. In Godard par Godard, vol. 2, 286–88.

Initial version of Fatale beauté (Fatal beauty), episode 2B of Histoire(s) du cinéma, 1994, 29 min., video. Screened at Museum of Modern Art, January 1994, and at the Locarno International Film Festival, August 1995.

"Histoire(s) du cinéma. Avec un s.," Le monde, 15 December 1994. Text derived from the soundtrack of episodes 1A, 1B, 2B, and 3A of Histoire(s) du cinéma, together with two passages not used in the series.

"Letter from Jean-Luc." Letter in English dated 21 January 1995 to Armond White, Chairman of the New York Film Critics Circle, refusing the NYFCC's inaugural career-achievement award. Published in Village Voice, 14 February 1995; Film Comment 31, no. 2, March/April 1995; and, in French (under the title "Lettre à un ami américain"), in Cahiers du cinéma, no. 490, April 1995. Anthologized in Godard par Godard, vol. 2, 344.

JLG/JLG: Autoportrait de décembre (JLG/JLG: December Self-Portrait), 1995, 56 min., 35 mm, color.

Trailer for JLG/JLG: Autoportrait de décembre, 1995, 58 sec., 35 mm, color.

"Lettre à une amie allemande" (Letter to a German friend), L'humanité, 8 March 1995. A copy of this letter to Christa Maerker of the Berlin International Film Festival was published in Cahiers du cinéma, no. 490, April 1995, and included in the pressbook for JLG/JLG:

Autoportrait de décembre. In Godard par Godard, vol. 1, 345–46.

Handmade A4 photocopied versions of the first three volumes of the Histoire(s) du cinéma books (150 copies), based on the first six episodes. Distributed at the Locarno International Film Festival, August 1995.

Initial version of La monnaie de l'absolu (Aftermath of the absolute), episode 3A of Histoire(s) du cinéma, 1995, 27 min., video. Screened at the Locarno International Film Festival, August 1995, and in the "Un certain regard" section at the Cannes Film Festival, May 1997.

Deux fois cinquante ans de cinéma français (2 × 50 Years of French Cinema, co-dir. Anne-Marie Miéville), 1995, 49 min., video, color.

Deux fois cinquante ans de cinéma français. Image-text book derived from the film. Partially reproduced in Godard par Godard, vol. 2, 323–34.

Letter to "A," 2 August 1995. Seven-page illustrated letter. In Godard par Godard, vol. 2, 347–53.

"À propos de cinéma et d'histoire" (On cinema and history), Trafic, no. 18, spring 1996. Text of the speech delivered by Godard when accepting the Adorno Prize in Frankfurt, 17 September 1995. In Godard par Godard, vol. 2, 401–5.

Espoir/Microcosmos and Le monde comme il ne va pas (Man's Hope/Microcosmos and What's Wrong with the World), 1996, 3 min. and 1 min., video, color and b/w. Two montage experiments broadcast on France 2 in the framework of Le cercle de minuit, January 1996.

Dialogue script for For ever Mozart, n.d., partially reproduced in Jean-Luc Godard: Documents, 370–72.

For ever Mozart, 1996, 80 min., 35 mm, color.

Trailer for For ever Mozart, 1996, 50 sec., 35 mm, color.

Pressbook for For ever Mozart, 1996. Includes the poem "Le film," reproduced in Jean-Luc Godard: Documents, 410.

Initial version of Une vague nouvelle (A new wave), episode 3B of Histoire(s) du cinéma, 1996, 28 min., video. Screeened at the Locarno International Film Festival, August 1995.

Adieu au TNS (Farewell to the Théâtre National de Strasbourg), 1996, 7 min. 20 sec., video, color.

"Adieu au TNS" (text of the film), in Godard par Godard, vol. 2, 398–99.

Plus Oh! 1996. Music video for the song "Plus haut" (Higher still) by France Gall, 4 min., video, color.

"Dit/vu," Cahiers du cinéma, no. 508, December 1996. Fourteen-page image/text collage letter to Cahiers du cinéma dated November 1996, published at the time of the release of For ever Mozart. The written component of this document is reproduced in *Godard par Godard*, vol. 2, 394–95.

JLG/JLG: Phrases. Paris: P.O.L., 1996.

For ever Mozart: Phrases. Paris: P.O.L., 1996.

Initial version of *Le contrôle de l'univers* (The control of the universe), episode 4A of *Histoire(s) du cinéma*, 1997, 28 min., video. Screened in the "Un certain regard" section at the Cannes Film Festival, May 1997.

Histoire(s) du cinéma: Extraits. A4-format pressbook made up of images and extracts of the soundtrack from episodes 3A and 4A, the layout of which differs in some instances from that used in the Gallimard books. Distributed at the Cannes Film Festival in May 1997 to accompany the screening of the near-final versions of episodes 3A and 4A.

Nouvelle vague, 2-CD set, ECM Records, 1997.

Early alternative version of *Les signes parmi nous* (The signs amongst us), episode 4B *Histoire(s) du cinéma*, 1997, 27 min., video. Projected at the Ciné Lumière, London, 27 September, 1997. Constructed around extracts of Godard's dialogue with Serge Daney recorded in Rolle, Switzerland, in 1988.

Four versions of the script for *Éloge de l'amour*, 1997–98. In *Godard par Godard*, vol. 2, 447–69.

Histoire(s) du cinéma, 1998, 264 min., video, color. (8 episodes: 1A *Toutes les histoires* [All the (hi)stories]; 1B *Une histoire seule* [A solitary (hi)story]; 2A *Seul le cinéma* [The cinema alone]; 2B *Fatale beauté* [Fatal beauty]; 3A *La monnaie de l'absolu* [Aftermath of the absolute]; 3B *Une vague nouvelle* [A new wave]; 4A *Le contrôle de l'univers* [The control of the universe]; 4B *Les signes parmi nous* [The signs amongst us].)

The Old Place: Small Notes Regarding the Arts at Fall of 20th Century, co-dir. Anne-Marie Miéville, 1998, 47 min., video, color.

Jean-Luc Godard par Jean-Luc Godard, vol. 2. Edited by Alain Bergala. Paris: Cahiers du cinéma/Éditions de l'Étoile, 1998.

Histoire(s) du cinéma. Paris: Gallimard-Gaumont, 1998. (4 vols.: 1 *Toutes les histoires/Une histoire seule*; 2 *Seul le cinéma/Fatale beauté*; 3 *La monnaie de l'absolu/Une vague nouvelle*; 4 *Le contrôle de l'univers/Les signes parmi nous*.)

"Deuxième lettre à Freddy Buache: Oh! Temps de l'utopie" (Second letter to Freddy Buache: Oh! Time of utopia), 1998. In *Godard par Godard*, vol. 2, 212–18.

2 × 50 ans de cinéma français: Phrases (sorties d'un film). Paris: P.O.L., 1998. Co-authored with Anne-Marie Miéville.

Les enfants jouent à la Russie: Phrases (sorties d'un film). Paris: P.O.L., 1998.

Allemagne neuf zéro: Phrases (sorties d'un film). Paris: P.O.L., 1998.

Letters to Gilles Sandoz, Claude Lanzmann, Bernard-Henri Lévy, and Julien Hirsch detailing plans for a film to be titled *Pas un dîner de gala* (Not a gala dinner) or *Un fameux débat* (A much talked-about debate) to be co-directed by Godard, Lanzmann, and Lévy, 18 March 1999, 18 June 1999, and 12 July 1999. In Bernard-Henri Lévy, "Pas un dîner de gala (troisième épisode, 1999)," *La règle du jeu*, 17 November 2010, laregledujeu.org/2010/11/17/3373/pas-un-diner-de-gala-troisieme-episode-1999.

Histoire(s) du cinéma. Munich: ECM Records, 1999. Box set of five CDs and four multilingual art books.

De l'origine du XXIe siècle (On the origin of the twenty-first century), 2000, 15 min., video, color.

Archéologie du cinéma et mémoire du siècle: Dialogue (Tours: Farago, 2000). Co-authored with Youssef Ishaghpour. First published in two parts in *Trafic* in 1999, and translated into English in 2005.

Lettre à Freddy Buache: À propos d'un court-métrage sur la ville de Lausanne (Lausanne: Éditions Demoures, 2001).

Éloge de l'amour (In Praise of Love), 2001, 94 min., 35 mm and digital video, b/w and color.

Trailer for Éloge de l'amour, 2001, 1 min. 20 sec., 35 mm, color.

Pressbook for *Éloge de l'amour*, 2001.

Éloge de l'amour: Phrases (sorties d'un film). Paris: P.O.L., 2001.

Moments choisis des Histoire(s) du cinéma (Selected moments of Histoire(s) du cinéma), 2001, 84 min., video transferred to 35 mm, color.

Dans le noir du temps (In the darkness of time, episode in Ten Minutes Older: The Cello), co-dir. Anne-Marie Miéville, 2002, 10 min., video, color.

Liberté et patrie (Freedom and fatherland), co-dir. Anne-Marie Miéville, 2002, 22 min., video, color.

"Our Music: Synopsis for a Film" (co-authored with Anne-Marie Miéville), n.d., in Steve Lake and Paul Griffiths, eds., *Horizons Touched: The Music of ECM* (London: Granta, 2007).

Notre musique (Our Music), 2004, 80 min., 35 mm, color.

Trailer for Notre musique, 2004, 1 min. 6 sec., 35 mm, color.

Pressbook for *Notre musique*, 2004.

"Regardezvoir, Godard" (Looksee Godard; co-authored with Gérard Lefort), *Libération*, 12 May 2004. In *Jean-Luc Godard: Documents*, 412–13.

"Collages de France," *Cahiers du cinéma*, no. 590, May 2004, 19. Early written outline of the project that would become *Voyage(s) en utopie*.

Prière pour refusniks (Prayer for refuseniks), 2004, 7 min., video, color.

Prière (2) pour refusniks (Prayer [2] for refuseniks), 2004, 3 min. 30 sec., video, color.

De l'origine du XXIe siècle, The Old Place, Liberté et Patrie, Je vous salue, Sarajevo. Hamburg: ECM Records, 2006. Co-authored with Anne-Marie Miéville. Includes a DVD containing the films of the title, together with a transcription in French and English of the soundtracks.

Reportage amateur (maquette expo) (Amateur report [exhibition model]), 2006, 47 min., video, color.

Voyage(s) en utopie: JLG, 1946–2006, À la recherche d'un théorème perdu (Travel(s) in Utopia: JLG, 1946–2006, In Search of a Lost Theorem), Galérie Sud, Pompidou Center, Paris, 11 May–14 August 2006.

Vrai faux passeport: Fiction documentaire sur des occasions de porter un jugement à propos de la façon de faire des films (True false passport: Documentary fiction on the opportunities for passing judgment about the manner in which films are made), 2006, 55 min., video, b/w and color.

Ecce homo, 2006, 2 min., video, b/w and color.

Une bonne à tout faire (A general dogsbody), new version, 2006, 8 min. 20 sec., video, color.

Une catastrophe, 2008, 1 min. 3 sec., video, b/w and color. Trailer for the 2008 Viennale.

Trailer for *Film socialisme,* 2009, 4 min. 15 sec., video, color.

C'était quand (It was when), 2010, 3 min. 26 sec., video. Homage to Éric Rohmer, screened at the Cinémathèque française, 8 February 2010.

Film socialisme (directorial committee: Jean-Luc Godard, Fabrice Aragno, Jean-Paul Battaggia, Paul Grivas), 2010, 102 min., HD video, color.

Five further trailers for *Film socialisme,* 2010 (4 min. 6 sec., 2 min. 10 sec., 1 min. 48 sec., 1 min. 11 sec., 1 min. 7 sec.), video, color.

Film socialisme: Dialogues avec visages auteurs. Paris: P.O.L., 2010.

Written reflection on digital technology, 8 June 2011, in Nicholas Cullinan, ed., *Tacita Dean: Film* (London: Tate, 2011), 75.

Dialogues sur le cinéma. Lormont: Bord de l'eau, 2011. Co-authored with Marcel Ophuls.

Deux ou trois voyages dans l'univers selon JLG (Two or three voyages into the universe according to JLG) (dir. Fabrice Aragno; written and supervised by Jean-Luc Godard), 2012, 27 min., video, color.

Notes

Introduction

1. Godard in conversation with Noël Simsolo on *À voix nue: Grands entretiens d'hier et d'aujourd'hui,* France Culture, 31 March 1998. This is the second in a series of five dialogues between Godard and Simsolo about *Histoire(s) du cinéma* that were broadcast on *À voix nue* from 30 March to 3 April 1998. These were transcribed by Nicole Brenez and Alain Philippon, with a view to their publication as a book entitled *L'humanité du cinéma: Jean-Luc Godard, entretiens.* This volume was also to have included a transcription of a previous series of ten dialogues between Godard and Simsolo about *Histoire(s) du cinéma,* which had been broadcast on *À voix nue* from 20 November to 1 December 1989. This earlier series had also been transcribed at the time, by Nicole Brenez, Cécile Carrega and Alain Philippon, again with a view to its publication in book form. That neither of these projects came to fruition is highly regrettable, since these interviews are undoubtedly among the richest contextual documents relating to *Histoire(s) du cinéma* available. I am very grateful to Nicole Brenez for having made a copy of the unpublished manuscript of *L'humanité du cinéma* available to me. When citing from these interviews, I will henceforth refer to the individual episodes of *À voix nue.*

2. "Godard fait son cinéma" (1998), 76–77.

3. Faulkner, *Requiem for a Nun,* 80. For Godard's use of this phrase in the series, see *Histoire(s),* vol. 3, 62–63.

4. Bresson, *Notes on the Cinematographer,* 41. Godard cites this phrase in the final episode of the series (*Histoire[s],* vol. 4, 265).

5. Godard, "Les cinémathèques," 287.

6. *À voix nue,* 20 November 1989.

7. Godard, *Histoire(s),* vol. 2, 159.

8. Godard's discussion with Hobsbawm, chaired by Marc Ferro, took place on *Histoire parallèle,* 6 May 2000.

9. "Le regard s'est perdu" (1987), 123.

10. "Propos rompus" (1980), 463.

11. The *Book of Kings,* also known as the *Morgan Bible, Maciejowski Bible,* and *Crusader Bible,* is a thirteenth-century picture bible made up of paintings depicting scenes from the Old Testament from Genesis to David. Its title is among those spoken by Godard on the soundtrack of 1A.

12. Warburg, *Der Bilderatlas Mnemosyne.*

13. Agamben, "Aby Warburg and the Nameless Science," 90.

14. I would like to acknowledge the pioneering research into Godard's sources conducted by other students of *Histoire(s) du cinéma,* especially Jacques Aumont, Bernard Eisenschitz, Roland-François Lack, Jean-Louis Leutrat, Suzanne Liandrat-Guigues, Céline

Scemama, Michael Temple, James Williams, and the team of researchers who worked on the Japanese DVD/DVD-ROM of the series instigated by Hayao Shibata and supervised by Akira Asada: Junji Hori, Tomoo Karube, Katsuhiko Sugihara and Erimi Fujiwara. The very impressive "score" of the series drawn up by Scemama (*La "partition" des Histoire(s) du cinéma de Jean-Luc Godard*, cri-image.univ-paris1.fr/celine/celinegodard.html) is an extremely useful research aid, but has to be treated with care, since it includes a significant number of omissions and misattributions.

15. Godard attributes the title to Malraux in "The Future(s) of Film" (2000), 26.

16. "Dialogue entre Godard et Daney" (1997), 53.

17. For a discussion by Godard of *The Great Sinner* in relation to the title of 2B, see *À voix nue*, 28 November 1989.

18. Malraux's study was published initially in three volumes: *Psychologie de l'art*, vol 1, *Le musée imaginaire* (1947); vol. 2, *La création artistique* (1948); and vol. 3, *La monnaie de l'absolu* (1949). It was published in English translation by Zwemmer in 1951, and republished in French by Gallimard the same year in a revised, less expensive single volume under the generic title *Les voix du silence,* which included an additional section, *Les métamorphoses d'Apollon.* Subsequent references are to the English translation of this second expanded version: *The Voices of Silence.*

19. Ramuz, *Les signes parmi nous.*

20. "Jean-Luc Godard: Une longue histoire" (2001), 32.

21. On the few occasions where I have found fuller citation to be preferable, I have translated directly from the soundtrack, and used the French-language transcription available in the ECM books for comparison. The latter is particularly valuable due to its relative fullness, and for the manner in which the book titles (and, at times, film titles) are distinguished from the surrounding material. Unfortunately, the English translation included in these volumes contains occasional significant errors.

22. "La légende du siècle" (1998), 23.

23. "Jean-Luc Godard: Une longue histoire" (2001), 31.

24. The order of the titles of the eight sections that make up *Moments choisis des Histoire(s) du cinéma* is as follows: (1) *Toutes les histoires,* (2) *Une histoire seule,* (3) *Fatale beauté,* (4) *Seul le cinéma,* (5) *Une vague nouvelle,* (6) *Le contrôle de l'univers,* (7) *La monnaie de l'absolu,* and (8) *Les signes parmi nous.* Each section lasts approximately ten minutes–apart from 2 and 3, which last a little under eight and nine minutes, respectively. Section 1 draws predominantly from 2A, section 2 from 1A, section 3

from 2B, section 4 from 3A, section 5 from 3B, section 6 from 4A, and sections 7 and 8 from 4B.

25. Godard and Ishaghpour, *Cinema,* 48.

26. "Jean-Luc Godard: Des traces du cinéma" (1999), 50.

27. Frodon, "Jean-Luc Godard, maître d'ouvrage d'art."

28. I am deeply indebted to Wendy Everett, who established a remarkable videotheque at the University of Bath in the 1980s, and inspired an intense curiosity among her students for the films it contained.

29. According to Alberto Farassino, Godard pitched this project to Radiotelevisione Italiana (RAI) ("Introduction," 52).

30. Witt, "Shapeshifter."

31. Doniol-Valcroze, "Jean-Luc Godard, cinéaste masqué."

32. Leutrat, "Retour sur *Histoire(s),* 3," 108–109.

1. *Histoire(s) du cinéma*

1. Godard, "Les cinémathèques," 286–87.

2. Godard on *Civilisation: L'homme et les images* (Éric Rohmer, 1967).

3. Aragon, "What Is Art?" 141.

4. For a description of this proposed book, see Baecque, *Godard: Biographie,* 483–84. Although this journalistic biography contains a good deal of valuable new information such as this, it lacks rigor and is at times highly derivative.

5. Farassino, "Introduction," 52.

6. Godard, *Introduction,* 42.

7. This document, read by cinematographer Armand Marco to David Faroult in the course of an interview on 2 August 2002, is cited in the latter's doctoral thesis ("Avant-garde cinématographique," 147). Godard's critique of Sartre through reference to Astruc returns in virtually identical terms in 2B.

8. Godard, *Introduction,* 162.

9. Godard, *Moi je,* 238.

10. "Godard arrêt sur images" (1988), 59.

11. Roud, *A Passion for Films,* 199.

12. I am indebted to Timothy Barnard for providing me with this information, and for sharing with me other important details regarding Godard's Montreal lectures.

13. Video recordings of the evening question and answer sessions with Godard that took place after the screenings of his films from 9 to 13 March are held in the Concordia University archives.

14. For an account of this visit, see Brody, *Everything Is Cinema,* 393–94.

15. Godard in Jean-Pierre Tadros, "Godard à

Montréal," *Le devoir* (Montreal), 25 August 1977. Quoted in Larouche, "Godard et le Québécois," 162.

16. Godard, *Introduction*, 165.

17. Godard, *Introduction*, 21–22, 24.

18. Narboni, Pierre, and Rivette, "Montage," in Rivette, *Jacques Rivette*.

19. Narboni, Pierre, and Rivette, "Montage," in Rivette, *Jacques Rivette*, 69.

20. "Le briquet de Capitaine Cook" (1992), 20.

21. Godard, *Introduction*, 165.

22. À voix nue, 20 November 1989.

23. À voix nue, 20 November 1989.

24. Godard, *Introduction*, 24.

25. Godard, *Introduction*, 144, 195.

26. À voix nue, 30 March 1998.

27. À voix nue, 30 March 1998.

28. "Entretien avec J-L Godard le 12 avril 1978," 26.

29. Godard, *Introduction*, 170–75.

30. See Alain Rémond's introduction to his and Jean-Luc Douin's seven-part interview with Godard in the summer of 1978 ("Godard dit tout," 4).

31. "Godard dit tout" (1978), 4. According to Richard Brody, Godard had already proposed a one-hour video about cinema history to INA in 1976 (*Everything Is Cinema*, 391).

32. Godard, *Introduction*, 170–75, 261.

33. Mitry, in Godard, "Les cinémathèques," 281.

34. Godard, *Introduction*, 124.

35. Godard, *Introduction*, 41.

36. Godard, *Introduction*, 21–22.

37. Godard, *Introduction*, 185.

38. Breton, "As in a Wood," 74.

39. Schefer, *L'homme ordinaire*, 99.

40. Cavell, *The World Viewed*, 154.

41. Rosenbaum, *Moving Places*.

42. In 1996 Godard suggested that Rosenbaum's *Moving Places* should be translated into French ("Parler du manque," 374). It was published in French in 2003.

43. Williams, "*Histoire(s) du cinéma*," 12 (original emphasis).

44. Godard, "Les cinémathèques."

45. Godard, "Les cinémathèques," 287.

46. Godard, "Les cinémathèques," 288.

47. Godard, *Introduction*, 23.

48. Godard, "Les cinémathèques," 287; Godard, *Introduction*, 166.

49. Godard, *Introduction*, 165.

50. Godard, "Les cinémathèques," 290.

51. "Les dernières leçons du donneur" (1979), 62.

52. Godard, *Introduction*, 166.

53. Godard, "Les cinémathèques," 287.

54. Godard, "Les cinémathèques," 289–90.

55. Godard, "Les cinémathèques," 287.

56. Païni, "Faire violence."

57. Godard, *Histoire(s)*, vol. 1, 70–71.

58. Godard, *Introduction*, 111–12.

59. This passage comes towards the end of 2A. It is faithfully transcribed in "Godard fait des histoires," interview by Serge Daney, *Libération*, 26 December 1988. In *Jean-Luc Godard par Jean-Luc Godard* (Hereafter *Godard par Godard*), vol. 2, 161–73. Published in English as "Godard Makes (Hi)stories" (quotation on 159). The Brecht poem Godard refers to is "Sorgfältig prüf ich" (1931), which he had previously cited in *Jean-Luc*, episode 2b of *Six fois deux*.

60. Godard, *Histoire(s)*, vol. 2, 144. The reference is to *Le secret du masque de fer*, in which Pagnol argued that the man in the mask was the King's twin brother.

61. Godard, "Grâce à Henri Langlois," 235.

62. À voix nue, 24 November 1989.

63. Godard in dialogue with Paul Amar at the Cannes Film Festival on 20h 10 May 1997. The partial transcription of this interview, as "Godard/Amar," elides Godard's key point here that cinema, even when made for a different purpose entirely, ended up archiving the twentieth century.

64. Godard, *Histoire(s)*, vol. 2, 96–97.

65. Godard, *Histoire(s)*, vol. 1, 190.

66. According to Godard, Edgar Degas used the term "fauxtographe" in conversation with Émile Zola as a means of criticizing the latter's enthusiasm for photography ("Jean-Luc Godard en liberté" [2010]). He attributed the celebrated phrase from *Vent d'est* to Gorin on À voix nue, 21 November 1989.

67. À voix nue, 30 March 1998.

68. Godard and Ishaghpour, *Cinema*, 87–88.

69. "Le cinéma est toujours une opération de deuil" (1996), 382.

70. À voix nue, 2 April 1998.

71. Godard, "Le ciné-fils."

72. Romains, "The Crowd at the Cinematograph," 53.

73. Henric, "L'image, quelle image?" 39.

74. See, for instance, "Dans Marie il y a aimer" (1985), 608.

75. "For me, he's St Paul," says Langlois of Godard in an archival interview included in *Le bon plaisir* (20 May 1995). Langlois's comments are not included in the partial transcript of this program, "Le bon plaisir."

76. Malraux, "The Creative Process," in *The Voices of Silence*, 273–466, quotation on 461. I am grateful to Derek Allan for pointing out to me the centrality of this idea within Malraux's œuvre.

77. Godard, *Histoire(s)*, vol. 1, 170.

78. Godard, "Jean Renoir," 63 (original emphasis).

79. Godard, *Histoire(s)*, vol. 2, 165.

80. Godard, *Histoire(s)*, vol. 1, 251–57. See also vol. 2, 188–201.

81. "Godard arrêt sur images" (1988), 59.

82. Godard, "Montage, mon beau souci."

83. See Bazin, "Editing Prohibited," in *What Is Cinema?* 73–86.

84. Tynjanov, "On the Foundations of Cinema," 90.

85. "Le briquet de Capitaine Cook" (1992), 19.

86. Merleau-Ponty, "The Film and the New Psychology," 58.

87. Bellour, "Godart or not Godard," 8.

88. Bazin, "The Evolution of Film Language," in *What Is Cinema?* 87–106, quotation on 104.

89. Malraux, "Sketch," 326.

90. Godard, *Introduction*, 175–76.

91. Godard, *Introduction*, 175.

92. "Godard Makes (Hi)stories" (1988), 160.

93. Interview with Joël Farges, 13 September 2011. All the information that follows regarding *Introduction à une véritable histoire du cinéma* is from this source.

94. A new full transcription and translation by Timothy Barnard of the videotapes of Godard's talks held in the Concordia University archives reveals the intrinsically dialogic nature of his method. This new version is forthcoming in English from Caboose Books.

95. Interview with Monica Galer, 1 September 2011. Monica Galer (Galer is Tegelaar's maiden name, to which she has reverted) went on to become a prominent television executive. She is currently CEO of Fremantle Media France.

96. Interview with Monica Galer, 1 September 2011.

97. Heijs and Westra, *Que le tigre danse*, 135.

98. See, for instance, Richard Roud, "Celebrity Hour," *The Guardian*, 27 February 1980.

99. Heijs and Westra, *Que le tigre danse*, 135.

100. Biette, "Godard et son histoire," v.

101. Heijs and Westra, *Que le tigre danse*, 136.

102. Heijs and Westra, *Que le tigre danse*, 136.

103. Martyn Auty, "First of the Festivals," *Time Out*, 27 February 1981, 21.

104. For a detailed description of the structure of *Sauve la vie (qui peut)*, see Tesson, "Rotterdam 81," 46.

105. Biette, "Godard et son histoire," v.

106. Biette, "Godard et son histoire," v.

107. Heijs and Westra, *Que le tigre danse*, 151.

108. Heijs and Westra, *Que le tigre danse*, 136, 151. It is difficult to ascertain precisely how much the Foundation invested in Godard's project. Although the initial figure was 150,000 guilders (a sum confirmed to me by Monica Galer), Bals indicated that by August 1981 the total had risen to 250,000 guilders.

109. See "J'ai fait une échographie" (1998), 36; "The Future(s) of Film" (2000), 26; and "La légende du siècle" (1998), 23.

110. "Parler du manque" (1996), 374.

111. Godard, "À propos de la coupure publicitaire," 92.

112. *Cinéma cinémas*, 20 December 1987.

113. Didi-Huberman, *Invention of Hysteria*.

114. Bergala, "L'Ange de l'Histoire," 231. Bergala and Buache also discussed these early versions at the conference organized by the former, "Godard entre terre et ciel: Les limites du sacré," at the Centre Thomas More, La Tourette monastery, L'Arbresle, November 1998.

115. See Mazabrard, "Histoires du cinéma sur Canal +," vi.

116. "Une boucle bouclée" (1997), 17.

117. Godard, "Le montage, la solitude," 242.

118. Rougemont, *Penser avec les mains*.

119. "Le chemin vers la parole" (1982), 503–504.

120. "Jean-Luc Godard: 'La France reste,'" (1990), 29.

121. This document is reproduced in *Godard par Godard*, vol. 1, 557–73.

122. "Une boucle bouclée" (1997), 17.

123. "Une boucle bouclée" (1997), 15; "Godard Makes (Hi)stories" (1988), 164.

124. "Une boucle bouclée" (1997), 17.

125. "Dialogue entre Godard et Daney" (1997), 51, 55.

126. The full list of titles is not given in 1A and 1B. Episodes 3B, 4A and 4B give all the titles, including *Montage, mon beau souci* and *La réponse des ténèbres*. Episodes 2A, 2B and 3A give all the titles, including the two additional ones, except for those of 1A and 1B.

127. See "Une boucle bouclée" (1997), 15; "La légende du siècle" (1998), 26; *À voix nue*, 1 April 1998; Godard and Ishaghpour, *Cinema*, 5, 18; and "Le cinéma me reste" (2005).

128. *À voix nue*, 1 April 1998.

129. Daney and Godard, *Microfilms*, 27 December 1987 and 3 January 1988.

130. "Dialogue entre Godard et Daney" (1997). The recording was retranscribed by Pauline le Diset and Alain Bergala. When citing this dialogue, I will henceforth refer mainly to this later version. However, since a good deal of important material included in the *Libération* version is omitted from the retranscription, there are times when it will be necessary to continue to cite from the earlier version.

131. "Dialogue entre Godard et Daney" (1997), 53.

132. Godard, "Le ciné-fils," 252.

133. Godard, *Histoire(s)*, vol. 2, 42.

134. Godard, "Tout seul," 613.

135. Godard, "Le ciné-fils," 252.

136. Godard and Ishaghpour, *Cinema*, 9.

137. Daney, *Postcards from the Cinema,* 54.

138. Daney, *L'exercice.* Jacques Aumont has also noted that some of the images inserted by Godard into this sequence in 2A function as a "gentle, discrete homage" to Daney (*Amnésies,* 106).

139. Baudelaire, "Le voyage," in *Les fleurs du mal,* 155–61.

140. "Le bon plaisir" (1995), 320.

141. This alternative early version of 4B was constructed around the exchange between Godard and Daney in "Godard Makes (Hi)stories" (1988), from Daney's "With the triumph of the audiovisual media . . ." (159) to Godard's ". . . because it needed a public immediately" (161). It also included lengthy passages not available in either transcription, together with the opening of the exchange transcribed in "Dialogue entre Godard et Daney" (1997), 49 (from the beginning of the text to Daney's "Est-ce que tu dis que tout cela est beau?").

142. For an account of the press launch, see "J'ai fait une échographie" (1998).

143. See Daney's introductory comments to "Godard fait des histoires" (1988), 24. These are not reproduced in the versions of this interview subsequently republished in French and English.

144. Duby, *History Continues,* 109.

145. Delage, "Librairie," 145.

146. "Un centre de recherche pour Godard," *La croix,* 5 April 1990. See also Godard, "Rapport d'inactivité."

147. See Eisenschitz, "Une machine." Eisenschitz was assisted in his work by Laurie Bloom, who was tasked with identifying the paintings.

148. Godard, "Les cinémathèques," 290.

149. See "C'est le cinéma" (1998).

2. The Prior and Parallel Work

1. "L'art à partir de la vie" (1985), 14.

2. This notion of "thinking oneself historically" can be traced to Brecht's parabolic prose fiction, *Me-ti, Buch der Wendungen,* which includes a section entitled "On looking at oneself historically." For a discussion of the influence of this book on Godard's work within the Dziga Vertov group, see Lesage, "Godard and Gorin's Left Politics."

3. Gorin in "Raymond Chandler, Mao Tse-Tung and *Tout va bien,*" 24.

4. Gorin in "Raymond Chandler, Mao Tse-Tung and *Tout va bien,*" 24.

5. Gorin in "Filmmaking and History," 19.

6. Miéville in "Un entretien avec la réalisatrice," 13.

7. Godard, "Voir avec ses mains" and "Le dernier rêve d'un producteur." The two images used in 1B

(recropped) from *Nord contre sud* are taken from page 71 (they are also used in larger format later in the same issue).

8. Attali, *Noise.*

9. Attali, *Noise,* 81.

10. Jacob, *The Logic of Life,* 309–10.

11. See "L'art à partir de la vie" (1985), 24; and Stevens, "The American Friend."

12. Godard recounted this anecdote during a talk at the Cinéma des cinéastes, Paris, on 8 June 2010.

13. See the radio program *Vidéo out, Vidéo 00, Vidéo cent fleurs, Vidéa et les insoumuses . . . ,* 19 September 2006.

14. Baecque, *Godard: Biographie,* 477, 519.

15. Godard and Ishaghpour, *Cinema,* 36.

16. "The Future(s) of Film" (2000), 24.

17. Godard, *Introduction,* 35.

18. "Jean-Luc Godard: L'important" (1975), 13.

19. "Jean-Luc Godard: Des traces du cinéma" (1999), 52.

20. Godard on *Droit d'auteurs,* 6 December 1998.

21. "The Future(s) of Film" (2000), 25–26.

22. "Le cinéma meurt, vive le cinéma!" (1987), 10.

23. "La chance de repartir" (1980), 408.

24. Godard, *Introduction,* 65.

25. Godard, *Introduction,* 65, 106.

26. Godard, *Introduction,* 264.

27. Godard confirmed to me via fax in 2006 that he had made the trailers for almost all his feature films since *À bout de souffle,* apart from those between 1968 and 1972 (with the exception, during this period, of *Tout va bien,* the trailer for which he made with Gorin), and excluding *Détective* and *King Lear.* For further discussion of Godard's trailers, see Hediger, "A Cinema of Memory."

28. Godard, *Introduction,* 144.

29. See for instance Alain Bergala's insightful "Hélas pour moi, ou De légères corrections du present," in *Nul mieux que Godard,* 171–82.

30. In reality Feldman had one daughter, but no son. See Feldman, *Journal de guerre,* 8.

31. See, for example, Godard's account of the failure of his collaborative venture with the Fémis, the concluding two paragraphs of which return virtually verbatim on the soundtrack of 3A ("Rapport d'inactivité" 251).

32. See Pourvali, *Godard neuf zéro,* which places particular emphasis on the relationship between *Histoire(s) du cinéma* and Godard's output between 1991 and 2004.

33. Godard described this clip to Bernard Eisenschitz simply as a "Russian soft porn film, 1990s." I am grateful to the latter for this information.

34. In this context see Bergala, "La réminiscence, ou Pierrot avec Monika," in *Nul mieux que Godard,* 183–210;

Bergala, "La figure de l'ange," 91; and Aumont, *Amnésies*, chapter 5.

35. *Zoya* was a film Godard remembered from his childhood. Since it had not been issued on video, he went to some lengths to track it down (at his request, Caroline Champetier contacted Bernard Eisenschitz in this regard). I am again grateful to the latter for this information.

36. Péguy, *Clio*.

37. The passage adapted by Godard is from the chapter on Dutch painting in Faure, *History of Art*, vol. 4, *Modern Art*.

38. Godard, "Boris Barnet," 140.

39. "Le regard s'est perdu" (1987), 126.

40. Godard on *Jean-Luc, racontez-nous la Russie*, 9 November 1993.

41. Bazin, "To Create a Public," in *French Cinema of the Occupation and Resistance*, 69.

42. Quoted in Ford, *Bréviaire du cinéma*, 29.

43. Godard, preface to *Cinémamémoire*, 210.

44. Broch, *The Death of Virgil*.

45. Godard, *Histoire(s)*, vol. 1, 183–84. For further discussion of Godard's use of *The Death of Virgil*, see Aumont, "La mort de Dante" and *Amnésies*, chapters 3 and 6; Scemama, *Histoire(s) du cinéma*, 157–59; and Liandrat-Guigues and Leutrat, *Godard simple comme bonjour*, 195–211.

46. See Godard, *Histoire(s)*, vol. 2, 44–51; and the working document relating to this sequence reproduced in Bellour and Bandy, *Son + Image*, 117.

47. *À voix nue*, 21 November 1989. Godard reveals here that he came across the story of Poncelet in a mathematics textbook (Dahan-Dalmédico and Peiffer, *Une histoire des mathématiques*.)

48. Weil, *Gravity and Grace*. I am grateful to Roland-François Lack for supplying me with the source of this quotation, which Godard has repeatedly attributed in interviews to Cézanne.

49. Bresson, *Notes on the Cinematographer*, 10, 20.

50. Sollers, *Women*, 12. There was talk in 1985 of Godard adapting this book as a film, but the project was not pursued.

51. Genet, "The Studio of Alberto Giacometti," in *Fragments of the Artwork*, 68.

3. Models and Guides

1. Gide's *Les faux-monnayeurs* (*The Counterfeiters*) is one of the first books mentioned in 1A, and the same passage from the soundtrack of this episode is reused in 2B. Faulkner is a recurrent reference in 1B, 2A and 3A. We hear Pound reciting an extract of "Canto 1" at the end of 4B. Broch's *The Death of Virgil* is central to 2B. The ending of Woolf's *The Waves*, previously cited in *King Lear*, is reused from this latter source in 3B.

2. Godard, "Malraux, mauvais français?" 75 (translation amended).

3. Virgil, *Aeneid*, 159.

4. Aumont, *Amnésies*, 36.

5. Bergala, "L'Ange de l'Histoire," 241–42.

6. Cocteau, *Orphée*, 10.

7. Godard, *Histoire(s)*, vol. 1, 154–56.

8. See Furet, "Lettre(s) à Godard." Rioux discussed the *Histoire(s) du cinéma* books with Godard on *Droit d'auteurs*, 1998. Godard's conversation with Vernant was broadcast on *Tout arrive!* 18 May 2004. He described his encounter with Vidal-Naquet in "Je reviens en arrière" (2001), 57. For his discussion with Hobsbawm, see *Histoire parallèle* (2000).

9. Furet, "Lettre(s) à Godard," 7.

10. Godard, "À propos de cinéma et d'histoire," 402.

11. "Le briquet de Capitaine Cook" (1992), 19.

12. "Les livres et moi" (1997), 437–38.

13. Péguy, *Clio*, 93, 100.

14. Péguy, *Clio*, 19–29.

15. Péguy, *Clio*, 45, 73.

16. Aronowicz, "The Secret of the Man of Forty," 101.

17. Godard in Agamben et al. "Face au cinéma et à l'Histoire," x.

18. Péguy, *Clio*, 229–38.

19. White, *Metahistory*.

20. Godard on *Tout arrive!* 18 May 2004.

21. See, for instance, Godard and Ishaghpour, *Cinema*, 84.

22. *À voix nue*, 30 March 1998.

23. Miéville reads two brief adapted passages from pages 153, 191, and 192 of *Clio*, and a longer passage from page 193.

24. Adapted by Godard from *Clio*, 193. In the interests of demonstrating Godard's fidelity to the original, as well as the slight changes he introduces, this quotation is a transcription and translation of Miéville's voice on the soundtrack, rather than the version reproduced in *Histoire(s)*, vol. 4, 260–75. Godard has added the opening sentence, together with the words "You see Péguy, she says . . ." and "my friend," and made two cuts indicated here by ellipses. The passage from "Or simply . . ." to "blood relationship" is repeated twice.

25. Godard, *Histoire(s)*, vol. 4, 276.

26. Benjamin, "Theses on the Philosophy of History," in *Illuminations*, 245–55. Alain Bergala argued that the "Theses" provide the most fruitful way of approaching Godard's historical work ("L'Ange de l'Histoire," 221). See also Douglas Morrey's discussion of the intellectual relationship between Godard and Benjamin in "Jean-Luc

Godard and the Other History of Cinema," 69–71, 97–101; and in *Jean-Luc Godard*, 202–204.

27. Benjamin, "Theses," 249.

28. Dall'Asta, "The (Im)possible History," 352.

29. Benjamin, "Theses," 252–53.

30. Benjamin, "Theses," 254.

31. Benjamin, "Theses," 255.

32. Benjamin, *The Arcades Project*.

33. Dall'Asta, "The (Im)possible History," 354.

34. For an important discussion of Michelet in relation to *Histoire(s) du cinéma*, see Temple, "Big Rhythm and the Power of Metamorphosis."

35. "Le bon plaisir" (1995), 316.

36. Michelet, "Préface de 1869," 59.

37. "Jean-Luc Godard en liberté" (2010).

38. Michelet, "Préface de 1869," 46.

39. "Jean-Luc Godard en liberté" (2010).

40. Godard and Ishaghpour, *Cinema*, 28.

41. See, for instance, "C'est le cinéma" (1998).

42. "Cultivons notre jardin" (1989), 82.

43. "Godard/Amar" (1997), 410.

44. See Godard in conversation with Thierry Jousse on *Surpris par la nuit*, 11 February 2000. Extracts of this program were subsequently released on CD as *Godard/Jousse: Les écrans sonores de Jean-Luc Godard* (France Culture and Harmonia Mundi, 2000).

45. "Faire un film" (1998), 3.

46. See Ferro, "Y-a-t-il une vision?" 225.

47. Braudel, "History and the Social Sciences: The *Longue Durée*," in *On History*, 25–54, quotation on 34 (translation amended).

48. See Godard's comments to Jean-Michel Frodon during their webcam dialogue on 8 December 2004, a recording of which is included on the DVD of *Morceaux de conversations avec Jean-Luc Godard*.

49. *La dernière leçon de Fernand Braudel*, 14 January 1992.

50. "La légende du siècle" (1998), 25.

51. See Braudel, "The Situation of History in 1950," in *On History*, 6–22.

52. Braudel, "History and the Social Sciences," 27.

53. Godard, *Histoire(s)*, vol. 4, 64–65. The source of this phrase is Braudel's introduction to his *A History of Civilizations*, xxxvi. It appears that Godard's use of it may have originated with André S. Labarthe, who cited it in a letter to the former in June 1995. See Baecque, *Godard: Biographie*, 739, where this letter is partially reproduced.

54. Godard, "À propos de cinéma et d'histoire," 403–404.

55. "La légende du siècle" (1998), 25.

56. The passage read by Ferdinand/Pierrot in *Pierrot le fou* is from Faure's *History of Art*, vol. 4, *Modern Art*, 124–25.

57. See "Le bon plaisir" (1995), 313; and "Les livres et moi" (1997), 432.

58. "Jean-Luc Godard: Des traces du cinéma" (1999), 50.

59. Faure, introduction to *History of Art*, vol. 5, *The Spirit of the Forms*, xvii.

60. Malraux, "Aftermath of the Absolute," in *The Voices of Silence*, 467–642, photographs on 538–39.

61. Temple, "Big Rhythm and the Power of Metamorphosis," 91.

62. Malraux, "Aftermath of the Absolute," 639.

63. Godard, *Introduction*, 114.

64. Faure, "Author's Note," *History of Art*, vol. 3, *Renaissance Art*, ix.

65. Malraux, *La métamorphose des dieux*, vol. 3, *L'intemporel*, 357.

66. Malraux, preface to *Saturn: An Essay on Goya*, 5.

67. "Jean-Luc Godard: 'La Nouvelle Vague'" (2000), 21.

68. Godard and Ishaghpour, *Cinema*, 36–37 (translation amended).

69. "Jean-Luc Godard: 'La Nouvelle Vague'" (2000), 21.

70. Malraux, "Aftermath of the Absolute," 577.

71. Malraux, "Museum without Walls," in *The Voices of Silence*, 11–128, quotation on 24.

72. In this context, see Païni, "The Cinema Museum," 33.

73. Malraux, *Picasso's Mask*, 133.

74. Malraux, "Museum without Walls," 121–27.

75. See Godard, "Textes à servir aux histoire(s) du cinéma."

76. Godard to Jean-François Lyotard on *Le cercle de minuit*, 26 November 1996.

77. Malraux, "Sketch," 323, 326, 327 (translations amended).

78. Bardèche and Brasillach, *Histoire du cinéma*.

79. Bardèche and Brasillach, "Avertissement," 5.

80. Interview with Sadoul by José Zendel, *L'écran français*, no. 348, March 1952.

81. Sadoul, "Matériaux," xiv.

82. Mitry in Godard, "Les cinémathèques," 290.

83. I am grateful to Nicole Brenez for having made it possible for me to view this film.

84. Langlois, "Préface," iv.

85. Godard in "Jean-Luc Godard rencontre Régis Debray" (1995), 429.

86. "Préface: Entretien" (1991), 6.

87. "Le bon plaisir" (1995), 305.

88. "Se vivre, se voir" (1980), 405.

89. Godard in Astruc et al., "Conférence de presse," 36.

90. Godard, "Grâce à Henri Langlois," 236, 237.

91. Godard, *Histoire(s)*, vol. 3, 139–49.

92. See Langlois, "Vingt ans après" and "Entretien avec Henri Langlois," interview by Éric Rohmer and Michel Mardore, in *Trois cent ans de cinéma*, 59, 62.

93. Godard, *Histoire(s)*, vol. 2, 182.

94. See the letter from Godard to Langlois dated 8–9 July 1975 reproduced in *Jean-Luc Godard: Documents*, 254; and Godard, "Les cinémathèques," 288–89.

95. "Préface: Entretien" (1991), 6; Godard, "Les cinémathèques," 289.

96. Mannoni, *Histoire de la Cinémathèque française*, 137.

97. Mannoni, *Histoire de la Cinémathèque française*, 224.

98. "Entretien avec Henri Langlois," 79.

99. See Langlois and Myrent, *Henri Langlois*, 182–85; and Roud, *A Passion for Films*, 82–83.

100. Letter from Godard to Langlois, in *Jean-Luc Godard: Documents*, 258.

101. Païni, *Conserver, montrer*.

102. Païni, "The Cinema Museum," 32.

103. Mannoni, *Histoire de la Cinémathèque française*, 263.

104. Mannoni, *Histoire de la Cinémathèque française*, 32–37.

105. Païni, *Le cinéma, un art moderne*, 169–84.

106. "Préface: Entretien" (1991), 6.

107. "Préface: Entretien" (1991), 5.

108. Truffaut in Roud, *A Passion for Films*, 178–79.

109. Païni, *Le cinéma, un art moderne*, 174.

110. Lack, "Sa voix," 325.

111. Godard, "Bergmanorama," 76.

112. See Eisenschitz, "Une machine," 52.

113. Michel Delain's report for *L'express* is reproduced in Langlois and Myrent, *Henri Langlois*, 397.

114. Leyda, *Films Beget Films*, 13. See also Patrik Sjöberg, according to whom compilation filmmaking can be traced to at least as early as 1898 (*The World in Pieces*, 23).

115. See Vertov, *Kino-Eye*.

116. "Jean-Luc Godard: Des traces du cinéma" (1999), 54. For an early outline of his proposed approach to the representation of the Holocaust, see Godard, "Feu sur *Les carabiniers*," 198.

117. For a useful discussion of these photographs, see Tec and Weiss, "The Heroine of Minsk."

118. "Jean-Luc Godard: Des traces du cinéma" (1999), 52.

119. Marker, *Le fond de l'air est rouge*, 5–7.

120. See, for instance, "The Artistic Act" (2002), 4.

121. Deleuze, "Qu'est-ce que l'acte de création?"

122. The text read in 4A is made up of lightly adapted extracts from across *Penser avec les mains*: 26, 51, 82, 131, 132, 134, 147, 150, 151, 164, 172, 173, 184, 190, 191, 200, 206, 207, 213, 232, 236, 240, 241, and 244.

123. Rougemont, *Penser avec les mains*, 150. See also 183, 190, and 206.

124. Godard and Miéville, *De l'origine*, 92.

125. Hugo, "Pour la Serbie," 949–50. For a useful discussion of Godard's use of this text in 3A, and of his broader engagement with Hugo elsewhere in his work, see Liandrat-Guigues and Leutrat, *Godard simple comme bonjour*, 109–20.

126. See Godard, "Rapport d'inactivité," 250; and "A Language before Babel" (1992), 415–16.

127. Agamben, "Difference and Repetition," 314–15.

128. B. Pertsov, "Filma-retsenzija," *Sovetskii ekran* (Soviet screen), no. 13 (1926): 3. Quoted in Tsivian, "The Wise and Wicked Game," 337–38.

129. Gauthier, "L'invention d'une discipline," 118.

130. See the letter from Duvivier and Lepage published in *Comœdia* on 26 March 1927. Cited in *Cinéopse*, no. 93, 1 May 1927, 399.

131. Duvivier and Lepage, *Comœdia*, 13 March 1924. Cited in *Le nouvel art cinématographique*, 26 November 1927.

132. Numerous articles relating to the controversy are reproduced in *Le nouvel art cinématographique*, 26 November 1927. See also *Cinéopse*, 7 November 1927; "Comment fut étouffé *L'histoire du cinéma par le cinéma*," supplement to *Le nouvel art cinématographique*, no. 2, 2nd series, April 1929; and Henry Lepage, "Un peu de pudeur, s.v.p.," *La griffe cinématographique*, 28 April 1927.

133. Godard, "Dictionnaire des cinéastes américains."

134. Godard, "No Synopsis" (1987), in the pressbook for *King Lear*.

135. Eisenschitz, "Une machine," 55.

136. Welles, quoted in Rosenbaum, "Orson Welles's Purloined Letter," 289.

137. Frampton, "For a Metahistory of Film: Commonplace Notes and Hypotheses," in *On the Camera Arts and Consecutive Matters*, 131–39.

138. Frampton, "For a Metahistory," 135; Godard, *Histoire(s)*, vol. 4, 290. Godard simplifies Frampton's argument somewhat, but he retains its central thrust.

139. Frampton, "For a Metahistory," 137.

140. Frampton, "For a Metahistory," 136.

141. Frampton, "For a Metahistory," 131.

142. Frampton, "For a Metahistory," 131.

143. Frampton, "For a Metahistory," 133.

144. Frampton, "For a Metahistory," 138.

4. The Rise and Fall of the Cinematograph

1. See Teitelbaum, *Montage and Modern Life*.

2. In this context, see "Se vivre, se voir" (1980), 405.

3. Godard, "Le montage, la solitude," 242, 246–47.

4. "La chance de repartir" (1980), 408.

5. À voix nue, 1 December 1989.

6. Michelson, "The Wings of Hypothesis," 62.

7. Godard, Histoire(s), vol. 1, 162.

8. Godard, Histoire(s), vol. 3, 156.

9. "Dialogue entre Godard et Daney" (1997), 49.

10. "Jean-Luc Godard rencontre Régis Debray" (1995), 425.

11. See Kirby, Parallel Tracks; Crary, "Unbinding Vision"; and Cavell, "Ideas of Origin" and "Baudelaire and the Myths of Film," in The World Viewed, 37–41, 41–6.

12. Baudelaire, "L'invitation au voyage," in Les fleurs du mal, 58–59; and Cros, Le collier de griffes.

13. Godard and Ishaghpour, Cinema, 56 (translation amended).

14. Godard noted the influence on his discourse on artistic childhood of Georges Bernanos's Les enfants humiliés on À voix nue, 28 November 1989.

15. À voix nue, 28 November 1989.

16. À voix nue, 31 March 1998.

17. Godard, Histoire(s), vol. 2, 123.

18. Godard, Histoire(s), vol. 1, 98–100.

19. Malraux, Felled Oaks, 24.

20. Godard, "La paroisse morte."

21. "Le cinéma est fait pour penser" (1995), 299.

22. "Faire les films possibles" (1975), 382.

23. Jean-Louis Leutrat identified the figures depicted in this photograph in his detailed discussion of the opening of 1A ("Retour sur Histoire(s), 4").

24. Freud, The Interpretation of Dreams, 652.

25. Breton, "As in a Wood," 84.

26. Breton, "As in a Wood," 84.

27. "Godard/Amar" (1997), 422.

28. Godard, Histoire(s), vol. 1, 166.

29. Rancière, Film Fables, 179.

30. Rancière, Film Fables, 180.

31. According to Jean-Louis Leutrat, this photograph derives from a scene cut from Griffith's Birth of a Nation: "Retour sur Histoire(s), 5," 81.

32. À voix nue, 28 November 1989.

33. Godard, Histoire(s), vol. 1, 51. In the audiovisual version, the same photograph and text are used in this sequence, but separately, and in different contexts.

34. For an entertaining account by Janet Leigh of her experiences with Hughes, see There Really Was a Hollywood.

35. Leutrat, "Retour sur Histoire(s), 6," 101.

36. Godard, Introduction, 177.

37. "Alfred Hitchcock est mort" (1980), 415 (original emphasis).

38. "Se vivre, se voir" (1980), 405.

39. Godard, "À propos de cinéma et d'histoire," 403.

40. Godard, Introduction, 70.

41. "Jean-Luc Godard rencontre Régis Debray" (1995), 425; À voix nue, 2 April 1998. By "everything," Godard refers primarily to the Spanish Civil War and World War II.

42. Godard in Godard and Kael, "The Economics of Film Criticism" (1981), 175. For a discussion by Epstein of the cinematograph as an instrument of justice, see "Le cinématographe dans l'Archipel," in Écrits sur le cinéma, vol. 1, 199.

43. "Godard Makes (Hi)stories" (1988), 162.

44. "ABCD . . . JLG," (1987), 330.

45. "Cultivons notre jardin" (1989), 83.

46. Godard, Histoire(s), vol. 3, 55–56.

47. Godard, Histoire(s), vol. 1, 78–113.

48. "Jean-Luc Godard rencontre Régis Debray" (1995), 425.

49. "Jean-Luc Godard: Des traces du cinéma" (1999), 54; À voix nue, 2 April 1998.

50. Godard, Histoire(s), vol. 1, 116–19.

51. "Jean-Luc Godard: Des traces du cinéma" (1999), 54.

52. "Dialogue entre Godard et Daney" (1997), 51.

53. "Godard Makes (Hi)stories" (1988), 165.

54. "Cultivons notre jardin" (1989), 83.

55. "Godard/Amar" (1997), 416–17.

56. "Cultivons notre jardin" (1989), 83.

57. "Cultivons notre jardin" (1989), 84.

58. Included on the Gaumont DVDs of Histoire(s) du cinéma.

59. À voix nue, 2 April 1998.

60. Both poems are included in Aragon, Le crève-cœur.

61. "Jean-Luc Godard: Des traces du cinéma" (1999), 54.

62. "Le cinéma est toujours une opération de deuil" (1996), 384. For a critique by Godard of the political films he made during and after May 1968, see À voix nue, 2 April 1998.

63. Godard, "Histoire(s) du cinéma: Avec un s."

64. Godard, "Histoire(s) du cinéma: Avec un s."

65. Comolli, "Le miroir à deux faces," in Comolli and Rancière, Arrêt sur histoire, 27.

66. Daney, "The Tracking Shot in Kapò," in Postcards from the Cinema, 17–35.

67. See, in this respect, Antoine de Baecque's overview of the significance of the Nazi concentration camps to Daney, and to postwar cinema history generally: "Le temps perdu du cinéma," in Baecque and Jousse, Le retour du cinéma, 11–47. See also his "Premières images des camps," "Des femmes qui nous regardent," and the opening chapter of L'histoire-caméra.

68. Godard, *Histoire(s)*, vol. 1, 122–44.

69. Rancière, *Film Fables*, 183.

70. Godard, *Histoire(s)*, vol. 1, 134.

71. Godard, *Histoire(s)*, vol. 1, 131–35.

72. *À voix nue*, 24 November 1989.

73. *À voix nue*, 21 and 28 November 1989.

74. Godard, *Histoire(s)*, vol. 1, 198–213. This passage is adapted from Wittgenstein, *Culture and Value*, 32e.

75. *À voix nue*, 29 November 1989.

76. Bellour, "(Not) Just an Other Filmmaker," 215.

77. Kerry Brougher in Chris Dercon's film *Still/A Novel* (1996).

78. Rancière, "The Saint and the Heiress," 116, 118.

79. Morrey, *Jean-Luc Godard*, 226–27.

80. Rancière, *Film Fables*, 183–84.

81. Heywood, "Holocaust and Image," 277.

82. Heywood, "Holocaust and Image," 275–77.

5. Cinema, Nationhood, and the New Wave

1. Godard on *Bouillon de culture*, 10 September 1993.

2. "Cinquante-neuf réalisateurs appellent à 'désobéir,'" *Le monde*, 12 February 1997.

3. Godard developed this idea in numerous interviews during and after the *sans-papiers* affair. See, for instance, "Une boucle bouclée" (1997), 29.

4. Godard in *Jean Cocteau, mensonges et vérités* (1996).

5. "Le cinéma n'a pas su remplir son rôle" (1995), 340.

6. Godard, *Histoire(s)*, vol. 4, 91, 85. Godard drew the title of this section of 4A from Paul Valéry's study of Leonardo de Vinci ("Trois fragments de l'introduction à la méthode de Léonard de Vinci," in *Morceaux choisis*, 63–95). As Rick Warner has noted, Godard's characterization of Hitchcock as the greatest inventor of forms of the twentieth century recalls a phrase from the conclusion of Rohmer and Chabrol's 1957 study *Hitchcock* (Warner, "Difficult Work," 67). The version of the phrase used by Godard (with its plural "forms") also recalls Truffaut, who used this variation in the title of his enthusiastic review of the book: "Réalisateur de 45 films," 7.

7. "Alfred Hitchcock est mort" (1980), 414.

8. Godard and Ishaghpour, *Cinema*, 16–17 (translation amended).

9. Godard, "Montage, mon beau souci," 39.

10. See, for instance, Godard, *Introduction*, 32.

11. Godard, *Introduction*, 101.

12. Godard, *Introduction*, 101.

13. See the introduction to Dyer and Vincendeau, *Popular European Cinema*.

14. "Godard à Venise," (1983), 6.

15. "Godard Makes (Hi)stories" (1988), 162.

16. "Cultivons notre jardin" (1989), 86.

17. "Cultivons notre jardin" (1989), 84.

18. "Le chemin vers la parole" (1982), 510.

19. "Le briquet de Capitaine Cook" (1992), 20.

20. Godard, *Introduction*, 245.

21. See Godard, "Le dernier rêve d'un producteur."

22. "Jean-Luc Godard in Conversation with Colin MacCabe" (1991), 102.

23. Included on the Gaumont DVDs of *Histoire(s) du cinéma*.

24. Godard, *Histoire(s)*, vol. 3, 78–86.

25. "Le briquet de Capitaine Cook" (1992), 20.

26. "Jean-Luc Godard: Des traces du cinéma" (1999), 54.

27. Godard, "Désespérant," 85–86.

28. Godard in John Ardagh, "An Alpha for Godard?" *The Guardian*, 12 December 1966.

29. Godard, "Désespérant," 86.

30. Bardèche and Brasillach, *Histoire du cinéma*, 275.

31. "J'ai fait une échographie" (1998), 38.

32. *Jean-Luc, racontez-nous la Russie* (1993).

33. *À voix nue*, 24 November 1989.

34. "Le briquet de Capitaine Cook" (1992), 20.

35. "Le briquet de Capitaine Cook" (1992), 20.

36. "L'art de (dé)montrer" (1988), 139; "Godard Makes (Hi)stories" (1988), 164; "Cultivons notre jardin" (1989), 84.

37. "Godard Makes (Hi)stories" (1988), 164.

38. Godard, *Histoire(s)*, vol. 3, 86.

39. "Week-end avec Godard" (1989), 179.

40. "Jean-Luc Godard: Des traces du cinéma" (1999), 54.

41. "Le briquet de Capitaine Cook" (1992), 20.

42. Eisenstein, "Montage 1938," in *Selected Works*, vol. 2, 296–326, quotation on 311.

43. Godard probably encountered this idea in the essay devoted to El Greco that opens Eisenstein, *Cinématisme*. It also informs texts by Eisenstein such as "Synchronization of Senses," in *The Film Sense*, 60–91.

44. See, for instance, Godard, "Le montage, la solitude," 248.

45. "Faire un film" (1998), 5.

46. Godard, "Boris Barnet."

47. "Le chemin vers la parole" (1982), 511.

48. "C'est notre musique" (2004), 32; "Le briquet de Capitaine Cook" (1992), 20.

49. "Le briquet de Capitaine Cook" (1992), 20.

50. Godard, "Panic in the Streets."

51. "C'est notre musique" (2004), 32.

52. Canudo, "Écrit par Canudo," 4.

53. "Godard Makes (Hi)stories" (1988), 164.

54. "Cultivons notre jardin" (1989), 84.

55. "Le briquet de Capitaine Cook" (1992), 20.

56. Quoted in Langlois and Myrent, *Henri Langlois*, 366.

57. "Godard Makes (Hi)stories" (1988), 159.

58. *Jean Cocteau, mensonges et vérités* (1996).

59. "Marguerite Duras et Jean-Luc Godard" (1987), 142.

60. *Cahiers du cinéma* (special issue: *Situation du cinéma français*), nos. 323/324, May 1981, 60–61.

61. *À voix nue,* 31 March 1998. See also *Jean Cocteau, mensonges et vérités* (1996).

62. "Je reviens en arrière" (2001), 57.

63. *Les écrans sonores.*

64. *À voix nue,* 2 April 1998.

65. *À voix nue,* 2 April 1998.

66. Astruc, "L'avenir du cinéma," in *Du stylo à la caméra,* 328–36, citation on 335; Bazin, "The Evolution of Film Language," in *What Is Cinema?* 87–106 (see especially 104).

67. Godard, "Jean Renoir," 63.

68. Epstein, "On Certain Characteristics of *Photogénie.*"

69. Epstein, "Le monde fluide de l'écran," in *Écrits sur le cinéma,* vol. 2, 145–58, quotation on 157.

70. Epstein, *Bonjour cinéma.*

71. Godard, *Histoire(s),* vol. 3, 128; Aumont, *Amnésies,* 183.

72. Langlois, "Jean Epstein," in *Trois cent ans de cinéma,* 239–60.

73. The song, "J'ai la mémoire qui flanche," is from Moreau's first album, *Jeanne Moreau* (1963).

74. "Jean-Luc Godard: 'La France reste'" (1990), 29.

75. Godard, *Histoire(s),* vol. 2, 126–27.

76. "Aujourd'hui, on cherche" (1996), 392.

77. *À voix nue,* 31 March 1998; "Godard/Amar" (1997), 414; "L'art de (dé)montrer" (1988), 134.

78. "The Future(s) of Film" (2000), 13.

79. Interview by Michael Witt, Rolle, Switzerland, 15 April 2005.

80. Godard in "For a Few Dollars Less" (1991), 20.

81. "Godard: Grandeur" (2001), 15.

82. "La légende du siècle" (1998), 26.

83. See, for instance, "Le bon plaisir" (1995), 311.

84. "Jean-Luc Godard: 'La Nouvelle Vague'" (2000), 19.

85. "Le briquet de Capitaine Cook" (1992), 20.

86. *La Nouvelle Vague,* France Culture, August 1987. Included in Simsolo, *La Nouvelle Vague.*

87. "Jean-Luc Godard: 'La Nouvelle Vague'" (2000), 19.

88. See chapter 2 in Andrew, *André Bazin.*

89. "Le cinéma est toujours une opération de deuil" (1996), 385.

90. See Godard, *Introduction,* 284.

91. Godard, *Introduction,* 284.

92. *À voix nue,* 28 November 1989.

93. "Aujourd'hui, on cherche" (1996), 391–92.

94. Biette, *Qu'est-ce qu'un cinéaste?*

95. Astruc, "L'avenir du cinéma," 329.

96. *À voix nue,* 29 November 1989.

97. The roundtable discussion was published as Domarchi et al., "Hiroshima, notre amour." The quotation from Godard is from "Le cinéma me reste" (2005).

98. "Cultivons notre jardin" (1989), 83.

99. "Faire un film" (1998), 3.

100. "L'art à partir de la vie" (1985), 9; "Godard/Amar" (1997), 411.

101. "Une place sur la terre" (1988), 51.

102. Godard, "Le montage, la solitude," 248.

103. "Le briquet de Capitaine Cook" (1992), 18.

104. "Le cinéma a été l'art des âmes" (2002).

105. "Aujourd'hui, on cherche" (1996), 393.

106. "Une boucle bouclée" (1997), 24; "The Future(s) of Film" (2000), 13.

107. Bazin, "Sacha Guitry a fait confiance!"

108. Astruc, "L'avenir du cinéma," 331. See also Orain, "Film, cinéma et télévision."

109. See Renoir and Rossellini, "Cinéma et télévision" (1958); and Rivette, "Letter on Rossellini," in Rivette, *Jacques Rivette,* 54–64.

110. Godard, "Jean Renoir: 'La télévision m'a révélé un nouveau cinéma.'"

111. "Le cinéma a été l'art des âmes" (2002; my emphasis).

112. See Zand, "Le dossier Philippine."

113. Godard, "Dans *Adieu Philippine.*" This rich text has been hitherto forgotten within the context of Godard studies.

114. This extract of Godard's presentation of the film is cited by Albert Cervoni in "Enfin *Adieu Philippine.*" It was not included in the version published previously in *Les lettres françaises.*

115. "Week-end avec Godard" (1989), 181.

116. See, for instance, "Une place sur la terre" (1988), 51.

6. Making Images in the Age of Spectacle

1. Godard on *L'invité du jeudi,* 15 September 1981; "The Carrots Are Cooked" (1984), 19.

2. See, for instance, Godard on *Ouvert le dimanche,* 6 June 1982.

3. Godard on *7/7,* 11 December 1983.

4. Godard, *Histoire(s),* vol. 3, 39.

5. See, for instance, "Travail-amour-cinéma" (1980), 450.

6. Godard, *Histoire(s),* vol. 1, 246–49.

7. *À voix nue,* 20 November 1989.

8. Labarthe, "Le triomphe d'Edison." Godard cited this article in "Le cinéma est fait pour penser" (1995),

299, and developed its central thesis in "Parler du manque" (1996), 371.

9. Godard, *Histoire(s)*, vol. 1, 231–33.

10. "Parti de chase" (1986), 97.

11. "Alfred Hitchcock est mort" (1980), 416.

12. "The Carrots Are Cooked" (1984), 19.

13. "Une place sur la terre" (1988), 54.

14. Godard, "Le montage, la solitude," 247.

15. Godard, "Le montage, la solitude," 247.

16. See Godard, *Histoire(s)*, vol. 1, 248–49.

17. "La télé selon Jean-Luc" (1986), 16.

18. Debord declared the cinema dead in *Hurlements en faveur de Sade* (1952). In 1953, Welles stated that he believed cinema to be dying. Cited in Mauriac, *L'amour du cinéma*, 44. At a press conference in 1963, Rossellini declared the cinema dead (Gallagher, *The Adventures of Roberto Rossellini*, 538).

19. Godard, "Qui? Pourquoi? Comment?" 36.

20. Godard, quoted on the final unnumbered page of Philippon, Laprévotte, and Egéa, *Made in Godard années 70/80*.

21. Godard, "Lettres écrites pendant le tournage," 613.

22. "Faire un film" (1998), 5.

23. Rivette, "Nous ne sommes plus innocents."

24. See, for instance, "Rolle over Godard" (1984), 9.

25. "Le chemin vers la parole" (1982), 504.

26. "Le chemin vers la parole" (1982), 517.

27. "Propos rompus" (1980), 466.

28. Daney in "Godard Makes (Hi)stories" (1988), 159.

29. Daney interviewed by Alain Veinstein on *Du jour au lendemain*, 4 February 1992.

30. Daney, "La rentrée des cases," in *Le salaire du zappeur*, 9–13, citation on 12.

31. Daney, "Avant et après l'image."

32. Daney, "Ce que produit *Out of Africa*," in *Devant la recrudescence des vols de sacs à main*, 13–14.

33. "Jean-Luc Godard: 'La France reste'" (1990), 29.

34. "Godard Makes (Hi)stories" (1988), 167 (translation amended).

35. For Eisenstein's definition of these terms, see "[Rhythm]" and "Montage 1938," in *Selected Works*, vol. 2, 227–48, 296–326. For an example of Godard's discussion of them, see *À voix nue*, 20 November 1989.

36. Shannon, "The Mathematical Theory of Communication," in Shannon and Weaver, *The Mathematical Theory of Communication*, 29–125.

37. Queneau, "L'explication des métaphores."

38. *Jean-Luc, racontez-nous la Russie* (1993).

39. For the original, see Reverdy, "L'image." See also the illuminating account of the poem's genealogy in the notes (280–83).

40. "Godard: Born-Again Filmmaker" (1980), 36.

41. Godard described himself as a maker of jigsaws in conversation with Stéphane Zagdanski on *Tout arrive!* 18 November 2004. The logic puzzle used in *Week-end*, and reprised in 1B, is number 54 in Carroll, *Symbolic Logic*, 122.

42. See "Juste une conversation" (2004), 20.

43. Deleuze, *Cinema 2*, 174.

44. See, for instance, Godard and Ishaghpour, *Cinema*, 7.

45. Benjamin, *The Arcades Project*, 463 (translation amended).

46. "Le bon plaisir" (1995), 318. Godard reveals here that when making this sequence he was inspired in part by a book written by Nemirovsky's youngest daughter about her mother: Gille, *Le mirador*.

47. Beckett, *L'image*.

48. "The Godard Interview" (2005), 30. Godard refers to Tillion, *Ravensbrück*.

49. Godard, letter to Elias Sanbar, 19 July 1977, 17. For a critical reading of Godard's use of the terms "Jew" and "Muslim" in 4B, see Scemama, *Histoire(s) du cinéma*, 181–89. Unfortunately, this discussion involves significant confusion, since it mistakes Godard's 1977 letter to Sanbar for a letter from Sanbar to Godard.

50. Levi, *The Drowned and the Saved*; Ryn and Klodzinski, *An der Grenze zwischen Leben und Tod*; Agamben, *Remnants of Auschwitz*, 165.

51. Agamben, *Remnants of Auschwitz*, 85.

52. Baudelaire, "Correspondances," in *Les fleurs du mal*, 13.

53. See, for instance, "The Godard Interview" (2005), 30.

54. "The Godard Interview" (2005), 30.

7. The Metamorphoses

1. Godard claimed in 2001 to have made *Moments choisis des Histoire(s) du cinéma* primarily for financial reasons ("Jean-Luc Godard: Une longue histoire" [2001], 31). Brenez made this observation in the program of the "L'image matière: Histoire du cinéma par lui-même, formes de la critique visuelle" event that she curated at the Louvre on 17–18 May 2008, which included a screening of *Moments choisis des Histoire(s) du cinéma*.

2. Leutrat, "Retour sur *Histoire(s)*, 3," 99.

3. Leutrat, "Retour sur *Histoire(s)*, 3," 101–102.

4. Agee's text is from his and Walker Evans's *Let Us Now Praise Famous Men*. As Jean-Louis Leutrat has noted, the other important new source introduced in *Moments choisis des Histoire(s) du cinéma* is an extract of an interview with Pier Paolo Pasolini ("Retour sur *Histoire[s]*, 3," 98).

5. Godard, *Introduction*, 105. See also 112 and 185.

6. Godard, letter to Serge Daney and Serge Toubiana, 14 April 1979, 3.

7. Godard, "Les cinémathèques," 288.

8. "Jean-Luc Godard: Des traces du cinéma" (1999), 50.

9. "Faire un film" (1998), 3.

10. Fromanger discussed these drawing lessons at the For Ever Godard conference at Tate Modern in 2001. See also his "Il faut créer un Vietnam dans chaque musée du monde," in Brenez and Lebrat, *Jeune, dure et pure!* 336–38.

11. Godard, *Introduction*, 187.

12. Godard in *Godard 1980*.

13. Epstein, *Bonjour cinéma*; Marker, "L'Amérique rêve."

14. "Entretien sur un projet–2" (1979), 29.

15. "Les dernières leçons du donneur" (1979), 64, 69.

16. Godard, "Voir avec ses mains," 39.

17. Aumont, *Amnésies*, 101–102.

18. Godard, "La 9ème symphonie"; "Colles et ciseaux"; "Dit/vu."

19. Anger, *Hollywood Babylon*.

20. Vedrès, *Images du cinéma français*.

21. Mannoni, *Histoire de la Cinémathèque française*, 194, 198.

22. Bataille, *Manet*.

23. Bataille, *Manet*, 85–95, 120.

24. Bataille, *Manet*, 83, 85; Godard, *Histoire(s)*, vol. 4, 49.

25. Godard on *À toute allure*, 15 May 2001.

26. "C'est le cinéma" (1998).

27. Maillot, "Je ne connais pas."

28. Maillot, "Je ne connais pas."

29. Maillot, "Je ne connais pas."

30. Bouquet, "Des livres, le Livre," 58.

31. Maillot, "Je ne connais pas."

32. Maillot, "Je ne connais pas." The four-volume set sold for 490 francs.

33. "C'est le cinéma" (1998).

34. Malraux, "Museum without Walls," in *The Voices of Silence*, 13–128, quotation on 14.

35. Jousse, "Godard à l'oreille."

36. "Jean-Luc Godard" (1968), 79.

37. Collet, "An Audacious Experiment."

38. "For a Few Dollars Less" (1991), 22.

39. See the film directed by Larry Sider, featuring François Musy in conversation with Chris Darke, entitled *François Musy on Sound, Direct Sound, Godard* (2003). I am grateful to Chris Darke for having made a copy of this film available to me.

40. *Le cercle de minuit* (1996). There was talk the following year of *For ever Mozart* being released on CD, but the plan was dropped.

41. Godard on *Faxculture*, 7 June 2001. I am grateful to Roland-François Lack for having made a copy of this program available to me.

42. See "The Audible Picture Show," Matt Hulse website, 1 February 2009, anormalboy.wordpress.com/2009/02/01/the-audible-picture-show.

43. Jullier, "JLG/ECM," 282n40.

44. An English translation of the transcription of the *Une femme est une femme* record, which is available as an extra on the Criterion DVD of the film, is given in *Godard on Godard*, 165–71. According to Tom Milne's notes, several copies of this ten-inch LP were cut, but it was never released commercially. A transcription of Godard's words on the cassette he sent to *Cinématographe* was published in the magazine as "Dernière minute" in 1983, and is reproduced in *Jean-Luc Godard: Documents*.

45. Swed, "Sharing Sound Theories."

46. Jousse, "Histoire(s) d'entendre"; Griffiths, "Godard's Mix."

47. "Marguerite Duras et Jean-Luc Godard" (1987), 146.

48. *Les écrans sonores*.

49. Williams, "Music, Love, and the Cinematic Event," 292.

50. Williams, "Music, Love, and the Cinematic Event," 305.

51. *Les écrans sonores*.

52. "Le cinéma de Jean-Luc Godard" (2004), 10.

53. Godard and Miéville made very clear their respect for Eicher in the outline of their unrealized film project on the "ECM Records World Orchestra" ("Our Music").

54. *Les écrans sonores*.

55. Godard and Miéville, "Our Music," 5.

56. *Les écrans sonores*.

57. Jullier, "JLG/ECM," 275–77.

58. *Les écrans sonores*.

59. *Les écrans sonores*.

60. Aragon, "What Is Art?" 144–45.

61. Valéry, "Psaume sur une voix," in *Morceaux choisis*, 58–59.

62. "Une boucle bouclée" (1997), 30.

63. Griffiths, "Godard's Mix."

64. *Les écrans sonores*.

65. Bartoli, "Le regard intérieur."

66. Epstein, "Slow-Motion Sound," 144.

67. Eicher, "La musique ECM chez Jean-Luc Godard," 411.

68. Swed, "Sharing Sound Theories," 50.

69. See in this context James Williams's astute early

observations on the *Histoire(s) du cinéma* books in "The Signs amongst Us," 315.

Envoi

1. Rohmer, "Renoir's Youth," in *The Taste for Beauty*, 186–93, citation on 187.

2. For an example of a book that both engages with and deploys Godard's montage method, see Mazierska, *European Cinema and Intertextuality*.

3. See "C'est le cinéma" (1998) and "Jean-Luc Godard: Des traces du cinéma" (1999).

4. Tavano and Yonnet, *Une chronique du temps à venir,* in *Quelques histoires de cinéma,* 11–15.

The emphasis in this bibliography is on works by and interviews with Godard cited in the text, on studies of *Histoire(s) du cinéma* and Godard's related later work, and on other items consulted for the purposes of this book.

Books by Godard

Godard, Jean-Luc. *Jean-Luc Godard par Jean-Luc Godard: Articles, essais, entretiens.* Edited by Jean Narboni. Paris: Éditions Pierre Belfond, 1968.

———. *Godard on Godard.* Edited by Jean Narboni and Tom Milne, translated by Tom Milne. London: Secker and Warburg, 1972. (Hereafter *Godard on Godard.*)

———. *Introduction à une véritable histoire du cinéma.* Paris: Albatros, 1980.

———. *Jean-Luc Godard par Jean-Luc Godard,* vol. 1. Edited by Alain Bergala. Paris: Cahiers du cinéma/Éditions de l'Étoile, 1985. (Hereafter *Godard par Godard,* vol. 1.)

———. *JLG/JLG: Phrases.* Paris: P.O.L., 1996.

———. *For ever Mozart: Phrases.* Paris: P.O.L., 1996.

———. *Jean-Luc Godard par Jean-Luc Godard,* vol. 2. Edited by Alain Bergala. Paris: Cahiers du cinéma, 1998. (Hereafter *Godard par Godard,* vol. 2.)

———. *Allemagne neuf zéro: Phrases (sorties d'un film).* Paris: P.O.L., 1998.

———. *Les enfants jouent à la Russie: Phrases (sorties d'un film).* Paris: P.O.L., 1998.

———. *Histoire(s) du cinéma.* 4 vols. Paris: Gallimard-Gaumont, 1998.

———. *Histoire(s) du cinéma.* 4 vols. Hamburg: ECM Records, 1999. (Includes the CDs of *Histoire[s] du cinéma.*)

———. *Éloge de l'amour: Phrases (sorties d'un film).* Paris: P.O.L., 2001.

———. *Film socialisme: Dialogues avec visages auteurs.* Paris: P.O.L., 2010.

Godard, Jean-Luc, ed. *Cahiers du cinéma,* no. 300, May 1979.

Godard, Jean-Luc, and Anne-Marie Miéville. *2 × 50 ans de cinéma français: Phrases (sorties d'un film).* Paris: P.O.L., 1998.

———. *De l'origine du XXIe siècle, The Old Place, Liberté et patrie, Je vous salue, Sarajevo.* Hamburg: ECM Records, 2006. (Includes a DVD containing the films of the title.)

Godard, Jean-Luc, and Marcel Ophuls. *Dialogues sur le cinéma.* Lormont, France: Bord de l'eau, 2011.

Godard, Jean-Luc, and Youssef Ishaghpour. *Cinema: The Archaeology of Film and the Memory of a Century.* Translated by John Howe. Oxford: Berg, 2005. (First published as "Archéologie du cinéma et mémoire du siècle," *Trafic,* nos. 29 and 30 [1999]).

Select Bibliography

Talks by and Interviews with Godard about *Histoire(s) du cinéma*

"Les cinémathèques et l'histoire du cinéma." *Travelling*, nos. 56–57 (1980). In *Jean-Luc Godard: Documents*, edited by Nicole Brenez, David Faroult, Michael Temple, James S. Williams, and Michael Witt, 286–91. Paris: Éditions du Centre Pompidou, 2006.

"Godard Makes (Hi)stories: Interview with Serge Daney." In *Jean-Luc Godard: Son + Image, 1974–1991*, edited by Raymond Bellour and Mary Lea Bandy, translated by Georgia Gurrieri, 159–67. New York: Museum of Modern Art, 1992. (First published as "Godard fait des histoires," interview by Serge Daney, *Libération*, 26 December 1988.)

"'Cultivons notre jardin': Une interview de Jean-Luc Godard." By François Albera. *CinémAction* (special issue: *Le cinéma selon Godard*), no. 52 (1989): 81–89.

"Entretien avec Jean-Luc Godard." By Noël Simsolo. In *Jean-Luc Godard: Un hommage du Centre culturel français et du Museo nazionale del cinema de Turin*, edited by Sergio Toffetti, 39–47. Turin: Centre culturel français de Turin, 1990.

"Le montage, la solitude et la liberté." In *Confrontations: Les mardis de la Fémis*, edited by Jean Narboni. Paris: Fémis, 1990. In *Godard par Godard*, vol. 2, 242–48.

"Le cinéma est toujours une opération de deuil et de reconquête de la vie." Interview by Frédéric Bonnaud and Serge Kaganski. *Les inrockuptibles*, 27 November 1996. In *Godard par Godard*, vol. 2, 380–90.

"Dialogue entre Jean-Luc Godard et Serge Daney." *Cahiers du cinéma*, no. 513, May 1997, 49–55.

"C'est le cinéma qui raconte l'histoire: Lui seul le pouvait." Interview by Jean-Michel Frodon. *Le monde*, 8 October 1998, 33.

"La légende du siècle." Interview by Frédéric Bonnaud and Arnaud Viviant. *Les inrockuptibles*, 21 October 1998, 20–28.

"Godard fait son cinéma." Interview by Pascal Merigeau. *Le nouvel observateur*, 29 October 1998, 76–78.

"J'ai fait une échographie." Interview by Pierre Murat and Jean-Claude Loiseau. *Télérama*, 11 November 1998, 34–38.

"Jean-Luc Godard: Des traces du cinéma." Interview by Michel Ciment and Stéphane Goudet. *Positif*, no. 456, February 1999, 50–57.

"Jean-Luc Godard: Une longue histoire." Interview by Jacques Rancière and Charles Tesson. *Cahiers du cinéma*, no. 557, May 2001, 28–36.

Articles and Collages by Godard Cited in the Text

Godard, Jean-Luc. "Panic in the Streets." *Gazette du cinéma*, no. 4, October 1950. In *Godard on Godard*, 20–21.

———. "Montage, mon beau souci." *Cahiers du cinéma*, no. 65, December 1956. In *Godard on Godard*, 39.

———. "Jean Renoir." *Cahiers du cinéma*, no. 78, December 1957. In *Godard on Godard*, 62–64.

———. "Malraux, mauvais français?" *Cahiers du cinéma*, no. 83, May 1958. In *Godard on Godard*, 75.

———. "Désespérant." *Arts*, no. 680, 30 July 1958. In *Godard on Godard*, 85–86.

———. "Bergmanorama." *Cahiers du cinéma*, no. 85, July 1958. In *Godard on Godard*, 75–80.

———. "Boris Barnet." *Cahiers du cinéma*, no. 94, April 1959. In *Godard on Godard*, 139–40.

———. "Jean Renoir: 'La télévision m'a révélé un nouveau cinéma.'" *Arts*, no. 718, 15 April 1959. Invented interview. In *Godard on Godard*, 143–46.

———. "Dans *Adieu Philippine* Rozier a trouvé le rapport des hommes et des choses." *Les lettres françaises*, no. 928, 24 May 1962, 12.

———. "Feu sur *Les carabiniers*." *Cahiers du cinéma*, no. 146, August 1963. In *Godard on Godard*, 196–200.

———. "Dictionnaire des cinéastes américains." *Cahiers du cinéma* (special issue: *Le cinéma américain*), nos. 150/151, December 1963–January 1964. In *Godard on Godard*, 201–204.

———. "Qui? Pourquoi? Comment? Questionnaire." *Cahiers du cinéma*, nos. 161/162, January 1965. In *Godard on Godard*, 208–10.

———. "Grâce à Henri Langlois." *Le nouvel observateur*, 12 January 1966. In *Godard on Godard*, 234–37.

———. *Moi je* (January 1973). In *Jean-Luc Godard: Documents*, edited by Nicole Brenez, David Faroult, Michael Temple, James S. Williams, and Michael Witt, 195–243. Paris: Éditions du Centre Pompidou, 2006.

———. Two letters to Henri Langlois, 9 April (no year given) and 8–9 July 1975. In *Jean-Luc Godard: Documents*, edited by Nicole Brenez, David Faroult, Michael Temple, James S. Williams, and Michael Witt, 248–58. Paris: Éditions du Centre Pompidou, 2006.

———. Letter to Elias Sanbar (19 July 1977). *Cahiers du cinéma*, no. 300, May 1979, 16–19.

———. *The Story* (1979). In *Godard par Godard*, vol. 1, 418–41.

———. Letter to Serge Daney and Serge Toubiana (14 April 1979). *Cahiers du cinéma*, no. 300, May 1979, 3.

———. "Le dernier rêve d'un producteur." *Cahiers du cinéma*, no. 300, May 1979, 70–78. Available in English in *"In the Poem about Love You Don't Write the Word Love,"* edited by Tanya Leighton, 56–64, 82–84. Berlin and New York: Sternberg Press, 2006.

———. "Voir avec ses mains: Comment joue Krystyna Janda." *Cahiers du cinéma*, no. 300, May 1979, 36–59.

———. "Dernière minute." *Cinématographe*, no. 95,

December 1983. In *Jean-Luc Godard: Documents,* edited by Nicole Brenez, David Faroult, Michael Temple, James S. Williams, and Michael Witt, 325–26. Paris: Éditions du Centre Pompidou, 2006.

———. "Tout seul." *Cahiers du cinéma* (special out-of-series issue: *Le roman de François Truffaut*), December 1984. In *Godard par Godard,* vol. 1, 613.

———. "Lettres écrites pendant le tournage de *Détective* et non envoyées à leurs destinaires (1984–85)." In *Godard par Godard,* vol. 1, 613–17.

———. "No Synopsis." (Included in the pressbook for *King Lear* [1987].)

———. Preface to *Cinémamémoire,* by Pierre Braunberger. Paris: CNC/Éditions du Centre Pompidou, 1987. In *Godard par Godard,* vol. 2, 208–10.

———. "La 9ème symphonie." *Cahiers du cinéma,* edited by Wim Wenders, supplement to *Cahiers du cinéma,* no. 400, October 1987, 28–29.

———. "Colles et ciseaux." *Cahiers du cinéma,* no. 402, December 1987. In *Godard par Godard,* vol. 2, 116–21.

———. "À propos de la coupure publicitaire à la télévision: Jean-Luc Godard, ses films, sa plume et ses ciseaux," *Le monde,* 3–4 July 1988. (Available in English in *"In the Poem about Love You Don't Write the Word Love,"* edited by Tanya Leighton, 89–92. Berlin and New York: Sternberg Press, 2006.)

———. "Textes à servir au(x) histoire(s) du cinéma." *Cahiers du cinéma* (special out-of-series issue: *Spécial Godard: 30 ans depuis*), supplement to no. 437, November 1990, 68–69.

———. "La paroisse morte." *Trafic,* no. 1 (1991). In *Godard par Godard,* vol. 2, 254.

———. "Rapport d'inactivité: Les mésaventures du centre de recherche sur les métiers de l'image et du son." *Le monde,* 8 October 1991. In *Godard par Godard,* vol. 2, 249–51.

———. "Le ciné-fils." *Libération,* 13–14 June 1992. In *Godard par Godard,* vol. 2, 252.

———. "Histoire(s) du cinéma: Avec un s." *Le monde* (special out-of-series issue: *Le siècle du cinéma*), January 1995. First published in *Le monde,* 15 December 1994.

———. "À propos de cinéma et d'histoire." *Trafic,* no. 18 (1996). In *Godard par Godard,* vol. 2, 401–405.

———. "Dit/vu." *Cahiers du cinéma,* no. 508, December 1996, 14–27.

———. "Deuxième lettre à Freddy Buache: Oh! Temps de l'utopie" (c. 1998). In *Godard par Godard,* vol. 2, 212–18.

Godard, Jean-Luc, and Anne-Marie Miéville. "Our Music: Synopsis for a Film." In *Horizons Touched: The Music of ECM,* edited by Steve Lake and Paul Griffiths, 5–6. London: Granta, 2007.

Books and Special Issues of Journals Largely or Wholly Devoted to *Histoire(s) du cinéma*

Art press (special out-of-series issue: *Le siècle de Jean-Luc Godard: Guide pour Histoire[s] du cinéma*), November 1998.

Aumont, Jacques. *Amnésies: Fictions du cinéma d'après Jean-Luc Godard.* Paris: P.O.L., 1999.

Cahiers du cinéma. Supplement to no. 537, July–August 1999 (copublished by Canal Plus).

Hardouin, Frédéric. *Le cinématographe selon Godard: Introduction aux Histoire(s) du cinéma ou réflexion sur le temps des arts.* Paris: Harmattan, 2007.

Heywood, Miriam. *Modernist Visions: Marcel Proust's À la recherche du temps perdu and Jean-Luc Godard's Histoire(s) du cinéma.* Bern and Oxford: Peter Lang, 2011.

Morrey, Douglas. "Jean-Luc Godard and the Other History of Cinema." Ph.D. diss., University of Warwick, 2002.

Prédal, René, ed. *CinémAction* (special issue: *Où en est le God-Art?*), no. 109 (2003).

Scemama, Céline. *Histoire(s) du cinéma de Jean-Luc Godard: La force faible d'un art.* Paris: Harmattan, 2006.

Temple, Michael, and James S. Williams, eds. *The Cinema Alone: Essays on the Work of Jean-Luc Godard, 1985–2000.* Amsterdam: Amsterdam University Press, 2000.

Articles on *Histoire(s) du cinéma*

Agamben, Giorgio, Florence Delay, Marie-José Mondzain, Jean Narboni, and Jacques Rancière. "Face au cinéma et à l'Histoire, à propos de Jean-Luc Godard: Cinq des contributions aux tables rondes organisées durant le Festival de Locarno à propos d'*Histoire(s) du cinéma* explorent différentes pistes ouvertes par l'œuvre du cinéaste." *Le monde,* 6 October 1995, *Supplément livres,* x–xi.

Aumont, Jacques. "La traversée des ruines." In *L'invention de la figure humaine–Le cinéma: L'humain et l'inhumain,* edited by Jacques Aumont, 25–35. Paris: Cinémathèque française, 1995.

———. "Beauté, fatal souci: Note sur un épisode des *Histoire(s) du cinéma.*" *Cinémathèque,* no. 12 (1997): 17–24.

———. "La mort de Dante." *CiNéMAS 8,* nos. 1/2 (1997): 125–45.

———. "Mortal Beauty." In *The Cinema Alone: Essays on the Work of Jean-Luc Godard, 1985–2000,* edited by Michael Temple and James S. Williams, 97–112. Amsterdam: Amsterdam University Press, 2000.

Baecque, Antoine de. "Le cinéma par la bande." *Cahiers du cinéma,* no. 513, May 1997, 37–38.

———. "À la recherche d'une forme cinématographique de l'histoire." *Critique*, nos. 632/633 (2000): 155–65.

———. "La théorie des étincelles: L'histoire en images selon Jean-Luc Godard." In *L'histoire-caméra*, 263–309. Paris: Gallimard, 2008.

Bergala, Alain. "Le choix de Godard" and "L'Ange de l'Histoire." In *Nul mieux que Godard*, 211–16, 221–49. Paris: Cahiers du cinéma, 1999.

———. "La figure de l'ange: Entretien avec Alain Bergala." Interview by René Prédal. *CinémAction* (special issue: *Où en est le God-Art?*), no. 109 (2003): 82–98.

Biette, Jean-Claude. "Godard et son histoire du cinéma." *Cahiers du cinéma*, no. 327, September 1981, "Le Journal des Cahiers du cinéma," v–vi.

Bouquet, Stéphane. "Des livres, le Livre." *Cahiers du cinéma*, no. 529, November 1998, 58–59.

Brenez, Nicole. "The Ultimate Journey: Remarks on Contemporary Theory," translated by William Routt. *Screening the Past*, no. 2 (1997), www.latrobe.edu.au/screeningthepast/reruns/brenez.html.

Brown, Alifeleti. "*Histoire(s) du cinéma*." *Senses of Cinema*, no. 46 (2008), sensesofcinema.com.

Callahan, Vicki. "The Evidence and Uncertainty of Silent Film in *Histoire(s) du cinéma*." In *The Cinema Alone: Essays on the Work of Jean-Luc Godard, 1985–2000*, edited by Michael Temple and James S. Williams, 141–58. Amsterdam: Amsterdam University Press, 2000.

Ciment, Michel. "*Histoire(s) du cinéma*." *Positif*, nos. 437/438, July–August 1997, 93.

Conley, Tom. "*Histoire(s) du cinéma* and the Polemical Image." *Dalhousie French Studies* 81 (2007), 9–18.

Dall'Asta, Monica. "The (Im)possible History." In *For Ever Godard*, edited by Michael Temple, James S. Williams, and Michael Witt, 350–63. London: Black Dog, 2004.

Darke, Chris. "*Histoire(s) du cinéma*." *Sight and Sound* 3, no. 7, July 1993, 57.

———. "Hearing the Invisible." *Sight and Sound* 7, no. 9, September 1997, 35.

Delage, Christian. "Librairie: Le vaste appétit de l'histoire de Jean-Luc Godard." *Vingtième Siècle*, no. 64 (1999): 145–48.

Dieckmann, Katherine. "Godard's Counter-Memory." *Art in America* 81, no. 10, 1993, 65–67.

Douin, Jean-Luc. "Jean-Luc Godard décrit l'Histoire à travers le prisme de l'imaginaire." *Le monde*, 20 April 2007, 27.

Eades, Caroline. "Godard, l'hommage au XIXe siècle." In *CinémAction* (special issue: *Où en est le God-Art?*), no. 109 (2003): 211–18.

Eisenschitz, Bernard. "Une machine à montrer l'invisible: Conversation avec Bernard Eisenschitz à propos des *Histoire(s) du cinéma*." Interview by Charles Tesson. *Cahiers du cinéma*, no. 529, November 1998, 50–56.

Farassino, Alberto. "Introduction à un véritable historien du cinéma." In *Jean-Luc Godard: Un hommage du Centre culturel français et du Museo nazionale del cinema de Turin*, edited by Sergio Toffetti, 49–57. Turin: Centre culturel français de Turin, 1990.

Frodon, Jean-Michel. "Jean-Luc Godard, maître d'ouvrage d'art." *Le monde*, 8 October 1998, 33.

Froger, Marion. "En attendant les *Histoire(s) du cinéma* de Jean-Luc Godard." *Ciné-Bulles* 18, no. 4, Summer 2000, 32–36.

Furet, François. "Lettre(s) à Godard." *Cahiers du cinéma* (special out-of-series issue: *Le siècle du cinéma*), November 2000, 6–9.

Gauville, Hervé. "Godard fait ses contes." *Libération*, 6–7 May 1989, 37.

Goudet, Stéphane. "Splendeurs et apories de la dernière écume." *Positif*, no. 456, February 1999, 58–59.

Grange, Marie-Françoise. "Un passeur à la dérive dans *Histoire(s) du cinéma* de J.-L. Godard." In *Arts platiques et cinéma: Les territoires du passeur*, edited by Marie-Françoise Grange and Éric Vandecasteele, 15–33. Paris: Harmattan, 1998.

Griffiths, Paul. "Godard's Mix of Movies and Music." *New York Times*, 2 July 2000, 25.

Guerin, Marie Anne. "Seul le cinéma." *La nouvelle revue française*, no. 536 (1997): 116–27.

Habib, André. "Before and After: Origins and Death in the Work of Jean-Luc Godard." *Senses of Cinema*, no. 16 (2001), sensesofcinema.com.

———. "Mémoire d'un achèvement. Approches de la fin dans les *Histoire(s) du cinéma*, de Jean-Luc Godard," *CiNéMAS* 13, no. 3 (2003): 9–31.

Heywood, Miriam. "World Literature as Video: Literary Quotation in Jean-Luc Godard's *Histoire(s) du cinéma*." In *World Literature, World Culture: History, Theory, Analysis*, edited by Karen-Margrethe Simonsen and Jakob Stougaard-Nielsen, 100–115. Aarhus, Denmark: Aarhus University Press, 2008.

———. "Holocaust and Image: Debates Surrounding Jean-Luc Godard's *Histoire(s) du cinéma* (1988–1998)." *Studies in French Cinema* 9, no. 3 (2009): 273–83.

———. "True Images: Metaphor, Metonymy and Montage in Marcel Proust's *À la recherche du temps perdu* and Jean-Luc Godard's *Histoire(s) du cinéma*." *Paragraph* 33, no. 1 (2010): 37–51.

Hill, Leslie. "'A Form That Thinks': Godard, Blanchot, Citation." In *For Ever Godard*, edited by Michael Temple, James S. Williams, and Michael Witt, 396–415. London: Black Dog, 2004.

Hori, Junji. "La géo-politique de l'image dans les

Histoire(s) du cinéma de Jean-Luc Godard." *European Studies,* Proceedings of the DESK Center for German and European Studies, vol. 3 (2003) (Graduate School of Arts and Sciences, University of Tokyo), 43–61, www.desk.c.u-tokyo.ac.jp/e/books_bk_es.html.

———. "Godard's Two Historiographies." In *For Ever Godard,* edited by Michael Temple, James S. Williams, and Michael Witt, 334–49. London: Black Dog, 2004.

Horwarth, Alexander. "The Man with the Magnéto-scope: Jean-Luc Godard's Monumental *Histoire(s) du cinéma* as SoundImageTextBook," translated by Aileen Derieg. *Senses of Cinema,* no. 15 (2001), sensesofcinema.com.

Ishaghpour, Youssef. "Jean-Luc Godard, Cinéaste of Modern Life: The Poetic in the Historical." In Jean-Luc Godard and Youssef Ishaghpour, *Cinema: The Archaeology of Film and the Memory of a Century,* translated by John Howe, 113–43. Oxford: Berg, 2005.

Jayamanne, Laleen. "Jean-Luc Godard's *Histoire(s) du cinéma,* or 'Memory of the World' (a lecture)." *Screening the Past,* no. 23 (2008), www.latrobe.edu.au/screeningthepast/23/histoires-cinema-lecture.html.

Jones, Kent. "Sound-Tracking Godard." *Film Comment* 36, no. 5, September–October 2000, 70.

Jousse, Thierry. "Histoire(s) d'entendre." *Cahiers du cinéma,* no. 541, December 1999, 11.

Kermabon, Jacques. "Tentatives incertaines pour aborder les *Histoire(s) du cinéma* de Jean-Luc Godard." *24 Images,* nos. 88/89, fall 1997, 54–57.

Labarthe, André S. "Dix sujets de méditation propagés à des étudiants imaginaires." *Art press* (special out-of-series issue: *Le siècle de Jean-Luc Godard: Guide pour Histoire[s] du cinéma*), November 1998, 8–12.

Leutrat, Jean-Louis. "*Histoire(s) du cinéma,* ou comment devenir maître d'un souvenir." *Cinémathèque,* no. 5 (1993): 28–39.

———. "Retour sur *Histoire(s),* 1." *Trafic,* no. 70 (2009): 52–62.

———. "Retour sur *Histoire(s),* 2." *Trafic,* no. 71 (2009): 129–39.

———. "Retour sur *Histoire(s),* 3." *Trafic,* no. 72 (2009): 96–116.

———. "Retour sur *Histoire(s),* 4." *Trafic,* no. 73 (2010): 77–94.

———. "Retour sur *Histoire(s),* 5." *Trafic,* no. 74 (2010): 78–90.

———. "Retour sur *Histoire(s),* 6." *Trafic,* no. 75 (2010): 98–106.

———. "Retour sur *Histoire(s),* 7." *Trafic,* no. 76 (2010): 68–82.

Lundemo, Trond. "The Index and Erasure: Godard's Approach to Film History." In *For Ever Godard,* edited by Michael Temple, James S. Williams, and Michael Witt, 380–95. London: Black Dog, 2004.

Maillot, Jacques. "Je ne connais pas de travail comparable sur un livre." Interview by Jean-Michel Frodon. *Le monde,* 8 October 1998, 33.

Martin, Adrian. "Godard's *Histoire(s) du cinéma,* Parts 1A and 1B: Tales from the Crypt." *Senses of Cinema,* no. 10 (November 2000), sensesofcinema.com.

Mazabrard, Colette. "Histoires du cinéma sur Canal +: Godard revigorant." *Cahiers du cinéma,* nos. 419/420, May 1989, "Le journal des cahiers," vi–vii.

Mercier, Christophe. "Les louanges du moine Godard." *Commentaire* 22, no. 85 (1999): 286–88.

Mondzain, Marie-José. "Histoire et passion." *Art press* (special out-of-series issue: *Le siècle de Jean-Luc Godard: Guide pour Histoire[s] du cinéma*), November 1998, 91–97.

Neer, Richard. "Godard Counts." *Critical Inquiry* 34, no. 1 (2007): 135–71.

Nel, Noël. "*Histoire(s) du cinéma* 1 et 2 de Godard." In *Godard et le métier d'artiste,* edited by Gilles Delavaud, Jean-Pierre Esquenazi, and Marie-Françoise Grange, 201–13. Paris: Harmattan, 2001.

Nettlebeck, Colin. "From La Nouvelle Vague to *Histoire(s) du cinéma:* History in Godard, Godard in History." *French History and Civilisation: Papers from the George Rudé Seminar* 1 (2005): 104–13.

Païni, Dominique. "The Cinema Museum and Aura." *Art press,* no. 221 (1997): 28–33.

———. "Que peut le cinéma?" *Art press* (special out-of-series issue: *Le siècle de Jean-Luc Godard: Guide pour Histoire(s) du cinéma*), November 1998, 4–7.

Pavsek, Christopher. "What Has Come to Pass for Cinema in Late Godard." *Discourse* 28, no. 1 (2006): 166–95.

Petit, Chris. "The History of Cinema *and* History in Cinema." *Vertigo* 4, no. 2, Spring 2009, 3–5.

Rancière, Jacques. "The Saint and the Heiress: A Propos of Godard's *Histoire(s) du cinéma.*" Translated by Timothy Murphy. *Discourse* 24, no. 1 (2002): 113–19.

———. "Godard, Hitchcock, and the Cinematographic Image." In *For Ever Godard,* edited by Michael Temple, James S. Williams, and Michael Witt, 214–31. London: Black Dog, 2004.

Ricciardi, Alessia. "Cinema Regained: Godard Between Proust and Benjamin." *Modernism/Modernity* 8, no. 4 (2001): 643–61.

———. "Godard's Histoire(s)." In *The Ends of Mourning: Psychoanalysis, Literature, Film,* 167–257. Stanford, Calif.: Stanford University Press, 2003.

Robbins, Alex. "Ce colporteur, c'était le cinéma." *French Studies Bulletin,* no. 87 (2003): 2–8.

Rohdie, Sam. "Intersections." *Screening The Past,* no. 23

(2008), www.latrobe.edu/screeningthepast/23/inter-sections.html.

———. "Deux ou trois choses. . . ." *Critical Quarterly* 51, no. 3 (2009): 85–99.

Romney, Jonathan. "Labyrinth of Sound." *The Guardian*, 19 January 2000, 15.

Rosenbaum, Jonathan. "His Twentieth Century: Go-dard's *Histoire(s) du cinéma*." In *Movies as Politics*, 318–22. Berkeley and Los Angeles: University of California Press, 1997.

———. "Trailer for Godard's *Histoire(s) du cinéma*." *Vertigo* 1, no. 7, Autumn 1997, 13–20.

———. "*Le vrai coupable*: Two Kinds of Criticism in Go-dard's Work." *Screen* 40, no. 3 (1999): 316–21.

———. "The Director's Cut: Jean-Luc Godard's Truncated Magnum Opus is Still Poetic." *Chicago Reader,* 10 March 2006, 26–27.

Saxton, Libby. "Anamnesis and Bearing Witness: Go-dard/Lanzmann." In *For Ever Godard,* edited by Mi-chael Temple, James S. Williams, and Michael Witt, 364–79. London: Black Dog, 2004.

Scemama, Céline. "Le roi n'est pas nu, il ne prétend pas être habillé: Lettres aux spectateurs." *CinémAction* (special issue: *Où en est le God-Art?*), no. 109 (2003): 99–105.

Shafto, Sally. "On Painting and History in Godard's *Histoire(s) du cinéma*." *Senses of Cinema,* no. 40 (2006), sensesofcinema.com.

Silverman, Kaja. "The Dream of the Nineteenth Cen-tury." *Camera Obscura* 51, vol. 17, no. 3 (2002): 1–29.

Sollers, Philippe. "Il y a des fantômes plein l'écran." In-terview by Antoine de Baecque and Serge Toubiana. *Cahiers du cinéma,* no. 513, May 1997, 39–48.

Stoneman, Rod. "Bon Voyage." *Sight and Sound* 3, no. 7, July 1993, 29.

Swed, Mark. "Sharing Sound Theories on Filmmaking." *Los Angeles Times,* 6 August 2000, 50, 52.

Temple, Michael. "It Will Be Worth It." *Sight and Sound* 8, no. 1, January 1998, 20–23.

———. "Big Rhythm and the Power of Metamorphosis: Some Models and Precursors for *Histoire(s) du cinéma*." In *The Cinema Alone: Essays on the Work of Jean-Luc Go-dard, 1985–2000,* edited by Michael Temple and James S. Williams, 77–95. Amsterdam: Amsterdam Univer-sity Press, 2000.

Temple, Michael, and James S. Williams. "Jean-Luc Go-dard: Images, Words, Histories." *Dalhousie French Stud-ies* 45 (1998): 99–109.

———. "Introduction to the Mysteries of Cinema, 1985–2000." In *The Cinema Alone: Essays on the Work of Jean-Luc Godard, 1985–2000,* edited by Michael Temple and

James S. Williams, 9–32. Amsterdam: Amsterdam University Press, 2000.

Tesson, Charles. "Rotterdam 81." *Cahiers du cinéma,* no. 322, April 1981, 45–48.

Toubiana, Serge. "Godard, le veilleur de rêves." In *Ca-hiers du cinéma,* supplement to issue no. 537, July–Au-gust 1999, 1.

Turner, Jenny. "Cinema's Rambling Man." *The Guardian,* 17 June 1993, 5.

Vincendeau, Ginette. "The World According to Godard." *Sight and Sound* 18, no. 12, December 2008, 84.

Warner, Charles R. "Shocking *Histoire(s)*: Godard, Sur-realism, and Historical Montage." *Quarterly Review of Film and Video* 25, no. 1 (2008): 1–15.

Warner, Rick. "Difficult Work in a Popular Medium: Go-dard on 'Hitchcock's Method.'" *Critical Quarterly* 51, no. 3 (2009): 63–84.

Williams, James S. "The Signs amongst Us: Jean-Luc Godard's *Histoire(s) du cinéma*." *Screen* 40, no. 3 (1999): 306–15.

———. "Beyond the Cinematic Body: Human Emotion Versus Digital Technology in Jean-Luc Godard's *Histoire(s) du cinéma*." In *Thinking the Inhuman,* edited by Scott Brewster and John Joughin, 188–202. Manches-ter, UK: Manchester University Press, 2000.

———. "European Culture and Artistic Resistance in *Histoire(s) du cinéma* Chapter 3A, *La monnaie de l'absolu*." In *The Cinema Alone: Essays on the Work of Jean-Luc Go-dard, 1985–2000,* edited by Michael Temple and James S. Williams, 113–39. Amsterdam: Amsterdam Univer-sity Press, 2000.

———. "Music, Love, and the Cinematic Event." In *For Ever Godard,* edited by Michael Temple, James S. Wil-liams, and Michael Witt, 288–311. London: Black Dog, 2004.

———. "*Histoire(s) du cinéma*." *Film Quarterly* 61, no. 3, spring 2008, 10–16.

Wilson, Emma. "Conclusion: Histories of Cinema." In *French Cinema Since 1950: Personal Histories,* 137–44. London: Duckworth, 1999.

Witt, Michael. "Montage, My Beautiful Care, or Histories of the Cinematograph." In *The Cinema Alone: Essays on the Work of Jean-Luc Godard, 1985–2000,* edited by Mi-chael Temple and James S. Williams, 33–50. Amster-dam: Amsterdam University Press, 2000.

———. "Qu'était-ce que le cinéma, Jean-Luc Godard? An Analysis of the Cinema(s) at Work in and around Godard's *Histoire(s) du cinéma*." In *France in Focus: Film and National Identity,* edited by Elizabeth Ezra and Sue Harris, 23–41. Oxford: Berg, 2000.

———. "Génèse d'une véritable histoire du cinéma." In *Jean-Luc Godard: Documents,* edited by Nicole Brenez,

SELECT BIBLIOGRAPHY

David Faroult, Michael Temple, James S. Williams, and Michael Witt, 265–80. Paris: Éditions du Centre Pompidou, 2006.

Wood, Michael. "After the Movies." *London Review of Books*, 4 December 2008.

Wright, Alan. "Elizabeth Taylor at Auschwitz: JLG and the Real Object of Montage." In *The Cinema Alone: Essays on the Work of Jean-Luc Godard, 1985–2000*, edited by Michael Temple and James S. Williams, 51–60. Amsterdam: Amsterdam University Press, 2000.

Other Interviews with Godard Cited in the Text

Domarchi, Jean, Jacques Doniol-Valcroze, Jean-Luc Godard, Pierre Kast, Jacques Rivette, and Eric Rohmer. "Hiroshima, notre amour." *Cahiers du cinéma*, no. 97, July 1959, 1–18.

Astruc, Alexandre, Marcel Carné, Claude Chabrol, Jean-Paul Le Chanois, Henri Chapier, Jacques Doniol-Valcroze, Jean-Luc Godard, Pierre Kast, Jean Jabely, Maître Kiejman, Maurice Lemaître, Nicholas Ray, Jean Renoir, Jacques Rivette, Jean Rouch, and Simone Signoret. "Conférence de presse." *Cahiers du cinéma*, no. 199, March 1968, 34–44.

"Jean-Luc Godard." Interview by Abraham Segal. *Image et son* (special issue: *Le son au cinéma*), no. 215, March 1968, 72–82.

"Jean-Luc Godard: L'important c'est les producteurs." Interview by Monique Annaud. *Le film français*, 14 March 1975, 13.

"Faire les films possibles là où on est." Interview by Yvonne Baby. *Le monde*, 25 September 1975. In *Godard par Godard*, vol. 1, 382–86.

"Godard dit tout." Seven-part interview by Jean-Luc Douin and Alain Rémond. *Télérama*, 8 July–19 August 1978.

"Entretien avec J-L Godard le 12 avril 1978." Interview by Jacques Richard. *Cinequanone*, no. 1, 10 May 1978, 25–29.

"Entretien sur un projet–2." Conversation between Jean-Luc Godard, Luc Béraud, and Claude Miller, 27 April 1979. *Ça cinéma*, no. 19 (1980), 17–30.

"Les dernières leçons du donneur: Fragments d'un entretien avec Jean-Luc Godard." *Cahiers du cinéma*, no. 300, May 1979, 60–69.

"Se vivre, se voir." Interview by Claire Devarrieux. *Le monde dimanche* (Radio-télévision), 30 March 1980. In *Godard par Godard*, vol. 1, 404–407.

"Alfred Hitchcock est mort." Interview by Serge July. *Libération*, 2 May 1980. In *Godard par Godard*, vol. 1, 412–16.

"La chance de repartir pour un tour." Interview by Claude-Jean Philippe. *Les nouvelles littéraires*, 30 May 1980. In *Godard par Godard*, vol. 1, 407–12.

"Propos rompus." *Cahiers du cinéma*, no. 316, October 1980. In *Godard par Godard*, vol. 1, 458–71.

"Travail-amour-cinéma." Interview by Catherine David. *Le nouvel observateur*, 20 October 1980. In *Godard par Godard*, vol. 1, 449–58.

"Godard: Born-Again Filmmaker." Interview by Jonathan Cott. *Rolling Stone*, 27 November 1980, 32–36.

"The Economics of Film Criticism: A Debate." Discussion between Godard and Pauline Kael, 7 May 1981. *Camera Obscura*, nos. 8/9/10 (1982): 163–84.

"Le chemin vers la parole." Interview by Alain Bergala, Serge Daney, and Serge Toubiana. *Cahiers du cinéma*, no. 336, May 1982. In *Godard par Godard*, vol. 1, 498–519.

"Godard à Venise." *Cinématographe*, no. 95, December 1983, 3–7.

"Rolle over Godard." Interview by Charles Tatum and Philippe Elhem. *Visions*, no. 17, 15 March 1984, 5–9.

"The Carrots Are Cooked: A Conversation with Jean-Luc Godard." Interview by Gideon Bachmann. *Film Quarterly* 37, no. 3, spring 1984, 13–19.

"Dans Marie il y a aimer." Interview by Antoine Dulaure and Claire Parnet. *L'autre journal*, no. 2, January 1985. In *Godard par Godard*, vol. 1, 597–609.

"L'art à partir de la vie: Nouvel entretien avec Jean-Luc Godard par Alain Bergala." 12 March 1985. In *Godard par Godard*, vol. 1, 9–24.

"Parti de chase." Interview by Marie Rambert. *Télérama*, 16 April 1986. In *Godard par Godard*, vol. 2, 95–99.

"La télé selon Jean-Luc." Interview by Catherine Humblot and Thomas Ferenczi. *Le monde radio-télévision*, 22–23 June 1986, 16–17.

"ABCD . . . JLG." Interview by Olivier Péretié. *Le nouvel observateur*, 18 December 1987. In *Jean-Luc Godard: Documents*, edited by Nicole Brenez, David Faroult, Michael Temple, James S. Williams, and Michael Witt, 330. Paris: Éditions du Centre Pompidou, 2006.

"Marguerite Duras et Jean-Luc Godard: Entretien télévisé." Dialogue with Marguerite Duras, 28 December 1987. In *Godard par Godard*, vol. 2, 140–47.

"Le cinéma meurt, vive le cinéma!" Interview by Danièle Heymann. *Le monde*, 30 December 1987, 1, 10.

"Le regard s'est perdu." Interview by Jean-Luc Douin. *Télérama*, 30 December 1987. In *Godard par Godard*, vol. 2, 122–27.

"L'art de (dé)montrer." Interview by Alain Bergala and Serge Toubiana. *Cahiers du cinéma*, no. 408, January 1988. In *Godard par Godard*, vol. 2, 128–39.

"Une place sur la terre." Interview by Hélène Merrick. *La revue du cinéma*, no. 434, January 1988, 51–55.

"Godard arrêt sur images: Le cinéaste commente quelques photos de *Soigne ta droite*." Interview by Michèle Halberstadt. *Première*, no. 130, January 1988, 56–59.

"Week-end avec Godard." Interview by Jean Daniel and Nicole Boulanger. *Le nouvel observateur*, 10 May 1989. In *Godard par Godard*, vol. 2, 175–81.

"Jean-Luc Godard: 'La France reste à l'avant-garde . . . de la régression.'" Interview by Frédéric Ferney. *Le monde*, 11 December 1990, 29.

"Préface: Entretien entre Jean-Luc Godard et Freddy Buache." In *Musée du cinéma Henri Langlois*, edited by Marianne de Fleury, Dominique Lebrun, and Olivier Meston, 4–6. Paris: Maeght Éditeur, 1991.

"Jean-Luc Godard in Conversation with Colin MacCabe." June 1991. In *Screening Europe: Image and Identity in Contemporary European Cinema*, edited by Duncan Petrie, 97–105. London: BFI, 1992.

"For a Few Dollars Less." Dialogue between Godard and Wim Wenders. *The Guardian/Sight and Sound: London Film Festival Special*, edited by Philip Dodd, October 1991, 20–22.

"Le briquet de Capitaine Cook." Interview by François Albera and Mikhail Iampolski. *Les lettres françaises*, no. 19, April 1992, 17–21.

"Le cinéma est fait pour penser l'impensable." Dialogue with André S. Labarthe. *Limelight*, no. 34, January 1995. In *Godard par Godard*, vol. 2, 294–99.

"Le cinéma n'a pas su remplir son rôle." Interview by Jean-Pierre Lavoignat and Christophe d'Yvoire. *Studio*, no. 156, March 1995. In *Godard par Godard*, vol. 2, 335–43.

"Le bon plaisir de Jean-Luc Godard." Interview by Jean Daive, 20 May 1995. In *Godard par Godard*, vol. 2, 305–322.

"Jean-Luc Godard rencontre Régis Debray." Interview by Régis Debray, October 1995. In *Godard par Godard*, vol. 2, 423–31.

"Parler du manque." Interview by Alain Bergala and Serge Toubiana, October 1996. In *Godard par Godard*, vol. 2, 360–79.

"Aujourd'hui, on cherche plus à interpréter qu'à regarder." Interview by Jean-Michel Frodon. *Le monde*, 3 December 1996. In *Godard par Godard*, vol. 2, 391–93.

"Les livres et moi." Interview by Pierre Assouline. *Lire*, no. 255, May 1997. In *Godard par Godard*, vol. 2, 437–38.

"Godard/Amar: Cannes 97." Interview by Paul Amar, 16 May 1997. In *Godard par Godard*, vol. 2, 408–22.

"Une boucle bouclée: Nouvel entretien avec Jean-Luc Godard par Alain Bergala." Interview dated October/December 1997. In *Godard par Godard*, vol. 2, 9–41.

"'Faire un film, c'est renoncer à tout': Points de vue du cinéaste sur son œuvre et sur son monde." Interview by François Armanet, Gérard Lefort, Mathieu Lindon, and Louis Skorecki. *Libération*, 7 October 1998, 3–5.

"The Future(s) of Film." Interview by Emmanuel Burdeau and Charles Tesson, 2 March 2000. In *The Future(s) of Film: Three Interviews, 2000/01*, translated by John O'Toole, 11–43. Bern: Gachnang and Springer, 2002.

"Jean-Luc Godard: 'La Nouvelle Vague, c'était l'ivresse du possible.'" Interview by François Gorin and Jean-Claude Loiseau. *Télérama*, 4 October 2000, 17–21.

"Godard: Grandeur d'un petit commerce de cinéma." Interview by Jean-Yves Gaillac, Tissy Morg, and Jean-Philippe Guerand. *Epok*, no. 16, May 2001, 8–14.

"Je reviens en arrière mais je vais de l'avant." Interview by Jean-Claude Loiseau and Jacques Morice. *Télérama*, 16 May 2001, 52–57.

"The Artistic Act Is an Act of Resistance." Interview by Michèle Halberstadt. *Enthusiasm*, no. 5, Winter 2002, 2–7.

"A Language before Babel: Film Conversation between Artavazd Peleshian and Jean-Luc Godard." 2 April 1992. In Artavazd Peleshian, *Our Century*, edited by Gerald Matt and Angela Stief, 415–19. Vienna: Ursula Blickle Stiftung/Kunsthalle Wien/Kerber Verlag, 2004.

"Le cinéma a été l'art des âmes qui ont vécu intimement dans l'Histoire." Interview by Antoine de Baecque. *Libération*, 6 April 2002, 44.

"C'est notre musique, c'est notre ADN, c'est nous." Interview by Serge Kaganski and Jean-Marc Lalanne. *Les inrockuptibles*, 5 May 2004, 30–39.

"Juste une conversation." Interview by Jean-Michel Frodon. *Cahiers du cinéma*, no. 590, May 2004, 20–22.

"Le cinéma de Jean-Luc Godard ne se joue pas à pile ou face." Interview by Michel Guilloux. *L'humanité*, 20 May 2004, 10.

Webcam dialogue between Jean-Luc Godard and Jean-Michel Frodon, 8 December 2004. Included as a bonus on the DVD of *Morceaux de conversations avec Jean-Luc Godard* (Alain Fleischer, 2006).

"Le cinéma me reste comme espérance." Interview by Jean-Pierre Dufreigne. *L'express*, 3 May 2005.

"The Godard Interview: I, a Man of the Image." Interview by Michael Witt. *Sight and Sound* 15, no. 6, June 2005, 28–30.

"Jean-Luc Godard en liberté." Interview by Sylvain Bourmeau, Ludovic Lamant, and Edwy Plenel. *Mediapart*, 10 May 2010, www.mediapart.fr.

Onstage talk at the Cinéma des cinéastes, Paris, 8 June 2010, following a screening of *Film socialisme*. Chaired by Edwy Plenel.

Selected Books and Articles on Godard

Aragon, Louis. "What Is Art, Jean-Luc Godard?" In *Focus on Godard,* edited and translated by Royal S. Brown, 135–46. Englewood Cliffs, N.J.: Prentice-Hall, 1972.

Art press. Out-of-series special issue no. 4: *Spécial Godard.* December 1984–January/February 1985.

Aumont, Jacques. "Godard peintre, ou l'avant-dernier artiste." In *L'œil interminable: Cinéma et peinture,* 223–48. Toulouse: Séguier, 1989.

———. "Autoportrait de l'artiste en théorichien." *La revue belge du cinéma* (special issue: *Jean-Luc Godard: Le cinéma*), nos. 22/23, 2nd ed., 1989, 171–76.

———. "The Medium." In *Jean-Luc Godard: Son + Image, 1974–1991,* edited by Raymond Bellour and Mary Lea Bandy, translated by Rachel Bowlby, 205–15. New York: Museum of Modern Art, 1992.

Baecque, Antoine de. *Godard: Biographie.* Paris: Grasset, 2010.

Bartoli, Claire. "Le regard intérieur: *Nouvelle vague* de Jean-Luc Godard." *Trafic,* no. 19 (1996): 75–92. (Available in English, translated by John M. King, in the booklet distributed with the CDs of *Nouvelle vague.*)

Bellour, Raymond. "Godart or not Godard." *Les lettres françaises,* 14 May 1964, 8.

———. "Autoportraits." In *L'entre-images: Photo, cinéma, video,* 327–87. Paris: La Différence, 1990.

———. "(Not) Just an Other Filmmaker." In *Jean-Luc Godard: Son + Image, 1974–1991,* edited by Raymond Bellour and Mary Lea Bandy, translated by Georgia Gurrieri, 215–32. New York: Museum of Modern Art, 1992.

———. "L'autre cinéaste: Godard écrivain." In *L'entre-images 2: Mots, images,* 113–38. Paris: P.O.L., 1999.

Bellour, Raymond, and Mary Lea Bandy, eds. *Jean-Luc Godard: Son + Image, 1974–1991.* New York: Museum of Modern Art, 1992.

Bergala, Alain. "Le juste milieu." *Cahiers du cinéma,* no. 307, January 1980, 39–42.

———. "The Other Side of the Bouquet." In *Jean-Luc Godard: Son + Image, 1974–1991,* edited by Raymond Bellour and Mary Lea Bandy, translated by Lynne Kirby, 57–73. New York: Museum of Modern Art, 1992.

———. *Nul mieux que Godard.* Paris: Cahiers du cinéma, 1999.

Bergala, Alain, with Mélanie Gérin and Núria Aidelman. *Godard au travail: Les années 60.* Paris: Cahiers du cinéma, 2006.

Bergstrom, Janet, Elisabeth Lyon, and Constance Penley, eds. *Camera Obscura: A Journal of Feminism and Film Theory* (special triple issue devoted to Godard and Miéville), nos. 8/9/10 (1982).

Brenez, Nicole. "Le film abymé: Jean-Luc Godard et l'Iconoclasme." In *De la figure en générale et du corps en particulier: L'invention figurative au cinéma,* 340–60. Paris and Brussels: De Boeck, 1998.

———. "The Forms of the Question." In *For Ever Godard,* edited by Michael Temple, James S. Williams, and Michael Witt, 160–77. London: Black Dog, 2004.

———. "Jean-Luc Godard, *Witz* et invention formelle (notes préparatoires sur les rapports entre critique et pouvoir symbolique)." *CiNéMAS* 15, nos. 2/3 (2005): 15–43.

Brenez, Nicole, David Faroult, Michael Temple, James S. Williams, and Michael Witt, eds. *Jean-Luc Godard: Documents.* Paris: Éditions du Centre Pompidou, 2006.

Brody, Richard. *Everything Is Cinema: The Working Life of Jean-Luc Godard.* London: Faber and Faber, 2008.

Brown, Royal S. ed. *Focus on Godard.* Englewood Cliffs, N.J.: Prentice-Hall, 1972.

Cerisuelo, Marc. "Godard et la théorie: Tu n'as rien vu à Pesaro. . . ." *CinémAction* (special issue: *Le cinéma selon Godard*), no. 52 (1989): 192–98.

———. *Jean-Luc Godard.* Paris: Quatres vents, 1989.

———. ed. *Études cinématographiques* (special issue: *Jean-Luc Godard [2]: Au-delà de l'image*), nos. 194–202 (1993).

Cohen-Halimi, Michèle, and Francis Cohen. "Juifs, martyrs, kamikazes: La monstreuse capture–Question à Jean-Luc Godard." *Les temps modernes,* no. 629 (2005): 301–10.

Collet, Jean. "An Audacious Experiment: The Sound Track of *Vivre sa vie.*" In *Focus on Godard,* edited and translated by Royal S. Brown, 160–62. Englewood Cliffs, N.J.: Prentice-Hall, 1972. (First published in *La revue du son,* no. 116, December 1962.)

Comolli, Jean-Louis. "Jouer à la Russie: Le corps projeté de Godard." *Trafic,* no. 18 (1996): 40–46.

Darmon, Maurice. *La question juive de Jean-Luc Godard.* Cognac, France: Le temps qu'il fait, 2011.

Delavaud, Gilles, Jean-Pierre Esquenazi, and Marie-Françoise Grange, eds. *Godard et le métier d'artiste.* Paris: Harmattan, 2001.

Deleuze, Gilles. "Three Questions about *Six fois deux.*" In *Jean-Luc Godard: Son + Image, 1974–1991,* edited by Raymond Bellour and Mary Lea Bandy, translated by Rachel Bowlby, 35–42. New York: Museum of Modern Art, 1992. (First published in *Cahiers du cinéma,* no. 271, November 1976.)

Doniol-Valcroze, Jacques. "Jean-Luc Godard, cinéaste masqué." *L'avant-scène cinéma,* no. 46, 1 March 1965, 6, 42.

Douin, Jean-Luc, ed. *Jean-Luc Godard.* Paris: Rivages, 1989.

Dubois, Philippe, ed. *La revue belge du cinéma* (special issue: *Jean-Luc Godard: Le cinéma*), nos. 22/23, 2nd ed., 1989.

———. "Video Thinks What Cinema Creates: Notes on

Jean-Luc Godard's Work in Video and Television."
In *Jean-Luc Godard: Son + Image, 1974–1991*, edited by
Raymond Bellour and Mary Lea Bandy, translated by
Lynne Kirby, 169–85. New York: Museum of Modern
Art, 1992.

Durgnat, Raymond. "Jean-Luc Godard: His Crucifixion
and Resurrection." *Monthly Film Bulletin* 52, no. 620,
September 1985, 268–71.

Eicher, Manfred. "'Jean-Luc Godard dépasse tous les
rêves des artistes du remix.'" Interview by Pierre
Gervasoni. *Le monde*, 4 December 1999, 33.

———. "Musikalische, nicht lineare Erzählstrukturen:
Manfred Eicher im Gespräch über Godard und
Musik." Interview by Christoph Egger. *Neue Zürcher
Zeitung*, 7 July 2000.

———. "Manfred Eicher, le solitaire du son." Interview by
Francis Marmande. *Le monde*, 4 October 2005.

———. "La musique ECM chez Jean-Luc Godard." Interview by James S. Williams. In *Jean-Luc Godard: Documents*, edited by Nicole Brenez, David Faroult, Michael
Temple, James S. Williams, and Michael Witt, 411.
Paris: Éditions du Centre Pompidou, 2006.

———. "The Periphery and the Centre." In *Horizons
Touched: The Music of ECM*, edited by Steve Lake and
Paul Griffiths, 8–9. London: Granta, 2007.

Eisenschitz, Bernard. "La réponse de Godard." *Cinéma*,
no. 12 (2006): 91–101.

Faroult, David. "Avant-garde cinématographique et
avant-garde politique: *Cinéthique* et le 'groupe' Dziga
Vertov." Ph.D. diss., Université de Paris III–Sorbonne
Nouvelle, 2002.

———. "Du vertovisme du Groupe Dziga Vertov." In
Jean-Luc Godard: Documents, edited by Nicole Brenez,
David Faroult, Michael Temple, James S. Williams,
and Michael Witt, 134–38. Paris: Éditions du Centre
Pompidou, 2006.

Fieschi-Vivet, Laetitia. "Investigation of a Mystery: Cinema and the Sacred in *Hélas pour moi*." In *The Cinema
Alone: Essays on the Work of Jean-Luc Godard, 1985–2000*,
edited by Michael Temple and James S. Williams,
189–206. Amsterdam: Amsterdam University Press,
2000.

———. "Transfigurations de l'invisible: Le sacré dans
l'œuvre de Jean-Luc Godard (1975–2000)." Ph.D. diss.,
Birkbeck College, University of London, 2005.

Fleischer, Alain. *Réponse du muet au parlant: En retour à
Jean-Luc Godard*. Paris: Seuil, 2011.

Gailleurd, Céline. "Du naufrage des utopies à
l'effondrement de l'œuvre totale." *Cinéma et cie: International Film Studies Journal* 9, no. 12 (2009): 27–34.

Giavarini, Laurence. "À l'ouest, le crépuscule." *Cahiers du
cinéma*, no. 449, November 1991, 82–86.

Gorin, Jean-Pierre. "Raymond Chandler, Mao Tse-Tung
and *Tout va bien*." Interview by Michael Goodwin
and Naomi Wise. *Take One* 3, no. 6, July–August 1971,
22–24.

———. "Filmmaking and History: Jean-Pierre Gorin."
Interview by Christian Braad Thomsen. *Jump Cut*, no.
3, September–October 1974, 17–19.

Goudet, Stéphane. "Splendeurs et apories de la dernière
écume." *Positif*, no. 456, February 1999, 58–59.

Graf, Frieda. "Whose History? Jean-Luc Godard Between
the Media." In *Documenta Documents 2*, edited by Jean
Christophe Bailly, Catherine David, and Paul Virilio,
4–11. Stuttgart, Germany: Cantz Verlag, 1996.

Habib, André. "Invitation au voyage: *Voyage(s) en utopie*,
JLG, Pompidou." *Hors champ*, 27 July 2006, www.hors-
champ.qc.ca.

———. "Un beau souci: Réflexions sur le montage de/
dans *Voyage(s) en utopie*." *Cinéma et cie: International
Film Studies Journal* 9, no. 12 (2009): 17–26.

Hediger, Vinzenz. "A Cinema of Memory in the Future
Tense: Godard, Trailers, and Godard Trailers." In *For
Ever Godard*, edited by Michael Temple, James S. Williams, and Michael Witt, 144–59. London: Black Dog,
2004.

Henric, Jacques. "L'image, quelle image? Énième épître
aux culs-de-plomb." *Art press* (special out-of-series
issue: *Spécial Godard*), December 1984–January/Febru-
ary 1985, 19–21.

James, Gareth, and Florian Zeyfang, eds. *I Said I Love.
That Is the Promise: The Tvideo Politics of Jean-Luc Godard*.
Berlin: B_Books, 2003.

Jameson, Fredric. "High-tech Collectives in Late Godard." In *The Geopolitical Aesthetic: Cinema and Space in
the World System*, 158–85. Bloomington: Indiana University Press, 1992.

Jousse, Thierry. "Godard à l'oreille." *Cahiers du cinéma*
(special out-of-series issue: *Spécial Godard: 30 ans
depuis*), supplement to *Cahiers du cinéma* no. 437, November 1990, 40–43.

Jousse, Thierry, and Serge Toubiana, eds. *Cahiers du
cinéma* (special out-of-series issue: *Spécial Godard: 30
ans depuis*), supplement to *Cahiers du cinéma* no. 437,
November 1990.

Jullier, Laurent. "Bande-son, attention travaux." In *Godard et le métier d'artiste*, edited by Gilles Delavaud,
Jean-Pierre Esquenazi, and Marie-Françoise Grange,
109–20. Paris: Harmattan, 2001.

———. "JLG/ECM." In *For Ever Godard*, edited by Michael
Temple, James S. Williams, and Michael Witt, 272–87.
London: Black Dog, 2004.

Lack, Roland-François. "Sa voix." In *For Ever Godard*,

edited by Michael Temple, James S. Williams, and Michael Witt, 312–29. London: Black Dog, 2004.

Larouche, Michel. "Godard et le Québécois." *CinémAction* (special issue: *Le cinéma selon Godard*), no. 52 (1989): 158–64.

Lesage, Julia. *Jean-Luc Godard: A Guide to References and Resources*. Boston: G. K. Hall, 1979.

———. "Godard and Gorin's Left Politics, 1967–72." *Jump Cut*, no. 28, April 1983, 51–58.

Leutrat, Jean-Louis. *Kaleidoscope: Analyses de films*. Lyon: Presses universitaires de Lyon, 1988.

———. *Des traces qui nous ressemblent*. Seyssel: Éditions Comp'Act, 1990.

———. "The Declension." In *Jean-Luc Godard: Son + Image, 1974–1991*, edited by Raymond Bellour and Mary Lea Bandy, translated by Rachel Bowlby, 23–33. New York: Museum of Modern Art, 1992.

———. "Ah! Les salauds!" *CINéMAS* 4, no. 3 (1994): 73–84.

———. "Un besoin de distance." *Vertigo*, no. 18 (1999): 124–28.

———. "The Power of Language: *Puissance de la parole, Le dernier mot* and *On s'est tous défilé*." In *The Cinema Alone: Essays on the Work of Jean-Luc Godard, 1985–2000*, edited by Michael Temple and James S. Williams, 179–88. Amsterdam: Amsterdam University Press, 2000.

Levi, Pavle. "The Crevice and the Stitch." *Critical Quarterly* 51, no. 3 (2009): 41–62.

Liandrat-Guigues, Suzanne, and Jean-Louis Leutrat. *Godard simple comme bonjour*. Paris: Harmattan, 2004.

MacCabe, Colin. *Godard: A Portrait of the Artist at 70*. London: Bloomsbury, 2003.

MacCabe, Colin, with Mick Eaton and Laura Mulvey. *Godard: Images, Sounds, Politics*. Bloomington: Indiana University Press, 1980.

Marquez, Anne. "L'impossible exposé selon JLG: Histoires d'expositions au centre Pompidou." *May*, no. 1 (2009), www.mayrevue.com.

McNeill, Isabelle. "Phrases, Monuments and Ruins: Melancholy History in *Éloge de l'amour* (2001)." *Studies in French Cinema* 3, no. 2 (2003): 111–20.

Miéville, Anne-Marie. "Un entretien avec la réalisatrice: 'Il faut parler de ce que l'on connaît.'" Interview by Danièle Heymann. *Le monde*, 18 January 1989, 13.

Morgan, Daniel. "The Place of Nature in Godard's Late Films." *Critical Quarterly* 51, no. 3 (2009): 1–24.

Morrey, Douglas. "History of Resistance/Resistance of History: Godard's *Éloge de l'amour*." *Studies in French Cinema* 3, no. 2 (2003): 121–30.

———. "An Embarrassment of Riches: Godard and the Aesthetics of Expenditure in *Le rapport Darty*." In *Formless: Ways In and Out of Form*, edited by Patrick Crowley and Paul Hegarty, 229–37. Bern and Oxford: Peter Lang, 2005.

———. *Jean-Luc Godard*. Manchester, UK: Manchester University Press, 2005.

Moullet, Luc. "Jean-Luc Godard." *Cahiers du cinéma*, no. 106, April 1960, 25–36.

Musy, François. "Les mouettes du pont d'Austerlitz." Interview by Alain Bergala. *Cahiers du cinéma*, no. 355, January 1984, 12–17.

Narboni, Jean. "Tous les autres s'appellent Meyer." *Trafic*, no. 3 (1992): 53–61.

Païni, Dominique. "D'après JLG. . . ." In *Jean-Luc Godard: Documents*, edited by Nicole Brenez, David Faroult, Michael Temple, James S. Williams, and Michael Witt, 420–26. Paris: Éditions du Centre Pompidou, 2006.

———. "De *Collage(s) de France* à *Voyage(s) en utopie*, retour d'exposition(s)." *Cinéma et cie: International Film Studies Journal* 9, no. 12 (2009): 11–16.

———. "Souvenirs de voyage en utopie: Note sur une exposition désœuvrée," *Cahiers du Musée national d'art moderne*, nos. 112/113 (2010).

Philippon, Alain, Gilles Laprévotte, and Jean-François Egéa, eds. *Made in Godard années 70/80: De 1972 à 1987, l'œuvre de Jean-Luc Godard*. Amiens, France: Maison de la culture d'Amiens, 1987.

Picard, Andréa. "Travels to Dystopia." *Cinema Scope*, no. 27 (2006), www.cinema-scope.com.

Pourvali, Bamchade. *Godard neuf zéro: Les films des années 90 de Jean-Luc Godard*. Biarritz, France: Atlantica, 2006.

Prédal, René, ed. *CinémAction* (special issue: *Le cinéma selon Godard*), no. 52 (1989).

Rosenbaum, Jonathan. "Theory and Practice: The Criticism of Jean-Luc Godard." *Sight and Sound* 41, no. 3, Summer 1972, 124–26.

———. "Eight Obstacles to the Appreciation of Godard in the United States." In *Jean-Luc Godard: Son + Image, 1974–1991*, edited by Raymond Bellour and Mary Lea Bandy, 197–204. New York: Museum of Modern Art, 1992.

———. "International Harvest." *Chicago Reader*, 22 November 1996, 38–41.

———. "Godard in the 1990s: An Interview, Argument, and Scrapbook." *Film Comment* 34, no. 5, September–October 1998, 52–61.

Roud, Richard. *Jean-Luc Godard*. 3rd ed. London: BFI, 2010.

Sanbar, Elias, "Vingt et un ans après." *Trafic*, no. 1 (1991): 109–19.

Schütte, Wolfram, and Peter W. Jansen, eds. *Jean-Luc Godard*. Munich: Carl Hanser Verlag, 1979.

Shafto, Sally. "Leap into Void: Godard and the Painter." *Senses of Cinema*, no. 39 (2006), sensesofcinema.com.

Silverman, Kaja. "The Author as Receiver." *October,* no. 96 (2001): 17–34.

Silverman, Kaja, and Harun Farocki. *Speaking about Godard.* New York: New York University Press, 1998.

Skoller, Jeffrey. "The Continuing Adventures of Lemmy Caution in Godard's *Germany Year 90 Nine Zero.*" *Film Quarterly* 52, no. 3, spring 99, 35–41.

Sollers, Philippe. "La 'Bonne Nouvelle' de Godard." *Le nouvel observateur,* 17 May 1985, 58.

———. "JLG/JLG, un cinéma de l'être-là." *Cahiers du cinéma,* no. 489, March 1995, 37–39.

Sterritt, David, ed. *Jean-Luc Godard: Interviews.* Jackson: University Press of Mississippi, 1998.

———. *The Films of Jean-Luc Godard.* Cambridge: Cambridge University Press, 1999.

Temple, Michael. "The Nutty Professor: Teaching Film with Jean-Luc Godard." *Screen* 40, no. 3 (1999): 323–30.

Temple, Michael, James S. Williams, and Michael Witt, eds. *For Ever Godard.* London: Black Dog, 2004.

Theweleit, Kaus. "Godard en Allemagne." *Trafic,* no. 18 (1996): 33–39.

———. *Un Plus Un.* Translated by Pierre Rusch with Bénédicte Vilgrain. Courbevoie, France: Théâtre typographique, 2000.

Toffetti, Sergio, ed. *Jean-Luc Godard: Un hommage du Centre culturel français et du Museo nazionale del cinema de Turin.* Turin: Centre culturel français de Turin, 1990.

Wajcman, Gérard. "'Saint Paul' Godard contre 'Moïse' Lanzmann, le match." *L'infini,* no. 65 (1999): 121–27.

Warner, Rick, ed. *Critical Quarterly* 51, no. 3 (special issue: *The Late Work of Jean-Luc Godard*) (2009).

Wheeler, Duncan. "Godard's List: Why Spielberg and Auschwitz are Number One." *Media History* 15, no. 2 (2009): 185–203.

Witt, Michael. "Godard, le cinéma, et l'ethnologie: Ou l'objet et sa representation." In *L'autre et le sacré: Surréalisme, cinéma, ethnologie,* edited by Christopher Thompson, 369–78. Paris: Harmattan, 1995.

———. "The Death(s) of Cinema According to Godard." *Screen* 40, no. 3 (1999): 331–46.

———. "'L'Image' selon Godard: théorie et pratique de l'image dans l'œuvre de Godard des années 70 à 90." In *Godard et le métier d'artiste,* edited by Gilles Delavaud, Jean-Pierre Esquenazi, and Marie-Françoise Grange, 19–32. Paris: Harmattan, 2001.

———. "Altered Motion and Corporal Resistance in *France tour détour deux enfants.*" In *For Ever Godard,* edited by Michael Temple, James S. Williams, and Michael Witt, 200–13. London: Black Dog, 2004.

———. "Shapeshifter: Godard as Multimedia Installation Artist." *New Left Review,* no. 29 (2004): 73–89.

———. "*Sauve qui peut (la vie),* œuvre multimedia." In *Jean-Luc Godard: Documents,* edited by Nicole Brenez, David Faroult, Michael Temple, James S. Williams, and Michael Witt, 302–306. Paris: Éditions du Centre Pompidou, 2006.

Wollen, Peter. "L'Éternel Retour." In *Jean-Luc Godard: Son + Image, 1974–1991,* edited by Raymond Bellour and Mary Lea Bandy, 187–96. New York: Museum of Modern Art, 1992.

———. "JLG." In *Paris-Hollywood: Writings on Film,* 74–92. London: Verso, 2002.

Documentary Audio and Audiovisual Material Cited in the Text

Film sur le montage (Jean Mitry, 1965, 95 min).

Civilisation: L'homme et les images (Éric Rohmer, ORTF, 1967, 34 min). With Godard, René Clair and Jean Rouch.

Parlons cinéma, a.k.a. *Les anti-cours d'Henri Langlois* (Harry Fischbach, 1976, 257 min).

Parlons cinéma: Hommage à Henri Langlois (Harry Fischbach, 1977, 43 min).

Godard 1980 (Jon Jost and Don Ranvaud, 1980, 17 min). Godard in conversation with Don Ranvaud and Peter Wollen.

L'invité du jeudi, Antenne 2, 15 September 1981. Godard in conversation with Antoine Vitez and Hélène Vida.

Ouvert le dimanche, FR3, 6 June 1982. Godard in conversation with Serge July and Maurice Achard.

7/7, TF1, 11 December 1983. Godard comments live on the news, and converses with Jean-Louis Burgat and Erik Gilbert. (Partially transcribed in *Jean-Luc Godard: Documents,* 326–27.)

Qu'est-ce que l'acte de création? (Arnaud de Pallières and Philippe Bernard, 1987, 49 min). (Based on a lecture delivered by Gilles Deleuze at the Fémis on 17 March 1987. Broadcast within the framework of the *Océaniques* series on FR3, 18 May 1989.)

Cinéma cinémas, Antenne 2, 20 December 1987. Directed by Claude Ventura. (Includes a sequence filmed in Godard's studio, in which he presents some of the materials he has compiled for use in *Histoire[s] du cinéma.*)

Microfilms, France Culture, 27 December 1987. Godard in conversation with Serge Daney (part 1).

Duras-Godard: 2 ou 3 choses qu'ils se sont dites (Jean-Daniel Verhaege, 1987, 62 min). (Broadcast within the framework of the *Océaniques* series on FR3, 28 December 1987. Transcribed in *Godard par Godard,* vol. 2.)

Microfilms, France Culture, 3 January 1988. Godard in conversation with Serge Daney (part 2).

À voix nue: Grands entretiens d'hier et d'aujourd'hui, France Culture, 20 November–1 December 1989. Godard in conversation with Noël Simsolo about *Histoire(s) du cinéma*.

La dernière leçon de Fernand Braudel, Antenne 2, 14 January 1992. Directed by Gérard Martin. Broadcast within the framework of the *25e heure* series.

Du jour au lendemain, France Culture, 4 February 1992. Serge Daney interviewed by Alain Veinstein.

Bouillon de culture, France 2, 10 September 1993. Godard in conversation with Bernard Pivot.

Jean-Luc, racontez-nous la Russie, Télévision Suisse Romande, 9 November 1993. Godard in conversation with Georges Nivat, chaired by Bertrand Theubet, before the television broadcast of *Les enfants jouent à la Russie*. (Broadcast within the framework of the *Tout va bien* series.)

Le bon plaisir, France Culture, 20 May 1995. Godard in conversation with Jean Daive. (Partially transcribed in *Godard par Godard*, vol. 2, 305–22.)

Vie et mort de l'image: Une histoire du regard en Occident, Arte, 14 October 1995. Directed by Pierre Desfons. Godard in conversation with Régis Debray. (Transcribed in *Godard par Godard*, vol. 2, 423–31.)

Still/A Novel (Chris Dercon, 1996, 2× 50 min).

Le cercle de minuit, France 2, 26 November 1996. Conversation, chaired by Laure Adler, between Godard, Jean-François Lyotard, Philippe Sollers and Jean-Claude Biette.

Jean Cocteau, mensonges et vérités (Noël Simsolo, 1996, 60 min). Broadcast on Arte, 18 February 1997. (Includes an interview with Godard about Cocteau.)

20h, Paris Première, 10 May 1997. Live interview with Godard by Paul Amar at the Cannes Film Festival. Partially transcribed in *Godard par Godard*, vol. 2, 408–22.

À voix nue: Grands entretiens d'hier et d'aujourd'hui, France Culture, 30 March to 3 April 1998. Godard in conversation with Noël Simsolo about *Histoire(s) du cinéma*.

Droit d'auteurs, La Cinquième, 6 December 1998. Godard in conversation with Jean-Pierre Rioux and others, chaired by Frédéric Ferney.

Noël Simsolo, *La Nouvelle Vague*, 2-CD set (INA/Radio France: 2000). A selection of radio interviews from the 1950s to the 1980s with members of the New Wave.

Surpris par la nuit, France Culture, 11 February 2000. Conversation between Godard and Thierry Jousse. (Extracts of this program were subsequently released on CD by France Culture and Harmonia Mundi in the "Signature" collection as *Godard/Jousse: Les écrans sonores de Jean-Luc Godard* [2000].)

Histoire parallèle, Arte, 6 May 2000. Conversation between Godard and Eric Hobsbawm, chaired by Marc Ferro.

À toute allure, France Inter, 15 May 2001. Live interview with Godard by Gérard Lefort and Marie Colmant from the Cannes Film Festival.

Faxculture, Télévision Suisse Romande, 7 June 2001. Godard in conversation with journalist Florence Heineger and linguist Henriette Walter.

François Musy on Sound, Direct Sound, Godard (Larry Sider, 2003, 40 min). François Musy in conversation with Chris Darke.

Tout arrive! France Culture, 18 May 2004. Godard in conversation with Elias Sanbar and Jean-Pierre Vernant.

Tout arrive! France Culture, 18 November 2004. Godard in conversation with Stéphane Zagdanski.

Vidéo out, Vidéo oo, Vidéo cent fleurs, Vidéa et les insoumuses . . ., France Culture, 19 September 2006. (Broadcast within the framework of the *Surpris par la nuit* series.)

Morceaux de conversations avec Jean-Luc Godard (Alain Fleischer, 2007, 125 min.).

On Cinema, Video, and Television

Abel, Richard. *French Film Theory and Criticism 1907–1939.* 2 vols. Princeton, N.J.: Princeton University Press, 1988.

Agamben, Giorgio. "Difference and Repetition: On Guy Debord's Films." In *Guy Debord and the Situationist International*, edited by Tom McDonough, translated by Brian Holmes, 314–15. Cambridge, Mass.: MIT Press, 2002.

Andrew, Dudley. *André Bazin.* New York: Oxford University Press, 1978.

Anger, Kenneth. *Hollywood Babylon.* 2 vols. London: Arrow, 1975/1984.

Astruc, Alexandre. *Du stylo à la caméra . . . et de la caméra au stylo: Écrits (1942–1984).* Paris: L'Archipel, 1992.

Aumont, Jacques, ed. *Pour un cinéma comparé: Influences et répétitions.* Paris: Cinémathèque française, 1996.

Aumont, Jacques, André Gaudréault, and Michel Marie, eds. *L'histoire du cinéma: Nouvelles approches.* Paris: Publications de la Sorbonne, 1989.

Auriol, Jean George. "Faire les films: Les origines de la mise en scène." *La revue du cinéma* 1, no. 1, 1 October 1946, 7–23.

Bardèche, Maurice, and Robert Brasillach. *Histoire du cinéma.* Paris: Denoël et Steele, 1935.

———. "Avertissement." In *Histoire du cinéma*, 5. 3rd ed. Paris: André Martel, 1948.

Bazin, André. "Sacha Guitry a fait confiance à la télévision comme il avait fait confiance au cinéma en 1914!" *Radio-Cinéma-Télévision*, no. 156, 11 January 1953, 34.

———. "Si c'était *vous*: Une des plus remarquables

émissions de notre T.V." *Radio-Cinéma-Télévision*, no. 413, 15 December 1957, 5.

———. *Jean Renoir*. Paris: Champ libre, 1971.

———. *Orson Welles*. Paris: Cerf, 1972.

———. *French Cinema of the Occupation and Resistance: The Birth of a Critical Esthetic*. Translated by Stanley Hochman. New York: Ungar, 1981.

———. *Bazin at Work: Major Essays and Reviews from the Forties and Fifties*. Edited by Bert Cardullo, translated by Alain Piette and Bert Cardullo. London and New York: Routledge, 1997.

———. *What Is Cinema?* Translated by Timothy Barnard. Montreal: Caboose, 2009.

Baecque, Antoine de. *Les cahiers du cinéma: Histoire d'une revue*. 2 vols. Paris: Cahiers du cinéma, 1991.

———. "Des femmes qui nous regardent." *Cahiers du cinéma* (special out-of-series issue: *Le siècle du cinéma*), November 2000, 68–69.

———. "Premières images des camps: Quel cinéma après Auschwitz?" *Cahiers du cinéma* (special out-of-series issue: *Le siècle du cinéma*), November 2000, 62–66.

———. *L'histoire-caméra*. Paris: Gallimard, 2008.

Baecque, Antoine de, and Christian Delage, eds. *De l'histoire au cinéma*. Paris: Complexe, 1998.

Baecque, Antoine de, and Thierry Jousse. *Le retour du cinéma*. Paris: Hachette, 1996.

Bellour, Raymond. *L'entre-images: Photo, cinéma, video*. Paris: La Différence, 1990.

———. *L'entre-images 2: Mots, images*. Paris: P.O.L., 1999.

Bellour, Raymond, Catherine David, and Christine van Assche, eds. *Passages de l'image*. Paris: Éditions du Centre Pompidou, 1990.

Bergstrom, Janet, ed. *Endless Night: Cinema and Psychoanalysis, Parallel Histories*. Berkeley and Los Angeles: University of California Press, 1999.

Biette, Jean-Claude. *Qu'est-ce qu'un cinéaste?* Paris: P.O.L., 1999.

Borde, Raymond, Freddy Buache, and Jean Curtelin. *Nouvelle Vague*. Lyon, France: Premier plan, 1962.

Braunberger, Pierre. *Cinémamémoire*. Paris: Éditions du Centre Pompidou/Centre nationale de la cinématographie, 1987.

Brenez, Nicole. *De la figure en général et du corps en particulier: L'invention figurative au cinéma*. Paris and Brussels: De Boeck, 1998.

———. "Montage intertextuel et formes contemporaines du remploi dans le cinéma expérimental." *CiNéMAS* 13, nos. 1/2 (2002): 49–67.

Brenez, Nicole, and Christian Lebrat, eds. *Jeune, dure et pure! Une histoire du cinéma d'avant-garde et expérimental en France*. Milan and Paris: Mazzotta/Cinémathèque française, 2001.

Bresson, Robert. "La question." Interview by Michel Delahaye and Jean-Luc Godard. *Cahiers du cinéma*, no. 178, May 1966.

———. *Notes on the Cinematographer*. Translated by Jonathan Griffin. London: Quartet, 1986.

Breton, André. "As in a Wood." In *The Shadow and Its Shadow: Surrealist Writings on the Cinema*, edited by Paul Hammond, 80–85. Edinburgh: Polygon, 1991.

Brougher, Kerry. "Hall of Mirrors." In *Art and Film since 1945: Hall of Mirrors*, edited by Russell Ferguson, 20–137. Los Angeles: Museum of Contemporary Art, 1996.

Burgin, Victor. *The Remembered Film*. London: Reaktion, 2004.

Cahiers du cinéma (special issue: *Serge Daney*), no. 458, July/August 1992.

Cahiers du cinéma (special out-of-series issue: *Nouvelle Vague: Une légende en question*), January 1999.

Cahiers du cinéma (special out-of-series issue: *Le siècle du cinéma*), November 2000.

Canudo, Ricciotto. "Écrit par Canudo (1907–1922)." *La revue du cinéma* 3, no. 13, May 1948, 3–9.

Cavell, Stanley. *The World Viewed: Reflections on the Ontology of Film*. Cambridge, Mass.: Harvard University Press, 1979.

Cendrars, Blaise. *Films sans images*. Paris: Denoël, 1959.

———. *Hollywood: La Mecque du cinéma*. Paris: Grasset, 2005.

Cervoni, Albert. "Enfin *Adieu Philippine*." *L'humanité*, 31 October 1980.

Chabrol, Claude, and Éric Rohmer. *Hitchcock: The First Forty-Four Films*. Translated by Stanley Hochman. New York: Frederick Unger, 1979.

Chapoulie, Jean-Marc, and Bruno Chibane, eds. *André S. Labarthe, TEMPO* (special out-of-series issue of *Limelight*), June 1993.

Cocteau, Jean. *Orphée: Film*. Paris: André Bonne, 1950.

———. *Beauty and the Beast: Diary of a Film*. Translated by Ronald Duncan. New York: Dover, 1972.

———. *Du cinématographe*. Edited by André Bernard and Claude Gauteur. Paris: Belfond, 1973.

———. *Entretiens sur le cinématographe*. Edited by André Bernard and Claude Gauteur. Paris: Belfond, 1973.

Comolli, Jean-Louis, and Jacques Rancière. *Arrêt sur histoire*. Paris: Éditions du Centre Pompidou, 1997.

Crary, Jonathan. "Unbinding Vision: Manet and the Attentive Observer in the Late Nineteenth Century." In *Cinema and the Invention of Modern Life*, edited by Leo Charney and Vanessa R. Schwartz, 46–71. Berkeley and Los Angeles: University of California Press, 1996.

Daney, Serge. *Ciné journal 1981–1986*. Paris: Cahiers du cinéma, 1986.

———. "Avant et après l'image." *Revue d'études palesti-niennes,* no. 40 (1991): 51–59.

———. *Devant la recrudescence des vols de sacs à main: Cinéma, télévision, information.* Lyon: Aléas, 1991.

———. "Le voyage absolu." In *Écrits, images et sons dans la Bibliothèque de France,* edited by Christian Delage, 87–89. Paris: IMEC/Bibliothèque de France, 1991.

———. *L'exercice a été profitable, Monsieur.* Paris: P.O.L., 1993.

———. *Le salaire du zappeur.* Paris: P.O.L., 1993.

———. *L'amateur de tennis: Critiques 1980–1990.* Paris: P.O.L., 1994.

———. *La rampe: Cahier critique 1970–1982.* Paris: Cahiers du cinéma/Gallimard, 1996.

———. "Survivre à la Nouvelle Vague." *Cahiers du cinéma* (special out-of-series issue: *Nouvelle Vague: Une légende en question*), January 1999, 62–66.

———. *La maison cinéma et le monde.* 2 vols. Edited by Patrice Rollet, with Jean-Claude Biette and Christophe Manon. Paris: P.O.L., 2001/2002.

———. *Postcards from the Cinema.* Translated by Paul Grant. Oxford: Berg, 2007.

Delage, Christian. "Cinéma, Histoire: La réappropriation des récits." *Vertigo* (special issue: *Le cinéma face à l'Histoire*), no. 16 (1997): 13–22.

Delavaud, Gilles. "André Bazin, critique de télévision." In *L'œil critique: Peut-on critiquer la télévision?,* edited by Jérôme Bourdon and Jean-Michel Frodon, 48–56. Paris and Brussels: De Boeck, 2001.

———. "L'influence de la télévision sur le cinéma autour de 1960." In *Nouvelle vague, nouveaux ravages: Permanences du récit au cinéma (1950–1970),* edited by Jean Cléder and Gilles Mouëllic, 145–57. Rennes, France: Presses universitaires de Rennes, 2001.

Deleuze, Gilles. "Optimisme, pessimisme et voyage: Lettre à Serge Daney." In Serge Daney, *Ciné journal 1981–1986,* 5–13. Paris: Cahiers du cinéma, 1986.

———. "Qu'est-ce que l'acte de création?" *Trafic,* no. 27 (1998): 133–42.

———. *Cinema 1: The Movement-Image.* Translated by Hugh Tomlinson and Barbara Habberjam. London and New York: Continuum, 2005.

———. *Cinema 2: The Time-Image.* Translated by Hugh Tomlinson and Robert Galeta. London and New York: Continuum, 2005.

Dubois, Philippe, and Jennifer Verraes, eds. *Cinéma et cie: International Film Studies Journal* 9, no. 12 (special issue: *Cinema and Contemporary Visual Arts III*) (2009).

Duras, Marguerite. *Les yeux verts.* Paris: Cahiers du cinéma, 1987.

Dyer, Richard, and Ginette Vincendeau, eds. *Popular European Cinema.* London and New York: Routledge, 1993.

Eisenschitz, Bernard. "Les meilleurs films sont ceux qu'on n'a pas vus." In *Pour un cinéma comparé: Influences et répétitions,* edited by Jacques Aumont, 13–24. Paris: Cinémathèque française, 1996.

Eisenstein, Sergei. *Cinématisme: Peinture et cinéma.* Edited by François Albera and Naoum Kleiman, translated by Anne Zouboff. Brussels: Éditions complexe, 1980.

———. *The Film Sense.* Edited and translated by Jay Leyda. London: Faber and Faber, 1986.

———. *Selected Works,* vol. 1, *Writings, 1922–34.* Edited and translated by Richard Taylor. London and Bloomington: BFI/Indiana University Press, 1991.

———. *Selected Works,* vol. 2, *Towards a Theory of Montage.* Edited by Michael Glenny and Richard Taylor, translated by Michael Glenny. London: BFI, 1991.

Eisner, Lotte H. *The Haunted Screen: Expressionism in the German Cinema and the Influence of Max Reinhardt.* Translated by Roger Greaves. Berkeley and Los Angeles: University of California Press, 1974.

Epstein, Jean. *Bonjour cinéma.* Paris: Éditions de la Sirène, 1921.

———. *Le cinématographe vu d'Etna.* Paris: Les Écrivains réunis, 1926.

———. *L'intelligence d'une machine.* Paris: Éditions Jacques Melot, 1946.

———. *Le cinéma du diable.* Paris: Éditions Jacques Melot, 1947.

———. *Écrits sur le cinéma.* 2 vols. Paris: Seghers, 1974/1975.

———. "Slow-Motion Sound." In *Film Sound: Theory and Practice,* edited by Elizabeth Weis and John Belton, translated by Robert Lamberton, 143–44. New York: Columbia University Press, 1985.

———. "On Certain Characteristics of *Photogénie*." In *French Film Theory and Criticism 1907–1939,* vol. 1, edited by Richard Abel, translated by Tom Milne, 314–18. Princeton, N.J.: Princeton University Press, 1988.

Ferro, Marc. "Société du 20e siècle et histoire cinématographique." *Annales, économies, sociétés, civilisations,* no. 23 (1968): 581–85.

———. "Y-a-t-il une vision filmique de l'histoire?" In *Fernand Braudel, Une leçon d'histoire de Fernand Braudel,* 225–30. Paris: Arthaud-Flammarion, 1986.

———. *Cinema and History.* Translated by Naomi Greene. Detroit: Wayne State University Press, 1988.

Ford, Charles, ed. *Bréviaire du cinéma: Soixante ans de pensée cinégraphique.* Paris: Contact, 1959.

Frampton, Hollis. "The Invention without a Future." *October,* no. 109 (2004): 65–75.

———. *On the Camera Arts and Consecutive Matters: The Writings of Hollis Frampton.* Edited by Bruce Jenkins. Cambridge, Mass.: MIT Press, 2009.

Gallagher, Tag. *The Adventures of Roberto Rossellini.* New York: Da Capo, 1998.

Garrel, Philippe, and Thomas Lescure. *Une caméra à la place du cœur.* Aix en Provence, France: Admiranda/ Institut de l'image, 1992.

Gauthier, Christophe. "L'invention d'une discipline: L'histoire du cinéma." *Vertigo* (special issue: *Le cinéma face à l'Histoire*), no. 16 (1997): 117–23.

Gerber, Jacques. *Anatole Dauman: Pictures of a Producer.* Translated by Paul Willemen. London: BFI, 1992.

Gunning, Tom. "Tracing the Individual Body: Photography, Detectives, and Early Cinema." In *Cinema and the Invention of Modern Life,* edited by Leo Charney and Vanessa R. Schwartz, 15–45. Berkeley and Los Angeles: University of California Press, 1995.

Hammond, Paul. "Available Light." In *The Shadow and Its Shadow: Surrealist Writings on the Cinema,* edited by Paul Hammond, 1–43. Edinburgh: Polygon, 1991.

Hauptman, Jodi. *Joseph Cornell: Stargazing in the Cinema.* New Haven, Conn.: Yale University Press, 1999.

Heijs, Jan, and Frans Westra. *Que le tigre danse: Huub Bals, A Biography.* Amsterdam: Otto Cramwinckel, 1996.

Kenez, Peter. "A History of *Bezhin Meadow.*" In *Eisenstein at 100: A Reconsideration,* edited by Al LaValley and Barry P. Scherr, 193–206. New Brunswick: Rutgers University Press.

Kirby, Lynne. *Parallel Tracks: The Railroad and Silent Cinema.* Exeter, UK: University of Exeter Press, 1997.

Kracauer, Siegfried. *From Caligari to Hitler: A Psychological History of the German Film.* London: Dennis Dobson, 1947.

———. *Theory of Film: The Redemption of Physical Reality.* London: Oxford University Press, 1960.

Kubler, Thierry, and Emmanuel Lemieux. *Cognacq-Jay 1940: La télévision française sous l'occupation.* Paris: Plume, 1990.

Kuleshov, Lev. *Kuleshov on Film: Writings by Lev Kuleshov.* Edited and translated by Ronald Levaco. Berkeley and Los Angeles: University of California Press, 1974.

Labarthe, André S. *Essai sur le jeune cinéma français.* Paris: Le terrain vague, 1960.

———. "Le triomphe d'Edison, la parenthèse Lumière." *Le monde,* 15 December 1994 (*Le monde des arts et des spectacles*), viii–ix.

———. "Le cinéma à vapeur (aide-mémoire)." *Limelight* (special out-of-series issue: *Florilège*), June 1997, 94–96.

Lagny, Michèle. *De l'histoire du cinéma. Méthode historique et histoire du cinéma.* Paris: Armand Colin, 1992.

Langlois, Georges P., and Glenn Myrent. *Henri Langlois: Premier citoyen du cinéma.* Paris: Denoël, 1986.

Langlois, Henri. "Préface." In Georges Sadoul, *Histoire du cinéma mondial: Des origines à nos jours.* 9th ed., i–iv. Paris: Flammarion, 1972.

———. *Trois cent ans de cinéma.* Edited by Jean Narboni. Paris: Cahiers du cinéma/Cinémathèque française/ Fémis, 1986.

Leenhardt, Roger. *Chroniques de cinéma.* Paris: Éditions de l'Étoile, 1986.

Leigh, Janet. *There Really Was a Hollywood.* New York: Doubleday, 1984.

Leighton, Tanya, ed. *"In the Poem about Love You Don't Write the Word Love."* Berlin and New York: Sternberg Press, 2006.

Lemaître, Maurice. *La véritable histoire créatrice du cinéma, ou les nouvelles escroqueries de Jean-Luc Godard.* Documents Lettristes, no. 76, May 1989. (Available for consultation in the Bibliothèque Nationale de France.)

Leyda, Jay. *Films Beget Films: Compilation Films from Propaganda to Drama.* London: Allen and Unwin, 1964.

L'Herbier, Marcel, ed. *Intelligence du cinématographe.* Paris: Corrêa, 1946.

Liandrat-Guigues, Suzanne, and Murielle Gagnebin, eds. *L'essai et le cinéma.* Seyssel: Champ Vallon, 2004.

Malraux, André. "Sketch for a Psychology of the Moving Pictures." In *Reflections On Art: A Source Book of Writings by Artists, Critics, and Philosophers,* edited by Susanne K. Langer, 317–27. Baltimore, Md.: Johns Hopkins University Press, 1958. (First published as "Esquisse d'une psychologie du cinéma," *Verve* 8, no. 2 [1940]: 69–73.)

———. *Espoir: Sierra de Teruel–Scénario du film.* Paris: Gallimard, 1996.

Mannoni, Laurent. *Histoire de la Cinémathèque française.* Paris: Gallimard, 2006.

———. "'Vends la Cinémathèque!'" In *Jean-Luc Godard: Documents,* edited by Nicole Brenez, David Faroult, Michael Temple, James S. Williams, and Michael Witt, 246–47. Paris: Éditions du Centre Pompidou, 2006.

Marker, Chris. "Orphée." *Esprit,* 18 November 1950, 694–701.

———. "L'Amérique rêve." In *Commentaires,* 88–121. Paris: Seuil, 1961.

———. *Le fond de l'air est rouge.* Paris: Maspero, 1978.

Matuszewski, Boleslaw. *A New Source of History/Animated Photography: What It Is, What It Should Be.* Translated by Ryszard Drzewiecki. Warsaw: Filmoteka Naradova, 1999.

———. *Écrits cinématographiques.* Edited by Magdalena Mazaraki. Paris: Association française de recherche sur l'histoire du cinéma/Cinémathèque française, 2006.

Mauriac, Claude. *L'amour du cinéma.* Paris: Albin Michel, 1954.

Mazierska, Ewa. *European Cinema and Intertextuality: History, Memory and Politics*. London: Palgrave Macmillan, 2011.

Merleau-Ponty, Maurice. "The Film and the New Psychology." In *Sense and Non-Sense*, translated by Hubert L. Dreyfus and Patricia Allen Dreyfus. Evanston: Northwestern University Press, 1973.

Michelson, Annette. "The Wings of Hypothesis: On Montage and the Theory of the Interval." In *Montage and Modern Life 1919–1942*, edited by Matthew Teitelbaum, 61–81. Cambridge, Mass.: MIT Press, 1992.

Mitry, Jean. *Esthétique et psychologie du cinéma*. 2 vols. Paris: Éditions universitaires, 1963/1965.

———. *Histoire du cinéma*. 3 vols. Paris: Éditions universitaires, 1967–1973.

Moss, Marilyn Ann. *Giant: George Stevens, a Life in Film*. Madison: University of Wisconsin Press, 2004.

Mulvey, Laura. "Detail, Digression, Death: the Movies in Chris Petit's Film *Negative Space*." *Afterall*, no. 5 (2002): 98–105.

———. *Death 24× a Second: Stillness and the Moving Image*. London: Reaktion, 2006.

Narboni, Jean, Sylvie Pierre, and Jacques Rivette. "Montage." *Cahiers du cinéma*, no. 208, March 1969, 17–35.

Neyrat, Cyril. "L'essai à la limite de la terre et de l'eau." In *L'essai et le cinéma*, edited by Suzanne Liandrat-Guigues and Murielle Gagnebin, 157–70. Seyssel, France: Champ Vallon, 2004.

"Niels Bohr va au cinéma," *Cinéma*, no. 4 (2002): 91–120. (Dossier of texts by Jacques Aumont, Leonid Kozlov, Viktor Listov, Igor Mantsov, and Vsevolod Pudovkin.)

Le nouvel art cinématographique, 26 November 1927. (Contains a dossier of articles and letters relating to the *Histoire du cinéma par le cinéma* affair.)

Nowell-Smith, Geoffrey. "On History and the Cinema." *Screen* 31, no. 2 (1990): 160–71.

Orain, Fred. "Film, cinéma et télévision." *Cahiers du cinéma*, no. 1, April 1951, 37–38.

Païni, Dominique. *Conserver, montrer*. Brussels: Yellow Now, 1992.

———. *Le cinéma, un art moderne*. Paris: Cahiers du cinéma, 1997.

———. "Faire violence: À propos du *Trafic* des cassettes video." *Cahiers du cinéma*, no. 524, May 1998, 92–97.

———. *Le temps exposé: Le cinéma de la salle au musée*. Paris: Cahiers du cinéma, 2002.

———. "Should We Put an End to Projection." Translated by Rosalind Krauss. *October*, no. 110 (2004): 23–48.

Païni, Dominique, with Pascale Pronnier and Ronan Le Régent, eds. *Projections, les transports de l'image*. Paris: Hazan/Le Fresnoy/AFAA, 1997.

Peleshian, Artavazd. "Distance Montage, or the Theory of Distance." In *Our Century*, edited by Gerald Matt and Angela Stief, translated by Hans Joachim Schlegel and Cheryce M. Kramer, 83–100. Vienna: Ursula Blickle Stiftung/Kunsthalle Wien/Kerber Verlag, 2004.

Positif (special out-of-series issue devoted to Michèle Firk), Spring 1970.

Rancière, Jacques. *Film Fables*. Translated by Emiliano Battista. Oxford: Berg, 2006.

———. *The Future of the Image*. Translated by Gregory Elliott. London: Verso, 2007.

Rappaport, Mark. "Mark Rappaport's Notes on *Rock Hudson's Home Movies*." *Film Quarterly* 49, no. 4, summer 1996, 16–22.

Renoir, Jean, and Roberto Rossellini. "Cinéma et télévision." Interview by André Bazin. *France-Observateur*, no. 442, 23 October 1958.

Rivette, Jacques. "Nous ne sommes plus innocents." *Bulletin du ciné-club du Quartier Latin*, January 1950.

———. "De l'abjection." *Cahiers du cinéma*, no. 120, June 1961, 54–55.

———. *Jacques Rivette: Texts and Interviews*, edited by Jonathan Rosenbaum. London: BFI, 1977.

Rohmer, Éric. *The Taste for Beauty*. Translated by Carol Volk. Cambridge: Cambridge University Press, 1989.

Romains, Jules. "The Crowd at the Cinematograph." In *French Film Theory and Criticism 1907–1939*, vol. 1, edited and translated by Richard Abel, 53. Princeton, N.J.: Princeton University Press, 1988.

Rosenbaum, Jonathan. "Criticism on Film." *Sight and Sound* 60, no. 1, winter 1990–91, 51–54.

———. "Talking Back to the Screen." *Film Comment* 28, no. 6, November–December 1992, 57–59.

———. *Placing Movies: The Practice of Film Criticism*. Berkeley and Los Angeles: University of California Press, 1995.

———. *Moving Places: A Life at the Movies*. Berkeley and Los Angeles: University of California Press, 1998.

———. *Movie Wars: How Hollywood and the Media Conspire to Limit What Films We Can See*. Chicago: A Cappella, 2000.

———. "Orson Welles's Purloined Letter: *F For Fake*." In *Discovering Orson Welles*, 289–95. Berkeley and Los Angeles: University of California Press, 2007.

Rosenbaum, Jonathan, and Adrian Martin, eds. *Movie Mutations: The Changing Face of World Cinephilia*. London: BFI, 2003.

Roud, Richard. *A Passion for Films: Henri Langlois and the Cinémathèque Française*. London: Secker and Warburg, 1983.

Rozier, Jacques. "*Adieu Philippine* est un film au présent." *Arts*, 16 October 1962.

———. "Après plus de deux ans de 'purgatoire,' *Adieu Philippine* va affronter Paris." Interview by Patrick Bureau. *Les lettres françaises,* 12 September 1963.

Rubin, Mathias. *Rassam le magnifique.* Paris: Flammarion, 2007.

Sadoul, Georges. "Les films de mise en scène comme sources historiques." In *L'histoire et ses méthodes,* edited by Charles Samaran, 1402–404. Paris: Gallimard, 1961.

———. *Histoire du cinéma français.* Paris: Club des Éditeurs, 1962.

———. "Matériaux, méthodes et problèmes de l'histoire du cinéma." In *Histoire du cinéma mondial: Des origines à nos jours,* v–xxix. 9th ed. Paris: Flammarion, 1972.

Saxton, Libby. *Haunted Images: Film, Ethics, Testimony and the Holocaust.* London: Wallflower, 2008.

Schefer, Jean Louis. *L'homme ordinaire du cinéma.* Paris: Cahiers du cinéma/Gallimard, 1997.

Sjöberg, Patrik. *The World in Pieces: A Study of the Compilation Film.* Stockholm: Aura förlag, 2001.

Skoller, Jeffrey. *Making History in Avant-garde Film.* Minneapolis: University of Minnesota Press, 2005.

Slide, Anthony. *Films on Film History.* Metuchen, N.J., and London: Scarecrow Press, 1979.

Smith, Grahame. *Dickens and the Dream of Cinema.* Manchester, UK: Manchester University Press, 2003.

Sorlin, Pierre. *The Film in History: Restaging the Past.* Oxford: Blackwell, 1980.

Stevens, Brad. "The American Friend: Tom Luddy on Jean-Luc Godard." *Senses of Cinema,* no. 44 (2007), sensesofcinema.com.

Tavano, Charles-Félix, and Marcel Yonnet. *Quelques histoires de cinéma.* Paris: Jules Tallendier, 1923.

Temple, Michael, and Michael Witt, eds. *The French Cinema Book.* London: BFI, 2004.

Terk, Boris. *Michèle Firk est restée au Guatemala.* Paris: Syllepse, 2004.

Trafic (special issue, *Serge Daney, après, avec*), no. 37 (2001).

Truffaut, François. "Réalisateur de 45 films en 34 ans, Hitchcock est le plus grand 'inventeur de formes' de l'époque." *Arts,* no. 647, 4 December 1957, 7.

———. Homage to Sacha Guitry. *Cahiers du cinéma* (special issue: *La situation du cinéma français*), nos. 323/324, May 1981, 60–61.

———. *Correspondence 1945–1984.* Edited by Gilles Jacob and Claude de Givray, translated by Gilbert Adair. New York: Farrar, Strauss and Giroux, 1990.

Truffaut, François, and Alfred Hitchcock. *Hitchcock.* London: Paladin, 1986.

Tsivian, Yuri. "The Wise and Wicked Game: Re-editing and Soviet Film Culture of the 1920s." *Film History* 8, no. 3 (1996): 327–43.

Tynjanov, Jurij. "On the Foundations of Cinema." In *Russian Formalist Film Theory,* edited by Herbert Eagle, 81–100. Michigan Slavic Publications 34. Ann Arbor: Department of Slavic Languages and Literatures, University of Michigan, 1981.

Ungaro, Jean. "La fille prodigue ou le cinéma après la télévision." In *La télévision dans la République: Les années 50,* edited by Marie-Françoise Lévy, 169–200. Paris: Complexe, 1999.

Vedrès, Nicole. *Images du cinéma français.* Paris: Éditions du Chêne, 1945.

Vertov, Dziga. *Kino-Eye: The Writings of Dziga Vertov.* Edited by Annette Michelson, translated by Kevin O'Brien. London: Pluto, 1984.

Zand, Nicole. "Le dossier Philippine." *Cahiers du cinéma,* no. 148, October 1963, 32–39.

Zryd, Michael. "History and Ambivalence in Hollis Frampton's *Magellan*." *October,* no. 109 (2004): 119–42.

On Literature, Art, Philosophy, and Culture

Adorno, Theodor. *Prisms.* Translated by Samuel and Shierry Weber. Cambridge, Mass.: MIT Press, 1981.

———. *The Culture Industry: Selected Essays on Mass Culture.* Edited by J. M. Bernstein. London and New York: Routledge, 1991.

Agamben, Giorgio. "Aby Warburg and the Nameless Science." In *Potentialities: Collected Essays in Philosophy,* edited and translated by Daniel Heller-Roazen, 89–103. Stanford, Calif.: Stanford University Press, 1999.

———. *Remnants of Auschwitz: The Witness and the Archive.* Translated by Daniel Heller-Roazen. New York: Zone, 2002.

Agee, James, and Walker Evans. *Let Us Now Praise Famous Men.* Boston: Houghton Mifflin, 1941.

Allan, Derek. *Art and the Human Adventure: André Malraux's Theory of Art.* Amsterdam: Rodopi, 2009.

Antelme, Robert. *The Human Race.* Translated by Jeffrey Haight and Annie Mahler. Evanston, Ill.: Marlboro Press/Northwestern, 1998.

Aragon, Louis. *Le crève-cœur/Le nouveau crève-cœur.* Paris: Gallimard, 1980.

———. *Le con d'Irène.* In *Œurvres romanesques complètes,* vol. 1, edited by Daniel Bougnoux, 437–75. Paris: Gallimard, 1997.

Arasse, Daniel. *Le détail: Pour une histoire rapprochée de la peinture.* Paris: Flammarion, 1992.

Aronowicz, Annette. "The Secret of the Man of Forty." *History and Theory* 32, no. 2 (1993): 101–18.

Attali, Jacques. *Noise: The Political Economy of Music.*

Translated by Brian Massumi. Minneapolis: University of Minnesota Press, 1985.

Balzac, Honoré de. *A Harlot High and Low*. Translated by Kathleen Raine. Harmondsworth, UK: Penguin, 1975.

———. *Le lys dans la vallée*. Paris: Livre de poche, 1984.

Bataille, Georges. *Manet*. Translated by Austryn Wainhouse and James Emmons. New York: Skira, 1955.

———. *Le bleu du ciel*. Paris: Éditions 10/18, 1999.

Baudelaire, Charles. *Les fleurs du mal*. Paris: Garnier, 1961.

Beckett, Samuel. *L'image*. Paris: Minuit, 1988.

Béguin, Albert. *L'âme romantique et le rêve: Essai sur l'âme romantique allemand et la poésie française*. Marseilles, France: Cahiers du sud, 1937.

Benjamin, Walter. "Some Motifs in Baudelaire." In *Charles Baudelaire: A Lyric Poet in the Era of High Capitalism*, translated by Harry Zohn, 107–54. London: Verso, 1983.

———. *Moscow Diary*. Edited by Gary Smith, translated by Richard Sieburth. Cambridge, Mass.: Harvard University Press, 1986.

———. *Illuminations*. Edited by Hannah Arendt, translated by Harry Zohn. London: Fontana, 1992.

———. *The Arcades Project*. Translated by Howard Eiland and Kevin McLaughlin. Cambridge, Mass.: Harvard University Press, 2002.

———. "The Metaphysics of Youth." In *Selected Writings*, vol. 1, *1913–1926*, edited by Marcus Bullock and Michael W. Jennings, translated by Rodney Livingston, 6–17. Cambridge, Mass.: Harvard University Press, 2004.

Bernanos, Georges. *Les enfants humiliés*. Paris: Gallimard, 1973.

Blanchot, Maurice. *Thomas l'obscur*. Paris: Gallimard, 1950.

———. "D'un art sans avenir." *Nouvelle revue française*, no. 51 (1957): 488–98.

———. "Time, Art, and the Museum." In *Malraux: A Collection of Critical Essays*, edited by R. W. B. Lewis, translated by Beth Archer, 147–60. Englewood Cliffs, N.J.: Prentice-Hall, 1964.

———. *Friendship*. Translated by Elizabeth Rottenberg. Stanford, Calif.: Stanford University Press, 1997.

Borges, Jorge Luis. *Other Inquisitions, 1937–1952*. Translated by Ruth L. C. Simms. Austin: University of Texas Press, 1988.

Braudel, Fernand. *On History*. Translated by Sarah Matthews. London: Weidenfeld and Nicolson, 1980.

———. *Une leçon d'histoire de Fernand Braudel*. Paris: Arthaud-Flammarion, 1986.

———. *L'identité de la France*. 3 vols. Paris: Flammarion, 1986–1992.

———. *A History of Civilizations*. Translated by Richard Mayne. Harmondsworth, UK: Penguin, 1993.

Brecht, Bertolt. "Lob der Dialektik." In *Gedichte*, vol. 3, 73. Frankfurt: Suhrkamp Verlag, 1961.

———. *Me-ti, Buch der Wendungen*. Frankfurt: Suhrkamp Verlag, 1965.

Breton, André. *Manifestes du surréalisme*. Paris: Gallimard, 1979.

Broch, Hermann. *The Death of Virgil*. Translated by Jean Starr Untermeyer. London: Penguin, 2000.

Brontë, Emily. *The Complete Poems of Emily Jane Brontë*. Edited by C. W. Hatfield. New York: Columbia University Press, 1995.

———. *Wuthering Heights*. London: Harper Collins, 2009.

Camus, Albert. *Le mythe de Sisyphe*. Paris: Gallimard, 1942.

———. *La peste*. Paris: Gallimard, 1947.

Canguilhem, Georges. *The Normal and the Pathological*. Translated by Carolyn Fawcett and Robert Cohen. New York: Zone, 1991.

Carroll, Lewis. *Symbolic Logic and Game of Logic*. New York: Dover, 1958.

Cervantes, Miguel de. *Don Quixote*. Translated by Edith Grossman. London: Vintage, 2005.

Chateaubriand, François René de. *Mémoires d'outre-tombe*. 4 vols. Paris: Livre de poche, 2001.

Chéroux, Clément, ed. *Mémoire des camps: Photographies des camps de concentration et d'extermination nazis (1933–1999)*. Paris: Marval, 2001.

Claudel, Paul. *L'œil écoute*. Paris: Gallimard, 1990.

Conrad, Joseph. *Heart of Darkness*. Edited by Robert Hampson. Harmondsworth, UK: Penguin, 2000.

Cros, Charles. *Le collier de griffes*. In *Œuvres complètes*, 165–245. Paris: Gallimard, 1970.

Dahan-Dalmédico, Amy, and Jeanne Peiffer. *Une histoire des mathématiques: Routes et dédales*. Paris: Seuil, 1986.

Darwich, Mahmoud. *La Palestine comme métaphore*. Translated by Elias Sanbar and Simone Bitton. Arles, France: Actes sud, 1997.

———. *La terre nous est étroite, et autres poèmes 1966–1999*. Translated by Elias Sanbar. Paris: Gallimard, 2000.

Debord, Guy. *La société du spectacle*. Paris: Gallimard, 1992.

Debray, Régis. *Vie et mort de l'image: Une histoire du regard en Occident*. Paris: Gallimard, 1992.

Deleuze, Gilles. *Pourparlers*. Paris: Minuit, 1990.

Descartes, René. *Discourse on Method and Related Writings*. Translated by Desmond M. Clarke. Harmondsworth, UK: Penguin, 1999.

Dickinson, Emily. *The Complete Poems of Emily Dickinson*. Edited by Thomas H. Johnson. New York: Little, Brown and Co., 1960.

Diderot, Denis. *Jacques le fataliste*. Paris: Flammarion, 1970.
———. *Lettre sur les aveugles*. Paris: Livre de poche, 1999.
Didi-Huberman, Georges. *L'image survivante: Histoire de l'art et temps des fantômes selon Aby Warburg*. Paris: Minuit, 2002.
———. *Images malgré tout*. Paris: Minuit, 2003.
———. *Invention of Hysteria: Charcot and the Photographic Iconography of the Salpêtrière*. Translated by Alisa Hartz. Cambridge, Mass.: MIT Press, 2003.
Dolto, Françoise. *L'évangile au risque de la psychanalyse*. 2 vols. Paris: Seuil, 1977.
Dostoyevsky, Fyodor. *The Insulted and Injured*. Translated by Constance Garnett. London: Grafton, 1987.
Duby, Georges. *History Continues*. Translated by Arthur Goldhammer. Chicago: University of Chicago Press, 1994.
———. *Women of the Twelfth Century*. 3 vols. Cambridge: Polity, 1997–1998.
Ducasse, Isadore, Comte de Lautréamont. *Poésies*. Edited by Georges Goldfayn and Gérard Legrand. Paris: Le terrain vague, 1960.
Dumbach, Annette, and Jud Newborn. *Sophie Scholl and The White Rose*. Oxford: Oneworld, 2006.
Färber, Helmut. "Une forme qui pense: Notes sur Aby Warburg." *Trafic*, no. 45 (2003): 104–20.
Faulkner, William. *Requiem for a Nun*. New York: Vintage, 1975.
———. *Light in August*. London: Vintage, 2000.
———. *The Wild Palms*. London: Vintage, 2000.
Faure, Élie. *History of Art*, 5 vols. Translated by Walter Pach. London: John Lane, 1923–1930.
———. *Fonction du cinéma: De la cinéplastique à son destin social*. Paris: Denoël, 1976.
Feldman, Valentin. *Journal de guerre, 1940–41*. Edited by Léone Teyssandier-Feldman and Pierre-Frédéric Charpentier. Tours, France: Farrago, 2006.
Focillon, Henri. *The Life of Forms in Art*. Translated by George Kubler. New York: Zone, 1992.
Foucault, Michel. *The Archaeology of Knowledge and The Discourse on Language*. Translated by Rupert Sawyer. New York: Barnes and Noble, 1993.
———. *The Order of Things: An Archaeology of the Human Sciences*. New York: Vintage, 1994.
Freud, Sigmund. *The Interpretation of Dreams*. Edited by James Strachey, Alan Tyson, and Angela Richards; translated by James Strachey. Harmondsworth, UK: Penguin, 1991.
Fromentin, Eugène. *Les maîtres d'autrefois*. Paris: Livre de poche, 1965.
Genet, Jean. *Un captif amoureux*. Paris: Gallimard, 1986.
———. *Fragments of the Artwork*. Translated by Charlotte Mandell. Stanford, Calif.: Stanford University Press, 2003.
Gide, André. *The Counterfeiters*. Translated by Dorothy Bussy. Harmondsworth, UK: Penguin, 1966.
Gille, Elisabeth. *Le mirador: Mémoires rêvées*. Paris: France loisirs, 1992.
Giraudoux, Jean. *Siegfried et le Limousin*. Paris: Grasset, 1959.
Goethe, Johann Wolfgang von. *The Sorrows of Young Werther*. Harmondsworth, UK: Penguin, 1989.
Goytisolo, Juan. *Cahier de Sarajevo*. Translated by François Maspero. Strasbourg, France: La Nuée bleue, 1993.
Hegel, Georg W. F. *The Philosophy of History*. Translated by J. Sibree. New York: Dover, 1956.
———. *Philosophy of Right*. Translated by S. W. Dyde. New York: Dover, 2005.
Heidegger, Martin. *Chemins qui ne mènent nulle part*. Translated by Wolfgang Brokmeier. Paris: Gallimard, 1949.
———. *On the Way to Language*. Translated by Peter D. Hertz. New York: Harper Collins, 1982.
———. *Basic Writings*. Edited by David Farrell Krell. New York: Harper Collins, 1993.
Hugo, Victor. "Pour la Serbie." In *Œuvres complètes: Actes et paroles III: Depuis l'exil*, 949–50. Paris: Robert Laffont, 1985.
Jacob, François. *The Logic of Life: A History of Heredity* and *The Possible and the Actual*. Translated by Betty Spillmann. Harmondsworth, UK: Penguin, 1989.
Kafka, Franz. *Metamorphosis and Other Stories*. Translated by Willa and Edwin Muir. Harmondsworth, UK: Penguin, 1987.
Koestler, Arthur. *Darkness at Noon*. Translated by Daphne Hardy. Harmondsworth, UK: Penguin, 1975.
Kofman, Sarah. *L'enfance de l'art: Une interprétation de l'esthétique freudienne*. Paris: Payot, 1975.
Koyré, Alexandre. *From the Closed World to the Infinite Universe*. Baltimore, Md.: Johns Hopkins University Press, 1957.
Lake, Steve, and Paul Griffiths, eds. *Horizons Touched: The Music of ECM*. London: Granta, 2007.
Lamarche-Vadel, Bernard. *Bernard Lamarche-Vadel: Entretiens, témoignages, études critiques*. Edited by Isabelle Rabineau. Paris: Méréal, 1997.
Larbaud, Valery. *Beauté, mon beau souci. . . .* Paris: Gallimard, 1920.
Leroux, Gaston. *Le parfum de la dame en noir*. Paris: Livre de poche, 1960.
———. *Le mystère de la chambre jaune*. Paris: Livre de poche, 1974.

Levi, Primo. *If This Is a Man.* Translated by Stuart Woolf. London: Bodley Head, 1966.

———. *The Drowned and the Saved.* Translated by Raymond Rosenthal. London: Abacus, 2007.

Leyda, Jay. *Melville Log: A Documentary Life of Herman Melville.* New York: Harcourt, Brace and Co., 1951.

London, Jack. *The Star Rover.* New York: Macmillan, 1915.

Lowenthal, David. *The Past is Another Country.* Cambridge: Cambridge University Press, 1985.

Lucretius. *On the Nature of Things.* Translated by Alicia Stallings. Harmondsworth, UK: Penguin, 1994.

Lütticken, Sven. "The Art of Theft." *New Left Review,* no. 13 (2002): 89–104.

Malherbe, François de. "Dessein de quitter une dame qui ne le contentait que de promesse." In *Œuvres,* edited by Antoine Adam, 21–22. Paris: Gallimard, 1971.

Malraux, André. *Psychologie de l'art,* 3 vols. Geneva: Skira, 1947–1949.

———. *Saturn: An Essay on Goya.* Translated by C. W. Chilton. London: Phaidon, 1952.

———. *Le musée imaginaire de la sculpture mondiale,* 3 vols. Paris: Gallimard, 1952–1954.

———. *The Voices of Silence.* Translated by Stuart Gilbert. London: Secker and Warburg, 1954.

———. *Antimemoirs.* Translated by Terence Kilmartin. Harmondsworth, UK: Penguin, 1970.

———. *Oraisons funèbres.* Paris: Gallimard, 1971.

———. *Felled Oaks: Conversation with de Gaulle.* Translated by Irene Clephane and Linda Asher. New York: Holt, Rinehart and Winston, 1972.

———. *La métamorphose des dieux,* 3 vols. Paris: Gallimard, 1957–1976.

———. *Lazarus.* Translated by Terence Kilmartin. London: Macdonald and Jane's, 1977.

———. *Man's Fate.* Translated by Haakon M. Chevalier. New York: Vintage, 1990.

———. *Picasso's Mask.* Translated by June Guicharnaud with Jacques Guicharnaud. New York: Da Capo, 1994.

Mann, Thomas. *Lotte in Weimar.* Translated by H. T. Lowe-Porter. London: Minerva, 1997.

———. *Joseph and His Brothers.* Translated by John E. Woods. New York: Knopf, 2005.

Marion, Denis, ed. *André Malraux.* Paris: Seghers, 1970.

Mendelsohn, Daniel. *The Lost: A Search for Six of Six Million.* London: Harper, 2007.

Michaud, Philippe-Alain. *Aby Warburg and the Image in Motion.* Translated by Sophie Hawkes. New York: Zone, 2004.

Michelet, Jules. *Histoire de la révolution française.* 4 vols. Paris: Chamerot, 1849.

———. "Préface de 1869." In *Histoire de France,* vol. 1, *Le moyen âge,* 39–63. Geneva: Édito-Service S.A., 1987.

Montaigne, Michel de. *Essays.* Translated by J. M. Cohen. Harmondsworth, UK: Penguin, 1993.

Musil, Robert. *L'homme sans qualités.* 4 vols. Paris: Seuil, 1995.

Musset, Alfred de. *On ne badine pas avec l'amour.* Paris: Livre de poche, 1999.

Némirovsky, Irène, *Le bal.* Translated by Sandra Smith. London: Vintage, 2007.

———. *Suite française.* Translated by Sandra Smith. London: Vintage, 2007.

Nietzsche, Friedrich. *Ecce Homo: How One Becomes What One Is.* Translated by R. J. Hollingdale. Harmondsworth, UK: Penguin, 1982.

Nora, Pierre. *Les lieux de mémoire.* 3 vols. Paris: Gallimard, 1997.

Onimus, Jean. *Péguy et le mystère de l'histoire.* Paris: Cahiers de l'Amitié Charles Péguy, 1958.

Pagnol, Marcel. *Le secret du masque de fer.* Paris: Presses pocket, 1977.

Péguy, Charles. *Clio: Dialogue de l'histoire et de l'âme païenne.* Paris: Gallimard, 1932.

———. "Clio I." In *Temporal and Eternal,* translated by Alexander Dru, 83–165. Indianapolis, Ind.: Liberty Fund, 2001.

Pessoa, Fernando. *The Book of Disquiet.* Edited and translated by Richard Zenith. Harmondsworth, UK: Penguin, 2001.

Pound, Ezra. *The Cantos of Ezra Pound.* New York: New Directions, 1996.

Proust, Marcel. *À la recherche du temps perdu.* Edited by Jean-Yves Tadié. Paris: Gallimard, 1999.

Queneau, Raymond. "L'explication des métaphores." In *Les ziaux,* 65–66. Boston: Twayne, 1985.

Rampley, Matthew. "Archives of Memory: Walter Benjamin's *Arcades Project* and Aby Warburg's *Mnemosyne Atlas.*" *de-, dis-, ex-* 3 (special issue: *The Optic of Walter Benjamin*) (1999): 94–117.

———. *The Remembrance of Things Past: On Aby M. Warburg and Walter Benjamin.* Wiesbaden, Germany: Harrassowitz Verlag, 2000.

Ramuz, Charles Ferdinand. *L'amour de la fille et du garcon.* In *Salutation paysanne,* 137–50. Paris: Grasset, 1929.

———. *Les signes parmi nous.* In *Œuvres complètes,* vol. 10, 45–172. Geneva: Slatkine, 1986.

———. *Aimé Pache, peintre vaudois.* Lausanne, Switzerland: L'Âge d'Homme, 1991.

Rappl, Werner. "Les sentiers perdus de la mémoire." *Trafic,* no. 9 (1994): 28–36.

Reverdy, Pierre. "L'image." In *Œuvres complètes,* 73–75. Paris: Flammarion, 1975.

Richter, Gerhard. *Atlas of the Photographs, Collages and Sketches.* New York: Distributed Art, 1997.

Rilke, Rainer Maria. *Letters to a Young Poet.* Translated by M. D. Herter Norton. New York: Norton, 2004.

Rougemont, Denis de. *Love Declared: Essays on the Myths of Love.* Translated by Richard Howard. New York: Pantheon, 1963.

———. *Love in the Western World.* Translated by Montgomery Belgion. New York: Fawcett, 1966.

———. *Penser avec les mains.* Paris: Gallimard, 1972.

Rousset, David. *Les jours de notre mort.* Paris: Le Pavois, 1947.

———. *The Other Kingdom.* Translated by Ramon Guthrie. New York: Reynal and Hitchcock, 1947.

Roy, Claude. *Moi je.* Paris: Gallimard, 1969.

Ryn, Zdzislaw, and Stanislaw Klodzinski. *An der Grenze zwischen Leben und Tod. Eine Studie über die Erscheinung des "Muselmanns" im Konzentrazionslager, Auschwitz-Hefte,* vol. 1. Weinheim, Germany, and Basel, Switzerland: Beltz, 1987.

Saint-Exupéry, Antoine de. *Night Flight.* Translated by Stuart Gilbert. New York: Signet Classic, 1961.

Sanbar, Elias. "Hors du lieu, hors du temps." In *La photographie d'une terre et de son people de 1839 à nos jours,* 7–32. Paris: Hazan, 2004.

Saroyan, William. *The Daring Young Man on the Flying Trapeze and Other Stories.* New York: New Directions, 1997.

Sartre, Jean-Paul. *La nausée.* Paris: Gallimard, 1938.

———. *Being and Nothingness: An Essay on Phenomenological Ontology.* Translated by Hazel E. Barnes. London and New York: Routledge, 2003.

Schneider, Monique. *Père, ne vois-tu pas?* Paris: Denoël, 1985.

Shakespeare, William. *King Lear.* Harmondsworth, UK: Penguin, 1994.

Shannon, Claude, and Warren Weaver. *The Mathematical Theory of Communication.* Urbana: University of Illinois Press, 1964.

Sollers, Philippe. *Women.* Translated by Barbara Bray. New York: Columbia University Press, 1990.

———. "Profond Marivaux." *Le monde des livres,* 20 May 1994.

Solzhenitsyn, Aleksandr. *The Gulag Archipelago, 1918–1956.* New York: Harper and Row, 1973.

Spengler, Oswald. *The Decline of the West.* Edited by Arthur Helps and Helmut Werner, translated by Charles F. Atkinson. New York: Oxford University Press, 1991.

Tec, Nechama, and Daniel Weiss. "The Heroine of Minsk: Eight Photographs of an Execution." *History of Photography* 23, no. 4 (1999): 322–30.

Teitelbaum, Matthew, ed. *Montage and Modern Life, 1919–1942.* Cambridge, Mass.: MIT Press, 1992.

Tillion, Germaine. *Ravensbrück.* Paris: Seuil, 1973.

———. "Introduction à trois 'Ravensbrück.'" *Ravensbrück,* 11–23. 2nd ed. Paris: Seuil, 1997.

Tolstoy, Leo. *Anna Karenina.* Translated by Richard Revear and Larissa Volokhonsky. Harmondsworth, UK: Penguin, 2003.

———. *War and Peace.* Translated by Anthony Briggs. New York: Viking Adult, 2006.

Valéry, Paul. *Morceaux choisis: Prose et poésie.* Paris: Gallimard, 1930.

Valtin, Jan. *Out of the Night.* Edinburgh and Oakland, Calif.: AK Press/Nabat, 2004.

Verne, Jules. *Les 500 millions de la Bégum.* Paris: Livre de poche, 1978.

Virgil. *The Aeneid.* Translated by C. Day Lewis. Oxford: Oxford University Press, 2008.

Vogt, Alfred van. *Destination: Universe!* London: Panther, 1960.

Warburg, Aby. *Der Bilderatlas Mnemosyne.* Edited by Martin Warnke with Claudia Brink. Berlin: Akademie Verlag, 2003.

Weil, Simone. *Gravity and Grace.* Translated by Emma Crawford and Mario von der Ruhr. London and New York: Routledge, 2002.

White, Hayden. *Metahistory: The Historical Imagination in Nineteenth-Century Europe.* Baltimore, Md.: Johns Hopkins University Press, 1973.

Wilde, Oscar. *The Critic As Artist.* New York: Mondial, 2007.

Wittgenstein, Ludwig. *On Certainty.* Edited by G. E. M. Anscombe and Georges Henrik von Wright, translated by G. E. M. Anscombe and Denis Paul. Oxford: Blackwell, 1969.

———. *Culture and Value.* Edited by G. H. Von Wright with Heikki Nyman, translated by Peter Winch. Chicago: University of Chicago Press, 1984.

Woolf, Virginia. *The Waves.* Harmondsworth, UK: Penguin, 2000.

Index

MICHAEL WITT is Reader in Cinema
Studies and Co-Director of the Centre for
Research in Film and Audiovisual Cultures
at the University of Roehampton in London.
His work has appeared in journals such as
Sight and Sound, Screen, Trafic, and *New
Left Review,* and he is co-editor of *For Ever
Godard* (Black Dog, 2004), *The French Cinema
Book* (BFI, 2004), and *Jean-Luc Godard:
Documents* (Centre Pompidou, 2006).

This book was designed by Jamison Cockerham and set in type by Tony Brewer at Indiana University Press and printed by Four Colour Imports, Ltd.

The text face is Arno, designed by Robert Slimbach in 2007. The captions are set in Caecilia, designed by Peter Matthias Noordzij in 1990. Titles are set in Avenir, designed by Adrian Frutiger in 1988. All were issued by Adobe Systems Incorporated.